Wars Without End

Wars Without End

Competitive Intervention, Escalation Control, and Protracted Conflict

NOEL ANDERSON

OXFORD
UNIVERSITY PRESS

Oxford University Press is a department of the University of Oxford.
It furthers the University's objective of excellence in research, scholarship,
and education by publishing worldwide. Oxford is a registered trade mark of
Oxford University Press in the UK and in certain other countries.

Published in the United States of America by Oxford University Press
198 Madison Avenue, New York, NY 10016, United States of America.

© Oxford University Press 2025

All rights reserved. No part of this publication may be reproduced, stored in a retrieval system,
transmitted, used for text and data mining, or used for training artificial intelligence, in any form or
by any means, without the prior permission in writing of Oxford University Press, or as expressly
permitted by law, by licence or under terms agreed with the appropriate reprographics rights
organization. Inquiries concerning reproduction outside the scope of the above should be sent
to the Rights Department, Oxford University Press, at the address above

You must not circulate this work in any other form
and you must impose this same condition on any acquirer

Library of Congress Cataloging-in-Publication Data
Names: Anderson, Noel (PhD in Political Science), author.
Title: Wars without end : competitive intervention, escalation control, and protracted
conflict / Noel Anderson.
Description: [New York, NY] : Oxford University Press, [2025] |
Includes bibliographical references. |
Identifiers: LCCN 2024039810 (print) | LCCN 2024039811 (ebook) |
ISBN 9780197798645 (hardback) | ISBN 9780197798676 |
ISBN 9780197798669 (epub)
Subjects: LCSH: Civil war–History–20th century–Case studies. | Prolonged war. |
Protracted conflicts (Military science) | Proxy war. | Angola–History–Civil
War, 1975-2002. | Afghanistan–History–Soviet occupation, 1979-1989. |
Syria–History–Civil War, 2011-
Classification: LCC JC328.5 .A53 2025 (print) | LCC JC328.5 (ebook) |
DDC 355.02/18–dc23/eng/20241101
LC record available at https://lccn.loc.gov/2024039810
LC ebook record available at https://lccn.loc.gov/2024039811

DOI: 10.1093/oso/9780197798645.001.0001

Printed by Sheridan Books, Inc., United States of America

Cover image: Joseph Eid/AFP via Getty Images

For Cass, always

Contents

List of Figures	viii
List of Tables	x
Acknowledgments	xi
List of Acronyms	xiv
1. Introduction	1
2. A Theory of Competitive Intervention in Civil War	28
3. External Meddling in Internal War: Tracking Global Trends, 1946–2009	59
4. Competitive Intervention and Protracted Civil War, 1946–2009	81
5. The Angolan MPLA–UNITA Civil War, 1975–1991	108
6. The Afghan Communist–Mujahideen Civil War, 1979–1992	153
7. Conclusion: Extensions, Implications, and Future Trajectories	204
Appendices	234
References	253
Index	283

List of Figures

1.1.	Trends in the global incidence and prevalence of internal conflict, 1946–2009	5
2.1.	Diagrammatic overview of the theory	30
3.1.	Rates of external intervention in civil wars, 1946–2009	68
3.2.	Rates of external intervention in civil wars by aid type, 1946–2009	69
3.3.	Trends in external military assistance in the form of competitive intervention and one-sided support to civil war combatants, 1946–2009	72
3.4.	Trends in one-sided support to government and rebel combatants, 1946–2009	73
3.5.	Prevalence of US–Soviet and lesser power competitive intervention during the bipolar and unipolar periods	75
3.6.	Percent of conflicts subject to an intervention with American participation in the unipolar period	78
4.1.	Distribution of civil war durations	85
4.2.	Estimated percent change in the hazard of civil war termination with 95% confidence intervals (core results)	94
4.3.	Estimated percent change in the hazard of civil war termination with 95% confidence intervals (additional results)	97
4.4.	Estimated percent change in the hazard of civil war termination with 95% confidence intervals (robustness checks)	99
4.5.	Year of competitive intervention onset for civil wars that were afflicted by competitive intervention at any time during their duration	104
4.6.	Trends in the yearly incidence, average duration, and prevalence of civil war, 1946–2009	105
5.1.	Angola and its neighbors	112
5.2.	Relationships between primary domestic combatants and competitive interveners during the Angolan civil war, 1975–1991	116
5.3.	Southern Angola	124
6.1.	Afghanistan and its neighbors	158
6.2.	Relationships between primary domestic combatants and competitive interveners during the Afghan civil war, 1979–1992	163
B.1.	Simulated percent change in the hazard of civil war termination given a one-unit change in LEGAL REBEL POLITICAL WING	237

B.2. Simulated percent change in the hazard of civil war termination given a one-unit change in UN PEACEKEEPING ... 239

B.3. Simulated percent change in the hazard of civil war termination given a one-unit change in UN PEACEKEEPING and REBEL TERRITORIAL CONTROL ... 241

C.1. Estimated percent change in the hazard of civil war termination with 95% confidence intervals; replication of core results using a two-year intermittency rule ... 245

C.2. Estimated percent change in the hazard of civil war termination with 95% confidence intervals; replication of additional results using a two-year intermittency rule ... 246

D.1. Estimated percent change in the hazard of civil war termination with 95% confidence intervals; replication of core results without a 1,000 cumulative battle-related deaths criterion ... 249

D.2. Estimated percent change in the hazard of civil war termination with 95% confidence intervals; replication of additional results without a 1,000 cumulative battle-related deaths criterion ... 251

E.1. Trends in the yearly incidence, average duration, and prevalence of internal conflicts without a 1,000 cumulative battle-related deaths criterion, 1946–2009 ... 252

List of Tables

2.1.	Predictions of the theory	53
4.1.	Cox model estimates, core results	92
4.2.	Cox model estimates, additional results	96
4.3.	Cox model estimates, robustness checks	99
6.1.	Pakistan Air Force air defense effort during the Afghan civil war	173
A.1.	Variable summary statistics	234
B.1.	Nonproportional hazards diagnostics for Models 1–5	236
B.2.	Nonproportional hazards diagnostics for Models 6–10	238
B.3.	Nonproportional hazards diagnostics for Models 11–15	240
C.1.	Cox model estimates; replication of core results using a two-year intermittency rule	243
C.2.	Cox model estimates; replication of additional results using a two-year intermittency rule	245
D.1.	Cox model estimates; replication of core results without a 1,000 cumulative battle-related deaths criterion	247
D.2.	Cox model estimates; replication of additional results without a 1,000 cumulative battle-related deaths criterion	250

Acknowledgments

This book is a testament to the enduring guidance, unwavering support, and boundless encouragement generously provided to me by family, friends, and colleagues. Through the many years dedicated to its creation, I have accumulated a large number of personal and professional debts of gratitude. It is with sincere appreciation that I acknowledge the ways in which this book is a reflection not only of my own efforts but also the collective influence and contributions of those who have helped me along the way.

The ideas I develop in the pages that follow have their origins in a dissertation that was cast and molded in an extraordinary graduate school environment at MIT. It was there that I met Roger Petersen, who from our very first meeting engaged my ideas in ways that not only improved my work but also encouraged me to think bigger, more creatively, and more carefully. I can't even begin to count the number of papers, chapters, and applications he has read over the years, and I am deeply thankful for his ever-constructive feedback, good humor, and friendship. Fotini Christia's mentorship and advice were equally critical, both for this book and for my academic career. A wellspring of motivation and an indispensable source of guidance, her suggestions substantially improved the framing and clarity of the manuscript. Finally, Barry Posen's encyclopedic knowledge of military affairs not only improved this book but also fundamentally changed my thinking about the use of military force in international affairs. I have benefited tremendously from working with him in research and in teaching, and I am grateful for his contributions to this project and to my career.

I also thank the incredible group of scholars who made up the MIT Political Science Department in general, and the Security Studies Program in particular, during my time in graduate school. The sense of community and collegiality I enjoyed at MIT was second to none, and my work has benefited tremendously from the input of thoughtful and incisive people like Dan Altman, Lena Andrews, Mark Bell, Chris Clary, James Conran, Fiona Cunningham, Brian Haggerty, Chad Hazlett, Sameer Lalwani, Marika Landau-Wells, Phil Martin, Tim McDonnell, Andrew Miller, Nick Miller, Cullen Nutt, Reid Pauly, Amanda Rothschild, Josh Shifrinson, Peter Swartz, Joseph Torigian, Steve Wittels, Alec Worsnop, Yiqing Xu, and Ketian Zhang.

Similarly, a tight-knit community of postdoctoral fellows and faculty at Dartmouth provided intellectual stimulation, professional guidance, and friendship during a rewarding year in Hanover, New Hampshire. Among others, Mary Barton, Suparna Chaudhry, Sean Fear, Jeff Friedman, Eric Hundman, Sabrina Karim, Jenny Lind, Daryl Press, David Wight, and Bill Wohlforth deserve special thanks.

Over the years, I've had the privilege of engaging with brilliant scholars whose insights and feedback have greatly influenced this book. I am particularly grateful for the enriching discussions and constructive input provided by Kyle Atwell, Austin Carson, Adam Casey, Alex Chinchilla, Stathis Kalyvas, Morgan Kaplan, Alexander Lanoszka, Julia Macdonald, Nic Marsh, Evan Perkoski, Sara Plana, Mike Poznansky, Kai Thaler, Rachel Whitlark, Cat Worsnop, and Anna-Mart van Wyk. I'm also indebted to a remarkable group of emerging scholars, including Sanjida Amin, Winston Bai, Michele St-Amant, and Cheng Xu, who provided excellent research assistance.

This book was completed at the University of Toronto, which has proven to be a wonderfully supportive and collegial intellectual home. I have benefited tremendously from the insights, advice, and support of many colleagues, with special thanks owed to Aisha Ahmad, Steven Bernstein, Nancy Bertoldi, Jacques Bertrand, Randy Besco, Phillip Lipsey, Emily Nacol, Andrea Olive, Alex Reisenbichler, Ed Schatz, and Alison Smith. However, my deepest gratitude is reserved for Matt Hoffmann, whose guidance and mentorship have played a pivotal role in shaping both my academic journey and the completion of this book.

At Oxford University Press, Angela Chnapko offered helpful advice throughout the review and publication process, and I also thank the anonymous reviewers for their time and thoughtful feedback. The comments and suggestions I received were stimulating and constructive; the final product is much stronger thanks to their input. Portions of this book draw on a previously published article in *International Studies Quarterly*, and I thank Oxford University Press for the permission to reprint this content.[1]

I also benefited from helpful feedback received during presentations at MIT's Strategic Use of Force Working Group; the University of Chicago's Program on International Politics, Economics, and Security; Yale's Program on Order, Conflict, and Violence; the University of Pennsylvania's Browne Center; Monash South Africa's Social Science Research Seminar; Dartmouth's International Relations Seminar Series; the University of Toronto's International Relations Workshop Series; and the Université de Montréal's Centre d'Études sur la Paix et la Sécurité Internationale.

---

[1] Anderson (2019).

I am grateful for the generous financial support provided by the Connaught Fund at the University of Toronto, the Harry Frank Guggenheim Foundation, the John Sloan Dickey Center for International Understanding at Dartmouth, the Miller Center at the University of Virginia, the MIT Center for International Studies, the MIT Department of Political Science, the Smith Richardson Foundation, the Social Sciences and Humanities Research Council, and the Tobin Project.

Finally, words cannot express my appreciation for my family's endless encouragement. My parents, Gerry and Ian, are models of hard work and perseverance whom I have always looked up to and sought to emulate. Their boundless confidence in my abilities pushed me to dream big and to set ambitious goals. I would not be where I am were it not for their love and support. Thanks also to my brothers Conor, Eóin, and Cameron, whose curiosity helped me stay motivated, and whose camaraderie helped me stay grounded. Above all, I owe an immeasurable debt of gratitude to my wife Cassidy, who shared in the trials, the tribulations, and the countless late nights. Her patience, optimism, and warm encouragement are what made this book possible. She has provided me with more happiness and love than I could possibly deserve. For this and for so much more, this book is dedicated to her.

List of Acronyms

ACD	Armed Conflict Dataset
AMISOM	African Union Mission in Somalia
CIA	Central Intelligence Agency
EESD	Extended External Support Dataset
FNLA	Frente Nacional de Libertação de Angola
GDP	Gross domestic product
HTS	Hayat Tahrir al-Sham
ISI	Inter-Services Intelligence
ISIS	Islamic State in Iraq and Syria
KGB	Komitet Gosudarstvennoy Bezopasnosti
MPLA	Movimento Popular de Libertação de Angola
NATO	North Atlantic Treaty Organization
NSC	National Security Council
NSDD-166	National Security Decision Directive 166
OAU	Organization of African Unity
PAF	Pakistan Air Force
PDPA	People's Democratic Party of Afghanistan
PHA	Proportional hazards assumption
PKK	Partiya Karkerên Kurdistanê
SADF	South African Defense Force
SDF	Syrian Democratic Forces
SFA	Syrian Free Army
SNA	Syrian National Army
SWAPO	South West Africa People's Organization
UCDP	Uppsala Conflict Data Program
UN	United Nations
UNITA	União Nacional para a Independência Total de Angola
USAID	United States Agency for International Development

1
Introduction

Many of the world's most pressing policy challenges stem from protracted civil wars. In Syria, the deliberate targeting of civilian populations has forced millions of refugees to flee their homes, creating a migration emergency of global proportion.[1] In Libya, a "nightmarish war" has generated widespread political instability, perpetuating criminality, human trafficking, and displacement.[2] And in Yemen, fighting between government and rebel forces has caused a humanitarian disaster dubbed "the worst in the world," with shocking levels of hunger and disease.[3]

And yet, despite untold human suffering, widespread destruction and loss, and far-reaching destabilization, the fires of today's most violent civil wars continue to burn. *Why are these wars without end?*

Given that the costs imposed by civil wars are a function of their duration, this question is of central importance for policymakers, politicians, and concerned citizens alike. The number of deaths inflicted by an internal conflict increases as it endures.[4] The intensity of violence—that is, a conflict's daily death rate—is likewise higher in longer civil wars.[5] Added to this brutality are the long-term economic costs imposed on suffering societies: higher military expenditure, capital flight, and declining (if not reversing) economic growth.[6] These effects have been shown to persist for years after fighting has come to an end, a direct consequence of the deterioration, if not total ruin, of a society's economic, political, and social institutions.[7] In light of these devastating effects, which only grow greater as a conflict persists, how can we explain the intractability of costly and stalemated—yet seemingly endless—civil wars?

This book provides an answer. By situating civil wars within the broader geopolitical environment in which they take place, it explains how protracted fighting *within* states is linked to enduring competition *between* them. It

---

[1] The United Nations Refugee Agency estimates that 6.6 million Syrians have been rendered refugees as a result of the civil war. This amounted to roughly one-quarter of all refugees in the world in 2020. See UNHCR (2020).
[2] Wehrey and Doherty (2019); US Department of State (2021: 613–615).
[3] UN Office for the Coordination of Humanitarian Affairs (2018: 4).
[4] Lacina (2006).
[5] Lujala (2009).
[6] Collier et al. (2003).
[7] Ghobarah, Huth, and Russett (2003).

reconsiders the conventional intrastate/interstate conflict distinction to better understand the behaviors of armed groups, the strategies of foreign interveners, and the trajectories of internal wars. In doing so, it offers a number of new and productive angles on civil war, third-party intervention, and conflict management and sheds fresh light on the international dimensions of domestic conflict, the determinants of intractable warfare, and the processes that underlie the waxing and waning of civil war in the international system.

A central finding that emerges concerns the critical role of what I call "competitive intervention"—*an opposing, simultaneous transfer of military assistance from different third-party states to both government and rebel combatants engaged in an ongoing civil war*—in the dynamics, duration, and prevalence of internal conflict. I provide a comprehensive theoretical and empirical account of this distinct form of external meddling that challenges traditional conceptions of "proxy war" by deriving new propositions about the strategic logics that motivate it. I explain competitive intervention's pernicious effects, document its consequences for civil wars, and derive policy prescriptions aimed at resolving some of today's most intractable conflicts.

Research Questions and Motivation

Two research questions lie at the heart of this book. The first explores the conditions under which domestic combatants and their foreign backers choose to delay negotiated settlement in favor of continued fighting. It asks: How does competitive intervention influence civil war duration?

Civil wars are exceedingly costly endeavors. They require the mobilization of thousands of fighters, often for many years; military equipment, weapons, and ammunition; extensive logistical support and means of resupply; medical supplies, nutritious food, and clean water; and miscellaneous spare parts, oils, and fuels. These resources must be acquired by state and non-state combatant organizations that are purposely built not to generate wealth, but to destroy it. Once the shooting starts, rebels often struggle to locate a source of supplies to replace worn-out equipment and replenish expended ammunition.[8] Governments in developing countries—the principal victims of intrastate conflict—likewise struggle to sustain campaigns against insurgents that employ asymmetric tactics, operate in remote regions, or hide among sympathetic

---

[8] Scarcity of weapons, ammunition, and other war materiel is a common theme in classical works on guerrilla warfare. See, for example, Mao (1965) and Guevara (1961). For a discussion on the critical role of conflict-specific capital in the prosecution of an insurgency, see Marsh (2007). Also see Kalyvas and Kocher (2007: 212), who highlight the constraining role of limited logistics and scarcity of weapons in rebel recruitment.

populations. For states and rebel groups alike, acute resource problems are a challenge inherent in armed struggle.

Precisely because warfare is so costly, opponents should have strong incentives to coordinate their expectations about a conflict's likely outcome as soon as possible.[9] Notably, this is the case not only for the rebel and government forces that are directly engaged in combat but also for the third-party interveners that support them. While interveners rarely pay the direct costs of war—troop casualties, civilian victimization, and the destruction of property—they nonetheless often invest substantial military and financial resources to affect battlefield outcomes. These investments make sense when they contribute to swift military victories, but they become more difficult to explain when interveners maintain their support at a level that results in intractable stalemates for many years, or even decades.

To better understand the strategic logics motivating domestic combatants and their international backers amid protracted fighting, I develop a theory that both explains the effects of foreign meddling on domestic bargaining processes and considers the wider strategic environment that shapes and constrains intervener decision-making. My account highlights the ways in which conflicting interests instigate divergent responses by rival third-party states, a phenomenon I call "competitive intervention." I describe the distortionary effects this form of external meddling imparts on domestic bargaining processes, identify the unique strategic dilemmas it entails for third-party interveners, and explain why belligerents often choose to continue to pay the high costs of war when *inter*state competition becomes intertwined with *intra*state conflict.

The second research question explored in this book considers the wider consequences of competitive intervention for internal conflict in the international system. It asks: How has competitive intervention affected temporal trends in the global prevalence of civil war?

Although the number of ongoing civil wars rose steadily between 1946 and 1990, it declined precipitously thereafter. The prevalence of civil conflicts generating at least 25 battle-related deaths per year declined by over 20% between 1991 and 2009, while that of civil wars generating 1,000 battle-related deaths per year declined by over 50%.[10] These reductions—together with analogous declines in the prevalence of interstate conflict, battle-related deaths, and other forms of interpersonal violence—have inspired bold claims about the waning of war.[11] The international community is "winning the war on war," writes

---

[9] Stated otherwise, a fundamental puzzle of war is its *ex post* inefficiency. See Fearon (1995).
[10] See Table 1 in Themnér and Wallensteen (2014: 543).
[11] On the waning of war, see Mueller (1989, 2004, 2009), Gurr, Marshall, and Khosla (2000), Payne (2004), Human Security Centre (2005), Fettweis (2006), Väyrynen (2006), N. Gleditsch (2008), Newman (2009), Goldstein (2011), Pinker (2011), Goldstein and Pinker (2011, 2016), Gat (2012),

one scholar.[12] It is conceivable that civil war "is going out of style," writes another.[13] Daily news headlines about warfighting in Afghanistan, Colombia, or Somalia mask the fact that "civil wars are increasingly rare."[14] And while it is acknowledged that they have not yet entirely disappeared, some scholars suggest that those conflicts that remain are not *real* civil wars; they are "closer to organized crime than traditional war."[15] They are, it is argued, merely "remnants of war"—opportunistic predation by thugs, hooligans, and other "residual combatants."[16]

Curiously, however, those proclaiming the decline of civil war have overlooked contradictory trends in the incidence and prevalence of internal conflict. These trends are documented in Figure 1.1, which plots the proportion of states experiencing *onsets* of armed conflict (incidence) and the proportion of states experiencing *ongoing* armed conflicts (prevalence) for all years from 1946 to 2009.[17] Three observations are of note. First, despite a relatively constant incidence rate, there was a gradual increase in the prevalence of internal conflict during the Cold War (1946–1990). In other words, states were subject to more or less the same risk of onset during this period; the increase in the prevalence of internal conflicts was driven by their growing accumulation over time.[18] Second, the increasing prevalence of conflict peaks in 1990, just as the Cold War comes to an end. It then declines precipitously in subsequent years. In fact, the sudden decline in civil war during the post–Cold War period is just as dramatic as its rise during the Cold War. Finally, and most surprisingly, the decline in the prevalence of conflict between 1991 and 2009 occurred despite an uptick in the incidence of armed conflict. In numbers, the average yearly incidence rate rose by nearly 40% in the post–Cold War period.[19] That the global decline

---

Tertrais (2012), Human Security Report Project (2014), and Mousseau (2019). For critical takes, see Braumoeller (2019), Fazal and Poast (2019), and the forum discussion in N. Gleditsch et al. (2013). Also see Hegre et al. (2013), who predict a continued decline in armed conflict between 2010 and 2050. On the related debate over the decline of combat deaths, see Lacina, N. Gleditsch, and Russett (2006), Gohdes and Price (2013), Lacina and N. Gleditsch (2013), and Fazal (2014).

[12] Goldstein (2011).
[13] Mueller (2009: 309).
[14] Tertrais (2012: 7).
[15] Goldstein and Pinker (2011). Also see Kaldor's (2012) distinction between "new" and "old" wars.
[16] Mueller (2004).
[17] The figure is compiled using data from the Uppsala Conflict Data Program (UCDP) Armed Conflict Dataset (N. Gleditsch et al. 2002; Themnér and Wallensteen 2014) and the Interstate System Membership Dataset (K. Gleditsch and Ward 1999).
[18] Fearon and Laitin (2003a: 75).
[19] From 1946 to 1990, the yearly incidence rate of conflict was 3.7%; from 1991 to 2009, it was 5.1%. This is a statistically significant difference ($t(36.819) = -2.011, p = 0.052$). In raw numbers, the former period experienced 4.5 outbreaks per year, while the latter period experienced 8.6 outbreaks per year.

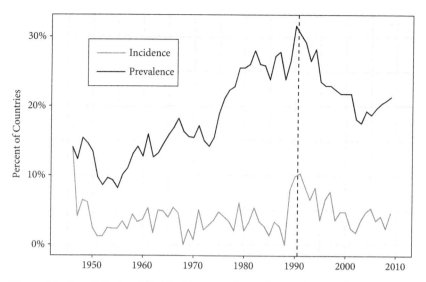

Figure 1.1 Trends in the global incidence and prevalence of internal conflict, 1946–2009.

in the prevalence of armed conflict occurred despite an *increase* in the rate of outbreaks begs for an explanation.

In this book, I highlight the role of competitive intervention. Linking changes in the international distribution of power to variation in patterns of external intervention in civil wars, I explain why fewer conflicts have been afflicted by competitive intervention in the post–Cold War period. As competitive intervention has waned, average conflict durations have decreased, and the global prevalence of civil war has therefore declined. Here again, understanding the bargaining distortions and strategic dilemmas inherent in competitive intervention is central to explaining why this has been the case.

The Argument

This book develops a generalizable theory of competitive intervention that explains protracted fighting, temporal variation in average conflict duration, and changing trends in the global prevalence of civil war. I argue that competitive intervention prolongs civil wars; that the prevalence of competitive intervention varies over time; and that as competitive intervention waxes and wanes, so too do the mechanisms linking it to protracted conflict—a dynamic that helps explain temporal variation in the average duration and global prevalence of civil war. The argument is presented in three steps and at three levels of analysis.

I begin at the level of the domestic combatants to explain how competitive intervention distorts civil war bargaining processes. Departing from the existing literature's emphasis on credible commitment problems as barriers to civil war settlement, I examine how competitive intervention exacerbates information problems among domestic combatants in ways that incentivize continued fighting.[20] In contrast to scholarship that conceives of interveners as third-party guarantors that facilitate negotiated settlements, I identify the mechanisms that link external meddling to bargaining failures. I argue that competitive intervention subsidizes domestic combatants' costs of war, balances their military capabilities, and amplifies information asymmetries. Together, these distortions increase combatants' willingness and ability to fight, negate decisive military advantages, and increase uncertainty over relative strength and resolve. They thereby prolong civil wars. This result helps to explain why rebel and government forces continue to bear the human and financial costs of fighting, even when conflicts become stalemated. It also uncovers the central role of persistent sources of uncertainty and asymmetric information in *ex post* decisions to keep fighting.

Next, I turn to the level of the third-party interveners, conceiving of competitive intervention as a mixed-motive strategic game of interdependent decision-making. I argue that while competitively intervening states have conflicting interests over the outcomes of civil wars, they also have common interests in the regulation of their confrontation with one another. Opposing preferences over which domestic combatant prevails on the civil war battlefield must be weighed by the mutual risks inherent in competitive intervention: conflict spirals, action–reaction dynamics, and direct confrontation. In the 1970s and 1980s, for example, Cuba and South Africa found themselves supporting rival government and rebel forces, respectively, in the Angolan civil war. Yet while both countries deployed combat forces to the country, neither entertained the prospect of fighting a war against the other.[21] Their challenge, therefore, was to pursue their individual national interests while at the same time avoiding mutually damaging and dangerous escalation. I explain how interveners navigate this dilemma by explicitly and tacitly communicating to establish limits in the scope of their support to domestic combatants. By signaling restraint through the force postures they adopt, the geographies they patrol, the targets they attack, and the types of aid they provision, competitive interveners find ways to control

---

[20] On credible commitment problems as an explanation for protracted civil war, see Walter (1997, 2002), Fearon (2004), McLauchlin (2018), and Keels and Wiegand (2020).
[21] I provide an in-depth analysis of the Angolan case in Chapter 5.

escalation and avoid costly confrontations. Yet while limits effectively regulate competition, they simultaneously—and paradoxically—prevent the interveners from conferring decisive military advantages on their domestic clients. This produces stalemated civil wars, as the interveners refrain from providing the level of support necessary to achieve positive objectives, such as battlefield victories, and instead provide a level of support sufficient only to achieve negative objectives, such as avoiding battlefield defeats. This result not only sheds new light on the determinants of protracted conflict but also helps explain why interveners often continue to invest in intractable conflicts in seemingly suboptimal ways.

Leveraging this inferential framework one step further, I consider how variation in the prevalence of competitive intervention has in turn affected the prevalence of civil war in the international system. Insofar as state decisions to intervene in civil wars reflect competitive state policymaking, temporal variation in geopolitical competition among states should affect patterns of external meddling in internal conflicts. I therefore explore how the transformation of the international system from a bipolar structure to a unipolar structure affects the prevalence of competitive intervention. I argue that there was a greater prevalence of competitive intervention during the Cold War owing to two effects emanating from the bipolar distribution of power: great power rivalry between the United States and the Soviet Union, and increased foreign adventurism among their client states. As competitive intervention proliferated, average conflict durations grew longer, and the global prevalence of civil war therefore increased. In the post–Cold War period, by contrast, unipolarity has both eliminated great power competition and moderated the interventionist tendencies of weaker states. As competitive intervention has become less prevalent, average conflict durations have decreased, and the global prevalence of civil war has therefore declined. Importantly, however, the mechanisms that link competitive intervention to protracted internal conflict have not disappeared—they continue to impact some of today's most violent civil wars. This underscores the importance of a generalizable theory of competitive intervention that not only explains past conflicts but also informs contemporary policy.

By bringing together battlefield bargaining dynamics, the escalatory pressures of interstate competition, and the systemic dimensions of geopolitical rivalry in civil wars, the theory produces a rich set of expectations about the behaviors of domestic combatants, the strategies of competitively intervening states, and the significance of the international distribution of power. I test these expectations empirically using a mixed-method, nested analysis approach that combines quantitative analyses with detailed qualitative case studies.[22] The

---

[22] On the nested analysis approach, see Lieberman (2005). On the value of mixed-method research designs in the study of political violence, see Thaler (2017).

quantitative component of the research design introduces a new dataset of external military assistance to civil war combatants that is global in scope for all conflicts fought between 1946 and 2009. It provides a range of descriptive and inferential statistics that confirm the theorized relationship between competitive intervention, protracted conflict, and the global prevalence of civil war. The qualitative component of the research design draws on a heterogeneous set of materials, including semi-structured interviews with former military commanders and political leaders, primary documents gathered from foreign archives and veterans' associations, declassified intelligence reports, and memoirs and personal accounts published by political and military veterans. It provides in-depth analyses of competitive interventions in the Angolan (1975–1991) and Afghan (1979–1992) civil wars, as well as an out-of-sample shadow case study of the Syrian conflict (2011–present). The case studies illustrate the theory in action and verify the proposed mechanisms linking competitive intervention to intractable conflict. Taken together, the combination of quantitative and qualitative methods—and their respective approaches to data collection, analysis, and inference—provides a more holistic view of competitive intervention, a more robust empirical grounding for theory testing, and ultimately greater confidence in the central findings of this book.

Scope and Definitions

This book introduces a new concept to the study of civil war: competitive intervention. This is a distinct configuration of external support to domestic combatants, characterized by *opposing, simultaneous transfers of military assistance from different third-party states to both government and rebel combatants engaged in an ongoing civil war.*

Competitive interventions are *competitive* insofar as they are attempts by third-party states to secure competing, rather than shared, interests in the outcome of a civil war.[23] These competitive dynamics, which distinguish competitive intervention from one-sided intervention, are significant for several reasons. First, competitive dynamics carry with them escalatory risks. The enmity underlying opposing interventions raises the specter of conflict spirals, growing costs, and enlarged conflict—up to and including direct confrontations

---

[23] Thus, interventions in which two or more states compete for the patronage of a single rebel group or government are not considered competitive interventions. Likewise, mutual interventions, in which two states simultaneously intervene in each other's intrastate conflicts by supporting rebel groups, are not considered competitive interventions (see Duursma and Tamm 2021). To fall within the scope of my theory, the domestic combatants must be opposing one another on the same battlefield and their external support must come from competing third-party states.

between the competitive interveners. Third-party states must account for these risks and confront the strategic dilemmas they entail. This, it will be demonstrated, has important implications for the strategies competitive interveners employ to influence conflict outcomes—the scale and scope of the aid they provision, the qualitative characteristics of the weapons they deliver, and the area of effect of their participation in foreign wars.

Second, competing flows of external military assistance render conflict dynamics more uncertain while simultaneously lowering the costs of fighting. And crucially, these effects are felt by *both* sides of an internal conflict. The chapters that follow unpack the significance of these effects for belligerents' willingness to delay negotiated settlements, even in the face of painful and persistent stalemates.

Third, competition among interveners renders peace negotiations more challenging. Agreements to terminate fighting must not only satisfy the domestic combatants but must also appease foreign interests. This adds an additional layer of complexity to bargaining dynamics, as opposing interveners endeavor to ensure that domestic resolutions align with their own desired ends. This, it will be shown, has significant policy implications for the sequencing of peace talks.

Fourth, a focus on the adversarial nature of competitive intervention draws attention to the interconnected nature of interstate competition and intrastate war. While by definition domestic conflicts, civil wars are part and parcel of a much larger geopolitical environment. As that environment undergoes change, the transnational linkages and interactions that influence civil war dynamics are subject to change as well. This insight sheds fresh light on the international systemic dimensions of internal conflict, as well as the ways in which changes at the level of the international system affect the character of intervention in civil wars.

Finally, greater attention to the competitive dynamics that distinguish competitive intervention from one-sided intervention is crucial for devising more effective conflict resolution strategies. By recognizing the unique strategic dilemmas that competitive intervention entails, policymakers and stakeholders can work toward minimizing the negative impacts of external meddling in internal wars while promoting more constructive and sustainable peace processes.

Competitive interventions are *interventions* insofar as they employ military and/or economic instruments to influence the dynamics and outcomes of civil wars in foreign countries by affecting the balance of power between government and rebel forces. This definition is in line with those regularly adopted in the literature, but note that my conception of intervention differs from existing studies in a number of ways. First, while I consider intervention to encompass the deployment of combat forces to directly assist one side of a civil war, I also include other forms of support that fall below that threshold, including the provision of weapons and ammunition transfers, financial aid, access to territory and military infrastructure, war materiel, logistical and intelligence support, training and advising, and other forms of military support, such as assistance with recruitment or arms trafficking. My more expansive definition of intervention distinguishes this book from those studies that focus exclusively on boots-on-the-ground military operations.[24] This broader conceptualization is also theoretically and empirically important: as I elaborate in the next chapter, competitively intervening states often constrain the scope of their support to domestic combatants for the purposes of escalation control. Consequently, a conception of intervention focused exclusively on foreign troop deployments misses much of the interventionism undertaken by third-party states.

Second, my emphasis on *competing* flows of external aid to opposing domestic combatants sets this book apart from studies that explore external support to only one side of a civil war.[25] It focuses attention on the ways in which strategic interactions among competitively intervening states condition the scale and scope of military assistance provided to domestic combatants. In doing so, it helps explain why the effectiveness of interventions is often constrained and why conflict stalemates often persist.

Finally, my conception of intervention is inclusive of all third-party state interveners, irrespective of their power status in world politics. Unlike some studies that focus their attention on great power interventions, this book additionally explores the impact of foreign meddling by regional powers and smaller states.[26] This broader perspective enriches the analysis by uncovering the pernicious role that competitive interventions by lesser powers have played in perpetuating civil wars, both in the past and in the contemporary international system.

The concept of competitive intervention is closely related to the concept of proxy war, but it is a limited variety of this form of warfare. While many conflicts around the globe and across time have been labeled proxy wars by pundits, politicians, and political scientists alike, surprisingly little theoretical work has been done to identify the defining properties of this form of conflict.[27]

---

[24] For examples of studies that define intervention in terms of boots-on-the-ground military operations, see Tillema (1989), Balch-Lindsay and Enterline (2000), Balch-Lindsay, Enterline, and Joyce (2008), Cunningham (2010), Metternich (2011), Peksen (2012), and Sullivan and Karreth (2015). This is also the definition used in widely cited civil war datasets, including the UCDP Armed Conflict Dataset (N. Gleditsch et al. 2002) and the Correlates of War Dataset (Sarkees and Wayman 2010).

[25] For examples of studies that focus attention on support to only one side of a conflict, see Byman et al. (2001), Saideman (2002), Bapat (2012), Carter (2012), Byman (2013), San-Akca (2016), and Grauer and Tierney (2018).

[26] For examples of studies with a focus on great power interventions, see Sullivan and Koch (2009), Kavanagh et al. (2017), and Kushi and Toft (2023).

[27] On the conceptual development of the proxy war literature, see Rauta (2021).

An important consequence of this omission has been the conceptual stretching of the proxy war concept to a myriad of often decidedly dissimilar cases.[28] For example, the term has been used to describe conflicts where one or more minor states fight at the behest of their great power ally. This application of the concept was popular during the Cold War, when scholars sought to interpret the role of the United States and Soviet Union in regional conflicts, such as the Arab-Israeli and Indo-Pakistani wars.[29] Proxy war has also been used as a label for conflicts in which a non-state actor fights a state opponent at the behest of another state patron.[30] This conceptualization is common in the "delegation of war" literature, which posits that states delegate warfighting to rebel groups to reduce the costs associated with advancing their foreign policy interests.[31] A closely related school applies principal-agent frameworks to understand foreign states' indirect control of local agents more broadly.[32]

Most troubling of all, proxy war has at times been used to describe cases in which *any* type of external party has indirectly engaged in a conflict to affect its outcome. One recent study, for example, includes under the rubric of "proxy wars" cases as diverse as the Thirty Years' War, the American Civil War, and the First World War; describes the American deployment of the Stuxnet virus against Iranian nuclear facilities as an "example of a proxy war strategy [...] in the cyber realm"; categorizes the US alliance with Taiwan as a "preventative proxy war" against China; and stylizes al-Qaeda's war against the West as "a religiously inspired proxy war" insofar as jihadists see themselves as "proxy clients of God."[33] Another recent volume extends the concept to include private military contractors, multinational corporations, and remotely piloted drones.[34] Such a broad conceptualization is problematic not only because it makes comparisons across cases exceedingly difficult but also because it renders the proxy war concept so elastic that it detracts from its analytic utility.[35]

---

[28] On conceptual stretching, see Sartori (1970) and Collier and Mahon (1993).
[29] See, for example, Bissell (1978), Vanneman and James (1978), Stein (1980), and Bar-Siman-Tov (1984).
[30] See, for example, Abbink (2003), Prunier (2004), Tubiana (2008), K. Gleditsch, Salehyan, and Schultz (2008: 484), Hughes (2012: 11–14), and Groh (2019: 29).
[31] See, for example, Salehyan (2010) and Hauter (2019). On delegation within a state's own borders, see Ahram (2011) and Eck (2015).
[32] See, for example, Byman and Kreps (2010), Salehyan, K. Gleditsch, and Cunningham (2011), Bapat (2012), Salehyan, Siroky, and Wood (2014), Popovic (2017), Rittinger (2017), Biddle, MacDonald, and Baker (2018), Berkowitz (2018), Berman and Lake (2019), Groh (2019), Marshall (2019), and Elias (2020). Also see San-Akca (2016) for a framework that conceives of state selection of rebel groups and rebel group selection of states as separate processes.
[33] Mumford (2013: 11–12, 88, 93, 105).
[34] See the contributions in Innes (2012).
[35] A related problem concerns the proliferation of labels for the actors participating in proxy wars, as well as their relationships to one another. See Rauta (2018).

My definition of competitive intervention is considerably more narrow in scope. First, I restrict the class of interveners to opposing third-party states. Second, I restrict the class of recipients of external support to rival government and rebel combatant forces engaged in combat. And third, I restrict the class of conflicts under examination to ongoing civil wars. While these restrictions scope out many of the "proxy wars" identified in the existing literature, they ensure that meaningful comparisons can be drawn across cases. Moreover, what is lost in empirical breadth is more than made up for in analytical depth: I move beyond popular anecdotes and derive theoretically grounded propositions about the strategic logics motivating intervener behaviors and their consequences for civil wars.

By "civil war," I refer to *an organized armed conflict between a state and domestic armed group(s) that results in fatalities.*[36] The question of "how many" fatalities are required to deem intrastate violence a civil war is an important one, not least because it has proven contentious.[37] In the wider literature, scholars have employed various fatality threshold criteria, ranging from 1,000 annual deaths per conflict, to 1,000 cumulative deaths per conflict, to 25 annual deaths per conflict.[38] This book takes the middle ground, adopting a fatality threshold criterion that includes both yearly minimums and cumulative totals: conflicts must inflict at least 25 battle-related deaths annually and at least 1,000 battle-related deaths cumulatively. While these scope conditions again reduce the generalizability of my theory, they are important for ensuring that the cases that are included in this study are sufficiently alike to merit meaningful comparisons. In the empirical chapters that follow, I also probe my findings at different battle-related death thresholds and demonstrate the robustness of my results to alternative definitions of civil war.

Situating the Argument: Complementary and Competing Perspectives

In developing a theory of competitive intervention in civil war, I engage with three broad strands of literature on conflict duration, third-party intervention

---

[36] This definition is in keeping with those widely employed in the existing literature. See, for example, N. Gleditsch et al. (2002), Fearon and Laitin (2003a), Doyle and Sambanis (2006), and Sarkees and Wayman (2010). It is inclusive of "internationalized civil wars"—that is, civil wars that attract the deployment of troops from other states on one or both sides (cf. N. Gleditsch et al. 2002; Themnér and Wallensteen 2014).

[37] For a discussion, see Anderson and Worsnop (2019).

[38] See, respectively, Collier, Hoeffler, and Söderbom (2004), Sambanis (2000), and N. Gleditsch et al. (2002).

and conflict management, and limited war. To situate my argument within this rich body of scholarship, I briefly turn to review existing approaches and identify gaps in our knowledge that are addressed by this book.

Civil War Duration

Civil wars exhibit remarkable variation in their duration. While some conflicts burn themselves out in only a few weeks or months, others rage on for decades. This has attracted the sustained attention of scholars, who have identified a number of variables correlated with protracted civil wars. For example, low gross domestic product (GDP) per capita has been linked to longer conflicts, whether because it reflects institutional weakness or because low per capita incomes decrease the opportunity costs of warfighting.[39] Democracies are likewise believed to suffer longer civil wars than their authoritarian counterparts, not least because they are constrained by domestic and international audiences in their ability to fight ruthlessly against insurgencies.[40] Large population sizes are associated with prolonged conflict, likely because state surveillance, policing, and control become more difficult as populations grow larger.[41] Multiparty conflicts are similarly more difficult to resolve, owing to their unique bargaining challenges.[42] Civil wars fought between ethnic groups are thought to be especially difficult to end—a finding that has given rise to calls for partition as the best, and perhaps only, solution to ethnonationalist conflict.[43] A related argument suggests that conflicts over territorial secession are more intractable than are wars in which rebel groups pursue goals that do not threaten the territorial integrity of the state.[44] And even a state's physical terrain has been linked to the dynamics of armed conflict: some suggest that rugged, mountainous terrain benefits rebels by providing a safe haven;[45] others link natural resource wealth to longer civil wars.[46]

Taken together, this rich body of scholarship provides a valuable contribution to our understanding of the determinants of civil war duration. It highlights the

[39] See Fearon and Laitin (2003a) and Collier, Hoeffler, and Söderbom (2004), respectively.
[40] For a review and critique of arguments linking democracy to prolonged civil war, see Lyall (2010).
[41] Collier, Hoeffler, and Söderbom (2004); Raleigh and Hegre (2009).
[42] Cunningham (2011).
[43] See C. Kaufmann (1996), Chapman and Roeder (2007), and Wucherpfennig et al. (2012). But also see Sambanis (2000), Fearon (2004), and Sambanis and Schulhofer-Wohl (2009).
[44] Weiner (1978); Licklider (1995); Balch-Lindsay and Enterline (2000); Toft (2002, 2006); Goddard (2006, 2010); Fearon and Laitin (2011). On the general relationship between territory and war, see Toft (2014).
[45] Fearon and Laitin (2003a); Buhaug and Lujala (2005); Lujala (2010); Bleaney and Dimico (2011); Tollefsen and Buhaug (2015).
[46] Ross (2004); Buhaug, Gates, and Lujala (2009); Lujala (2010).

wide range of political, economic, and social contexts in which intrastate conflicts are fought; it identifies which of these contexts correlate with protracted fighting; and it provides an empirical foundation upon which to develop new insights about the dynamics of internal wars.

But there is a problem: most of these explanations privilege structural variables that change much too slowly to fully account for the decline in the prevalence of civil war documented above. Unless we have strong reasons to believe that post–Cold War civil wars are breaking out in countries that are fundamentally dissimilar from their Cold War predecessors, variables subject to gradual change—such as GDP per capita, population size, or ethnic diversity—are ill-suited to explain the sharp discontinuity in the number of ongoing internal wars that coincides with the end of the Cold War.

A second problem is the "closed polity" approach that is adopted in many existing studies of civil war duration.[47] Because they are by definition *intra*state conflicts, much of the literature has been dominated by a theoretical perspective that stresses domestic factors. Yet, this overlooks the international actors, structures, and processes that shape the dynamics and outcomes of internal conflict: the tens of thousands of troops deployed to foreign war zones; the millions of rounds of ammunition shipped to foreign combatants; and the billions of dollars of aid transferred to foreign governments and rebel groups alike. That the recent reversal in the prevalence of civil war coincides with the collapse of the Soviet Union, the termination of the Cold War, and the dawn of the unipolar moment only underscores the point that there is a need to widen the theoretical aperture beyond the borders of the state afflicted by internal conflict to better understand why some civil wars last so long.

By taking the intrastate/interstate conflict nexus seriously, this book makes a number of contributions to the existing literature. First, the analysis that follows generates new insights on the determinants of civil war duration by explicitly incorporating actors, structures, and processes that originate beyond the civil war battlefield into a comprehensive account of protracted conflict. It integrates the international system into the study of civil war duration by specifying its impact on state decisions to intervene in foreign conflicts and, in turn, on domestic combatants' willingness to continue fighting. I demonstrate that variation in the structural incentives and constraints of bipolar and unipolar systems significantly affects the configuration of external aid flows to civil wars, which has crucial implications for domestic combatants' costs of war, relative military capabilities, and private information. This result sheds new light on the drivers of protracted fighting by incorporating the influence of external meddling into a bargaining model of internal conflict.

---

[47] For a critique and discussion of the "closed polity" approach to civil war, see K. Gleditsch (2007).

Second, this book demonstrates empirically that foreign meddling has been a ubiquitous and consistent feature of the ostensibly "internal" civil war process across time. Employing new data on external military assistance to civil war combatants with a broad temporal scope, it reveals that the vast majority of internal conflicts—an average of nearly 75% per year—attracted external aid of some kind. This striking result presents a powerful challenge to the traditional distinction that is drawn between intrastate and interstate conflicts. It underscores that, far from being exclusively internal affairs, intrastate conflicts are intimately linked to the dynamics of interstate coercion and bargaining.

Finally, this book's theoretical and empirical findings highlight a severe omitted variable bias problem afflicting existing studies that fail to account for the international determinants of civil war duration. Insofar as the "internationalization" of civil wars is the rule, rather than the exception, a failure to account for external aid flows to civil war combatants risks incomplete and misleading inferences about the drivers of conflict dynamics and outcomes. In the pages that follow, I provide a corrective by empirically estimating the substantive and statistical significance of different configurations of third-party intervention for trends in the average duration and global prevalence of civil war.

Third-Party Intervention and Conflict Management

While the domestic determinants of civil war duration have dominated the literature, interest in the international dimensions of intrastate conflict has been long-standing.[48] One prominent argument emphasizes the facilitative role of third parties in helping to end—rather than prolong—civil wars. This perspective contends that peace settlements ultimately fail because domestic combatants are unable to guarantee the terms of their own mutually arranged settlements. This incentivizes defection from agreements, since neither side can credibly commit to abide by a peace treaty's terms. Third-party interveners, it is argued, help to overcome this problem by guaranteeing agreements, monitoring compliance, and protecting against defection. In these ways, they "solve" the credible commitment problem faced by domestic combatants, thereby facilitating bargaining and war termination.[49]

Support for these arguments can be found in the peacekeeping literature, which confirms the ameliorative effects peacekeeping operations can have in conflict zones.[50] Peacekeepers can serve as third-party guarantors of peace treaties, physically separating and disarming domestic combatants to make a

---

[48] For early examples, see Eckstein (1964), Rosenau (1964), and Luard (1972).
[49] Walter (1997, 2002).
[50] For recent reviews of this literature, see Sandler (2017) and Walter, Howard, and Fortna (2021).

resumption of fighting more difficult. In this way, peacekeeping can help to overcome credible commitment problems by reassuring belligerents, deterring violations of negotiated settlements, and protecting against defections from agreements. In the post–Cold War period, the United Nations (UN) has also moved beyond "traditional peacekeeping" by expanding the civilian component of its operations to include election monitoring, police training, and civilian administration. This new wave of "robust" (or multidimensional) peacekeeping has had a significant impact on civil wars. First, it has decreased conflict recidivism and contributed to the prolongation of peace.[51] Second, it has lowered levels of violence and civilian victimization.[52] Third, it has reduced the time to negotiate resolutions between combatants.[53] And fourth, it has prevented the spread of conflict.[54] Taken together, the joint effect of these outcomes supports the claim that peacekeeping has a significant peace-enhancing role to play in conflict-afflicted societies.[55] Some scholars suggest these findings also help to explain the recent decline in the prevalence of civil war.[56]

Perhaps because the logic and evidence of the commitment problem argument is so compelling, information problems—of the type emphasized in this book—have been downplayed as an explanation for protracted civil wars. A number of scholars have claimed that asymmetric information provides a poor account of lengthy conflict, since information about the relative strength and resolve of the combatants should be revealed quickly on the battlefield.[57] Credible commitment problems, it is argued, are *the* critical barrier to civil war settlement. Accordingly, it has been suggested that civil wars that attract third-party interventions are likely to be shorter, not longer.[58]

There are major limitations to this perspective, however. First, the literature on third-party intervention and credible commitment problems tends to conflate "third party" with "international organization," failing to incorporate the strategies and incentives of other actors—especially other states.[59] This overlooks the vast majority of third-party intervention that occurs during civil wars. A second limitation, which stems directly from the first, is

---

[51] Fortna (2004, 2008); Doyle and Sambanis (2006); Gilligan and Sergenti (2008); Hultman, Kathman, and Shannon (2016).
[52] Hultman, Kathman, and Shannon (2013, 2014).
[53] Ruggeri, Dorussen, and Gizelis (2017); Kathman and Benson (2019).
[54] Beardsley (2011); Beardsley and K. Gleditsch (2015).
[55] Hegre, Hultman, and Nygård (2019).
[56] Goldstein (2011).
[57] See, for example, Reiter (2003: 32), Fearon (2004: 290), Powell (2006: 172–176), Walter (2009: 246, 254), Blattman and Miguel (2010: 12), and Schulhofer-Wohl (2020: 34, 36).
[58] Walter (2009: 254–256).
[59] Relatedly, the focus of much of this literature is the duration of post-conflict *peace*, not the duration of conflict itself. Fortna (2008: 6), for example, is explicit about this in her study on the effectiveness of UN peacekeeping: "I am examining the effects of whether peace lasts, not on whether peace is achieved in the first place."

this perspective's assumption that international interventions are intended to expedite the resolution of conflict, either by suppressing violence or by improving the prospects for negotiation. While this may be a reasonable assumption for multilateral interventions led by international organizations like the UN, it is untenable when we expand the set of third-party interveners to include other states. Indeed, states are strategic actors that may have incentives to empower insurgents, destabilize regimes, and impose costs on interstate rivals.[60] Empirically, studies have found that state intervention can make conflicts more difficult to resolve; that troop deployments to both government and rebel forces can generate battlefield stalemates; and that fungible support to rebels can prolong conflict.[61] More generally, foreign powers can struggle to positively influence the behavior of local actors, resulting in unsuccessful interventions, policy failures in counterinsurgency wars, and quagmires on civil war battlefields.[62] And even when undertaken as well-intentioned humanitarian operations, third-party intervention can do more harm than good.[63]

Thus, there remains a real tension in the literature between those who argue that interventions help ameliorate bargaining challenges in civil wars, and those who argue that they can have opposite effects. To help resolve this tension, and to deepen our understanding of the link between third-party intervention and civil war duration, this book departs from the existing literature in a number of ways.

First, I challenge the established view that information problems provide a poor account of lengthy conflict, making the case for the renewed study of uncertainty and asymmetric information in *ex post* decisions to keep fighting. Existing bargaining model accounts conceive of the costly learning process of war as a unidirectional flow of information: from initial conditions, the belligerents cumulatively learn about their opponent's relative capabilities and resolve, with combatant expectations converging monotonically. This, I argue, ignores the ways in which dynamic processes *exogenous* to the battlefield—such as competitive intervention—distort the information-transmission function of fighting. Moreover, the existing literature's emphasis on credible commitment problems overlooks the fact that many protracted civil wars are characterized by the *absence* of meaningful negotiation, often for many years or even decades. This presents a challenge to the credible commitment perspective insofar as it suggests that the primary hurdle in bargaining for domestic combatants is not the inability to commit credibly to mutually agreed terms, but rather their lack

---

[60] Akcinaroglu and Radziszewski (2005); Lee (2020).
[61] See, respectively, Regan (2002) and Cunningham (2010); Balch-Lindsay and Enterline (2000) and Balch-Lindsay, Enterline, and Joyce (2008); and Sawyer, Cunningham, and Reed (2017).
[62] Petersen (2011); Elias (2020); Schulhofer-Wohl (2020).
[63] Betts (1994); Luttwak (1999); Kuperman (2008); Paris (2014).

of willingness to engage in negotiations in the first place. Relatedly, many civil wars end in the *absence* of third-party guarantees.[64] This suggests that while credible commitment problems can be an important barrier to civil war settlement, they are not the only one. Scholars have also identified conditions under which long wars can result even though both sides *can* credibly commit to a settlement.[65] This again highlights the need to more carefully explore how information problems afflict domestic bargaining in the context of protracted fighting.

Second, while existing studies examine the consequences of interventions with a focus on the patron–client relationship of interveners and domestic combatants, my approach additionally considers the strategic interactions of the interveners themselves—that is, the ways in which *intervener competition* over the stakes of a conflict affects its dynamics and outcomes. Exploring this additional dimension of the intervention process sheds new light on the intrastate/interstate conflict nexus by identifying the strategic logic that informs intervener behaviors. I uncover the conditional nature of intervention under the shadow of inadvertent escalation and explain why intervening states often refrain from providing the level of support necessary for military success, instead providing a level of support sufficient only to avoid battlefield defeat. By additionally connecting these behaviors to domestic bargaining distortions, I demonstrate how the strategic dilemmas interveners confront vis-à-vis *one another* affect civil war combatants' value for fighting, estimates of future battlefield outcomes, and assessments of relative power and resolve, as well as the set of mutually acceptable settlements. These results not only improve our understanding of the relationship between third-party intervention and civil war duration but also challenge prominent views—advanced by scholars and policymakers alike—that hold that interveners can help end civil wars by fostering "mutually hurting stalemates" that are "ripe" for conflict resolution.[66]

Third, while existing distinctions between multilateral peacekeepers and state interveners have facilitated progress in our understanding of third-party intervention, I call attention to the importance of greater theoretical and empirical disaggregation in the study of foreign support and protracted conflict. To date, many existing studies remain overly limited in scope, whether due to an exclusive focus on boots-on-the-ground military operations or one-sided interventions.[67] By adopting a broader conceptualization of military assistance—one

---

[64] See Toft (2009: 31).
[65] Findley (2013); Krainin et al (2020).
[66] E.g., Zartman (1985, 2000).
[67] See, for example, Balch-Lindsay and Enterline (2000), Balch-Lindsay, Enterline, and Joyce (2008), and Cunningham (2010). An important exception is Regan (2002). Unfortunately, monotone likelihood afflicts the study, which results in inflated parameter estimates that diverge to infinity for variables recording the presence or absence of intervention. For a detailed discussion, see Anderson, Bagozzi, and Koren (2021).

that incorporates external aid below the threshold of troop deployments, that is inclusive of all third-party state interveners, and that captures variation in the configuration of external aid flows—this book demonstrates the distinctive impacts of one-sided and competitive interventions, the significance of external meddling by lesser powers, and the effects of international systemic change on global trends in external military assistance to civil war combatants.

Finally, while scholars have called attention to the booming peacekeeping industry that has developed in the post–Cold War period, the existing literature has remained largely silent on the question of whether and how patterns of state intervention have changed over time. Conventional accounts assume that the end of the Cold War put a premium on domestic sources of warfighting capacity in light of the termination of great power support.[68] Yet to date, this assumption has gone untested in the empirical literature. In this book, I demonstrate that the transition from a bipolar to a unipolar international system did have an important effect on the nature of third-party intervention—but not in the ways one might expect. Contrary to the established view, the percentage of civil wars attracting foreign military assistance remained virtually unchanged as the Cold War came to a close. What did change, however, was the *configuration* of external aid flows to civil war combatants: the frequency of competitive intervention was cut in half, while the rate of one-sided intervention increased by over one and a half times. As will be explained in the pages that follow, these changes have had profound implications for conflict management, the average duration of internal conflicts, and the global prevalence of civil war.

Limited War

Escalation and its control lie at the heart of my account of competitive intervention and protracted conflict. But while recognized as a strategic problem since Clausewitz, the study of escalation dynamics largely fell out of fashion as the Cold War came to a close. This book makes a case for its revival. In doing so, it engages with an older literature concerned with limiting the scope of war in the nuclear age. It also speaks to a newer literature on the challenges posed by "hybrid wars" in the twenty-first century.

The modern study of limited war emerged in opposition to the Eisenhower administration's "New Look" national security strategy, which sought to deter communist aggression in third areas with threats of "massive retaliation." Critics argued that the strategy lacked credibility given that the Soviet Union could

---

[68] See, for example, Regan (2000: 51–52), Kalyvas (2001: 117), Collier and Hoeffler (2004: 568), Human Security Centre (2005), Lacina (2006: 285), Lacina, N. Gleditsch, and Russett (2006: 678), and Kalyvas and Balcells (2010: 421–422).

retaliate in kind. The US–Soviet nuclear stalemate meant that to fulfill a threat of massive retaliation was to suffer costs as great as those inflicted. Assuming both sides accepted that the interests at stake were not worth mutually assured destruction—as they undoubtedly would in peripheral wars of lesser strategic significance—any effort to protect national interests with a strategy of massive retaliation would fail.[69] These realities necessitated finding ways to successfully prosecute wars *without* resorting to the full military potential of the US armed forces.

The question of how military force could be limited became an important subject of inquiry.[70] While some highlighted the need for formal diplomacy, others observed that tacit communication could coordinate state behavior even in the absence of explicit bargaining.[71] During the Korean War, for example, belligerents found ways to limit the scope of war without formal talks: the principal northern political boundary was marked by a river that served to geographically constrain fighting; the thirty-eighth parallel served as a focus for military stalemate; and weapons were distinguished by the qualitative differences between nuclear and non-nuclear armaments.[72] The observation of these limits by belligerents reflected their mutual recognition that while either side *could* have expanded the war, doing so would have benefited neither. For limited war theorists, the Korean case demonstrated the role that tacit bargaining and communication could play in controlling escalation.

Limited war theory was a product of its time, shaped by the pressures of the nuclear age. Its scope was narrowly centered on wars in which the US would square off against the Soviet Union or China; the key limitation of interest centered on the (non-)use of nuclear weapons; and there were few historical cases with which to empirically assess the theory. By the late 1960s, the popularity of the approach began to wane.[73] With the end of East–West confrontation in the early 1990s, the limited war school faded further. The dawn of the unipolar moment presented new strategic problems to consider—in the 1990s, humanitarian interventions in countries like Somalia and the Former Yugoslavia, and in the 2000s, the "return" of counterinsurgency operations in countries like Afghanistan and Iraq.

Nonetheless, limited war theory provides valuable insights on the interplay of explicit and tacit bargaining and communication; the importance of limited aims in the development of military strategy; and the critical role of escalation

---

[69] For early critiques of this kind, see Brodie (1954), W. Kaufmann (1954), Morgenthau (1954), and Kissinger (1955).

[70] See, for example, W. Kaufmann (1956), Osgood (1957, 1979), Kissinger (1957), Brodie (1959), and Halperin (1963a).

[71] For the former, see Kissinger (1957). For the latter, see Schelling (1957, 1960) and Rathjens (1958: 187–188).

[72] Schelling (1957: 33); Halperin (1963b).

[73] For a discussion, see Trachtenberg (1989).

control in constraining the scope of war. And while nuclear strategy may seem divorced from the study of civil conflict, many of the strategic questions examined by limited war theorists in the 1950s and 1960s remain relevant in the contemporary period. For example, recent work has applied limited war theory in new and exciting ways to better understand states' strategic use of secrecy to control escalation.[74] There is also a proliferating literature on "hybrid war" (or "gray war"), in which adversaries eschew large-scale conventional confrontations in favor of a tailored mix of conventional, irregular, and covert means.[75] Considerable concern has centered on the supposedly "new" challenge that this form of conflict entails. Yet, the central elements of a hybrid war struggle are in many ways akin to those identified by the limited war school: upper bounds are established on overt violence; fears of inadvertent escalation to general war drive strategic decision-making; and tacit bargaining and communication play a central role in the interactions of adversaries. In short, insights from the past have retained their relevance for contemporary conflicts.

This book therefore extends limited war theory in a number of novel and productive ways. First, it explores limited war dynamics in a unique empirical setting: civil wars. Second, it assesses the consequences of interveners' limited war strategies for a heretofore unexplored outcome variable: civil war duration. Third, it looks beyond the great powers to better understand how escalatory risks affect the intervention strategies of all states, regardless of their power status. Fourth, it looks beyond the Cold War period to develop a more generalizable account that bears insights for civil wars both past *and* present. And fifth, it relaxes the focus on the non-use of nuclear weapons to explore other limiting processes, including in contexts where nuclear use would be impossible owing to a lack of capability. Taken together, these innovations significantly expand the applicability of earlier insights on limited war dynamics while shedding new light on the consequences of interveners' limited war strategies for internal conflicts.

Contributions

In addition to its engagement with the diverse literature on civil war duration, third-party intervention, and limited war, the theoretical and empirical findings presented in this book make a number of contributions to policy and to scholarship.

---

[74] Carson (2016, 2018).
[75] See, for example, Hoffman (2007), Murray and Mansoor (2012), Freedman (2014), Monaghan (2015), Thornton (2015), Lanoszka (2016), Renz (2016), Freier et al. (2016), Johnson (2018), Hicks and Friend (2019), and McCarthy, Moyer, and Venable (2019). These concepts have also gained currency in policy and military circles. See, for example, North Atlantic Treaty Organization (2015) and US Special Operations Command (2015).

My results are of immediate relevance to some of today's most deadly and protracted conflicts: in Libya, where Turkey supports a Government of National Unity against the Russian-backed House of Representatives and its Libyan National Army; in Sudan, where the United Arab Emirates arms the Rapid Support Forces in a rebellion against the Egyptian-backed Sudanese Armed Forces; in Syria, where the Russian- and Iranian-backed Assad regime fights opposition groups armed by Turkey and the US; and in Yemen, where Saudi Arabia bolsters a Yemeni regime fighting Iranian-backed Houthi rebels. This book helps to explain why these conflicts persist. In doing so, it identifies pathways to their resolution.

My theory and empirics also draw attention to a problematic assumption held among pundits, policymakers, and political scientists alike—that backing friendly governments or rebel movements can help to end civil wars by manipulating the costs of fighting and the benefits of negotiated settlement.[76] By facilitating a "mutually hurting stalemate" through the selective application of butter and guns, it is argued, interveners can create the preconditions necessary for peace.[77] Yet, empirical reality does not comport with this theoretical claim: even when a civil war has become a costly, protracted battle of attrition, rebel and government forces regularly choose to continue to bear the human and financial costs of war. This suggests that conceiving of external military aid as a tool to manipulate the payoffs of war and peace is incomplete; there is a need to more rigorously identify how external aid affects domestic bargaining dynamics. This book explains why the effectiveness of interventions is often constrained: under the shadow of inadvertent escalation, interveners must balance their desire to intervene with their need to control the risk of enlarged conflict. Far from facilitating negotiated settlements, this prevents the conferral of decisive military advantages while simultaneously distorting domestic bargaining processes. Protracted war results.

My results also speak to ongoing debates over the utility of military assistance as a foreign policy instrument in an age of shifting security strategies. The political will needed to sustain large troop deployments has waned following costly interventions in Iraq and Afghanistan. In their place, policymakers have increasingly turned to security force assistance programs, which bolster allied forces at lower political and financial cost. These programs train, equip, and advise partner forces to meet security challenges without depending on foreign combat troops. Over the past decade, security force assistance has become increasingly popular, emerging as a central plank of the national defense strategies of middle

---

[76] See, for example, Licklider (1995), Walter (1997, 2002), Rothchild (1997), Carment and Rowlands (1998), Regan (2002), Siqueira (2003), Amegashie and Kutsoati (2007), and Sisk (2009).
[77] Zartman (1985, 2000).

and great powers alike.[78] Yet, while the delegation of war might reduce the annual budgetary cost of a given foreign policy outcome, these short-term fiscal benefits must be weighed against long-term consequences—the possibility of unintended effects, the risk of retaliatory responses from interstate rivals, and the potential for prolonged military campaigns.[79] By adopting a broad conceptualization of military assistance and a wide temporal scope, this book tracks variation in patterns of military aid to uncover its varying effects on civil wars over time. My results suggest that the benefits of security force assistance programs should not be oversold. Especially in an era of increasing competition among interstate rivals, understanding the challenges posed by competitive intervention is crucial to shaping realistic expectations about the efficacy of military assistance as a foreign policy tool.

For scholars, this book contributes to a growing body of scholarship that explores the ways in which the international system conditions intrastate conflicts. To date, existing research has linked the dynamics of the international system to changes in conflict intensities, outcomes, and technologies of rebellion.[80] My theory of competitive intervention complements these findings, developing an argument that moves beyond popular anecdotes about Cold War era "proxy wars" by deriving theoretically grounded propositions about the effect of international systemic change on global trends in intervention, as well as the strategic logics motivating competitive interventions. By drawing attention to the pernicious role that competitive interventions by lesser powers have played in civil wars, it also underscores the importance of a generalizable theory applicable across time and irrespective of the power status of the interveners.

In a related vein, this book's examination of competitive intervention from domestic, international, and systemic perspectives demonstrates the value of linking multiple levels of analysis to advance our understanding of civil war dynamics.[81] It calls attention to the inferential leverage to be gained through multi-level theoretical integration in the study of civil war and the careful consideration of the nested interactions of domestic combatants, intervening states, and the international distribution of power. In doing so, it helps to fill a gap in the existing literature while also contributing to the theoretical and empirical development of both the interstate and civil conflict research fields.

---

[78] For example, Canada's most recent national defense policy lists "capacity building to support the security of other nations" as one of the Canadian Armed Forces' "core missions" (Canadian Department of National Defense 2017: 82, 86). Similarly, the growing significance of security force assistance for US defense strategy can be seen in the US Army's formation of Security Force Assistance Brigades within the Security Force Assistance Command in 2018.

[79] On the delegation of war, see Salehyan (2010).

[80] On intensity, see Lacina (2006). On outcomes, see Kreutz (2010) and Howard and Stark (2018). On technologies of rebellion, see Kalyvas and Balcells (2010) and Balcells and Kalyvas (2014).

[81] On the value of linking levels of analysis in the study of civil war, see Balcells and Justino (2014).

This book also contributes to a burgeoning literature on escalation and its control. Recent work has explored the microfoundations that underpin escalation dynamics.[82] Other studies consider the implications of emerging technologies—such as drones and cyberattacks—on escalatory risks.[83] Related work examines the strategic use of secrecy as a device for sustaining limits in war.[84] This book builds on these and related contributions by developing a distinct argument about escalation and its control in the context of competitive intervention. It draws a link between the symbolic significance of "thresholds"— salient limits that interveners use to signal their intentions—and the characteristics of aid provision. This approach yields new insights about intervener decision-making and behavior under the shadow of inadvertent escalation. It also draws attention to a largely overlooked consequence of the war-limiting process: conflict prolongation.

An important empirical contribution of the book is its presentation of new data on third-party intervention in civil wars. It introduces the Extended External Support Dataset, which provides global coverage of external military aid flows to civil wars for all years from 1946 to 2009. Drawing on a broad range of quantitative and qualitative sources, the dataset captures a wide variety of types of external support, including troop deployments, weapons and ammunition transfers, financial aid, access to territory and/or military infrastructure, and the provision of war materiel, logistical support, intelligence, and training. Observations are recorded at a yearly resolution for both government and rebel combatants. The dataset also records which state(s) provisioned aid. The net result is a comprehensive record of external aid flows to civil war combatants that reveals the scope and scale of foreign meddling in internal conflicts over the course of more than six decades of warfare.

Finally, this book contributes to our understanding of the continued evolution of the security landscape of the twenty-first century. The decline of civil wars across the globe is a good news story for the international community, but without a theoretical and empirical understanding of the causes of the decline, it is impossible to know whether this trend will continue. Policy debates over the global diffusion of power and its implications for international stability have unfolded against the backdrop of Russian interventions and Chinese military modernization. Russia's renewed foreign policy assertiveness and China's global rise represent new challenges to existing global governance structures that risk the proliferation of ungovernable spaces in weak states. By studying the processes that drive trends in the average duration and global prevalence

---

[82] Lin-Greenberg (2022, 2023).
[83] Talmadge (2019); Kreps and Schneider (2019); Lin-Greenberg (2022).
[84] Carson (2016, 2018); Cormac and Aldrich (2018).

of intrastate conflict, this book stands to inform new policy solutions that can guide engagement with international competitors in future civil wars.

Looking Ahead

This book is organized into seven chapters. This introductory chapter has overviewed the book's research questions and motivation, previewed its central arguments, defined key terms, identified scope conditions, and discussed its contributions for scholarship and for policy. It is followed by Chapter 2, which presents my theory of competitive intervention in full. I develop a framework that integrates the nested interactions of domestic combatants, third-party interveners, and the international distribution of power. I detail the distortionary effects that competitive intervention entails for domestic bargaining processes, explain the escalation dilemma confronting competitively intervening states, and link variation in the prevalence of competitive intervention to international systemic change. I conclude the chapter by deriving hypotheses from my theory, identifying the observable implications of my argument, and describing the research design I employ to test my claims in subsequent chapters.

In Chapter 3, I introduce the Extended External Support Dataset, a new dataset that records information on external military assistance to civil war combatants for all years from 1946 to 2009. I then present a range of descriptive data that chronicles how patterns of intervention have varied over time. I demonstrate, for example, that external intervention has been a ubiquitous feature of the ostensibly "internal" civil war process since the end of the Second World War. Moreover, I show that the percentage of conflicts attracting external aid remained virtually unchanged even as the international system transitioned from a bipolar to a unipolar distribution of power. However, while rates of intervention remained consistent, the *configuration* of military aid flows to domestic combatants changed dramatically: the rate at which competitive intervention afflicted civil wars was halved in the unipolar period, while the rate of one-sided intervention increased by over one and a half times. I also show that the popular notion that great power "proxy wars" pervaded the Cold War period is correct, but incomplete; competitive interventions by less powerful states were in fact more common. Finally, I demonstrate that the phenomenon of competitive intervention did not disappear with the end of the Cold War—a finding that underscores this book's importance for the study of contemporary civil wars.

Chapter 4 builds on the descriptive data analysis by presenting a series of statistical tests that assess my theory against rival explanations drawn from the existing literature. I analyze the Extended External Support Dataset to estimate the effect of competitive intervention on conflict duration and to probe its connection to the global prevalence of civil war. My results provide statistically and substantively significant evidence in support of my theory's core claims. Competitive intervention is shown to be a robust predictor of protracted civil war. Likewise, temporal variation in average conflict duration is shown to be a key driver of the waxing and waning of civil war over time. By testing my theory with a global sample of over six decades of internal conflict, these findings confirm the generalizability of my argument across the wide range of political, economic, and social contexts in which civil wars are waged.

Chapter 5 takes the analysis one step further, shifting from *between*-case analyses of a global sample to a *within*-case analysis of one of the deadliest conflicts of the past century: the Angolan civil war (1975–1991). Drawing on declassified intelligence and military reports, memoirs of military veterans, and original interviews with former military commanders, diplomats, and political elites, I show that while battlefield victory was undoubtedly the primary objective for Angola's domestic combatants, fears of uncontrolled escalation led third-party interveners to pursue more limited objectives. I document how the need to avoid direct confrontations prompted South Africa and the United States, on one side, and Cuba and the Soviet Union, on the other, to condition the scope of their support for rebel and government forces, respectively. While this restraint was successful in helping the interveners manage escalatory risks with one another, it simultaneously prevented them from conferring decisive military advantages on their domestic clients. The net result was a stalemated civil war that would go on for decades, inflicting hundreds of thousands of deaths, displacing millions, and decimating Angola's economic, political, and social institutions.

Sadly, this narrative of protracted death and destruction is repeated in Chapter 6, which takes the analysis to one of the most infamous battlefields afflicted by competitive intervention: the Afghan civil war (1979–1992). Drawing on archival documents, declassified intelligence reports, and memoirs of former military and political elites, I unpack the strategic logic motivating the Soviet Union's intervention in support of the Afghan communist regime as it faced off against the mujahideen rebels that were backed by Pakistan and the United States. I explain how the interveners navigated the strategic dilemmas inherent in competitive intervention in this case by signaling restraint through the imposition of limitations on the scope of their support to the domestic combatants. While limits proved fruitful in controlling escalation between the interveners, its consequences for the dynamics and outcomes of the Afghan conflict were significant: with the aid of their external backers, neither rebel nor government forces faced the resource constraints inherent in war; yet precisely because the interveners sought to avoid escalation, neither side was conferred a decisive military advantage that could help them attain victory. As was true in Angola, this resulted in a bloody and protracted conflict, with little hope for compromise or negotiated agreement. These arguments challenge conventional accounts of the conflict while shedding new light on a classic case of Cold War era "proxy war" between the US and Soviet Union. In doing so, the chapter further demonstrates the mechanisms and logic of my argument and shows how the dilemmas of competitive intervention afflict even the most powerful states in the international system.

Chapter 7 concludes the book by summarizing my key findings and deriving policy implications from my argument. It presents a shadow case study of competitive intervention in the Syrian civil war (2011–present) that further illustrates the veracity of my theory. This ancillary case provides valuable out-of-sample testing by examining the dynamics of competitive intervention in a civil war that falls outside the universe of cases included in the Extended External Support Dataset. In doing so, it provides additional within-case analysis in the service of my broader empirical results. Leveraging my findings, I suggest practical proposals for international engagement in contemporary civil wars afflicted by competitive intervention, explain the implications of my argument for conflict management, and close with some suggestions for future research on civil war, interstate competition, and competitive intervention.

2
A Theory of Competitive Intervention in Civil War

Competitive interventions have fueled the fires of some of the world's most deadly and destructive civil wars. They have been a dominant mechanism linking interstate competition to intrastate violence. And their varying frequency has been a key driver of changing trends in the average duration and global prevalence of internal conflicts. To explain wars without end, we must understand the logic and dynamics of this form of external meddling. To that end, this chapter develops a generalizable theory of competitive intervention in civil war, which I present in three steps.

I begin at the domestic level of the civil war combatants. Conceiving of violent armed struggle as a costly learning process that ends when opponents coordinate their expectations about the likely outcome of future rounds of fighting, I explain how competitive intervention distorts domestic bargaining processes in ways that delay negotiated settlement. By subsidizing the costs of war, balancing military capabilities, and amplifying information asymmetries, competitive intervention increases domestic combatants' willingness and ability to fight, precludes decisive military advantages, and increases uncertainty over relative strength and resolve. These distortions generate powerful incentives to forgo settlement today in the interest of greater returns tomorrow. This, I argue, leads to protracted civil wars.

Next, I turn to the international level of the third-party states, identifying a unique strategic problem confronting competitive interveners: the *escalation dilemma*. I show that while battlefield victory may be the primary objective for a civil war's domestic combatants, the need to avoid large-scale confrontations with one another leads third-party interveners to pursue more limited objectives. The establishment of thresholds serves to effectively limit confrontation between the interveners, but it simultaneously prevents the provision of decisive military advantages on the domestic combatants. This, I argue, leads to stalemated civil wars, as interveners refrain from providing the level of support necessary to enable military success, and instead provide a level of support sufficient only to avoid battlefield defeat.

Finally, I turn to the systemic level to explore how variation in the structural incentives and constraints of bipolar and unipolar systems affects the

Wars Without End. Noel Anderson, Oxford University Press. © Oxford University Press (2025).
DOI: 10.1093/oso/9780197798645.003.0002

global prevalence of competitive intervention. I argue that bipolar systems are positively associated with the prevalence of competitive intervention owing to intense geopolitical rivalry among the great powers and increased foreign adventurism among their client states. Unipolar systems, by contrast, are negatively associated with the prevalence of competitive intervention owing to the elimination of great power rivalry and the moderation of interventionist tendencies among weaker states. As competitive intervention waxes and wanes alongside variation in system structure, so too do the domestic- and international-level mechanisms that link it to protracted conflict. This, I argue, explains variation in the average duration and global prevalence of civil war over time.

Figure 2.1 provides a diagrammatic overview of the theory, which is elaborated from the bottom up in the sections that follow. In the penultimate section of this chapter, I derive a set of hypotheses associated with the outcomes predicted by the theory, as well as a set of observable implications associated with the proposed mechanisms that link its explanatory and outcome variables. I conclude by providing an overview of the research design that is adopted to test the theory in subsequent chapters.

The Domestic Level: Competitive Intervention and Civil War Bargaining Distortions

What explains protracted conflict in the face of mounting costs for domestic combatants? The bargaining approach to war provides a powerful framework to examine this question for three reasons.[1] First, it integrates battlefield dynamics with bargaining table behaviors, underscoring the purposive function of warfare and focusing attention on a critical insight of military strategists dating back to Clausewitz: that war is a political act, fought in pursuit of political goals, representing "nothing but the continuation of policy with other means."[2] Second, by uncovering the conditions that lead to bargaining failures, it provides a logical, deductively sound, and generalizable explanation for why combatants fight despite war's *ex post* inefficiency.[3] Third, the bargaining model of war has proven to be especially insightful for researchers studying the strategic interaction of combatants across the many dimensions of civil war disputes, from onset to termination.[4] It thereby provides a formidable foundation upon which to explore the consequences of competitive intervention in civil war.

---

[1] For examples of earlier work on the bargaining approach, see Schelling (1960, 1966) and Pillar (1983). For more recent examples, see Fearon (1995), Wagner (2000), Filson and Werner (2002), Slantchev (2003), Powell (2004), and Reiter (2009). For a general review, see Reiter (2003).
[2] Clausewitz (1989: 69).
[3] Fearon (1995: 383–384).
[4] For a review of the bargaining approach to civil war, see Walter (2009).

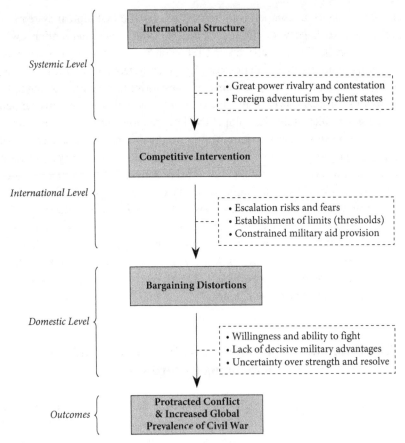

Figure 2.1 Diagrammatic overview of the theory.

The bargaining approach models violent conflict as a costly process that ends when opponents coordinate their expectations about the likely outcome of future rounds of fighting.[5] While combatants would prefer to avoid the costs of war, coordination of expectations is delayed because they possess private information about their willingness and ability to fight. This generates powerful incentives for both sides to misrepresent their capabilities and resolve in order to

---

[5] Earlier work modeled *prewar* bargaining and conceived of war as a game-ending "costly lottery," whereby the winner of a war is determined by a random draw from a probability distribution that reflects the balance of power (e.g., Fearon 1995; Powell 1996; Bueno de Mesquita et al. 1999). Later work relaxed this costly lottery assumption to explore bargaining *during* war, conceiving of fighting as a "costly learning process" that serves to converge combatants' expectations about the likely outcome of the war (e.g., Wagner 2000; Filson and Werner 2002; Werner and Yuen 2005). Because I am interested in the duration of ongoing wars, I adopt the latter approach here.

secure a better settlement than they would otherwise receive. Assuming that they value the future sufficiently and that different types of opponents meaningfully vary in their probabilities of victory, combatants will opt to delay settlement to accrue additional information about their opponent to avoid settling prematurely on worse terms.[6] This information is attained through fighting, which reveals each side's ability to endure and impose costs.

War is therefore conceptualized as the means through which information is revealed about the combatants' capabilities and resolve. As they win or lose battles, combatants update their beliefs about the likely outcome of continued periods of fighting. Victories in battle embolden a combatant to raise its war-terminating demands; defeats encourage less demanding settlement terms. Over time, the sequence of victories and defeats coordinates the expectations of both sides. In effect, warfare serves as a costly learning process through which combatants signal their capability and resolve and accrue information about their opponent.[7] Conflict termination becomes possible once opponents learn enough about their prospects in the war that they decide that its continuation will not earn additional concessions.[8] Insofar as a war ends once fighting has lost its informational content and the expectations of combatants have converged, the timing of its termination will be a function of the rate at which fighting transmits information between the combatants.

In the bargaining literature, it is usually assumed that information is revealed quickly on the battlefield. This has given rise to a prominent view that information problems provide a poor account of lengthy conflict.[9] However, as previously discussed in Chapter 1, existing private-information models generally conceive of the costly learning process of war as a unidirectional flow of information in which belligerents cumulatively learn about their opponent through combat, and in which expectations about the likely outcome of future battles converge monotonically. This overlooks the

---

[6] Both of these assumptions are necessary for the arguments that follow. If combatants do not value the future sufficiently, they do not have incentives to bear costly delays to secure better outcomes. Likewise, if different types of opponents are equally likely to prevail in battle, combatants have little incentive to delay agreement in order to accrue information about the type of opponent they are facing. For war to persist, combatants must be both sufficiently patient and prefer to engage in strategic screening and signaling. See Slantchev (2003).

[7] It can be shown empirically that the longer a civil war lasts, the more likely it is to end (i.e., fighting exhibits positive duration dependence). See, for example, Fearon (2004: 285). This aligns with the argument that information is revealed as a function of fighting. As combatants engage in the costly learning process of war, they become increasingly likely to terminate the conflict.

[8] Note that it is not necessary for both sides to agree on who will *win* the war; rather, all that is necessary is agreement on the relative likelihood of various outcomes. See Slantchev (2003).

[9] See, for example, Reiter (2003: 32), Fearon (2004: 290), Powell (2006: 172–176), Walter (2009: 246, 254), Blattman and Miguel (2010: 12), and Schulhofer-Wohl (2020: 34, 36).

dynamism of warfare and processes exogenous to the battlefield that distort the information-transmission function of fighting—and that thereby delay the convergence of combatants' expectations. I argue that competitive intervention in civil war has three such effects, which prolong the period of fighting.

Subsidizing the Costs of War

Competitive intervention prolongs internal conflict by subsidizing the domestic combatants' costs of war, thereby increasing their willingness and ability to fight.[10] Lost equipment, expended ammunition, and other consumables are replaced with war materiel shipped in from abroad; troop numbers are replenished with foreign deployments; and financial shortages are offset with international money transfers. For governments and rebels alike, the ability to mobilize labor and capital exogenous to the local battlefield serves to insulate against the economic and political burden of sustaining a costly war effort. The combatants become less susceptible to coercion, less reliant on local taxation, and liberated from domestic material constraints. In simple terms, competitive intervention renders the costly learning process of war less costly. This has two effects on bargaining dynamics.

First, as the domestic combatants' costs of fighting decline, their value for war relative to peace increases.[11] Accordingly, both sides will raise their war-terminating demands while offering fewer concessions to the other side. This shrinks the bargaining range—that is, the set of agreements that both sides prefer to war—thereby increasing the likelihood of continued bargaining failure. In effect, decreasing war costs encourage combatants to dig in their heels and drive a harder bargain, necessitating that a greater number of battles be fought to converge expectations about relative capability and resolve. That both sides have private information about the level of support they are receiving from external sources only compounds this problem, as neither side can be certain about their opponent's true costs of war.

Second, decreasing war costs encourage the domestic combatants to delay negotiated settlement. Precisely because aid from the competitive interveners subsidizes the costly learning process of war, the price for postponing agreement

---

[10] For a complementary argument that conceives of external aid as a subsidy that expands the conditions under which belligerents can continue to fight in the context of quagmire (a concept related to, but distinct from, conflict duration), see Schulhofer-Wohl (2020: chapter 2).

[11] A combatant's value for war is the sum of the expected outcome of the war less its costs. Thus, a combatant's value for war grows positively as the expected costs of fighting decline.

declines—and it does so for *both* sides. In practice, this means that the domestic combatants can afford to be more patient, choosing continued fighting today in the interest of greater concessions in the future. This behavior is especially likely when combatants recognize that there is a large variance around their estimates of the relative balance of power, which discourages rapid changes in beliefs following individual battles.[12] As it happens, such recognition is most likely to occur under conditions of competitive intervention, for reasons I now turn to discuss.

Balancing Combatant Capabilities

Competitive intervention prolongs conflict by balancing combatant capabilities, thereby precluding decisive military advantages. Quantitative and qualitative deficiencies in weapons or equipment can be corrected with military transfers from allied patrons; supply limitations can be overcome with logistic support from external states; and weaknesses in combat skills and tactics can be strengthened in training camps run by foreign advisors. Here, "balance" need not mean the delivery of equivalent quantities or qualities of military supplies, nor does it require equality in the number of troops fighting on either side of the war. It simply entails the provision of countermeasures capable of curtailing an opponent's military advantages. For example, man-portable air-defense systems—rather than fighter jets and helicopters—might be provided to counter an opponent's air superiority. Likewise, man-portable fire-and-forget antiarmor weapons—rather than tanks—might be provided to counter an opponent's advantages in armored fighting vehicles.[13]

As military capabilities become balanced, stalemates set in. No clear trend in battlefield outcomes can emerge, and individual battles reveal less information. Uncertainty about the likely outcome of future clashes increases, and the significance of unobservables—such as resolve, strategy, and tactics—is enhanced.[14] Under these conditions, combatants with private information are

---

[12] Reiter (2009: 222).
[13] Here I follow Kalyvas and Balcells (2010: 421) in conceiving of external aid as benefiting both combatants, but asymmetrically. In a civil war context, states generally remain militarily superior to rebels. However, competitive intervention shifts the military balance toward parity by turning rebels' "deep weakness," which undermines their capacity to meaningfully challenge the state, into "relative weakness," which enables them to mount effective military challenges and impose meaningful costs via "robust insurgency."
[14] Here I follow Reed (2003) in assuming that the variance of the domestic combatants' estimates of the probability of victory is a function of the distribution of power. If there is no variance in combatants' estimates of the probability of victory, the significance of private information is null and there is little incentive to delay agreement. Thus, I assume that increases in the variance of a

strongly incentivized to misrepresent to secure more favorable concessions. In turn, additional battles must be fought to acquire information about their opponent and to signal their own capability and resolve. Conflict is prolonged as combatants delay negotiated agreement to avoid settling prematurely on inequitable terms.[15]

Notably, a balance in domestic combatants' military capabilities is especially likely to obtain under conditions of competitive intervention owing to the unique strategic dilemmas this form of external meddling entails for third-party states. As I elaborate below, upward pressure for competitive interveners to provide their domestic clients with decisive military advantages is offset by downward pressure to constrain the scope of their support for the purpose of escalation control. This leads the competitive interveners to provision a level of support sufficient to enable their domestic clients to counter an opponent's military advantages, but insufficient to enable battlefield victory. Stated otherwise, the domestic military balance tends toward parity under conditions of competitive intervention. This increases uncertainty about the probability of victory, which encourages continued fighting.

Amplifying Information Asymmetries

Competitive intervention complicates domestic bargaining processes by amplifying information asymmetries among combatants, thereby increasing uncertainty over relative strength and resolve. The details of military aid programs are often cloaked in secrecy and obscured by illicit networks. The inability to fully observe the quantity and quality of external support provisioned to the domestic combatants complicates efforts to estimate relative capabilities. At the same time, the covert nature of external support encourages recipients to misrepresent the advantages they have accrued from foreign sources. Domestic combatants often deny receiving military supplies from state patrons.[16] Even when these patron–client relationships are "open secrets," combatants are incentivized to

---

combatant's estimate of the probability of victory increases the likelihood of continued conflict by increasing the differences among combatant types that must be screened through the costly learning process of fighting. This is consistent with evidence of the conflict-prolonging effect of balances of power. See, for example, Bennett and Stam (1996), Slantchev (2004), Christia (2012), Findley (2013), and Weisiger (2016).

[15] These expectations, derived from the logic of the bargaining model of war, run contrary to the argument that "mutually hurting stalemates" are "ripe" for conflict resolution (e.g., Zartman 1985, 2000). I return to this point in Chapter 7.

[16] For example, for many years, Houthi rebels fighting in Yemen denied their relationship with Tehran, despite the fact that the latter began shipping weapons to the former as early as 2009 (Landry 2015). To this day, the rebels still do not acknowledge the details of the Iranian military aid program.

withhold key information about their supplies for military advantage.[17] In this way, the competitive interveners' contributions serve as exogenous shocks to private information, complicating estimates of relative strength and resolve.

Questions about the reliability and variability of foreign support, and about whether aid might be withdrawn in the future, further amplify information asymmetries. While battlefield wins and losses can be used to update beliefs about the likely outcome of future clashes with a domestic opponent, they do not reveal information about intervener resolve. For this reason, there may be uncertainty about the extent to which a foreign backer will continue to shore up its client, especially as a conflict becomes protracted. A patron's regime may collapse, its alliance portfolio may change, or its level of support may vary in response to internal or external constraints.[18] Domestic combatants may come to believe that they can outlast their opponent's foreign ally, thereby gaining a military advantage when the flow of aid dries up in the future. In short, external support is not only subject to obscurity—it is also subject to variation. This variation generates uncertainty, which encourages continued fighting.

Even in the unlikely case that external transfers are fully observable, uncertainty about an opponent's capacity to effectively deploy provisioned capabilities, exploit military technology, or execute strategy complicates estimates of the probability of victory. Domestic combatants often lack the requisite skills, tactical training, and discipline needed to effectively employ the weapons and equipment provided to them by external backers.[19] They may suffer from insufficient combat leadership, logistics, or maintenance capacities.[20] More generally, there can be a mismatch in the priorities and preferences of domestic combatants and

---

[17] For example, mujahideen commanders fighting in Afghanistan initially concealed the fact that they were receiving training on and access to US Stinger antiaircraft weapons. This was strategically wise: by keeping this information hidden, it ensured that their first use of the weapons would catch enemy pilots entirely by surprise. The rebels revealed this new military capability during an ambush in September 1986, downing three Mi-24 Hind gunships in a single attack (Yousaf and Adkin 1992: 175–176). I discuss the Stinger missile's role in the Afghan civil war in detail in Chapter 6.

[18] Consider, for example, the gradual decay of the Soviet regime and subsequent collapse of the Soviet Union. This event led to the termination of Soviet aid flows to former Cold War clients—government and rebel alike—all over the globe (see Westad 2007: 384).

[19] Consider, for example, the stunning collapse of Iraqi government forces when confronted by the Islamic State in Iraq and Syria (ISIS) in June 2014. Notwithstanding a massive US train-and-equip program, the Iraqi army disintegrated in the face of a numerically inferior ISIS offensive. On the collapse itself, see Fraiman, Long, and Talmadge (2014). On the failures of the US train-and-equip program and the ineffectiveness of Iraqi security forces, see Biddle, Macdonald, and Baker (2018: 113–118).

[20] This was the case for Frente Nacional de Libertação de Angola (FNLA) forces in Angola, for example. Consider the exasperated assessment of one US Marine Corp major, as quoted in Stockwell (1978: 176): "You would have to see it to believe it. I drove around in a jeep with Commandant Lukenge, who is supposed to be the FNLA's best soldier. I picked his M-79 grenade-launcher up one time and tried to open it; you know it breaks open like a single-barrel shotgun. It was rusted shut! He had had it only a few weeks and it was rusted so tight I couldn't force it open. The same thing is happening to their rifles, mortars, and vehicles. They need help!"

their international backers, which can generate persistent tensions over how best to leverage provisioned capabilities.[21] The influx of money and arms can also exacerbate local corruption, illegality, and patronage networks that hinder the development of military strength and battlefield proficiency. Taken together, these weaknesses and sources of uncertainty increase the variance of domestic combatants' estimates of the probability of victory, even when external transfers are fully observable.

Finally, in addition to uncertainty about their opponent's capabilities and resolve, domestic combatants also confront uncertainty about how much their opponent knows about their *own* capabilities and resolve. Have enemy informants penetrated the internal security apparatus? Were a patron's weapons shipments detected? Has the presence of foreign advisors been uncovered? How is the opponent interpreting this intelligence? Precisely because information about foreign assistance is difficult to acquire, domestic combatants can rarely be certain of what their adversary knows about them. There are also strategic reasons to hide what one knows about the other side, especially when revealing such knowledge would disclose classified collection techniques, identify informers, or compromise an intelligence source. Domestic combatants are therefore incentivized to misrepresent not only their own capabilities and resolve but also their beliefs about the other side as well. This "uncertainty about uncertainty"— which is amplified by foreign covert aid programs—can delay the convergence of expectations among the domestic combatants, even when both sides are informed of the other's capabilities and resolve.[22]

Summary

Competitive intervention subsidizes domestic combatants' costs of war, balances their capabilities, and amplifies information asymmetries. Taken together, these distortions increase combatants' willingness and ability to fight while precluding decisive military advantages and increasing uncertainty over relative strength and resolve. This generates powerful incentives to forgo settlement today in the interest of greater returns tomorrow. Protracted civil war is the result.

This account of bargaining under conditions of competitive intervention helps explain why domestic combatants continue to fight even when conflicts become intractable. But why do external states invest in costly and protracted civil wars? This behavior is especially difficult to explain when states maintain

---

[21] See the examples documented in Elias (2020).
[22] On the breakdown of bargaining due to "uncertainty about uncertainty," see Chadefaux (2020).

their support for domestic combatants over the course of many years, or even decades. Why do interveners continue to invest in stalemated conflicts in seemingly suboptimal ways, providing just enough resources to fuel the fighting, but not enough to terminate the war? It is to this question that I now turn.

The International Level: Interstate Competition and Escalation Control

That national and strategic interests motivate interventionist policies among states is a classic argument found in the international relations literature.[23] Revolutionary outcomes of civil wars not only challenge existing power relations within a country—they can also dramatically shift the relative balance of power among third-party states. Civil wars present a number of threats (such as conflict spillovers, refugee flows, and criminality), as well as opportunities (to overthrow rival regimes, capture disputed territories, or seize natural resource deposits), that incentivize foreign states to intervene in an effort to shape their dynamics and outcomes.

Like any other international policy issue, however, the interests of third-party states in the outcomes of civil wars are often overlapping and competing. While some states profit from the persistence of the status quo, others are advantaged by its revision. Competing interests generate divergent responses, which can take the form of competitive interventions. In the following sections, I develop the argument that this form of external meddling presents a unique strategic dilemma for intervening states. While the challenge it entails is not insoluble, its management comes at a cost for foreign interveners and domestic combatants alike.

The Escalation Dilemma

Third-party states that find themselves engaged in a competitive intervention against an interstate rival confront a strategic dilemma: the *escalation dilemma*. By "escalation," I refer to an action that crosses a threshold that determines the current limits of a war and that is considered significant by one or more actors.[24] Because an escalation in support to a domestic client can improve its battlefield situation and impose additional costs on its adversary—higher military expenditure, increased destruction, and additional lives lost—deviations

---

[23] See, for example, Morgenthau (1967), Feste (1992), Byman et al. (2001), MacFarlane (2002), and Henderson (2015).

[24] Cf. Schelling (1960: 192), Smoke (1977: 35), and Morgan et al. (2008: 8).

from existing thresholds can tip the balance of power and resolve among the domestic combatants in ways favorable to the interveners' interests. In the context of a civil war, escalation can take two forms.[25] First, interveners can provide greater quantities of war materiel, more sophisticated weapon systems, rigorous training operations, or troop deployments to improve a client's battlefield performance and enhance its lethality (vertical escalation). Second, interveners can expand the geographic area afflicted by the war, capturing territory in areas previously unaffected by fighting or attacking enemy sanctuaries that lie outside the conflict zone (horizontal escalation). By expanding the scale and scope of their support, an intervener can confer military advantages on its client. This increases the probability of the client's victory on the battlefield—a victory that can deliver an intervener the spoils of war.[26]

However, in the strategic environment of a competitive intervention, an intervener's desire to escalate must be balanced by the uncertainty surrounding how an opposing intervener might respond. Viewing the increasing scope of its competitor's intervention, an opponent is incentivized to expand its own participation in the war. The opponent may respond in kind, increasing its own level of support to negate the military gains achieved by its competitor through increasing levels of violence. In this scenario, strategic stability is maintained via offsetting investments, but the costs of participation in the war increase for both sides; the competitive interveners would have been better off had the instigating intervener forgone the original escalation. More worryingly, however, an opponent may not simply reciprocate an escalation—it might counter-escalate, further expanding the scope of its intervention to affect a reprisal. In this scenario, the original escalation has not only increased the costs of intervention but has also proven strategically counterproductive: now the instigating

---

[25] On the two forms of escalation, see Smoke (1977: viii). Also see Kahn (1965: 4–6), Carson (2018: 28–30), and Talmadge (2019: 867).

[26] Here I assume that competitive interveners ultimately seek to see their domestic clients through to victory. This is a simplification that has three important advantages. First, it is useful for the purposes of theory building and clarity of exposition—it simplifies a complex reality to make the argument tractable. Second, it captures the most interesting and puzzling case: one where both interveners are committed to see their domestic client through to victory, yet behave in ways that undermine that objective. And third, it captures what is arguably the most representative case—one where both sides would prefer their client's victory rather than protracted engagement in a foreign quagmire. This assumption will not always hold; interveners may seek more limited objectives, such as sowing instability or bleeding the resources of a rival (see Groh 2019: 34–37). However, no generality is lost. Regardless of the objective, an intervener's opponent is likely to see all such behavior as hostile to its interests. This increases the chance of responses in kind and counter-escalations, necessitating that both sides avoid provoking inadvertent escalation. As I demonstrate in Chapter 6, relaxing the assumption that competitive interveners ultimately seek to see their domestic clients through to victory does no damage to the theory. In fact, more limited objectives should amplify the dynamics of tacit and explicit signaling, patterned actions, and strategic restraint I describe below. It is precisely in those cases where total victory is less valuable that the search for limits on the scope of violence should be most important.

intervener must double down, lest its own domestic client be put in a militarily disadvantageous position.

The latter response is especially precarious insofar as it risks a spiraling of actions and reactions in the interveners' quest for strategic advantage in the civil war. These dynamics can produce unanticipated tactical and strategic situations, which raise the risk of ever-larger clashes. As both sides bid up their respective investments, the hazard of direct confrontation between the interveners grows. This threat of inadvertent escalation—perhaps to the level of war between the interveners—looms in the background of a competitive intervention.[27]

An agreement between the interveners to mutually terminate their support to the domestic combatants would resolve the escalation dilemma, but two problems impede agreement on the mutual cessation of aid. The first is the *collaboration problem*: even if the competitive interveners prove capable of reaching an agreement to end their participation in the war, both are unilaterally incentivized to defect from it to gain an advantage over the other. Were one side to terminate its support, the other would be tempted to exploit that restraint by continuing to arm its own domestic client, thereby securing a favorable outcome in the war. And because both interveners reason the same way, both must fear that their own restraint will be exploited. Given the incentives of unilateral defection, and fearful of losses from unrequited cooperation, both interveners can be expected to defect from any such agreement.

Collaboration problems of this type can be overcome through iterated interactions and strategies of reciprocity.[28] However, the conditions for these strategies are rarely met in the context of competitive intervention due to a second impediment to intervener cooperation: the *momentum problem*. Even in the absence of external aid, civil war processes have their own internally driven motion. A decision to terminate aid is a decision to let a civil war run its course based on the relative capabilities and resolve of the domestic combatants at the time of aid termination. While this stands to benefit the intervener supporting the combatant that is relatively stronger when support is cut off, it stands to undermine the intervener supporting the combatant that is relatively weaker at that time. This generates powerful incentives for the latter side to renege on any such agreement—incentives that grow larger as the weaker combatant edges closer to defeat. Knowing this to be true, the opposing intervener is unlikely to terminate aid to its own client. In effect, the momentum problem undermines strategies of reciprocity by changing the relative costs and benefits of

---

[27] This is akin to Schelling's "threat that leaves something to chance" and "competition in risk taking." See Schelling (1960: chapter 8, 1966: chapter 3).

[28] On the general form of collaboration problems, see Stein (1982) and Oye (1985). There is an extensive literature on cooperative non-equilibrium behavior in collaboration problems of the type discussed here. For one of the most prominent expositions, see Axelrod (1984).

(non)intervention as a civil war runs its natural course. For this reason, agreement on the mutual cessation of aid is unlikely to hold, even where collaboration problems can be overcome.

Competitive interveners must therefore confront the escalation dilemma. While their national interest generates upward pressure to provide support at a level sufficient to ensure their domestic client enjoys battlefield advantages, the risks of responses in kind, spiraling costs, counter-escalations, action–reaction dynamics, and enlarged conflict generate downward pressure to constrain the scope of intervention to control escalation. Faced by these contradictory upward and downward pressures, how should an intervener respond?

Covert operations present one option. Recent research highlights the utility of secrecy as a device for sustaining limits in war, demonstrating that interveners often purposely conceal evidence of foreign involvement for the purposes of escalation control. By individually and collectively creating a "backstage" to an ongoing war, interveners can hide discrepant incidents and manage the impressions of observing audiences. This helps to resist hawkish domestic pressures to escalate while at the same time communicating restraint.[29] Yet, secrecy is not always possible. Logistics, for example, may preclude it. Nor is secrecy always desirable. Covert communication brings with it unique escalatory risks that states may prefer to avoid. For example, ambiguity about responsibility for specific decisions and outcomes, even among adversaries that are carefully tracking each other, can ratchet up escalatory pressures.[30] Overlapping logics for the use of secrecy can also undermine its escalation-control function. For example, states often employ secrecy to foster "strategic uncertainty" for bargaining advantages, thereby amplifying the risk of war.[31] Covert operations also risk forgoing the bargaining benefits of publicity: the ability of state leaders to tie hands, generate audience costs, and thereby credibly signal resolve and commitment.[32]

Finally, there is the problem of exposure: even when concealing evidence of involvement is desirable, an opponent that detects a covert intervention may be unwilling to collude in the secret. Exposure, after all, may justify the imposition of political or economic sanctions. This was the case during the Angolan civil war, when captured South African Defense Force troops were paraded in front of international media in the aftermath of the Operation Savannah intervention in 1975. The worldwide exposure of South African involvement

---

[29] Carson (2016, 2018). Also see Cormac and Aldrich (2018).
[30] "Counter-escalation risk" is one reason states employ covert communication to credibly signal resolve. See Carson and Yarhi-Milo (2017).
[31] Meirowitz and Sartori (2008).
[32] Fearon (1994, 1997). Note, however, that covert signaling does not entirely forgo the ability to credibly convey resolve. See Carson and Yarhi-Milo (2017).

gave rise to widespread condemnation in international forums, as well as public humiliation for the apartheid regime, which was forced to publicly acknowledge participation in the affair.[33]

I therefore focus on an alternative approach states employ to control escalation in the context of competitive intervention in civil wars. My formulation helps connect insights from the limited war literature with outcomes from civil war battlefields. In particular, I draw a link between the symbolic significance of "thresholds"—that is, salient limits with symbolic significance that serve as signaling devices—and the characteristics of aid provision during competitive interventions.[34] To be clear, I see this alternative as complementing, rather than competing with, the logic of secrecy in limited wars. In fact, the thresholds I describe below may be observed by interveners to help keep covert interventions plausibly deniable (and thereby keep escalation controlled). My account, however, presents a more general framework—one that is applicable to interventions both overt and covert. Moreover, in contrast to work that explores how secrecy can be used to sustain limits in war, my approach focuses on the features of the limits themselves. My objective is to draw attention to a largely overlooked consequence of the war-limiting process—conflict prolongation.

Solving the Dilemma

The structure of the escalation dilemma facing the competitive interveners can be conceived of as a mixed-motive strategic game of interdependent decision-making. It is *mixed-motive* insofar as the interveners' preferences among the set of possible outcomes are both opposed and coincident: they have conflicting interests over the outcome of the civil war, but they have a common interest in the avoidance of a mutually damaging outcome. It is *strategic* in two respects. First, each intervener's "best" choice with regard to the level of support to provide their client is dependent on the level of support it expects the other intervener will provide to its own client. That is, intervener behaviors must be both "purposive" and "contingent"—they must be directed toward the pursuit of the intervener's preferences, but they are constrained by the behaviors of the other side.[35] Second, both interveners know that each side is conditioning its behavior based on what the other is doing. Consequently, intervener behaviors can serve as signals with which to coordinate with the other side.

---

[33] Baines (2012).
[34] On thresholds, see Schelling (1966: 135) as well as the discussion of "saliencies" in Smoke (1977: 13–18).
[35] Schelling (1978: 17).

I posit that competitive interveners value escalation control. This is not to suggest that escalation never occurs—it does. Rather, the point is that the risks of action–reaction dynamics, growing costs, and enlarged conflict encourage competitive interveners to view escalatory spirals as contrary to the national and strategic interests that motivated their intervention in the first place. Their challenge, therefore, is to pursue their individual interests while avoiding collectively damaging and dangerous escalation. They must together find ways to constrain the scope of their interventions and, thereby, limit their competition with each other.

I argue that competitive interveners manage their confrontation through the establishment of thresholds that possess symbolic significance and that serve as signaling devices that communicate restraint. Thresholds are most easily coordinated via explicit communication and debate. However, formal contact with an opponent is often complicated in times of war: talk is cheap, enforcement is uncertain, and a willingness to negotiate can be mistaken for weakness. Where explicit communication is limited or non-viable, tacit coordination and bargaining can be adopted in its place.[36] Through a sequence of patterned behaviors, competitive interveners can establish thresholds that strategically signal their intentions, manage expectations, and limit confrontation.

The establishment of thresholds is fundamentally a process of social construction. Because escalation is context-dependent and relational, what constitutes a threshold in any given conflict environment will be conditioned by time, by place, and by actor identities.[37] In this sense, thresholds are social constructs rather than objective facts—they must be intersubjectively negotiated, mutually recognized, and shared in the minds of actors to be meaningful. A failure to envision an opponent's expectations and perspective can result in unintentional escalation when actions violate thresholds that are unknown to, or misunderstood by, one or both sides. For this reason, competitive interveners are best served by establishing thresholds that are conspicuous (in the sense that they are prominent and both sides ought to be reasonably well aware of them) and unique (in the sense that they are novel, discrete, or discontinuous).[38] Precisely because these characteristics are the mark of focal points, each side can reasonably expect that the other will also perceive them as natural saliencies at

---

[36] On tacit coordination and bargaining in general, see Schelling (1960: chapter 3). On tacit bargaining during times of war, see Schelling (1960: 74–77, 1966: 136–141).

[37] As Smoke (1977: 252, emphasis in original) explains, "[t]here are different [escalation] ladders for every conflict, and they bear only a loose resemblance to one another. Controlling escalation in any particular conflict will often depend crucially on identifying the particular twists and protuberances of *that* conflict's misshapen ladder." Also see Morgan et al. (2008: 11–14). For recent cross-national survey evidence, see Lin-Greenberg (2023).

[38] Schelling (1960: 57–58 and appendix A, 1966: 137–138).

which to establish limits. Once thresholds have been identified, restraint can be signaled by conveying intentions through actions, behaving in predictable ways, and acquiescing to existing rules, thereby (re)producing shared understandings about thresholds that limit the scope of the war.

While detailed expositions of the role of thresholds in the war-limiting process must await empirical examination in the chapters that follow, a few examples can help elucidate the form and function of these credible signals of restraint:

> GEOGRAPHIC BOUNDARIES OF CONTESTATION VERSUS CONTROL: It has long been observed that geography and topography provide natural focal points that can be used to limit the scope of war. Bodies of water, deserts, and mountains can serve to delimit areas of operation and control. Even cartographic principles of latitude and longitude can function in such a role. In the 1980s, for example, France and Libya found themselves supporting opposing government and rebel forces, respectively, during the Chadian civil war. While both states deployed combat forces to the country, neither entertained the prospect of fighting a war against the other. To minimize the risk of direct confrontation, a demarcation line (the so-called "Red Line") was established at the fifteenth, and later sixteenth, parallel. French forces remained south of the line; Libyan forces remained north of it. While this agreement amounted to a *de facto* partition of Chad, it effectively managed escalation by circumscribing areas of operation for intervening forces.[39]
>
> LIGHT VERSUS HEAVY WEAPONS: Interveners are often at pains to communicate restraint by exploiting the qualitative characteristics of different weapon systems. Schelling highlights the distinction between nuclear weapons and all other types, which was first made during the Korean War, but lesser distinctions are regularly observed in a civil war context.[40] For example, during the Syrian civil war, American transfers of massive quantities of small arms and light weapons (such as assault rifles, mortars, and grenade launchers) to rebels fighting the Russian-backed Assad regime were banal. The question of whether to provision rebel forces with heavy weapons (such as advanced ground-to-air antiaircraft weapons), however, was subject to heated debate. While introducing these weapons

---

[39] Nolutshungu (1996: 189–91).
[40] Schelling (1960: 76). The aversion to the use of nuclear weapons has only grown in strength over the last number of decades, reinforced by their non-use in deadly and expensive interventions, such as the US campaign in Vietnam and the Soviet campaign in Afghanistan. On this "nuclear taboo," see Tannenwald (2007).

would have enabled the rebels to fend against crippling air strikes, US officials feared that they would end up shooting down Russian planes, thereby triggering a wider confrontation with Moscow.[41]

ADVISORS VERSUS COMBAT TROOPS: That there exists a general proscription against combat between competitive interveners' troops is evident in how rarely interveners supply ground forces to both sides of a civil war. In those cases where one intervener has deployed troops, its foreign opponent almost never responds in kind. Technical and military "advisors," however, have regularly been exempt from this rule—ostensibly because of the "non-combat" roles they serve. To reinforce the distinction, advisors are usually strictly prohibited from participating in direct ground combat and often restricted in their movement on the battlefield. For example, Turkey refrained from sending combat troops to Azerbaijan's First Nagorno-Karabakh War, both to avoid direct confrontation with Armenian soldiers who were supporting the secessionist rebellion and to prevent escalating the war into "the larger dimension of a Christian-Muslim conflict."[42] Ankara did, however, permit retired army officers to deploy in non-combat roles as "advisors," thereby assisting Azerbaijani government forces.[43]

INCLUSIVE VERSUS EXCLUSIVE TARGETING: When competitive interveners do deploy combat forces to foreign wars, the targets they attack send clear signals to an opponent. While attacks to degrade a domestic combatant's forces are to be expected, striking a rival intervener's troops or advisors risks retaliation in kind. Consequently, interveners regularly take pains to carefully select their targets. For example, Israel has sought to limit Iranian casualties during its participation in the Syrian civil war, targeting infrastructure rather than personnel to "avoid giving the Iranians a reason to retaliate."[44] Israeli officials have also issued pre-strike warnings to rival interveners' forces, making surprise phone calls to inform them of impending air strikes. An especially interesting approach has been the use of so-called "knock-on-the-bumper" tactics, in which warning shots are fired in advance of targeted strikes. These warnings encourage opposing forces to flee their vehicles and abandon their supplies, which are subsequently destroyed in follow-on strikes. According to Israeli officials,

---

[41] Entous (2016); Miller and Entous (2016); Jaffe and Entous (2017).
[42] The quotation is from the then Turkish Prime Minister Süleyman Demirel, as quoted in Kohen (1992).
[43] Aves (1998: 181).
[44] Pfeffer (2019).

these tactics have been adopted to limit the risk of a wider war in the region.[45]

These distinctions serve as signaling devices that regulate confrontation between states engaged in competitive intervention. They are discrete limits with symbolic significance that are easily recognized even in the absence of explicit communication; they provide clear guidelines for one's own commanders; and they make violations by the enemy relatively easy to detect. They are the unwritten "rules of the game" that bound the scope of competition between the interveners.

But these thresholds are not only symbolically significant—they also have tactical implications on the civil war battlefield. Geographic limits circumscribe the area of effect of supporting combat troops; restrictions on heavy armaments prevent the provision of advanced weapon systems; decisions to withdraw advisers under fire undermine a domestic client's morale; and pre-strike warnings forgo the military advantages of initiative and surprise. In effect, the ways in which competitive interveners signal restraint to control escalation results in their forfeiting of military options. In turn, both domestic combatants become blocked from receiving the quality and quantity of aid needed to attain battlefield advantages. This produces stalemated conflicts, as the interveners refrain from providing the level of support necessary for military success, opting instead to provide a level of support sufficient only to enable continued fighting. When combined with the distortionary effects of competitive intervention on domestic bargaining processes, protracted civil wars result.

This outcome, while tactically suboptimal, is nonetheless strategically rational.[46] To invest in a conflict at a level required to ensure a domestic client's battlefield victory risks the spiraling of costs and mutual destruction of potential gains—this is the escalation dilemma. To attempt to reach a mutual agreement on the cessation of aid risks exploitation by the opposing intervener—this is the collaboration problem. To forgo investing at any level risks forfeiting the interests at stake in the war—this is the momentum problem. In the face of these strategic trade-offs, an intervener's optimal solution is a limited intervention strategy, which while prolonging involvement in the civil war nonetheless provides higher net payoffs than the alternative options of doing nothing (and

---

[45] "Knock-on-the-bumper" tactics are an evolution of "knock-on-the-roof" strikes, in which a non- or low-yield explosive is dropped on the roof of a civilian building prior to it being bombed. The ostensible objective of the latter tactic is to warn the inhabitants of the building to leave in advance of a major strike. On Israeli pre-strike warnings, see Hubbard and Bergman (2020).

[46] Formally, the outcome is a Pareto-deficient equilibrium, but one in which all actors are playing their dominant strategy.

risking the stakes), collaborating with an opponent (and risking exploitation), or fighting to win (and risking mutual destruction of potential gains).

Summary

Third-party states competitively intervene in civil wars to secure their national interests. To affect the dynamics and outcomes of these conflicts, they provide military aid to domestic combatants. While they would generally prefer to provision military advantages that enable their domestic client to prevail on the battlefield, the escalation dilemma inherent in competitive intervention cautions restraint. Accordingly, interveners establish mutually recognizable thresholds to limit their confrontation and control escalation. This restraint provides strategic stability, but at the cost of tactical efficiency, as interveners refrain from providing a level of support necessary to enable decisive military victories, and instead provide a level of support sufficient only to avoid battlefield defeat. Given the distortionary effects of competitive intervention on domestic bargaining processes, this limited intervention strategy generates protracted fighting.

By integrating a domestic-level argument about bargaining distortions with an international-level account of the dilemma states face under the shadow of inadvertent escalation, the theory explains why rebels, governments, and third-party interveners often continue to invest in costly and protracted conflicts. But this framework is not limited to explaining conflict dynamics and outcomes—it also lays a foundation to better understand broader trends at the level of the international system. If competitive intervention prolongs civil wars, then the varying prevalence of competitive intervention should in turn explain temporal variation in *average* conflict duration, which is itself a key driver of trends in the global prevalence of civil war. It is this proposition that I now turn to explore.

The Systemic Level: The Varying Prevalence of Competitive Intervention

International politics vary as a function of different structures of power. A voluminous literature documents the interplay between the anarchic character of the international system and the distribution of capabilities in determining state behavior and, in turn, international outcomes.[47] Different distributions of

---

[47] See, for example, Kaplan (1957), Deutsch and Singer (1964), Rosecrance (1966), Waltz (1979), Walt (1987), Christensen and Snyder (1990), Mearsheimer (2001), Ikenberry, Mastanduno, and Wohlforth (2011), and Monteiro (2014). Also see the contributions in Græger et al. (2022). On the link between international structure and civil war, see Kalyvas and Balcells (2010) and Posen (2017).

power generate different incentives for conflict and cooperation, spur different types of balancing behaviors, and give rise to varying levels of geopolitical competition among states. Insofar as state decisions to aid combatants are patterned in ways consistent with competitive state policymaking, temporal variation in geopolitical competition between states should affect patterns of external military aid over time. As strategic rivalries intensify and decline, and as alliance agreements are inked and dissolved, the nature of external meddling in third-party conflicts should change. Accordingly, I consider how the transformation of the international system from a bipolar structure to a unipolar structure affects the prevalence of competitive intervention in civil wars.[48]

Bipolarity and the Proliferation of Competitive Intervention

Bipolarity is characterized by intense geopolitical confrontation between two great power states that together control so much of the international system's economic and military resources that alignments among other states cannot meaningfully alter the relative balance of power between them.[49] With only two states capable of projecting power and influence on a truly global scale, "anything that happens anywhere is potentially of concern to both of them."[50] Bipolarity extends the geographic scope of concern and broadens the range of factors included in the great powers' competition with one another.[51] It encourages the great powers to perceive change anywhere in the world as a potential crisis, driving a tendency toward overreaction given that only the great powers can contain one another.[52] Since a loss for one appears as a gain for the other, neither side can allow challenges to the status quo to even appear to

---

[48] Scholars typically distinguish between three types of international power structures: multipolar systems, which are characterized by three or more great powers of relatively equal capability; bipolar systems, which are characterized by the predominance of two great powers of relatively equal capability; and unipolar systems, which are characterized by the supremacy of a single great power. Because this book seeks to explain the rising prevalence of civil war during the bipolar Cold War period and the subsequent declining prevalence of civil war in the unipolar post–Cold War period, I omit consideration of multipolar systems in the discussion below. However, I return to explore the implications of diffusing power in the international system in Chapter 7.
[49] Morgenthau (1954: 362–363).
[50] Waltz (1979: 171).
[51] Waltz (1979: 171).
[52] Waltz (2000: 13); Posen (2011: 319). As US Secretary of State Dean Rusk explained to a press conference in 1961 amid the US–Soviet rivalry of the bipolar Cold War period, "if you don't pay attention to the periphery, the periphery changes. And the first thing you know the periphery is the center [...] [W]hat happens in one place cannot help but affect what happens in another" (as quoted in Gaddis 1982: 202).

succeed against their will, lest it undermine the credibility of their deterrent threats elsewhere.[53] Precisely because political commitments are understood to be interdependent in this way, the great powers are compelled to stand firm in the periphery of their spheres of influence, if only to deter challenges in more strategic areas.[54]

These structural incentives and constraints affect the global prevalence of competitive intervention in two ways. First, they generate a proliferating number of great power competitive interventions. Since any crisis, anywhere in the world, threatens to overturn the status quo between the great powers, it must be responded to. Yet, because any action by one great power is perceived by its opponent to be an attempt to gain a geostrategic advantage, it must be resisted. The net result is an action–reaction dynamic, whereby both great powers find themselves committing military and financial resources to otherwise strategically marginal areas.[55] And precisely because this aid flows to crises as a function of the *interaction* of the great powers and their *competition with one another*, it often takes the form of competitive intervention—the simultaneous transfer of military assistance to opposing government and rebel forces.[56]

Second, bipolar international structures enable competitive intervention among the great powers' client states. Constrained by the need to both deter and avoid direct confrontation, the great powers must employ indirect strategies to project power and assert influence. Military aid programs—which train,

---

[53] Hironaka (2005: 107–111).
[54] Feste (1992: 15).
[55] This was precisely the language used by US policymakers during the bipolar Cold War. Consider the following passage from a statement by the then Secretary of State Henry Kissinger (1976: 176): "When one great power attempts to obtain special positions of influence based on military interventions, the other power is sooner or later bound to act to offset this advantage in some other place or manner. This will inevitably lead to a chain of action and reaction typical of other historic eras in which great powers maneuvered for advantage, only to find themselves sooner or later embroiled in a major crisis and often in open conflict."
[56] This expectation is consistent with the wider literature's characterization of many Cold War-era civil wars as "US–Soviet proxy wars" (see, for example, Litwak and Wells 1988; Hironaka 2005; Kanet 2006; Westad 2007; Kalyvas and Balcells 2010). The Cold War coincided with a bipolar distribution of power. Accordingly, it was associated with intense geopolitical competition between the two great powers of that era: the US and the Soviet Union. What is missing in existing accounts, however, is an explanation for why these great power proxy wars might be associated with longer conflicts. If the Cold War balances of power and credibility hinged on great power interventions, why would the US and Soviet Union do just enough to prevent their sides from losing, but not enough to ensure their preferred sides won their wars? The escalation dilemma outlined above provides an answer: while compelled to intervene, they were simultaneously—and paradoxically—compelled to do so with restraint. This led to stalemated conflicts, as the great powers opted to trade tactical advantages on civil war battlefields for strategic stability in their wider competition with each other.

equip, and advise client states' military forces to meet security challenges *without* depending on the patron's combat troops—are an essential tool for these purposes. These programs can be employed to maintain local or regional balances of power, to influence the political orientation of other states, to help secure strategic resources, to strengthen the internal stability of allies, and to help secure foreign basing, overseas facilities, and transit rights—all while avoiding the commitment of military forces.[57] In this way, they secure the great powers' strategic objectives while avoiding their direct confrontation. Yet, these benefits are not without associated costs, as the provision of military aid also empowers client states to pursue independent foreign policy objectives.[58] Great powers competing under bipolarity struggle to control this adventurism on the part of their clients, as the latter can exploit the former's fears of defection to commandeer money and arms for their own self-interested ends.[59] As interventionism proliferates, a growing number of civil wars attract the attention of client states associated with opposing blocs. The net result is an increasing number of competitive interventions that, while waged by otherwise weak states, are indirectly underwritten by the great powers.

The growing prevalence of competitive intervention in bipolar systems has important implications for the global prevalence of civil war. Indeed, insofar as this form of external meddling prolongs civil war through the domestic- and international-level mechanisms identified above, its growing global prevalence increases *average* conflict durations, which in turn affects the total number of civil wars being fought year-over-year. Notably, this provides a theoretically grounded explanation for the growing prevalence of internal conflict during the Cold War, which I document in Chapter 1. Simply put, as competitive intervention proliferated under bipolarity, the average conflict grew longer, and the global prevalence of civil war therefore increased.[60]

---

[57] On the use of military aid programs for strategic objectives, see Mott (1999).

[58] Interventionism by weaker states was both widespread and undertaken at shocking distance during the bipolar Cold War. Cuba, for example, was not only active in Latin America but also in Angola, Ethiopia, and Zaire; Libya supplied rebels fighting not only in North Africa but also in Northern Ireland and the Philippines; and Vietnam intervened in civil wars not only in Southeast Asia but also as far afield as El Salvador.

[59] This phenomenon has been dubbed "reverse leverage" or "reverse influence." See, for example, Carr (1977), Lewis (1979: 187), Pierre (1982: 17–19), and Paul (1992: 1081). For an extended discussion of power and influence in arms transfer relationships, see Krause (1991).

[60] This follows from the fact that prevalence (the proportion of a population that is afflicted by a condition in a given period of time) is a function of incidence (the proportion of the population that is diagnosed with a new instance of the condition) *and* average duration (the time it takes, on average, to be "cured" of the condition). The argument assumes a relatively constant rate of new conflict outbreaks year-over-year. Empirically, this assumption is valid. See my discussion on this issue in Chapters 1 and 4.

Unipolarity and the Decline of Competitive Intervention

The defining characteristic of a unipolar system is the existence of a lone great power.[61] A single state—the unipole—enjoys such a preponderance of the international system's economic and military resources that it faces no meaningful competitor. No other state can threaten the security of the unipole, assemble feasible counterbalancing coalitions, or pursue war as a viable means for changing the structure of the system.[62] This does not mean that the unipole enjoys hierarchical domination; other states are juridically equal, maintain autonomy under anarchy, and can refuse to accommodate the unipole's preferences.[63] But no other state possesses the capacity to sustain prolonged politico-military operations on a global scale. Consequently, no other state is capable of opposing the unipole's preferences across multiple theaters.[64]

The absence of great power competition in unipolar systems affects the global prevalence of competitive intervention in three ways. First, precisely because the unipole faces no great power competitor, unipolar systems are characterized by an absence of great power competitive intervention. Since no other state is capable of challenging the unipole's primacy, competitive intervention among great powers cannot occur. This is not to suggest that interventionism on the part of the unipole will decline: if the vice to which great powers succumb under bipolarity is overreaction, under unipolarity it can be overextension.[65] Geopolitically unconstrained, the unipole can be more easily drawn toward discretionary foreign policy goals and an interventionist global strategy.[66] But precisely because the unipole faces no peer competitors, the potential for competitive intervention among great powers is eliminated, and the degree to which this form of external meddling afflicts civil wars therefore declines.

Second, the structural characteristics of unipolar systems discourage weaker states from competitively intervening against each other. While client states can leverage the great powers' money and arms for self-interested ends under bipolarity, they have a harder time commandeering military assistance under

---

[61] Hansen (2011: 5); Monteiro (2014: 40).

[62] Wohlforth (1999); Jervis (2009: 195); Walt (2009: 96–97).

[63] In this sense, unipolarity reflects "incomplete power preponderance" (Monteiro 2014: 40). This is an important characteristic that distinguishes unipolarity (a particular distribution of material capabilities in the international system) from hegemony or empire (types of hierarchical political relationships).

[64] Monterio (2014: 45).

[65] Waltz (2000: 13). On the ways in which unipolarity reduces constraints on the unipole, see Jervis (2009) and Walt (2009).

[66] This possibility is not structurally determined—unipolarity provides the unipole with greater freedom of action, and it can refrain from management of the system if it so chooses. But a unipolar structure conditions the odds of more ambitious foreign policy postures on the part of the lone great power. On the grand strategic options available to a unipole, see Posen and Ross (1996), Art (2003), Monteiro (2014: 65–70, 212–225), and Posen (2014).

unipolarity. Lacking an alternative great power patron, weaker states can no longer prey on the unipole's fears of defection to an opposing bloc.[67] The unipole has greater choice in which states it chooses to support and enjoys greater flexibility to sanction adventurism. And while the international arms market provides an alternative source of supplies, recalcitrant states are more likely to be subject to military, economic, and political isolation. The unipole's "command of the commons"—its predominance at sea, in space, and in the air—enables it to restrict external aid flows around the globe.[68] Together, these features of unipolar systems constrain interventionism by lesser powers, further reducing the global prevalence of competitive intervention.[69]

Finally, the absence of a great power competitor capable of balancing the unipole's military might encourages weaker states to avoid competitively intervening against it. Mindful of the unipole's unrivaled capabilities, weaker states must be wary of militarily threatening its interests and allies in foreign civil wars. Unlike in bipolar systems, there are no other great powers with which to turn for protection, military resupply, or financial support should they become subject to sanction. Weaker states need not always bandwagon with the unipole—they will still resist threats to their survival and security.[70] But relative to their behavior under bipolarity, weaker states must adopt more prudent and accommodating foreign policies vis-à-vis the unipole's interests, if only to avoid confronting its power.[71] While they may competitively intervene against the unipole in neighboring civil wars—where their security interests are most at risk—they are far less likely to competitively intervene against it further afield.

Intervention in civil war remains an important foreign policy tool that states employ to secure their national interests in unipolar systems. Nothing discussed above suggests that the prevalence of intervention *in general* must decline. But transitions from bipolarity to unipolarity are associated with changes in the

---

[67] Walt (2009: 98).

[68] Posen (2003). As one example, since the onset of the Yemeni civil war in 2015, the current unipole—the United States—has repeatedly interdicted Iranian weapons bound for Houthi rebels fighting the Yemeni regime. See, for example, Fitch (2016), Fotre (2018), Baldor (2019), Landay and Pamuk (2020), Snow (2020), and Gambrell (2021).

[69] To be clear, the argument is not that these features of unipolarity *eliminate* competitive intervention among weaker states, but rather that they *reduce* its frequency. It is possible that the prevalence of competitive intervention among lesser powers could increase under unipolarity if the unipole were to completely and globally disengage from the international system. In such a scenario, the unipole's disengagement could unleash competitive regional pressures that produce more frequent countervailing interventions among states in different regions. Yet while theoretically plausible, we have no empirical record of a globally disengaged unipole in the modern international state system. For a discussion of pathways to conflict amid a disengaged unipole, see Monteiro (2014: 170–174, 202–203).

[70] On bandwagoning in general, see Walt (1987: chapters 2 and 5). On bandwagoning under unipolarity, see Walt (2009: 108–111).

[71] As Mowle and Sacko (2007: 71) put it, "[i]f one cannot fight the unipolar power, then it is reasonable to try to stay off its target list."

configuration of external aid flows owing to variation in structural incentives and constraints across the two systems. While interventions regularly provoke countervailing responses in the form of competitive interventions under bipolarity, this is less likely to occur in a unipolar system. An important implication naturally follows: as competitive intervention becomes less common under unipolarity, so too do the domestic- and international-level mechanisms that link it to protracted conflict. This results in a decrease in *average* conflict durations, which in turn affects the total number of wars being fought year-over-year. Notably, this provides a theoretically grounded explanation for the declining prevalence of internal conflict during the post–Cold War period, which I document in Chapter 1. In short, as competitive intervention waned under unipolarity, average conflict durations decreased, and the global prevalence of civil war therefore declined.

Summary

Bipolar systems are associated with a higher prevalence of competitive intervention owing to intense geopolitical rivalry among the great powers and increased foreign adventurism among their client states. Unipolar systems, by contrast, eliminate the potential for great power competitive intervention and moderate the interventionist tendencies of weaker states. As the prevalence of competitive intervention waxes and wanes across the two systems, so too do the domestic- and international-level mechanisms that link it to protracted conflict—an outcome that helps explain temporal variation in the average duration and global prevalence of civil war.

Predictions of the Theory

The preceding sections yield a rich set of expectations about the nested interactions of domestic combatants, intervening states, and the international distribution of power. The theory's core claims can be summarized as a set of logically sequential *hypotheses* associated with the outcomes predicted by the theory and a set of *observable implications* associated with the proposed mechanisms that link the theory's explanatory and outcome variables (see Table 2.1).[72]

---

[72] I follow Gerring (2008: 178) in defining mechanisms as "the pathway or process by which an effect is produced or a purpose is accomplished." The distinction between "outcomes" and "mechanisms" is regularly drawn in the existing literature, albeit often with different turns of phrase. For example, Mahoney and Goertz (2006: 230–232) suggest "effects of causes" and "causes of effects," while Gerring (2004: 348–349) considers "causal effects" and "causal mechanisms."

Table 2.1 Predictions of the theory

Testable hypotheses associated with outcomes
There is a higher prevalence of competitive intervention in bipolar systems relative to unipolar systems.
Competitive intervention prolongs civil wars.
The prevalence of competitive intervention is positively associated with the prevalence of civil war through the duration channel.
Observable implications associated with proposed mechanisms
DOMESTIC LEVEL (BARGAINING DISTORTIONS)
Competitive intervention subsidizes domestic combatants' costs of war, increasing their willingness and ability to fight.
Competitive intervention balances domestic combatants' military capabilities, precluding decisive military advantages.
Competitive intervention amplifies information asymmetries, increasing uncertainty over relative strength and resolve.
INTERNATIONAL LEVEL (ESCALATION CONTROL)
Competitive interveners constrain the scope of the assistance they provide to domestic combatants.
Restraint on the part of the interveners is driven by fears of conflict escalation vis-à-vis opposing interveners.
Limits on the scope of support are constructed around thresholds that signal restraint to opposing interveners.
SYSTEMIC LEVEL (PREVALENCE OF COMPETITIVE INTERVENTION)
The termination of great power rivalry decreases the prevalence of competitive intervention in unipolar systems.
Weaker states are less likely to competitively intervene against each other in unipolar systems.
Weaker states are less likely to competitively intervene against the lone great power in unipolar systems.

With respect to *hypotheses* associated with outcomes, the theory first predicts a discontinuity in the percentage of civil wars afflicted by competitive intervention coinciding with transitions from bipolarity to unipolarity. In particular, it expects that there is a higher prevalence of competitive intervention in bipolar systems relative to unipolar systems. Second, the theory predicts that competitive intervention prolongs civil wars. Importantly, this is a generalized expectation: it should hold across time, irrespective of the structure of the international system (bipolar/unipolar) and the power status of the interveners (great power/weaker state). Finally, owing to its effects on conflict duration, the theory anticipates that the prevalence of competitive intervention in the international system is positively associated with the global prevalence of civil war.

The *observable implications* associated with the theory's proposed mechanisms can be subdivided into the three levels of analysis at which the theory operates. At the domestic level, the theory holds that competitive intervention distorts civil war bargaining processes in ways that protract conflict. In particular, I should find evidence that competitive intervention (1) subsidizes combatants' costs of war, thereby increasing their willingness and ability to keep fighting; (2) balances combatants' military capabilities, thereby precluding decisive military advantages; and (3) amplifies information asymmetries, thereby undermining combatants' abilities to correctly estimate their opponent's relative strength and resolve.

At the international level, the theory contends that escalation fears condition the behavior of competitive interveners. In particular, I should find evidence that competitive interveners (1) constrain the scope of the support they provide to the domestic combatants, even when doing so is tactically disadvantageous; (2) exercise caution due to fears of conflict escalation vis-à-vis opposing interveners; and (3) explicitly and tacitly limit the scope of their aid around thresholds that are mutually recognized as credible signals of strategic restraint.

Finally, at the systemic level, the theory holds that the prevalence of competitive intervention declines as the international system transitions from bipolar to unipolar distributions of power owing to variation in structural incentives and constraints across the two systems. In particular, I should find evidence that (1) the termination of great power rivalry decreases the prevalence of competitive intervention in unipolar systems; (2) weaker states are less likely to competitively intervene against each other in unipolar systems; and (3) weaker states are less likely to competitively intervene against the lone great power in unipolar systems. Importantly, these expectations relate to the *configuration* of external support flowing to civil wars, not rates of intervention overall. The theory anticipates that intervention *in general* remains an important foreign policy tool employed by states in unipolar systems. The key difference is that while interventions regularly provoke countervailing responses under bipolarity, this becomes less common under unipolarity.

Having derived my theory's hypotheses and identified its observable implications, I now turn to overview the research design adopted to test my claims in the remaining chapters.

Research Design

This book tests the theory outlined above with a mixed-method, nested analysis research design that combines cross-national statistics with detailed case studies.[73] The central strength of this design is its ability to leverage the inferential opportunities afforded by both large- and small-N research within a single framework, combining the generalizability of quantitative models with the nuance of qualitative case studies. A mixed-method approach enables more rigorous testing of rival explanations, improves concept measurement, and ultimately increases confidence in empirical findings by leveraging quantitative and qualitative tools in ways that preserve their respective strengths while overcoming their respective limitations.

In line with best practice, I begin the nested analysis with a quantitative assessment of the relationship between competitive intervention and civil war. This component of the design tests my argument against rival explanations, exploring the relationships between variables and identifying levels of uncertainty around estimated parameters. Uniquely, quantitative analyses can adjudicate between competing explanations where analytic constraints prevent qualitative assessment, assess the extent to which partial explanations or control variables explain patterns of variation in the outcome variable of interest, and estimate the conditional relationships among covariates. To those ends, an important objective of this component of the design is to test the hypotheses associated with the outcomes predicted by the theory and to verify the external validity of my argument.

I present the large-N component of the research design in the next two chapters, which provide a range of descriptive and inferential statistics. In Chapter 3, I introduce the Extended External Support Dataset, a novel dataset that records information on external military aid to government and rebel combatants for all years from 1946 to 2009. I then present a range of descriptive data that capture trends in foreign intervention over time, which I employ for the purposes of hypothesis testing and to verify the theory's observable implications at the systemic level. Specifically, the chapter examines whether international systemic change is associated with variation in the prevalence of competitive intervention; it then examines the processes that underlie that association. Next, in Chapter 4, I present a set of statistical analyses that empirically test the hypothesized relationship between competitive intervention and civil

---

[73] Lieberman (2005). On the advantages of mixed-method research designs in the study of civil war, see Thaler (2017).

war duration. I demonstrate the robustness of my results across various model specifications, alternative definitions of civil war, unobserved decade-specific confounders, unobserved conflict-specific heterogeneity, and the inclusion of a rich set of competing explanatory variables and controls. Finally, drawing together the evidence amassed in both large-N chapters, I examine whether temporal variation in the prevalence of competitive intervention is positively associated with the global prevalence of civil war.

Upon establishing the empirical relationship between competitive intervention and civil war, I turn to the second stage of the nested analysis approach—small-N analysis using qualitative case studies.[74] This component of the design entails a shift from *between*-case analyses that broadly examine my full sample of civil wars to *within*-case analyses that intensively examine the civil war process in individual cases.[75] Country-level quantitative analyses are often plagued by problems of endogeneity, concerns about the quality of concept measurement, and questions about causal ordering. Small-N analyses provide an opportunity to counter criticisms of this kind by verifying the plausibility of proposed mechanisms and providing a sense for whether the logic of the theory is compelling. Qualitative research tools are especially helpful for identifying the causal processes that link explanatory and outcome variables.[76] To those ends, an important objective of this component of the design is to test my theory's observable implications at the domestic and international levels and to verify the internal validity of my theoretical claims.

I present the small-N component of the research design in Chapters 5–7, which present intensive case studies of competitive intervention in the Angolan (1975–1991) and Afghan (1979–1992) civil wars, as well as an out-of-sample shadow case study of competitive intervention in the Syrian conflict (2011–present). These chapters scrutinize a heterogeneous set of materials—archival documents, declassified intelligence reports, original interviews, participant accounts, memoirs, media reports, and secondary sources—to shed light on the mechanisms that connect competitive intervention to protracted conflict. They employ a process tracing methodology to examine fine-grained evidence

---

[74] Following Gerring (2004: 342), I define a case study as "an intensive study of a single unit for the purpose of understanding a larger class of (similar) units."

[75] The small-N component of the nested analysis approach can take one of two forms: small-N model *testing* or small-N model *building*. The former is to be employed when the specification and fit of the large-N analysis is demonstrated to be appropriate and the goal of the in-depth analysis is to further test the robustness of those findings; the latter is to be employed when the state of the theory is initially weak or refuted by the large-N analysis. See Lieberman (2005: 442–443).

[76] On the advantages of qualitative methods for identifying causal mechanisms, see McKeown (1999: 172–174, 185), Gerring (2004: 348–349), George and Bennett (2004: 21–22), Bennett (2013: 211–212), and Bennett and Checkel (2015).

of events and behaviors, confirm the temporal sequencing of causal processes, and provide narrative assessments of theoretical claims.[77] This approach adds analytic depth that complements the analytic breadth provided by the large-N analysis. The shadow case study further illustrates the plausibility of the theory, providing valuable out-of-sample testing in a case that falls outside the large-N component's sample.[78]

Just as multiple sources of inferential leverage provide a stronger basis for theory testing, so too does the careful triangulation of data strengthen confidence in empirical findings.[79] In this book, I have sought to triangulate in two ways. First, I draw on a heterogeneous set of primary and secondary materials. The persuasiveness of a given piece of evidence is enhanced when it is confirmed across multiple types of sources—for example, when interviewees recall events that are also noted in declassified intelligence reports written during a war and reiterated in independent participant memoirs published in the interim. Second, I draw on materials provided by both sides of each war that I examine. Confidence in a given piece of evidence is strengthened when opposing sides concur on a particular event or outcome. To be sure, triangulation of sources is no panacea, but by including a diverse set of independent primary and secondary sources originating from opposing sides of a war, there is greater confidence in empirical claims.

Conclusion

Despite their *ex post* inefficiency and incalculable cost, many of the world's most violent internal conflicts have been protracted wars, seemingly without end. This chapter developed a theoretical framework to explain why rebels, governments, and third-party interveners often continue to invest in costly and stalemated conflicts, rather than sue for peace. It unpacked the ways in which *inter*state competition affects *intra*state conflict through competitive intervention—two-sided, simultaneous military assistance from different third-party states to both government and rebel combatants. It identified the distortionary effects competitive interventions have on domestic bargaining

---

[77] I follow Collier (2011: 824) in defining process tracing as "an analytic tool for drawing descriptive and causal inferences from diagnostic pieces of evidence—often understood as part of a temporal sequence of events or phenomena" (for a similar definition, see George and Bennett 2004: 6). In my use of the process tracing method, I have sought to follow the advice and best practices outlined by Bennett and Checkel (2015).

[78] On the advantages of shadow cases in political science research, see Soifer (2020).

[79] On the need for careful triangulation of sources, with applications to the study of civil war, see Checkel (2013: 23–25).

processes, described the strategic dilemmas they entail for third-party interveners, and linked their varying prevalence to international systemic change. In doing so, it provided a comprehensive theoretical account that explains protracted warfare, temporal variation in average conflict durations, and the waxing and waning of civil war in the international system over time. Having laid out the theory in full, I now turn to empirical illustrations and tests of this book's central claims.

3
External Meddling in Internal War
Tracking Global Trends, 1946–2009

Have global trends in external support to civil war combatants changed over time? Who have been the primary recipients of foreign weapons transfers and financing? Did the transition of the international system from a bipolar to a unipolar structure affect the frequency or form of external meddling in internal conflicts? Has the prevalence of competitive intervention varied over time? This chapter sets out to answer these and related questions, providing an empirical overview of global trends in external intervention in internal wars between 1946 and 2009. It introduces a novel dataset that records military aid transfers to civil war combatants, describes how patterns of intervention have changed over time, and establishes the nature of temporal variation in the book's key independent variable of interest—competitive intervention. In doing so, it begins the work of empirically testing my theory by examining whether international systemic change is associated with variation in the prevalence of competitive intervention. An additional objective of the chapter is to verify the observable implications of the theory's proposed mechanisms at the systemic level.

Several striking findings emerge. First, I demonstrate that external intervention has been a central dimension of the ostensibly "internal" civil war process over time. Indeed, the vast majority of internal conflicts—an average of nearly 75% per year—attracted external aid of some kind. This result presents a powerful challenge to the traditional distinction that is often drawn between *intra*state and *inter*state conflicts. It also highlights the importance of processes exogenous to the domestic battlefield that shape and constrain the dynamics of civil wars.

Second, I show that the end of bipolarity and the transition to a unipolar international structure had a profound effect on the nature of external aid flows—but not in the ways one might expect. While many have linked the termination of great power competition to decreased foreign interference in civil wars, I demonstrate that the percentage of conflicts attracting external support remained virtually unchanged between the bipolar and unipolar periods. However, while foreign meddling remained a ubiquitous feature of the civil war process, the *configuration* of military aid flows to domestic combatants changed dramatically. In particular, the rate at which civil wars attracted competitive

Wars Without End. Noel Anderson, Oxford University Press. © Oxford University Press (2025).
DOI: 10.1093/oso/9780197798645.003.0003

interventions was halved in the unipolar period, while the rate of one-sided interventions increased by over one and a half times. I show that government combatants were the primary beneficiaries of these changing trends—an outcome driven by the United States' foreign policy activism, as well as the reluctance of weaker states to challenge it, in the unipolar era.

Finally, I demonstrate that the widely held belief that US–Soviet "proxy wars" pervaded the Cold War period is correct, but incomplete. Great power competitive intervention was a defining feature of the bipolar international system, afflicting over 11% of conflicts per year, on average. What has been overlooked in the wider literature, however, is the prevalence of competitive intervention by less powerful states, which was in fact more common. This latter form of external meddling afflicted an average of 30.5% of conflicts per year under bipolarity—a finding that draws attention to the pernicious role that lesser powers have played in civil wars. Under unipolarity, weaker states have been less likely to competitively intervene against each other. Yet, competitive intervention still afflicts one-fifth of conflicts each year, on average. Taken together, these findings highlight the importance of a generalizable approach to the study of competitive intervention—one that is capable of explaining its dynamics, irrespective of the structure of the international system and the power status of the interveners.

In what follows, I present evidence to support each of the above assertions. In doing so, I confirm the veracity of this book's theoretical claims that link international systemic change to variation in the prevalence of competitive intervention. I begin by introducing the Extended External Support Dataset (EESD), a novel dataset that records information on external military assistance to civil war combatants for all years from 1946 to 2009. Next, I present descriptive statistics that demonstrate the ubiquity of external meddling in internal conflict over time. I then show that the prevalence of competitive intervention has varied in ways that are anticipated by the theory. I also verify the observable implications associated with the theory's mechanisms at the systemic level. I conclude with a summary of my findings, which set the stage for further quantitative testing in the next chapter.

The Extended External Support Dataset

This book introduces the EESD—a cross-national, time-series dataset of external military assistance to civil war combatants. The EESD builds off the pioneering work of Högbladh, Pettersson, and Themnér (2011) by extending the temporal scope of the Uppsala Conflict Data Program (UCDP) External Support Dataset, which compiles records of external aid flows to civil war combatants between 1975 and 2009.[1] The EESD supplements the UCDP External Support Dataset with three additional decades of data (1946–1974), providing temporal coverage for the full period from 1946 to 2009. This enables a more comprehensive assessment of external meddling in internal conflicts over time—and especially during the bipolar era—while providing additional statistical leverage for scholars studying third-party intervention in intrastate conflict.

A second contribution of the EESD is its introduction of a conflict-level data structure. The UCDP External Support Dataset is organized by warring party, a data structure that is ideal for analyses of the receiver or sender of support, but which is less well-suited for analyses of conflict-level outcomes.[2] By restructuring the data by conflict, the EESD enables researchers to study the effect of external aid flows on a variety of conflict-level outcomes, including total battle deaths, violence intensity, and—an outcome variable of interest in this book—war duration. For each conflict in the dataset, yearly observations record external aid flows to both government and rebel combatants for a variety of types of aid, including the provision of combat troops as secondary warring parties; weapons and ammunition transfers; financial aid; access to territory and/or military infrastructure; war materiel, logistical support, and/or intelligence; training and/or advising; and other forms of support. The dataset also records which state(s) sent a particular type of support to either government or rebel forces in a given conflict-year, enabling researchers to track patron–client relationships over time.

In the following subsections, I provide a detailed overview of the EESD and its construction. I identify the universe of civil war cases it includes, define key concepts, explain variable operationalization, review source materials, and overview its advantages relative to other datasets.

Universe of Cases: Civil Wars, 1946–2009

When does violent intrastate conflict constitute a "civil war"? Defining and operationalizing civil war presents a vexing challenge for scholars. While most would agree with the definition of civil war introduced in Chapter 1—*an organized*

---

[1] For details on the UCDP External Support Dataset, see Croicu et al. (2011) and Högbladh, Pettersson, and Themnér (2011).

[2] The UCDP External Support Dataset comes in two versions: the Primary Warring Party Dataset and the Disaggregated/Supporter Level Dataset. In the former, each row in the dataset provides observations for one warring party (i.e., one recipient of external support) in a given year, aggregating all external supporters; in the latter, external supporters are disaggregated in separate rows in the dataset for each recipient-supporter dyad. Thus, the Primary Warring Party Dataset is best suited for analyses of recipients of support, while the Disaggregated/Supporter Level Dataset is best suited for analyses of supporters. Neither is structured for conflict-level analyses.

armed conflict between a state and domestic armed group(s) that results in fatalities—the question of "how many" fatalities must be inflicted would likely be subject to dispute. At the heart of debates over fatality thresholds are concerns about relative trade-offs. Higher fatality thresholds help set civil wars apart from other forms of intrastate conflict, such as violent riots, terrorist attacks, or coups. However, they risk the introduction of a selection bias against smaller countries, which often fail to reach high threshold requirements despite suffering large fatality rates relative to their population size. Lower fatality thresholds guard against this small country selection bias. However, they introduce an opposite complication: the threshold is so low that it is not limited to civil wars.[3]

To address these competing trade-offs, while at the same time maximizing comparability with existing studies, two versions of the EESD are provided. The first adopts a low threshold of twenty-five annual battle-related deaths. This version of the dataset draws its sample from the widely used UCDP Armed Conflict Dataset (ACD), which defines armed conflict as "a contested incompatibility that concerns government or territory or both, where the use of armed force between two parties results in at least 25 battle-related deaths in a calendar year. Of these two parties, at least one has to be the government of a state."[4] A threshold of twenty-five annual battle-related deaths increases the number of cases included in the EESD, guards against small country selection bias, and maximizes the usability of the dataset for researchers studying political violence, broadly conceived. The trade-off, however, is that such a low threshold increases unit heterogeneity, risking comparisons of dissimilar cases that are inappropriate for some research questions.

To address unit heterogeneity concerns, a second version of the EESD is provided. This version also draws its sample from the ACD, but adds an additional requirement of 1,000 cumulative battle-related deaths to the case inclusion criteria. This cumulative requirement serves to exclude low-magnitude intrastate conflicts, such as coups or violent riots. While this decreases the sample size of the dataset, it helps to ensure that cases are sufficiently alike to merit meaningful comparison in empirical analyses of high-magnitude intrastate conflicts, such as civil wars. It thereby serves to reduce both the bias and variance of empirical estimates by reducing sampling variability and ameliorating concerns about unobserved bias.[5]

This book's research focus is on the dynamics and consequences of competitive intervention in civil wars. Precisely because we would not expect

---

[3] For a discussion on the perils of battle death threshold criteria in the civil war literature, see Anderson and Worsnop (2019).
[4] N. Gleditsch et al. (2002); Themnér and Wallensteen (2014).
[5] Anderson and Worsnop (2019: 98). For a general discussion of the effect of unit heterogeneity on sampling variability and unobserved bias, see Rosenbaum (2005: 150).

competitive interventions to afflict low-magnitude intrastate conflicts of other kinds, such as coups or individual terrorist attacks, including those cases in the discussion and analysis below would be inappropriate. For this reason, in the following sections I employ the second version of the EESD, which includes only those conflicts that inflict 25 battle-related deaths annually *and* at least 1,000 battle-related deaths cumulatively over the course of their duration.[6]

Military Aid Flows to Civil War Combatants: Definitions, Variables, and Sources

To date, much of the existing large-N research on third-party intervention in civil war has focused on the effects of boots-on-the-ground military operations.[7] Until recently, external meddling below the level of troop deployments, such as weapons and equipment transfers, financial aid, and advising, garnered less attention.[8] This gap in the literature is understandable, owing to the political and normative significance of foreign troop deployments. But it is unfortunate, given that such operations represent only a minority of intervention cases.[9]

The EESD offers a richer conceptualization of third-party intervention. Following in the footsteps of the UCDP External Support Dataset, it records yearly observations of military assistance to government and rebel combatants for a variety of types of external support, including:

> COMBAT TROOPS: The provision of combat troops to assist a domestic combatant in warfighting. Importantly, this category excludes troops sent as military advisors and trainers (which fall under the training and/or advising category), and also excludes technicians or troops serving other non-combat roles (which fall under the war materiel/logistical support/intelligence category). It includes only those troops that are actively fighting alongside either government or rebel forces.

---

[6] Unit heterogeneity concerns notwithstanding, it is valuable to probe empirical findings at different thresholds to examine whether results align with theoretical predictions. To those ends, I confirm the robustness of my empirical results using both versions of the EESD in the statistical analyses presented in the next chapter.

[7] As a few examples of this work, see Tillema (1989), Pearson and Baumann (1993), Walter (1997), Balch-Lindsay and Enterline (2000), Talentino (2005), Balch-Lindsay, Enterline, and Joyce (2008), Pickering and Kisangani (2009), Sullivan and Koch (2009), Cunningham (2010), and Sullivan and Karreth (2015).

[8] For an important exception, see Regan (2002). Since the publication of the UCDP External Support Dataset in 2011, a growing body of scholarship has begun to explore the effects of external military aid of varying forms on a number of outcome variables of interest. For a few examples, see Sawyer, Cunningham, and Reed (2017) and Karlén (2017, 2019).

[9] Below, I show that troop deployments are the least common type of external support provided to civil war combatants (see Figure 3.2).

WEAPONS AND/OR AMMUNITION TRANSFERS: Arms transfers, donations, or loans of weapons and/or ammunition of any kind. This category includes sales on conciliatory terms (such as deferred payments and/or offsets), but excludes standard commercial arms sales.

FINANCIAL AID: Any type of economic aid provided to a domestic combatant to help fund the war. This category includes money, military loans, grants, and intercession via multilateral financial institutions or other lenders. It does not include humanitarian, development, or balance of payments aid or loans.

ACCESS TO TERRITORY AND/OR MILITARY INFRASTRUCTURE: The intentional provision of sanctuary by a state to a domestic combatant that allows the latter to establish bases on the former's territory, undertake cross-border military actions, or otherwise concedes territorial sovereignty in favor of the supported party.[10] This category also includes cases where an external backer has permitted a domestic combatant to use its military infrastructure, such as bases, outposts, or intelligence gathering stations.[11]

WAR MATERIEL, LOGISTICAL SUPPORT, AND/OR INTELLIGENCE: War materiel refers to non-weaponry and non-ammunition supplies that are used in combat and/or serve a military purpose, such as vehicles, uniforms, tents, field hospitals, medical supplies, counter-battery radars, night vision goggles, and so on. Logistical support refers to logistics assistance, such as troop transport, repair facilities, and the provision of technicians for servicing and/or support of advanced weaponry. Intelligence refers to materials that assist in the planning and/or conduct of military operations, such as maps, information on enemy positions or capabilities, cryptographic codes, satellite imagery, or signals intelligence of any kind.[12]

TRAINING AND/OR ADVISING: Training and/or advising of any kind, whether in the civil war state or in the supporter's country. This category

---

[10] Intentionality is essential. In cases where borders are porous and/or a state has only very limited control of its territorial boundaries, evidence that a warring group attained access to a state's territory is not sufficient to consider that state to have provided access to territory. The support must be intentional.

[11] The UCDP External Support Dataset records access to territory and access to military infrastructure as separate categories. The EESD complies with these coding rules, but I combine them here to reflect the fact that territorial access is a type of support provided almost exclusively to rebels, while access to military infrastructure is a type of support provided almost exclusively to governments. That is, these are similar types of external aid that differ in form, but not function.

[12] The UCDP External Support Dataset records war materiel and logistical support as distinct from intelligence support. The EESD complies with these coding rules, but I combine them here to reflect an important shared characteristic: all three are non-lethal forms of assistance that facilitate the planning and conduct of military operations.

includes the deployment of expert personnel and/or advisors engaged in military planning, but excludes troops that are engaged in combat operations (which fall under the combat troops category) or that are serving in other non-combat roles (which fall under the war materiel/logistical support/intelligence category).

OTHER FORMS OF SUPPORT: Other forms of support that are not easily captured by the above categories. For example, this could include assisting domestic combatants with recruitment activities, running a radio station that belongs to a rebel movement, serving as an intermediary between arms dealers and warring parties, and so on.[13]

Each type of aid is separately coded for both government and rebel combatants in a series of indicator variables, measured at a yearly resolution. The dataset also records which third-party state(s) sent a particular type of military aid to either government or rebel forces in a given year. Finally, and again in line with the UCDP External Support Dataset, the EESD distinguishes between substantiated instances of support and alleged (unsubstantiated) instances of support. The latter category includes unconfirmed allegations of support originating from other states, in media, or from other sources, but excludes clearly outrageous claims.[14] In the following sections, I exclude alleged instances of support from my discussion and analysis, but I confirm the robustness of my empirical results to their inclusion in the statistical analyses presented in the next chapter.

The EESD draws on a wide variety of open source quantitative and qualitative materials. These include the Non-State Actor Dataset,[15] the Non-State Armed Groups Dataset,[16] the Mapping Militants Project,[17] the Dynamic Analysis of Dispute Management Project,[18] the Autocratic Client Regime Dataset,[19] detailed

---

[13] I also include an "unknown" support type in this category, which captures those cases where there are reliable sources indicating that support was provided, but the type of aid goes unspecified. The UCDP External Support Dataset records other forms of support and unknown forms of support as distinct variables. The EESD complies with these coding rules.

[14] Croicu et al. (2011: 6).

[15] Cunningham, K. Gleditsch, and Salehyan (2009).

[16] San-Akca (2016). The Non-State Armed Groups Dataset distinguishes between *intentional* support and *de facto* support. The former type refers to cases in which a state directly and purposefully provides support to a rebel group; the latter type refers to cases in which a state does not directly support a rebel group, but the group nonetheless finds ways to support itself on that state's territory (e.g., due to lax border controls, weakness of the central government, etc.). Because the EESD complies with the UCDP External Support Dataset coding rules (which only include support that is actively given to strengthen a domestic combatant), it includes instances of *intentional* support, but excludes instances of *de facto* support.

[17] The Mapping Militants Project provides a database of detailed and documented group profiles. For an index of groups covered by the project, see https://cisac.fsi.stanford.edu/mappingmilitants/profiles.

[18] Mullenbach (2020).

[19] Casey (2020).

insurgency case studies compiled by RAND researchers,[20] and numerous peer-reviewed academic articles and books on individual conflicts. Each conflict-year observation in the dataset was manually coded by a minimum of three independent coders, with accompanying documentation and explanations recorded for all coding decisions. The end product is an exhaustive record of external aid flows to civil war combatants, which the EESD compiles in accordance with the coding rules developed by the UCDP External Support Dataset project.

Like the UCDP External Support Dataset on which it is based, the EESD offers a number of advantages over alternative datasets. First, the EESD incorporates a wide range of both direct *and* indirect forms of external assistance, such as weapons transfers, economic aid, and logistical support. This provides an advantage over datasets that are limited in scope to foreign troop deployments, enabling a more comprehensive assessment of the effects of external support on civil wars.[21] Second, the EESD's yearly resolution provides researchers with more fine-grained information about variation in the flows of external aid over the course of a conflict's full duration. This is an advantage over datasets that provide more limited (or no) temporal variation in external assistance.[22] Third, the EESD provides information on external aid flows to both rebel *and* government combatants. Given that the provision of aid to one side of a civil war often triggers countervailing responses to the other, this attribute of the EESD provides an advantage over datasets that focus on just one of the domestic combatants.[23] It is also an essential feature for the study of competitive intervention. Finally, the EESD's wide time frame (1946–2009), its global scope, and its adoption of the ACD's battle-related death threshold criterion provides more extensive coverage relative to other datasets that are more limited in temporal or global scope or which adopt higher battle-related death threshold criteria.[24]

---

[20] Paul et al. (2013).

[21] Data projects that are limited in scope to troop deployments include the Overt Military Intervention Dataset (Tillema 1989), the International Military Intervention Dataset (Pearson and Baumann 1993; Pickering and Kisangani 2009), the UCDP Armed Conflict Dataset (N. Gleditsch et al. 2002), the Military Intervention by Powerful States Dataset (Sullivan and Koch 2009), and the RAND US Ground Intervention Dataset (Kavanagh et al. 2017). The Non-State Actors Dataset (Cunningham, K. Gleditsch, and Salehyan 2009) distinguishes between "troops," "military," and "non-military" aid; however, it does not disaggregate military and non-military aid into their component parts.

[22] For example, the insurgency data collected by Byman et al. (2001), Lyall and Wilson (2009), and Jones (2017) do not provide time-varying measures of external support.

[23] The Non-State Armed Groups Dataset (San-Akca 2016), for example, only records external support to rebel forces—it does not include external support to government combatants.

[24] The data compiled by Regan (2000, 2002), for example, are restricted to conflicts with at least 200 battle-related deaths between 1944 and 1999, while the data compiled by Sousa (2015) are limited to conflicts in Africa in the post–Cold War period.

Having provided an overview of the EESD and its advantages, I now turn to present a variety of descriptive statistics. I first explore the general prevalence of external meddling in internal conflict over time. I then examine how patterns in military aid flows to civil war combatants have varied, focusing in particular on changing rates of competitive intervention and one-sided support.

The Ubiquity of External Intervention in Internal Wars

Many of the most influential studies of civil war produced over the past twenty years focus their analysis on domestic variables, such as a state's level of development, its regime type, the size and diversity of its population, or its physical terrain.[25] This internal orientation of the civil war literature is understandable. After all, civil wars are by definition domestic conflicts. Yet, we might question its validity. Many civil wars exhibit an international character, with participation by foreign troops or the provision of external military assistance by third-party states. The nature of civil warfare in contemporary conflicts in Libya, Sudan, Syria, or Yemen, for example, would seem to challenge the traditional distinction drawn between *intra*state and *inter*state conflict processes. Each of these wars has been vulnerable to foreign interference, which has transformed local fighting into regional- and even global-level conflicts among interstate rivals.[26] But just how common is external meddling in internal wars? Is foreign interference *typical* of the civil war process?

To help answer these questions, Figure 3.1 plots rates of external intervention in civil wars since the end of the Second World War. It charts the percentage of conflicts that received some form of external military aid in a given year, whether to government forces, rebel combatants, or both. Two important results emerge. First, the figure reveals that the vast majority of civil wars—an average of 74.3% per year—attracted external support of some kind between 1946 and 2009. This is a staggering finding. It suggests that, far from being strictly "internal" conflict processes, most civil wars are subject to exogenous pressures that originate outside of the civil war state. Indeed, the "internationalization" of civil wars appears to be the rule, not the exception. A failure to account for this fact risks incomplete and misleading inferences about the drivers of conflict dynamics, durations, and outcomes, calling into question the validity of "closed polity" approaches to the study of civil war.[27]

---

[25] This is true of both cross-national studies and subnational analyses. See, for example, the highly influential studies by Fearon and Laitin (2003a), Collier and Hoeffler (2004), and Kalyvas (2006).

[26] Each of these conflicts has been branded a "proxy war." See, for example, Hughes (2014), Tisdall (2015), Kharief (2020), and Mohammad (2023).

[27] For a critique of the "closed polity" approach, see K. Gleditsch (2007).

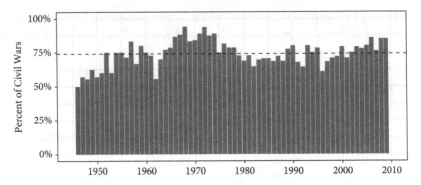

Figure 3.1 Rates of external intervention in civil wars, 1946–2009. The yearly average is indicated by the horizontal dashed line.

Second, the figure reveals that external meddling has been a pervasive feature of the civil war process over time. While there is yearly variation, with somewhat lower rates in the late 1940s and early 1950s, and somewhat higher rates during the late 1960s and early 1970s, the prevalence of intervention has been consistently high.[28] Notably, this is true even when comparing the bipolar period to the unipolar era. Indeed, while an average of 73.8% of conflicts received external support each year during the Cold War, this rate of intervention was largely unchanged in the post–Cold War period, which saw an average of 75.3% of conflicts receive external aid each year. A difference-in-means test confirms that there is no statistically significant difference between the two periods—a surprising finding in light of conventional accounts that suggest that the end of the Cold War put a premium on domestic sources of warfighting capacity.[29] Contrary to such views, external military assistance has remained a key foreign policy instrument employed by states to secure their national interests, which has continued to benefit civil war combatants in the post–Cold War period.

What types of military aid are most commonly provided to domestic combatants? Figure 3.2 disaggregates external support into its component parts, separately plotting the yearly percentage of conflicts receiving weapons and/or ammunition transfers, war materiel/logistical support/intelligence, training

---

[28] Note that the increased variability of the earlier decades in the dataset is also a function of a smaller number of observations per year during that period (i.e., there were significantly fewer civil wars in the 1950s than in the 1980s).

[29] $t(50.544) = -0.649$, $p = 0.519$. For examples of such conventional accounts, see Regan (2000: 51–52), Kalyvas (2001: 117), Collier and Hoeffler (2004: 568), Human Security Centre (2005), Lacina (2006: 285), Lacina, N. Gleditsch, and Russett (2006: 678), and Kalyvas and Balcells (2010: 421–422).

EXTERNAL MEDDLING IN INTERNAL WAR 69

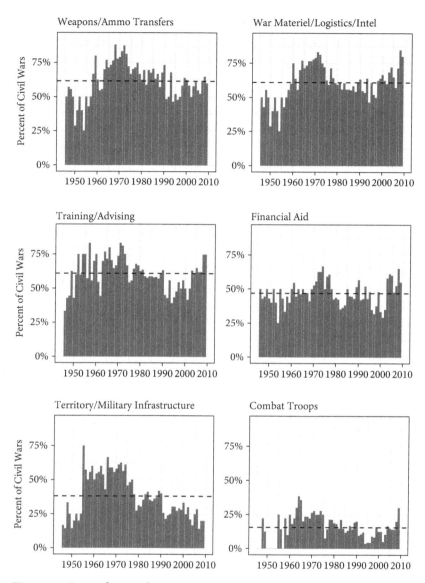

Figure 3.2 Rates of external intervention in civil wars by aid type, 1946–2009. The yearly average for each type of aid is indicated by the horizontal dashed line.

and/or advising, financial aid, access to territory and/or military infrastructure, and troop deployments. Of the six aid categories, the provision of weapons and/or ammunition transfers has been the most common—an average of 61.6% of conflicts have received this type of support each year since 1946. War materiel/logistical support/intelligence and training/advising have also been common, with provisions to an average of 61.0% and 60.9% of conflicts per year, respectively. Financial aid and access to territory and/or military infrastructure have been somewhat less common, with provisions to an average of 46.9% and 38.0% of conflicts per year, respectively. Finally, troop deployments have been the least common form of external support, with an average of just 15.6% of conflicts per year attracting this form of assistance—a finding that underscores the importance of a broader conceptualization of intervention that extends beyond boots-on-the-ground military operations.

In sum, foreign interference is a ubiquitous feature of the civil war process. A *majority* of conflicts have attracted external military aid of some kind since the end of the Second World War. This finding highlights the need for a theoretical orientation that incorporates factors exogenous to the domestic battlefield into the study of internal wars. In the next section, I develop this point further by digging deeper into the data to examine whether and how international systemic change has affected patterns of external aid flows to civil war combatants over time.

Changing Patterns in External Military Aid

My theory of competitive intervention posits that changes in the international distribution of power affect the configuration of third-party intervention in internal conflicts. In particular, it expects that bipolar systems are associated with a higher prevalence of competitive intervention relative to unipolar systems. Bipolarity gives rise to action–reaction dynamics among the great powers, which find themselves reflexively responding to perceived challenges in the peripheries of their spheres of influence, only to become mired in foreign entanglements. The great powers' reliance on military assistance as a foreign policy instrument, together with their fears of client state defections to the opposing bloc, also empowers otherwise weak client states that can leverage their great power patron's money and arms for their own self-interested ends. The net result is a proliferation of competitive interventions, by the great powers and weaker states alike, under bipolarity. Unipolarity, by contrast, eliminates great power competitive intervention and curbs the interventionist tendencies of weaker states. In light of the unipole's unrivaled power and command of the global commons, weaker states are less likely to competitively intervene against the unipole and each other. The theory therefore predicts a decreased prevalence of competitive intervention under unipolarity. Are these theoretical expectations supported by empirical evidence? In what follows, I employ the data compiled in the EESD to examine each in turn.

The Decline of Competitive Intervention in the Unipolar Era

To test for changing trends in the prevalence of competitive intervention, I construct indicator variables that record all cases of competitive intervention and one-sided intervention in the EESD. The former are defined as instances in which both the government and the rebels receive simultaneous support from different third-party states in a given conflict-year; the latter are defined as instances in which only the government or only the rebels receive external support in a given conflict-year. Figure 3.3 presents linear fits of the data, plotting the percentage of civil wars experiencing competitive intervention (top panel) or one-sided assistance to government or rebel forces (bottom panel) for both the bipolar and unipolar periods.

The figure uncovers a striking discontinuity in the configuration of military aid flows coinciding with the end of the bipolar international system. While the percentage of civil wars attracting competitive intervention increased between 1946 and 1990, this trend reversed dramatically beginning in 1991. Indeed, the dawn of the unipolar era was attended by a stark drop in the prevalence of competitive intervention, followed by a continued decline in this form of external meddling over the next two decades. In numbers, the percentage of conflicts experiencing competitive intervention decreased from a yearly average of 41.6% under bipolarity to a yearly average of only 20.6% under unipolarity. In other words, the degree to which competitive intervention afflicted civil wars was cut in *half* with the termination of the bipolar international system. A difference-in-means test confirms a statistically significant difference between the two periods.[30]

In contrast to the reduction in the prevalence of competitive intervention, the percentage of conflicts experiencing one-sided aid flows increased dramatically after 1990, rising from a yearly average of 32.2% under bipolarity to a yearly average of 54.7% under unipolarity. Here again, the trend reversal is striking. While the prevalence of one-sided support was in steady decline between 1946 and 1990, it increased sharply thereafter, forming a V-shaped pattern centered at the transition between the bipolar and unipolar periods. A difference-in-means test once again confirms a statistically significant difference between the two periods.[31]

---

[30] $t(57.880) = 8.181, p = 0.000$.
[31] $t(39.375) = -6.890, p = 0.000$.

72 WARS WITHOUT END

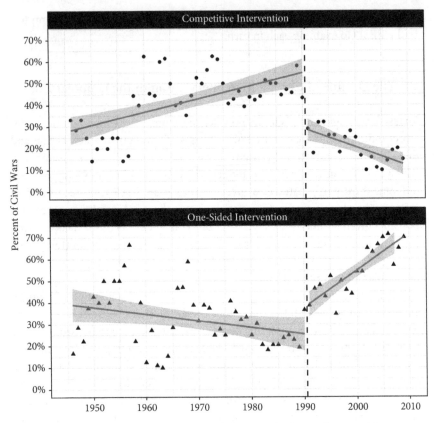

Figure 3.3 Trends in external military assistance in the form of competitive intervention and one-sided support to civil war combatants, 1946–2009.

Which side benefited from the growth in one-sided support in the unipolar era? Figure 3.4 distinguishes between one-sided support to governments and one-sided support to rebels, plotting linear fits of the data for both the bipolar and unipolar periods. It reveals that one-sided support to governments nearly doubled after 1990, rising from a yearly average of 19.6% of conflicts under bipolarity to a yearly average of 37.9% of conflicts under unipolarity—a statistically significant difference.[32] The increase is notable throughout the 1990s, but stands out even more starkly in the 2000s. One-sided support to rebels also saw an increase in the unipolar period, albeit of lesser magnitude.

---

[32] $t(32.380) = -5.383, p = 0.000$.

EXTERNAL MEDDLING IN INTERNAL WAR 73

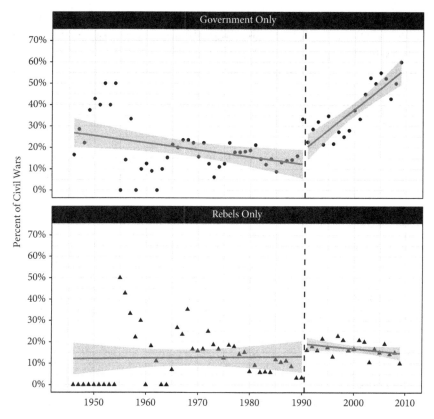

Figure 3.4 Trends in one-sided support to government and rebel combatants, 1946–2009.

While seeing an initial jump in the early 1990s, it slowly declined thereafter.[33] In numbers, one-sided support to rebels increased from a yearly average of 12.7% of conflicts in the bipolar period to a yearly average of 16.8% of conflicts in the unipolar period—once again, a statistically significant difference.[34]

---

[33] One contributing factor to the jump in one-sided support to rebels in the early 1990s was the decline of competitive intervention. Governments supported by the Soviet Union during the Cold War saw external aid dry up suddenly as that country collapsed. Support to rebel groups fighting Soviet-backed governments, on the other hand, sometimes continued apace. The Afghan communist government, for example, was cut off from Soviet aid even as a Pakistani aid program to the mujahideen rebels remained ongoing. In effect, a competitive intervention transformed into a one-sided intervention in support of the rebels as the Cold War came to an end.

[34] $t(57.338) = -2.074, p = 0.043$.

The growth in one-sided support for governments in the 2000s coincides with the US-led "global war on terror." Following al Qaeda's 2001 terrorist attacks in New York and Washington, the US launched a global campaign to identify, locate, and destroy militant organizations that employ terrorist tactics. In support of these objectives, Washington began to partner with weak states that were threatened by domestic insurgencies, while also implementing policies designed to deny state sponsorship, support, and sanctuary to terrorists. Figure 3.4 captures these policy shifts, demonstrating that governments fighting in civil wars were increasingly likely to attract external support in the post-9/11 period, while rebel groups (i.e., "terrorists" in US foreign policy lingo) found it more difficult to secure external aid in the same period. I return to this point in more detail below.

In sum, and in line with theoretical expectations, a closer look at the data reveals that while the transition from a bipolar to a unipolar international system had little effect on the percentage of conflicts attracting external aid, the *configuration* of those external aid flows changed in a substantively and statistically significant way, with a stark decline in competitive intervention and increasing rates of one-sided intervention in the unipolar period. From the theory, I derived three observable implications associated with the mechanisms linking international systemic change to these changing trends in external support to civil war combatants: the termination of great power rivalry and associated competitive interventions; the decreased likelihood that weaker states competitively intervene against each other; and the unwillingness of weaker states to competitively intervene against the unipole. I now turn to verify each of these observable implications in turn.

The Termination of Great Power Rivalry and Associated Competitive Interventions

During the Cold War, the Global South served as a principal arena of East–West rivalry between the US and Soviet Union. Accordingly, many civil wars of the time have been understood as US–Soviet "proxy wars"—that is, conflicts fought as part of the wider bipolar competition between the great powers.[35] When the Cold War ended, these conflicts also came to an end. This presents one explanation for the decline of competitive intervention in the post–Cold War era. But just how pervasive were US–Soviet proxy wars? To what extent

---

[35] For general discussions on this point, see Litwak and Wells (1988), Hironaka (2005), Kanet (2006), Westad (2007), and Kalyvas and Balcells (2010).

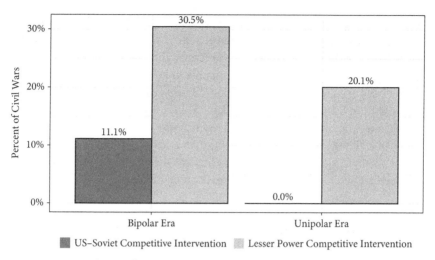

Figure 3.5 Prevalence of US–Soviet and lesser power competitive intervention during the bipolar and unipolar periods.

does their termination explain the general decline of competitive intervention since 1990?

The EESD records information about which state(s) sent military aid to a civil war combatant in a given conflict-year. This enables me to differentiate between competitive interventions waged between the great powers and competitive interventions waged among weaker states. The former are defined as all instances in which the US and Soviet Union supported opposing domestic combatants in a given conflict-year; the latter are defined as all other instances of competitive intervention. Figure 3.5 plots the percentage of conflicts afflicted by either type of competitive intervention for both the bipolar and unipolar periods.

The data confirm that US–Soviet competitive interventions were a characteristic feature of the bipolar international system. This manifestation of great power rivalry afflicted an average of 11.1% of conflicts each year during the Cold War. In raw numbers, this amounts to ninety-five conflict-years of fighting, rendering the US–Soviet dyad the most frequent competitive intervener dyad in the EESD. What is more, the great powers' meddling was global in scope, infusing civil wars in Africa, Asia, Central and South America, and the Middle East with American and Soviet money and arms.

Naturally, when the Soviet Union collapsed, these great power competitive interventions terminated. In June 1990, the Supreme Soviet ordered cuts to all forms of foreign aid, especially military assistance, to allies around the globe.[36] Economically and politically weakened at home, Moscow was no longer willing or able to continue to challenge US interests abroad. An almost immediate consequence was the settlement of a number of long-standing civil wars, often with direct or indirect Soviet mediation.[37] For its part, and in light of the dramatic shift in Soviet—and then Russian—policy, Washington reduced its own involvement in foreign conflicts. With its great power competitor gone, the outcome of civil wars on the periphery of the American sphere of influence was of lesser strategic significance. The net result was the elimination of great power competitive intervention at the dawn of the unipolar era.

The Decreased Likelihood that Weaker States Competitively Intervene Against Each Other

Importantly, however, the general decline of competitive intervention in the aftermath of the Cold War is not only attributable to the termination of US–Soviet "proxy wars." Indeed, Figure 3.5 reveals that bipolarity was associated with pervasive levels of competitive intervention by less powerful states as well. An average of 30.5% of civil wars attracted competing flows of external military assistance from weaker states each year between 1946 and 1990. Stated otherwise, the prevalence of competitive intervention by less powerful states was three times as common as great power competitive intervention during the Cold War. This finding is important: it calls attention to the fact that competitive intervention is not simply a US–Soviet phenomenon. Empowered by the assistance they received from their great power patrons, and emboldened by their alliances with Moscow and Washington, client states found ways to commandeer their sponsor's military and economic resources for their own self-interested ends. Fearing defection to the opposing bloc, the great powers struggled to contain this adventurism. An important consequence was an increase in the rate of intervention by lesser powers, which contributed to the higher prevalence of competitive intervention during the bipolar period.

In the unipolar period, by contrast, the prevalence of competitive intervention among weaker states became less common. Declining by nearly one-third, it afflicted an average of 20.1% of conflicts. This represents a statistically significant decline relative to the bipolar period.[38] With access to great power money and arms either eliminated (in the case of former Soviet client states) or reduced (in the case of some American client states), the foreign policies of

---

[36] Westad (2007: 384).
[37] For a discussion, see Westad (1992), Chernick (1996), Hironaka (2005), and Kanet (2006).
[38] $t(47.221) = 4.858, p = 0.000$.

lesser powers became increasingly constrained. Simultaneously, US command of the global commons—that is, its capacity to restrict access to external flows of economic, military, and political assistance—circumscribed the geographic scope of interventionism among weaker states.[39] Together, these features of the unipolar system constrained foreign adventurism by lesser powers relative to the bipolar period, thereby reducing the prevalence of competitive intervention among weaker states.

Competitive intervention has not been eliminated in the unipolar period: one-fifth of all conflict-years attracted opposing flows of military assistance between 1990 and 2009. The phenomenon is therefore not unique to the Cold War. But as geopolitical competition has waned, the nature of external meddling in civil wars has changed. In line with theoretical expectations, the data show that there was a decline in the prevalence of competitive intervention in the unipolar period, among the great powers and weaker states alike.

The Unwillingness of Weaker States to Competitively Intervene Against the Unipole

The US declaration of a "global war on terror" in the aftermath of the September 11 attacks has been dubbed "the single most ambitious reordering of America's foreign policy objectives since the Second World War."[40] In a speech to Congress less than two weeks after the attacks, former US President George W. Bush articulated the defeat of terrorism to be a critical national interest, including an ominous warning to the rest of the world: "[e]very nation, in every region, now has a decision to make. Either you are with us, or you are with the terrorists."[41] The years that followed would see Washington unleash an international military campaign against militant groups that employ terrorist tactics, as well as the "rogue states" that support them. The US also began extending military and financial assistance to governments fighting their own domestic militant threats, and additionally expanded the scope of military training programs for allied clients worldwide.[42] It was suggested above that the EESD captures these policy shifts, documenting a rise in one-sided support to governments. A closer examination of the data confirms the determining role played by the US, especially after 2001.

---

[39] On US command of the global commons, see Posen (2003).
[40] Boyle (2008: 191).
[41] Bush (2001). Also see the 2002 National Security Strategy of the United States, which codified US objectives in the "global war on terror" (The White House 2002).
[42] On trends in US foreign military training, see McLauchlin, Seymour, and Martel (2022).

Figure 3.6 plots the percentage of conflicts that were subject to an intervention with American participation in the unipolar period, separately plotting one-sided US support to governments, one-sided US support to rebels, and competitive interventions that included US support to one of the domestic combatants. It shows that one-sided US military aid to government combatants more than *tripled* in the years following the September 11 attacks, relative to the preceding decade. The figure also reveals the expansive scope of US foreign policy activism during the "global war on terror." Indeed, between 2002 and 2009, the US intervened in over *half* of all civil war conflict-years.

Crucially, and in line with theoretical expectations, the data confirm that the vast majority of these US interventions went uncontested by other third-party states—that is, they did *not* give rise to competitive interventions. Unencumbered by a great power counterweight, and in command of the global commons, the US embarked on a truly expansive campaign that sought to lower the costs of military cooperation with states suffering civil wars while simultaneously undermining support for insurgent groups. External aid programs were a key policy tool employed to this end, and accordingly, government-to-government transfers of American weapons, financing, war materiel, and training increased dramatically after 2001, without an offsetting increase in support to rebel groups over the same period. This is not to suggest that third-party states always bandwagoned with the unipole; to the contrary, they have competitively intervened against the US in an average of 9.0% of civil wars during the unipolar period. But while willing to challenge the unipole in neighboring conflicts—where their

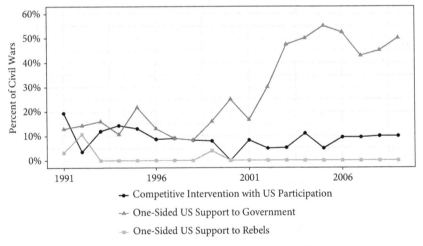

Figure 3.6 Percent of conflicts subject to an intervention with American participation in the unipolar period.

security interests are most at risk—weaker states have been less willing to competitively intervene against it further afield. This has contributed to the general decline in competitive intervention in the unipolar period, as anticipated by the theory.

Conclusion

This chapter presented new data on external military assistance to civil war combatants. In doing so, it uncovered a number of striking findings about continuity and change in patterns of foreign meddling in internal conflicts. First, notwithstanding their local roots, the vast majority of civil wars—an average of 74.3% per year—attracted external aid of some kind between 1946 and 2009. The ubiquity of external interference in internal conflict calls into question traditional distinctions drawn between intrastate and interstate conflict processes and highlights the shortcomings of a "closed polity" approach to the study of civil war. To better understand the dynamics and outcomes of internal conflict requires an account that incorporates factors that lie beyond the domestic battlefield—a key task taken up by this book.

Second, the transition from a bipolar to a unipolar international system had a profound effect on the nature of third-party intervention in intrastate conflict, but not in the ways one might expect. Contrary to conventional wisdom, the percentage of civil wars attracting foreign military assistance remained virtually unchanged in the post–Cold War period. What did change, however, was the *configuration* of external aid flows to civil war combatants. In particular, while the rate at which competitive intervention afflicted civil wars was cut in half in the unipolar period, the percentage of conflicts experiencing one-sided support increased dramatically. Governments have been the primary beneficiaries of these changing trends, with one-sided interventions in support of governments nearly doubling since 1990. These trends began to emerge in the first decade of the unipolar era, before quickly accelerating following the onset of the US-led "global war on terror."

Finally, while it is true that great power competitive intervention was a characteristic feature of the bipolar international system, one must not overlook the prevalence of competitive intervention by weaker states during the Cold War, which was in fact more common. In the unipolar period, the prevalence of competitive intervention has declined significantly in light of the termination of great power competitive intervention, a decreased likelihood that weaker states competitively intervene against each other, and a general unwillingness among lesser powers to competitively intervene against the unipole. Yet, the phenomenon has not disappeared and continues to impact some of today's most violent civil wars. This underscores the continued relevance of competitive intervention in the contemporary period.

Taken together, the findings reported above provide confirmatory evidence in support of this book's theoretical claims that link international systemic change to variation in the prevalence of competitive intervention. The data likewise verify the observable implications associated with the theory's mechanisms at the systemic level. Having established how trends in external military assistance to domestic combatants have changed over time, I now turn to explore the consequences of this variation for the average duration and global prevalence of civil wars.

4
Competitive Intervention and Protracted Civil War, 1946–2009

In the previous chapters, I first laid a theoretical foundation for an empirical understanding of protracted conflict under conditions of competitive intervention—a distinct configuration of external support to domestic combatants characterized by opposing, simultaneous transfers of military assistance from different third-party states to both government and rebel combatants engaged in an ongoing civil war. Next, I introduced new data on external support to civil war combatants and documented the changing nature of foreign meddling in internal wars over six decades. This chapter takes the analysis one step further, leveraging the data compiled in the Extended External Support Dataset (EESD) to examine the consequences of competitive intervention for the duration and global prevalence of civil war. It presents the results of a series of quantitative analyses that rigorously test my theory using a global sample of internal conflicts fought between 1946 and 2009.

I find robust empirical support for this book's central arguments. Across numerous model specifications that employ alternative measures of civil war, account for unobserved decade-specific confounders, and control for unobserved conflict-specific heterogeneity, competitive intervention is shown to systematically prolong conflict. The magnitude of this effect is large: the estimated hazard of conflict termination is reduced by *more than 50%* across every point in time over a conflict's duration. What is more, these findings are shown to be remarkably robust, even when constraining the data sample by time period and disaggregating competitive interveners by their great power status.

An additional objective of this chapter is to assess the explanatory power of my argument relative to alternatives. To that end, I incorporate a range of competing explanations and control variables highlighted by the existing literature into the models. By doing so, the analyses presented below provide an assessment of the impact of competitive intervention that accounts for the wide range of political, economic, and social contexts in which intrastate conflicts are waged. By testing the theory using a global sample of civil wars, the analyses also verify the external validity of my argument.

The chapter proceeds as follows. I first describe the methods and models I employ, highlighting their advantages for the research questions examined in this book. Next, I overview the variables included in the statistical tests presented below, explaining the logic of their inclusion and their connections to alternative explanations of civil war duration found in the existing literature. I then undertake an extensive set of quantitative analyses that test the relationship between competitive intervention and civil war duration, taking care to provide accessible expositions of the results. In the penultimate section, I explain why the relationship between competitive intervention and protracted conflict helps to explain variation in the global prevalence of civil war between 1946 and 2009. I conclude with a brief summary of my findings, which set the stage for the in-depth case studies presented in subsequent chapters.

Models and Methods

Does competitive intervention prolong civil wars? To answer that question, I adopt an empirical strategy that employs a duration model design. Duration models provide estimates of the conditional probability of an event occurring—in this case, the termination of a civil war—given the length of elapsed time since the start of a duration. These models provide a number of advantages relevant to the analysis of time-to-event data.[1] First, they explicitly model the effects of time on a dependent variable of interest. For obvious reasons, the termination of a conflict is intimately tied to the history that precedes it. Duration models provide a method for incorporating this history into a study's statistical design to account for the duration dependence that characterizes conflict data. Second, duration models elegantly account for the problem of "censoring." While the dataset analyzed in this chapter has a wide temporal scope, covering all years from 1946 to 2009, some wars were still ongoing at the end of the study period (that is, they are "right-censored"). Censoring is akin to a missing data problem insofar as parts of a case's event history go unobserved. Duration models correct for this problem, alleviating concerns about selection bias arising from missing data. Finally, duration models facilitate the inclusion of time-varying covariates. This enables me to capture variation in covariates not only *between* cases but *within* cases as well.

I employ semi-parametric Cox models, which are generally regarded as the preferred choice among alternatives for applied duration modeling.[2] A limitation of fully parametric approaches—such as exponential, Weibull, or log-logistic models—is the need to assume the distributional form of the baseline

---

[1] For a detailed overview of duration modeling in the social sciences, see Box-Steffensmeier and Jones (2004).

[2] For the original derivation of the Cox model approach, see Cox (1972). On the advantages of Cox models over other event history modeling approaches, see Box-Steffensmeier and Jones (2004), Golub (2008), and Metzger and Jones (2022).

hazard in the data. Unfortunately, there is no way of knowing *a priori* which distributional form best fits the data. Cox models are partial likelihood estimators that do not require assumptions about the baseline hazard, which is left unparameterized. This liberates researchers from the need to impose a distributional form on the data. The model is *semi*-parametric because (ordered) duration times are still parameterized in terms of a set of covariates. Although the resulting estimates are not as efficient as maximum likelihood estimates for a correctly specified fully parametric hazard model, this trade-off is more than compensated for by the fact that researchers can avoid imposing arbitrary assumptions about the form of the baseline hazard.

The Cox models reported below estimate the hazard of civil war termination at time t for a given conflict episode i, which is defined as

$$h_i(t \mid X_{it}) = h_0(t) \exp(\beta' X_{it})$$

where $h_0(t)$ is the baseline hazard function, β is a vector of coefficients, and X_{it} is a vector of covariates for conflict episode i at time t. The hazard is assumed to be proportional under a Cox model framework; that is, the effect of a change in any covariate on the hazard of event occurrence is assumed to be constant over time.[3] I employ tests based on Schoenfeld residuals to assess whether this proportional hazards assumption is met for the models reported below.[4] Where the assumption is violated, I follow best practice and create an interaction between the offending variable and (logged) time.[5] This relaxes the proportional hazards assumption to capture any nonlinear effects.

Sample and Dependent Variable

As noted in the previous chapter, the EESD draws its sample from the Uppsala Conflict Data Program (UCDP) Armed Conflict Dataset (ACD), which defines armed conflict as "a contested incompatibility that concerns government or territory or both, where the use of armed force between two parties results in at least 25 battle-related deaths in a calendar year. Of these two parties, at least one has to be the government of a state."[6] To minimize concerns over the heterogeneity of cases inherent in such a low fatality threshold, I add a one thousand cumulative battle-related deaths requirement to my case selection criteria in my

---

[3] For a discussion of this proportional hazards assumption, see Box-Steffensmeier, Reiter, and Zorn (2003) and Licht (2011).
[4] The results of these tests are reported in full in Appendix B.
[5] Note that in the context of Cox duration models, and unlike standard interaction tests, one includes x and the interaction $x^*\ln(t)$, but not $\ln(t)$ itself, in the model to relax the proportional hazards assumption.
[6] N. Gleditsch et al. (2002); Themnér and Wallensteen (2014: 541).

main series of analyses.[7] However, I also confirm the robustness of my results to the exclusion of this cumulative requirement below.[8]

The dataset is cross-national time-series in structure, with yearly observations and time-varying covariates for the full period 1946–2009. I follow existing studies by analyzing conflict episodes, defined as "continuous period[s] of active conflict-years."[9] A conflict's start date is recorded once the ACD criteria are met; it is considered terminated once it ceases to meet the criteria for one full year. By employing these criteria, I adopt a negative conception of peace—my interest lies in the absence of sustained, violent armed conflict, not necessarily the resolution of a conflict's underlying incompatibilities.[10] Elsewhere in the literature, scholars require the absence of conflict for at least two full years. I demonstrate the robustness of my results to this alternative coding criterion below.[11]

The dependent variable, CIVIL WAR DURATION, is calculated using the start and end dates recorded in the ACD and is measured at a daily resolution.[12] Figure 4.1 provides a visual overview of the variation in civil war duration that is captured by the sample. In total, there are 1,256 unique observations divided between 133 conflict episodes, with an average duration of 3,137 days (8.59 years). This raw average should be interpreted with care, however, as it includes both terminated conflicts as well as those that were still ongoing at the end of the dataset's observation period of December 31, 2009 (i.e., those that are right-censored). The shortest conflict in the dataset is the South Yemeni civil war, an exceptionally intense conflict that inflicted thousands of deaths in just over a week's time. The longest conflict in the dataset is the Israeli–Palestinian conflict, which spans multiple decades.

Explanatory Variables

My core explanatory variable, COMPETITIVE INTERVENTION, is generated using the data compiled in the EESD, as described in the previous chapter. For each conflict-year observation, I generate an indicator variable that marks instances

---

[7] On the methodological challenges posed by unit heterogeneity in the quantitative study of civil war, see Anderson and Worsnop (2019).

[8] Also see Appendix D.

[9] Kreutz (2010: 244).

[10] The latter approach, which adopts a positive conception of peace, is generally understood to be the absence of indirect (or structural) violence. This simple negative/positive peace dichotomy is widely applied in peace and conflict research. For an elaboration on these concepts, see the foundational work by Galtung (1969).

[11] Also see Appendix C.

[12] Most start and end dates are coded to a specific day in the ACD. Where precise information about dates is lacking, the ACD sets the date to the last day of a known period, usually a month. To eliminate any bias this may introduce, I set any imprecise dates to the middle of the known period.

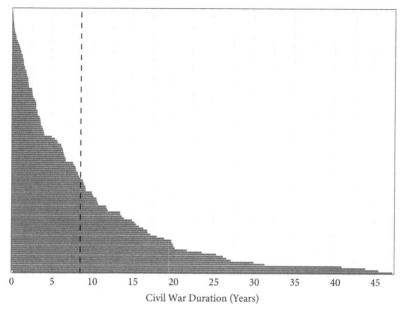

Figure 4.1 Distribution of civil war durations. The mean duration (8.59 years) is indicated by the vertical dashed line. Note that the figure includes both terminated conflicts as well as those that were still ongoing at the end of the dataset's observation period.

of simultaneous support of any kind to both government and rebel combatants from different third-party states. In my main analyses, I include only substantiated instances of support when constructing this variable, excluding alleged instances of support. However, I confirm the robustness of my results to an alternative coding criterion that includes alleged support as well.[13] To examine the duration effects of competitive intervention relative to other configurations of support, I also construct indicator variables that mark conflicts in which NEITHER SIDE WAS SUPPORTED, ONLY GOVERNMENT WAS SUPPORTED, and ONLY REBELS WERE SUPPORTED. Finally, because the EESD records which state(s) sent military aid to civil war combatants in a given conflict-year, I generate additional indicator variables to distinguish between US–SOVIET COMPETITIVE INTERVENTION and LESSER POWERS COMPETITIVE INTERVENTION. This enables me to test whether the effects of competitive intervention vary as a function of the interveners' great power status.[14] Summary statistics for these and all other variables included in the analyses below are reported in Appendix A.

---

[13] See Model 11 in Table 4.3.
[14] See Model 10 in Table 4.2.

Alternative Explanations and Control Variables

Scholarship on the determinants of civil war duration is voluminous. For this reason, an important task in the empirical assessment of my theoretical claims is the adjudication of my argument against alternatives. There are three broad classes of factors against which I must test my theory: the characteristics of the state suffering the civil war; the characteristics of the conflict itself; and the characteristics of the rebels that are fighting the state.

STATE-LEVEL CHARACTERISTICS

The literature has identified a range of state-level factors that affect civil war duration, including regime type, population size, topography, geography, and natural resource endowments. These variables affect the viability of armed rebellion and the local resource base upon which combatants can wage their wars.

In light of arguments that democracies are inferior counterinsurgents due to constraints inherent in their domestic structures and their sensitivity to casualties, I include an indicator for whether the state prosecuting the civil war is a DEMOCRACY.[15] Following standard practice, I identify democracies using the Polity2 scores compiled in the Polity5 dataset.[16] Scores range from −10 (a totalitarian regime) to +10 (a consolidated democracy). For the purposes of the analyses below, democratic regimes are defined as those that achieve a score greater than or equal to 6.[17] To minimize endogeneity concerns, I lag this indicator by one year.

Research has shown that countries with larger populations also tend to suffer longer civil wars owing to increased combatant recruitment pools and the challenges of surveilling, policing, and controlling larger numbers of people.[18] I therefore include a measure of a state's POPULATION SIZE (in thousands) using data provided by the Correlates of War National Military Capabilities Dataset.[19] To improve interpretability of the results, I log transform the variable.

---

[15] On domestic structural constraints, see Merom (2003). On casualty sensitivity, see Mueller (2005). For a critical take, see Lyall (2010).

[16] Marshall and Gurr (2020).

[17] This is the threshold commonly employed in the wider literature (e.g., Wucherpfennig et al. 2012; Fortna 2015). Others require a Polity2 score greater than or equal to 7 (e.g., Lyall 2010). Using the higher threshold has no meaningful effect on the results reported below.

[18] See, for example, Collier, Hoeffler, and Söderbom (2004) and Cunningham, K. Gleditsch, and Salehyan (2009). Also see Raleigh and Hegre (2009).

[19] Singer, Bremer, and Stuckey (1972). I use version 5 of the dataset.

Existing work also suggests that low gross domestic product (GDP) per capita serves as a proxy for weak state financial, administrative, and military capabilities, while high GDP per capita identifies developed states that are more easily policed, monitored, and disciplined.[20] An alternative argument suggests that low per capita incomes lower the opportunity costs of fighting, which can make participation in violence more lucrative.[21] I therefore control for a state's REAL GDP PER CAPITA, which is measured in millions of 2005 US dollars at chained purchasing power parity rates. I use data originally compiled by K. Gleditsch (2002) and subsequently extended to cover the full period 1946–2009.[22] To minimize endogeneity concerns and to improve interpretability, I lag the variable by one year and log transform it.

I also control for RUGGED TERRAIN, which has been identified as an important factor affecting both states' abilities to project power and rebels' abilities to evade government forces. I employ a measure developed by Shaver, Carter, and Shawa (2019) that records all elevation changes at a one-kilometer by one-kilometer grid-square resolution. Terrain ruggedness is calculated by taking the sum of all squared differences between a given grid square and all contiguous grid squares. These calculations are then aggregated at the country level to generate a variable recording variance in a state's terrain ruggedness.[23] This measure improves on traditional indicators, which have relied exclusively on mountains as a proxy for terrain ruggedness and have thereby overlooked the possibility that sharp, localized variation in elevation (both mountainous *and* non-mountainous) can render terrain more advantageous for rebels.[24] The new measure is also time-varying, which enables me to capture changes in a state's terrain resulting from secession (e.g., Ethiopia losing Eritrea in 1993), unification (e.g., North Yemen and South Yemen joining in 1990), and collapse (e.g., the dissolution of the Soviet Union in 1991), as well as conquest, cession, and the negotiated resolution of interstate border disputes.

I additionally control for OIL PRODUCTION for two reasons. First, oil production has been empirically linked to civil war duration.[25] Oil is a lucrative

---

[20] See, for example, Fearon and Laitin (2003a) and Cunningham (2011).
[21] See, for example, Collier, Hoeffler, and Soderbom (2004) and Dube and Vargas (2013).
[22] K. Gleditsch (2002). I use version 6 of the Expanded GDP Data, which covers all years 1950–2009. For data coverage during the years 1946–1949, I follow the approach adopted by Fearon and Laitin (2003a) and regress the log of real GDP per capita on year and the log of per capita energy consumption, as provided by the Correlates of War National Capabilities Dataset (Singer, Bremer, and Stuckey 1972; I use version 5 of the dataset). I then use predicted values as estimates for missing values. For details on this approach, see the discussion in Fearon and Laitin (2003b).
[23] Shaver, Carter, and Shawa (2019: 199–201).
[24] See, for example, the commonly used measures compiled by Gerrard (2000) and subsequently extended (and popularized) by Fearon and Laitin (2003a).
[25] Buhaug, Gates, and Lujala (2009); Lujala (2010).

resource that can finance the prosecution of a costly counterinsurgency campaign, enabling governments to dig in their heels, avoid settling prematurely, and thereby prolong a conflict. Second, the presence of oil has been shown to increase the likelihood of third-party intervention in civil wars.[26] It is therefore important that I control for this factor in my analyses below. I employ data provided by Wimmer and Min (2006) and construct an oil production indicator for each conflict-year.[27]

Finally, because states are more likely to be concerned about political instability in neighboring countries relative to those further afield, I control for the number of CONTIGUOUS BORDERS states afflicted by civil war share with others. Shared borders increase the risk of conflict spillovers, provide more opportunities for interactions between states, and reduce the logistical burden associated with intervention.[28] For all these reasons, the number of contiguous borders a state shares with others increases the likelihood of intervention. Moreover, the number of states neighboring a civil war has been previously correlated with conflict duration.[29] I therefore employ data compiled in the Correlates of War Direct Contiguity Dataset and include a count variable of the number of direct land contiguities of every civil war state for each conflict-year.[30]

Conflict-level factors

A conflict's own features and characteristics have been shown to affect its intractability. These include whether the conflict is organized along ethnic lines, whether the incompatibility of interests between the government and rebels concerns secession or irredentism, and whether a peacekeeping operation is deployed.

One prominent argument in the literature contends that civil wars fought between ethnic groups are uniquely difficult to end due to the "hardened" nature of ethnic identities during wartime.[31] Ethnic wars erupt when group myths that justify hostility, fears of extinction, and chauvinist mobilization take hold.[32] In turn, violence (re)constructs ethnic identities in more antagonistic and rigid ways. This polarizes group preferences, enabling ethnic elites to make more extremist demands while fostering images of ethnic opponents as

---

[26] Bove, K. Gleditsch, and Sekeris (2016).
[27] This data was subsequently updated in Wimmer, Cederman, and Min (2009). I use version 3 of that dataset.
[28] On conflict spillovers, infection risk, and intervention by contiguous neighbors, see Kathman (2010).
[29] Balch-Lindsay and Enterline (2000: 632).
[30] Stinnett et al. (2002). I use version 3.2 of the dataset.
[31] Kaufmann (1996).
[32] Kaufman (2001, 2006).

intractably hostile.[33] In effect, ethnic violence acts as a discursive practice that produces—and reproduces—the identities, interests, and norms necessary for its perpetuation.[34] In line with this argument, research has shown that ethnic fractionalization prolongs wars when rebel organizations become linked to groups that are excluded by the state along ethnic lines.[35] Regime ethnic exclusion can also generate credible commitment problems that protract fighting.[36] Ethnically based conflicts may also be more likely to attract external state sponsors in light of shared kinship ties.[37] I therefore control for whether a civil war is an ETHNIC CONFLICT. I employ the criteria and codings provided by Wimmer, Cederman, and Min (2009), who distinguish ethnic conflicts by the objectives of the combatants and their recruitment strategies.[38] With respect to the former, ethnic wars are those fought over ethnonational self-determination or autonomy, the ethnic balance of power in government, ethnically based discrimination, and/or language and cultural rights. With respect to the latter, ethnically based armed groups are those that recruit fighters predominantly from their own ethnic group.[39] Armed organizations must both pursue ethnic objectives and employ ethnic recruitment strategies for a civil war to be classified as an ethnic conflict.

A related argument holds that secessionist and irredentist conflicts are more intractable than are wars that are fought by center-seeking rebel groups, especially when control over a homeland territory becomes socially constructed as an "indivisible good." Existing research has found that the rhetorical legitimation strategies political leaders employ to justify their claims to territory can alter coalition politics in ways that make cooperation more difficult. When this occurs, political leaders can become locked into zero-sum bargaining positions, unable to recognize the legitimacy of their opponent's demands. In turn, territory that once appeared divisible is (re)constructed as indivisible, transforming territorial disputes into intractable conflicts.[40] Other work has shown that central governments are driven to forcefully retain secessionist and irredentist regions to ensure access to fuel or mineral resources located in those territories.[41]

---

[33] On the social construction of ethnic violence, see Fearon and Laitin (2000).

[34] Jackson (2004). This discursive practice can be guided by "ethnic entrepreneurs" that instrumentalize ethnic identities to mobilize popular support for their own self-interested ends. On the instrumentalization of ethnic identities and its connection to violence, see Brass (1997).

[35] Wucherpfennig et al. (2012).

[36] McLauchlin (2018).

[37] Saideman (2002).

[38] I use the updated version 3 of the Wimmer, Cederman, and Min (2009) dataset.

[39] Cederman, Min, and Wimmer (n.d.: 1-2).

[40] Goddard (2006, 2010). On the connection between the indivisibility of territory and ethnic war, see Toft (2002).

[41] These are the "sons of the soil" conflicts highlighted by Weiner (1978) and Fearon and Laitin (2011).

States are also likely to fear that a successful secessionist or irredentist attempt on their territory will set a dangerous precedent for additional attempts in the future.[42] I therefore control for whether a war is a SECESSIONIST/IRREDENTIST CONFLICT. I employ the criteria and codings provided by Wimmer, Cederman, and Min (2009), who define such wars as those "fought by armed organizations that aim at establishing a separate, independent, internationally recognized state or that want to join another existing state."[43]

I also control for the deployment of peacekeeping missions to civil wars. Existing research has highlighted the ameliorative effects of peacekeeping on conflict recidivism and violence levels. Peacekeeping deployments increase domestic combatants' costs of war by physically separating and disarming them, making it more difficult for the belligerents to engage militarily.[44] Peacekeepers also serve as third-party monitors and security guarantors, helping domestic combatants overcome credible commitment problems that protract civil wars.[45] Taken together, these effects can reduce civil war duration.[46] When peacekeepers are tasked to secure a country's borders, their presence may additionally restrict the flow of external support from foreign patrons.[47] Some scholars have also suggested that the growth of peacekeeping in the post–Cold War period helps to explain the decline of internal conflict during the 1990s and 2000s.[48] I therefore include an indicator variable for UN PEACEKEEPING deployments for each conflict-year using data provided in the Third-Party Peacekeeping in Intrastate Disputes Dataset.[49]

Of course, not all peacekeeping is undertaken by the UN—regional intergovernmental organizations, such as the African Union, also deploy peacekeepers to conflict zones. I therefore construct an additional indicator variable marking a REGIONAL PEACEKEEPING deployment in a given conflict-year, once again using data provided in the Third-Party Peacekeeping in Intrastate Disputes Dataset.[50]

GROUP-LEVEL FACTORS

Characteristics of the rebels fighting civil wars have also been linked to conflict duration. Beyond access to external military aid, other variables, such as whether the rebels control territory, the degree of their factionalism, and whether they possess a legal political wing, can also play a key role in their willingness and capacity to keep fighting.

---

[42] Balch-Lindsay and Enterline (2000: 623).
[43] Cederman, Min, and Wimmer (n.d.: 2). I use the updated version 3 of the Wimmer, Cederman, and Min (2009) dataset.
[44] Hultman, Kathman, and Shannon (2014).
[45] Fortna (2008).
[46] Ruggeri, Dorussen, and Gizelis (2017); Kathman and Benson (2019).
[47] Beardsley (2011: 1053).
[48] Goldstein (2011).
[49] Mullenbach (2013).
[50] Mullenbach (2013).

Territorial control provides rebel groups with a safe haven to rest, regroup, and refit for military operations. It also provides security from the coercive reach of the state. This can prolong civil wars if and when government forces prove unable to target and repress insurgents. Research also suggests that external support can encourage domestic combatants to pay the additional costs associated with fighting to seize and hold territory.[51] I therefore control for REBEL TERRITORIAL CONTROL, constructing an indicator variable using data provided by the Non-State Actor Dataset.[52]

Research has also convincingly shown that an increase in the number of rebel factions participating in a war increases its duration.[53] By their very nature, multiparty conflicts are more complex, rendering bargaining more difficult in a number of ways. First, additional parties at the bargaining table make it harder to find an agreement that all sides prefer to fighting. Second, information problems are more acute when there are multiple combatants, making it more difficult to estimate the relative balance of power and resolve. Third, when there are more parties that must agree to the final terms of a treaty, there are stronger incentives to delay agreement and be the last to sign on. Finally, shifting combatant alliances can result in bargaining breakdown when worries about each group's share of postwar power begin to take hold. I therefore construct a count variable of the NUMBER OF REBEL FACTIONS participating in each conflict-year observation using data provided by the ACD.[54]

Finally, I control for the ability of rebel groups to substitute strategies of violence with nonviolent political action. A legal political wing provides insurgent organizations with the ability to pursue their group interests through peaceful means that are formally recognized by the state. Existing work has shown that the presence of this alternative to violence is associated with a greater likelihood of conflict termination.[55] I therefore construct an indicator variable marking the presence of a LEGAL REBEL POLITICAL WING using data provided by the Non-State Actor Dataset.[56]

Empirical Results

What is the effect of competitive intervention on civil war duration? Table 4.1 reports results obtained from running Cox models on the dataset described above. Because the coefficient estimates report the effects of the covariates on the

---

[51] Schulhofer-Wohl (2020).
[52] Cunningham, K. Gleditsch, and Salehyan (2009). I use version 3.4 of the dataset.
[53] Cunningham (2011); Christia (2012).
[54] N. Gleditsch et al. (2002); Themnér and Wallensteen (2014).
[55] Cunningham, K. Gleditsch, and Salehyan (2009). On the effectiveness of nonviolent political action, see Chenoweth and Stephan (2011).
[56] Cunningham, K. Gleditsch, and Salehyan (2009). I use version 3.4 of the dataset.

Table 4.1 Cox model estimates, core results.

	Model 1 (bivariate)	Model 2 (state factors)	Model 3 (conflict factors)	Model 4 (group factors)	Model 5 (fully specified)
COMPETITIVE INTERVENTION	−0.662*** (0.228)	−0.876*** (0.235)	−0.735*** (0.220)	−0.624*** (0.234)	−0.845*** (0.233)
DEMOCRACY		−0.953*** (0.361)			−0.791** (0.349)
POPULATION (LOGGED)		−0.130 (0.095)			−0.109 (0.101)
GDP PER CAPITA (LOGGED)		−0.039 (0.121)			0.012 (0.138)
RUGGED TERRAIN		−0.071 (0.183)			−0.038 (0.209)
OIL PRODUCTION		1.560 (1.071)			1.566 (1.128)
OIL PRODUCTION*LN(T)		−0.206 (0.142)			−0.215 (0.149)
CONTIGUOUS BORDERS		−0.001 (0.037)			0.003 (0.041)
ETHNIC CONFLICT			0.029 (0.239)		0.009 (0.271)
SECESSIONIST–IRREDENTIST CONFLICT			−0.225 (0.225)		−0.172 (0.286)
UN PEACEKEEPING			0.904*** (0.331)		0.660* (0.389)
REGIONAL PEACEKEEPING			0.118 (0.383)		0.335 (0.417)
REBEL TERRITORIAL CONTROL				0.274 (0.200)	0.203 (0.201)
NUMBER OF REBEL FACTIONS				−0.542*** (0.206)	−0.643*** (0.208)
LEGAL REBEL POLITICAL WING				2.594*** (0.988)	2.361** (1.008)
LEGAL REBEL POLITICAL WING*LN(T)				−0.290** (0.144)	−0.274* (0.147)
NUMBER OF CONFLICTS	133	133	133	133	133
NUMBER OF TERMINATIONS	114	114	114	114	114
OBSERVATIONS	1,256	1,256	1,256	1,256	1,256

Note: Coefficient estimates with robust standard errors, clustered on conflict, in parentheses. *$p < 0.1$; **$p < 0.05$; ***$p < 0.01$.

hazard of a civil war's termination, positive coefficient estimates imply increases in the hazard of conflict termination (i.e., shorter durations), while negative estimates imply decreases in the hazard of conflict termination (i.e., longer durations). I adopt a step-wise approach, reporting multiple specifications with and without different sets of state-, conflict-, and group-level controls to demonstrate that the results do not rely on any particular combination of covariates. In the discussion below, I first provide a brief overview of the direction and statistical significance of the estimates before turning to substantive interpretations of the effects of variables of interest.

The theory presented in Chapter 2 posits a positive association between competitive intervention and civil war duration; I find strong empirical support for this prediction. Model 1 reports a simple bivariate specification. The coefficient estimate for competitive intervention is negative and strongly statistically significant at the $p < 0.01$ level. Model 2 examines how the incorporation of state characteristics—regime type, population size, real GDP per capita, rugged terrain, oil production, and contiguous borders—affects the findings of the baseline model.[57] The coefficient estimate for competitive intervention increases in magnitude in this model while remaining negative and statistically significant at the $p < 0.01$ level. Model 3 explores whether conflict-level factors—whether the war is an ethnic conflict, whether the war is a secessionist or irredentist conflict, whether a UN peacekeeping mission is deployed, and whether a regional peacekeeping mission is deployed—moderate the relationship between competitive intervention and civil war duration. The coefficient estimate for competitive intervention once again remains negative and statistically significant at the $p < 0.01$ level. Model 4 examines how group-level factors—whether the rebels control territory, the number of rebel factions, and whether the rebels possess a legal political wing—condition the relationship.[58] Competitive intervention is again found to have a substantively negative and statistically significant association with civil war duration at the $p < 0.01$ level. Finally, Model 5 presents a fully saturated model that includes all three groups of factors. In line with theoretical expectations, the coefficient estimate for competitive intervention remains negative and statistically significant at the $p < 0.01$ level. Taken together, these results confirm that competitive intervention prolongs civil war and that this is a generalizable relationship that holds across the wide range of contexts in which civil wars are fought.

[57] Note that this model also includes an interaction between OIL PRODUCTION and (logged) time to correct for violations of the proportional hazards assumption. For a full discussion, see Appendix B.
[58] Note that this model also includes an interaction between LEGAL REBEL POLITICAL WING and (logged) time to correct for violations of the proportional hazards assumption. For a full discussion, see Appendix B.

To evaluate these findings substantively, I use the coefficients reported for Model 5 to calculate the estimated percent change in the hazard of conflict termination given a one-unit increase in each variable included in the model.[59] I plot the results, along with 95% confidence intervals, in Figure 4.2. The figure shows that competitive intervention is estimated to decrease the hazard of civil war termination by an average 57% relative to conflicts that were not experiencing competitive intervention. Stated otherwise, competitive intervention cuts the hazard of conflict termination *in half* at every point in time over a conflict's duration. These are substantively large effects. Indeed, they are comparable in magnitude to a shift from non-democracy to democracy, the addition of another rebel faction to the civil war, or the deployment of a UN peacekeeping operation. These findings lend considerable support to this book's central argument:

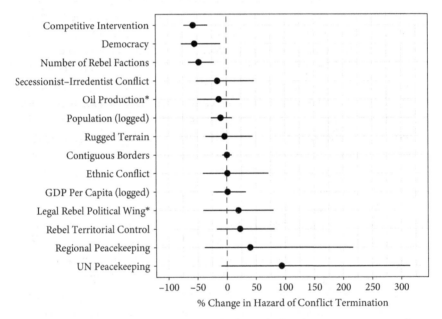

Figure 4.2 Estimated percent change in the hazard of civil war termination with 95% confidence intervals (core results, Model 5). Note that the changes in hazard for OIL PRODUCTION and LEGAL REBEL POLITICAL WING, both of which vary as a function of time, are estimated at the sample mean duration.

[59] To calculate this quantity of interest, I exponentiate the reported coefficients to recover hazard ratios for each covariate. Next, I subtract 1 from the hazard ratio and multiply by 100 to calculate the percent change in the hazard of conflict termination. Note that log-transformed covariates are interpreted as percentage, rather than unit, increases.

competitive intervention imparts large, substantively meaningful effects that protract civil wars.

The results reported here also find support for existing explanations of civil war duration. For example, in line with arguments connecting regime type to protracted conflict, democracies are found to fight longer wars than non-democracies.[60] In numbers, a shift from non-democracy to democracy is estimated to decrease the hazard of civil war termination by 55%. Likewise, increasing numbers of rebel factions is strongly associated with protracted fighting. Each additional faction is found to decrease the hazard of conflict termination by 47%, lending empirical support to arguments linking multiparty conflicts to longer civil wars.[61] I also find evidence for existing arguments about the constructive role peacekeepers can play in war zones.[62] Indeed, UN peacekeeping deployments are found to increase the hazard of conflict termination by an average 94%, though there is greater uncertainty surrounding these estimates ($p = 0.090$).

Finally, the results indicate that rebels with legal political wings fight shorter wars than those without them. This lends support to arguments linking the ability of rebel groups to substitute strategies of violence with nonviolent political action to an increased likelihood of conflict termination.[63] However, there is an important qualifier to this result: the negative coefficient on the interaction between the legal rebel political wing indicator and (logged) time indicates that the effect of this variable is moderated over time. In particular, legal rebel political wings are found to increase the hazard of civil war termination only in the earlier stages of a conflict. Indeed, as shown in Figure 4.2, at the sample mean duration, the effect of this variable is no longer statistically significant (for a full discussion of this latter result, see Appendix B).

Table 4.2 extends the analysis by (i) comparing the duration effect of competitive intervention to other configurations of external support, (ii) constraining the data sample by time period, and (iii) disaggregating the competitive intervention variable by the great power status of the intervening states. To translate these additional results into substantively meaningful quantities of interest, Figure 4.3 plots the estimated percent change in the hazard of conflict termination given a shift from a conflict without competitive intervention to a conflict with competitive intervention.

---

[60] E.g., Merom (2003).
[61] E.g., Cunningham (2011); Christia (2012).
[62] E.g., Fortna (2004, 2008); Hultman, Kathman, and Shannon (2014).
[63] E.g., Cunningham, K. Gleditsch, and Salehyan (2009).

Table 4.2 Cox model estimates, additional results.

	Model 6 (CI vs. only gov't)	Model 7 (CI vs. only rebels)	Model 8 (bipolar era)	Model 9 (unipolar era)	Model 10 (disaggregated)
COMPETITIVE INTERVENTION	−0.711** (0.284)	−0.864*** (0.277)	−0.882*** (0.251)	−1.234** (0.490)	
NEITHER SIDE SUPPORTED	0.231 (0.262)	0.078 (0.282)			
ONLY REBELS SUPPORTED	0.153 (0.284)				
ONLY GOVERNMENT SUPPORTED		−0.153 (0.284)			
US–SOVIET COMPETITIVE INTERVENTION					−0.832* (0.428)
LESSER POWERS COMPETITIVE INTERVENTION					−0.848*** (0.257)
OTHER CONTROLS INCLUDED?	YES	YES	YES	YES	YES
NUMBER OF CONFLICTS	133	133	95	65	133
NUMBER OF TERMINATIONS	114	114	68	46	114
OBSERVATIONS	1,256	1,256	820	436	1,256

Note: Coefficient estimates with robust standard errors, clustered on conflict, in parentheses. *$p < 0.1$; **$p < 0.05$; ***$p < 0.01$.

My theory highlights the strategic dilemmas and bargaining distortions that are unique to competitive intervention and that distinguish it from other forms of foreign meddling. To empirically assess the duration effect of competitive intervention relative to other configurations of external support, Models 6 and 7 compare conflicts afflicted by competitive intervention with conflicts in which only the government or only the rebels receive external support, respectively. These models confirm that civil wars experiencing competitive intervention are systematically longer than conflicts in which only one of the domestic combatants enjoys external support. In numbers, competitive intervention is found to decrease the hazard of conflict termination by 51% relative to conflicts in which only the government receives external support, and by 58% relative to conflicts in which only the rebels receive external support.

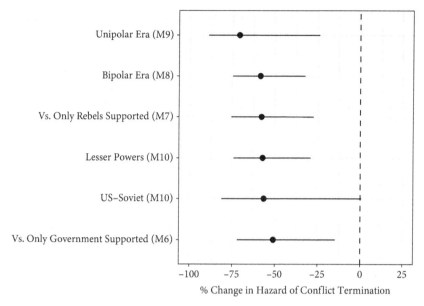

Figure 4.3 Estimated percent change in the hazard of civil war termination with 95% confidence intervals (additional results).

Models 8–10 further probe the generalizability of the results. My theory holds that the link between competitive intervention and protracted conflict should hold across time, irrespective of the structure of the international system (bipolar/unipolar) and the power status of the interveners (great powers/weaker states). Putting these expectations to the test, Models 8 and 9 examine whether the relationship between competitive intervention and protracted conflict is dependent on time period by constraining the data sample to the bipolar and unipolar eras, respectively. The effect of competitive intervention is consistently negative and statistically significant in these models, notwithstanding the reduced sample size. In numbers, competitive intervention is found to decrease the hazard of conflict termination by 59% in the bipolar era sample and by 71% in the unipolar era sample. These results are worth underscoring: they confirm that the duration effects of competitive intervention are not unique to the bipolar period. While the prevalence of competitive intervention has declined since 1990, its consequences for internal conflict remain potent.

Finally, Model 10 disaggregates the competitive intervention variable, distinguishing between competitive intervention among great powers (the US and Soviet Union) and competitive intervention among lesser powers. The results show that great power competitive intervention decreased the hazard of civil war termination by an average 56% relative to those conflicts that were not experiencing competitive intervention, albeit there is greater uncertainty around this estimate ($p = 0.052$). For their part, competitive interventions by lesser powers are estimated to decrease the hazard of conflict termination by an average 57% relative to those conflicts that were not experiencing competitive intervention. Thus, while great power proxy warfare prolonged internal conflicts, so too do competitive interventions by lesser powers. This demonstrates that the model estimates reported above are not being driven solely by US/Soviet rivalry; competitive intervention by less powerful states is also a significant predictor of longer wars, underscoring the value of a generalizable theory applicable to interveners of all types.

Taken together, the results reported here lend considerable empirical support to this book's central argument: competitive intervention prolongs civil wars. This effect holds even when controlling for a large number of alternative explanations, when comparing competitive intervention to alternative configurations of external support, when restricting the data sample by time period, and when disaggregating the competitive intervention variable into its great power and lesser power varieties.

Robustness Checks

To further probe the robustness of my findings, Table 4.3 presents an additional set of results that examine alternative model specifications and coding criteria. The substantive significance of these robustness checks is evaluated in Figure 4.4, which plots the estimated percent change in the hazard of conflict termination when moving from a conflict without competitive intervention to a conflict with competitive intervention.

Including Alleged Instances of Support

Like the UCDP External Support Dataset on which it builds, the EESD draws a distinction between *substantiated* instances of third-party support to civil war combatants and *alleged* instances of support. The latter category captures those cases where allegations of external sponsorship have been made by other states, media, or other sources, but it was not possible to find confirmatory evidence in support of those claims.[64] To test whether the inclusion of alleged instances of

---

[64] Croicu et al. (2011: 6). While alleged instances of support are unsubstantiated by the empirical record, note that this category excludes clearly outrageous claims.

Table 4.3 Cox model estimates, robustness checks.

	Model 11 (incl. alleged)	Model 12 (decade FEs)	Model 13 (shared frailty)	Model 14 (2-year rule)	Model 15 (25-threshold)
COMPETITIVE INTERVENTION		−0.770*** (0.237)	−0.845*** (0.234)	−1.021*** (0.239)	−0.954*** (0.155)
COMPETITIVE INTERVENTION (INCL. ALLEGED SUPPORT)	−0.788*** (0.238)				
OTHER CONTROLS?	YES	YES	YES	YES	YES
DECADE FIXED EFFECTS?	NO	YES	NO	NO	NO
SHARED FRAILTY?	NO	NO	YES	NO	NO
NUMBER OF CONFLICTS	133	133	133	130	365
NUMBER OF TERMINATIONS	114	114	114	109	337
OBSERVATIONS	1,256	1,256	1,256	1,365	1,754

Note: All models report coefficient estimates with robust standard errors, clustered on conflict, in parentheses with the exception of Model 13, which reports coefficient estimates with conventional standard errors in parentheses. *p < 0.1; **p < 0.05; ***p < 0.01.

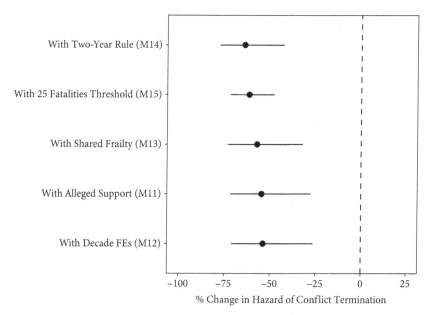

Figure 4.4 Estimated percent change in the hazard of civil war termination with 95% confidence intervals (robustness checks).

support affect the results, Model 11 reruns the analysis while incorporating all instances of support, both those that were corroborated in the empirical record and those that remain unsubstantiated. The results confirm that my findings are insensitive to the inclusion of alleged instances of support. Indeed, the substantive and statistical significance of the effect of competitive intervention on civil war duration is virtually unchanged in this model.

Unobserved Decade-Specific Confounders

There may be concerns that unobserved differences across decades could affect the results. For example, perhaps civil war duration exhibits variability over time that is unrelated to the variables included in the analyses. To control for this possibility, Model 12 reruns the analysis with decade fixed effects, which capture any potential decade-to-decade shocks to the outcome of interest.[65] The coefficient on competitive intervention remains negative and statistically significant. Substantively, competitive intervention is found to decrease the hazard of conflict termination by an average 54% relative to conflicts that were not experiencing competitive intervention in this model. In short, even when controlling for potential decade-specific confounders, the relationship between competitive intervention and civil war duration is found to be substantively and statistically robust.

Unobserved Conflict-Specific Heterogeneity

There may also be concerns that unobserved heterogeneity specific to individual conflicts in the dataset could affect the results. For example, there may be factors unique to individual conflicts that affect duration that are otherwise unaccounted for in the analyses. One way to address this concern is to employ a shared frailty model, which introduces a random component to account for variability due to potential unobserved group-specific factors.[66] The intuition

---

[65] In a Cox model context, decade fixed effects are preferable to year fixed effects, as the latter risks the introduction of monotone likelihood as the number of binary parameters increases. This problem is akin to that which afflicts the use of time dummies in binary outcome models, which can inadvertently introduce separation. On bias in fixed effects Cox regression with dummy variables, see Allison (2002). On monotone likelihood, see Anderson, Bagozzi, and Koren (2021). On the risk of separation with time dummies and logistic regression, see Carter and Signorino (2010: 275).

[66] A frailty model is akin to a random effects model for survival data, where the random effect (the frailty) has a multiplicative effect on the baseline hazard.

behind this approach is that some conflicts may be particularly susceptible to shorter durations (i.e., they are more "frail"). To account for this possibility, a shared frailty model modifies the hazard function, such that

$$h_i(t \mid X_{it}, v_i) = h_0(t)\, v_i \exp\left(\beta' X_{it}\right)$$

where $v_i = \exp(\psi'\omega)$ and denotes shared frailties, with a gamma distribution and mean equal to 1. Notably, as a parameter of the model, one can estimate the variance of v_i, traditionally denoted as θ. If $\theta = 0$, the model reduces to a standard Cox model, implying the absence of group-level heterogeneity.

Model 13 reruns a fully specified model with the inclusion of a shared frailty. As shown in Figure 4.4, the substantive and statistical significance of the relationship between competitive intervention and civil war duration remains essentially unchanged. In numbers, competitive intervention is estimated to reduce the hazard of conflict termination by an average 57% relative to conflicts that were not afflicted by competitive intervention. Moreover, the results indicate that unobserved, conflict-specific heterogeneity is unlikely to be driving the results. Indeed, the variance of the random effect θ is insignificant.[67] Simply put, the link between competitive intervention and civil war duration is once again found to be robust.

Increasing the Conflict Episode Intermittency Window: The "Two-Year Rule"

The definition of civil war I employ measures conflict duration using the start and end dates provided in the UCDP ACD. A conflict's start date is recorded once the ACD inclusion criteria are met; it is considered terminated once it ceases to meet these criteria for one full year. Notably, however, some conflicts in the dataset fail to meet the ACD inclusion criteria for just one year, only to reignite shortly thereafter. While it is this book's objective to explain the determinants of *sustained* violent conflict, it is reasonable to ask whether a one-year lull in fighting is sufficient to merit coding a war as "terminated." To strike a balance between treating one-year lulls in fighting as terminations and treating distinct onsets of armed violence as the same conflict, a number of scholars

---

[67] $\chi^2 = 0.000$, $p = 0.921$.

employ a two-year intermittency rule—that is, a conflict is considered terminated only when it has failed to meet the inclusion criteria for two full years.[68] To confirm my results are not inadvertently driven by my use of a one-year intermittency rule, I reanalyze my results using the two-year intermittency rule. I report the results of a fully specified model here; replications of all Models 1–10 are reported in Appendix C.

Model 14 confirms that my empirical results are consistent with theoretical predictions regardless of whether a one- or two-year intermittency rule is used to identify conflict terminations. The negative and statistically significant relationship between competitive intervention and civil war duration persists. In fact, the magnitude of the effect of competitive intervention is marginally increased when using the two-year rule: competitive intervention is estimated to reduce the hazard of conflict termination by an average 64% relative to conflicts that were not afflicted by competitive intervention. This underscores the robust relationship between competitive intervention and civil war duration and confirms that my findings are insensitive to alternative measures of conflict termination.

Relaxing the 1,000 Cumulative Fatalities Criterion

The dataset analyzed above includes all civil wars fought between 1946 and 2009 with at least 25 battle-related deaths per year *and* a minimum of 1,000 cumulative battle-related deaths over the course of their full duration. The latter criterion serves an important purpose: it minimizes concerns over the heterogeneity of cases inherent in a low, twenty-five battle-related deaths threshold, thereby ensuring that cases are sufficiently alike to merit meaningful comparison in empirical analyses. Indeed, one methodological concern inherent in adopting a low battle-related death threshold is the inclusion of arguably dissimilar forms of political violence, such as coups, violent riots, isolated terrorist attacks, and civil wars. Precisely because we would not expect competitive intervention to afflict the former varieties of intrastate conflict—all of which tend to be short in duration—including these cases in empirical analyses risks overstating the substantive effect of competitive intervention on the hazard of civil war termination. Nonetheless, it is valuable to probe empirical findings at different thresholds to confirm that results align with theoretical predictions.[69] To those ends, I reanalyze my results using a threshold of

---

[68] E.g., Fearon (2004); Sambanis (2004); Cunningham, K. Gleditsch, and Salehyan (2009); Cunningham (2011); Wucherpfennig et al. (2012).

[69] For a discussion, see Anderson and Worsnop (2019).

twenty-five battle-related deaths per year *without* a cumulative requirement. My expectation is that the inclusion of additional, low-fatality conflicts will increase the magnitude of the effect of competitive intervention on civil war duration. I report the results of a fully specified model here; replications of all Models 1–10 without the cumulative fatalities criterion are reported in Appendix D.

Model 15 confirms that the magnitude of the effect of competitive intervention is indeed larger in the absence of the cumulative fatalities criterion, while the statistical significance of the relationship between competitive intervention and civil war duration is strengthened. Competitive intervention is found to decrease the hazard of conflict termination by an average 61% relative to conflicts that were not experiencing competitive intervention. Empirical results therefore align with theoretical predictions. Competitive intervention is shown to have a substantively and statistically significant relationship with civil war duration, regardless of the threshold criteria employed.

Reverse Causality

Finally, there may be concerns about reverse causality. In particular, it may not be the case that competitive intervention prolongs civil war; rather, it might be argued, civil wars that have *already* been waged for long periods of time may disproportionately attract competitive interventions. If the latter case were true, the link between competitive intervention and longer conflict would be a spurious one.

There are two responses to this critique. First, the cross-national time-series structure of the dataset alleviates this concern by allowing the competitive intervention variable to vary across years of a civil war. The models reported above estimate the hazard of conflict termination by comparing conflicts with competitive intervention at time t against conflicts without competitive intervention at time t. As a result, even if it were true that competitive intervention only afflicted conflicts that had already been waged for long periods of time, the model would capture this temporal lag in the onset of competitive intervention in the estimates it derives.

Second, it can be empirically demonstrated that the majority of competitive interventions begin in the early years of a civil war. Figure 4.5 plots the year of competitive intervention onset for all civil wars that were afflicted by this form of external meddling in the dataset. The figure reveals that in the majority (66.2%) of cases, the onset of a competitive intervention occurred in the *first year* of a conflict. In 86.8% of cases, the onset of a competitive intervention occurred by the third year of a conflict. Recall that the average duration of civil wars in the dataset is 8.59 years. It is therefore not the case that long-standing

104　WARS WITHOUT END

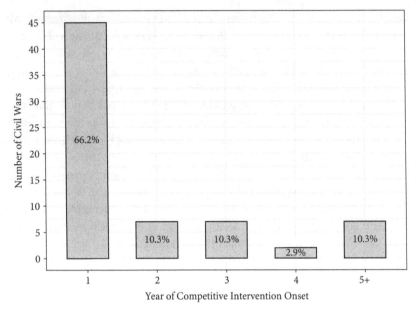

Figure 4.5 Year of competitive intervention onset for civil wars that were afflicted by competitive intervention at any time during their duration.

conflicts tend to disproportionately attract competitive intervention; rather, competitive intervention systematically prolongs civil wars.

Competitive Intervention, Protracted Conflict, and the Global Prevalence of Civil War

The results presented above are unanimous: competitive intervention prolongs civil wars. The task that remains, therefore, is to assess whether competitive intervention and its relationship to protracted conflict can in turn help to explain the rise and decline in the global prevalence of civil war witnessed between 1946 and 2009. Prevalence is a statistical concept that refers to the proportion of a population that is afflicted by a condition in a given period of time. It is a function of two quantities: the incidence of the condition and its average duration. Incidence refers to the proportion of the population that is diagnosed with a new instance of the condition (thereby becoming part of the prevalent population). Average duration refers to the time it takes, on average, to be "cured" of the condition (thereby moving out of the prevalent population). If the incidence of a condition is high, but its average duration is short, then its prevalence will largely mirror its incidence. Conversely, if the incidence of a condition is low, but its average duration is long, then its prevalence will largely mirror its average duration.

How have the incidence, average duration, and global prevalence of civil war varied over time? Figure 4.6 plots all three quantities over the full period from 1946 to 2009. It reveals a striking result: the global prevalence of civil war has been predominantly driven by changes in the average duration of conflict, rather than its incidence.[70] Indeed, while there has been some interannual variability, the incidence of civil war has remained remarkably low over time. Average conflict duration, on the other hand, has noticeably trended upwards and downwards during different periods. From 1946 to 1990, there was a clear rise in the average yearly duration of civil war; over the following decade there was a downward trend; and through the 2000s average conflict duration rose once more. These patterns are largely mirrored by the prevalence of civil war,

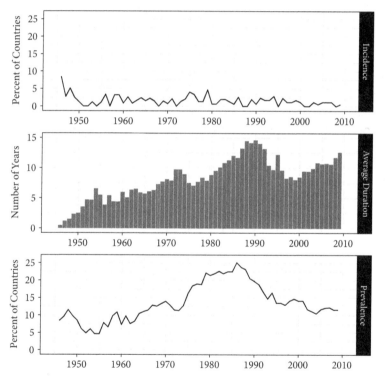

Figure 4.6 Trends in the yearly incidence, average duration, and prevalence of civil war, 1946–2009.

---

[70] The same conclusion holds when employing a threshold of 25 battle-related deaths per year without a 1,000 cumulative fatalities criterion. For a discussion, see Appendix E.

which similarly rose and fell, before leveling out in the 2000s—this, despite the fact that the incidence of new conflict outbreaks during the latter decade was just 0.70%.

What, then, is the relationship between competitive intervention and the global prevalence of civil war? My theory posits a positive association; three lines of evidence support this conclusion. First, Chapter 3 demonstrated that there was a significantly higher prevalence of competitive intervention in civil war during the bipolar period relative to the unipolar period. In numbers, competitive intervention was shown to afflict an average of 41.6% of conflicts in the former period, but an average of just 20.6% of conflicts in the latter period. Stated otherwise, competitive intervention was more common when the prevalence of civil war was rising, and it was less common when the prevalence of civil war was declining. Second, in the quantitative analyses reported above, I find robust empirical support for a substantively and statistically significant relationship between competitive intervention and protracted civil war. This form of external meddling was shown to decrease the hazard of conflict termination by more than 50% across every point in time over a conflict's duration. In effect, when the prevalence of competitive intervention increases, so too does average conflict duration. Finally, an overview of trends in the incidence, average duration, and global prevalence of civil war confirms that, between 1946 and 2009, the latter was predominately driven by how long conflicts lasted, rather than by how many broke out. In short, as the prevalence of competitive intervention has varied, so too have its conflict prolonging effects—a dynamic that helps to explain temporal variation in the global prevalence of civil war through the duration channel.

Conclusion

The quantitative analyses presented in this chapter confirm the critical role competitive interventions have played in sustaining civil wars. By testing my theory against the universe of civil wars fought between 1946 and 2009, the analyses verify its external validity across space and time. Similarly, by testing my argument against those found in the existing literature, the analyses confirm its generalizability across the wide range of political, economic, and social contexts in which intrastate conflicts are waged.

Together with my findings reported in Chapter 3, the empirical evidence presented here demonstrates that there was a greater prevalence of competitive intervention in the bipolar period relative to the unipolar period; that competitive intervention has large duration effects on internal conflicts; and that temporal variation in average conflict duration has been the predominant driver of the prevalence of civil war. Drawing these three lines of evidence together provides an integrated explanation for the waxing and waning of civil war over time.

Having found strong support for each of the hypotheses associated with the outcomes predicted by the theory, the next step in my nested analysis research design is to test the observable implications associated with the proposed mechanisms of the theory, which link competitive intervention to protracted conflict—both at the international level of the competitive interveners and at the domestic level of the civil war combatants. My argument highlights the conditional nature of intervention under the shadow of inadvertent escalation, arguing that competitive interveners constrain the scope of their support to domestic combatants to control escalation vis-à-vis opposing interveners and to avoid mutually destructive outcomes. This prevents the conferral of decisive military advantages on clients while distorting domestic bargaining processes by decreasing combatants' costs of war, shifting their capabilities toward parity, and amplifying information asymmetries. Validating these observable implications requires a shift from *between*-case analyses (i.e., the study of a cross-national time-series dataset) to *within*-case analyses (i.e., the in-depth study of the civil war process in individual cases). To those ends, Chapter 5 turns to explore the dynamics of competitive intervention in one of the deadliest conflicts of the past century: the Angolan civil war (1975–1991).

5
The Angolan MPLA–UNITA Civil War, 1975–1991

That third-party states would invest billions of dollars and risk the lives of thousands of soldiers, yet seek only to avoid their domestic client's defeat, rather than ensure their victory, may strike some as fanciful. After all, scholars and practitioners generally assume that states intervene to either help one side win militarily or to facilitate a negotiated settlement—outcomes that terminate civil wars.[1] But as my theory explains, what is distinct about competitive intervention is the escalatory risk it entails. While battlefield success may be the primary objective for a conflict's domestic combatants, the need to avoid large-scale confrontations with one another leads competitive interveners to pursue more limited objectives. Limits serve to constrain intervener confrontation, but they simultaneously prevent the provision of decisive military advantages to domestic clients. This leads to deadlocked conflicts and prolonged interventions, as interveners abstain from provisioning the level of support necessary to secure a decisive military victory, and instead provide a level of support sufficient only to sustain continued fighting. When combined with the distortionary effects of competitive intervention on domestic bargaining processes, protracted civil wars result.

The Angolan civil war is an illuminating example of these dynamics in action. While battlefield victory was undoubtedly the primary objective for the Angolan government and its rebel challengers, fears of uncontrolled escalation led competitive interveners—on one side, Cuba and the Soviet Union, and on the other, South Africa and the United States—to constrain the scope of their interventions. As I demonstrate below, strategic restraint manifested in the distinctions interveners drew between advisory and combat missions, geographic areas of control and contestation, offensive and defensive deployment patterns and force postures, and acceptable and prohibited targets. In line with theoretical expectations, the need to avert the dangers of escalation generated a set of interventions that aimed to sustain the rebel insurgency rather than propel it to victory, and a corresponding set of interventions that aimed to prevent the

---

[1] See, for example, Licklider (1995), Walter (1997, 2002), Carment and Rowlands (1998), Regan (2002), Siqueira (2003), and Amegashie and Kutsoati (2007).

Wars Without End. Noel Anderson, Oxford University Press. © Oxford University Press (2025).
DOI: 10.1093/oso/9780197798645.003.0005

dislodging of the Angolan government rather than end the civil war. In turn, these behaviors distorted domestic bargaining processes by subsidizing local war costs, balancing combatant capabilities, and enhancing information asymmetries. The net result was a bloody and protracted conflict, with little hope for victory or negotiated settlement.

The Angolan war is an important case for this book for theoretical and empirical purposes. Representing one of the clearest examples of the nexus between interstate competition and the civil war process, between 1975 and 1991 Angola was the site of a complex system of conflicts that simultaneously took place at the national, regional, and systemic levels. These conflicts were distinct but interrelated, exerting important conditioning effects on one another. By exploring how competitive intervention manifested on the battlefields of Angola, this chapter demonstrates that the combatants and interveners were not simply reacting to developments inside the country—neither the strategic logics motivating their warfare nor the scope and form of their interventions can be directly inferred from the internal orientation of the conflict. To explain the dynamics and duration of the war necessitates an understanding of the escalation dilemma at the heart of competitive intervention, as well as its distortionary effects on domestic bargaining processes.

The case also provides a "least-likely" test for my argument relating escalation fears to intervener restraint.[2] The conflict was disturbingly violent, inflicting hundreds of thousands of deaths.[3] Accounts of the war are replete with images of homicidal violence and omnipresent death. As one Angolan observer recounts, "The killing was big! Killing! Killing so many people!"[4] In addition to its vast human toll, the war decimated the country's political, social, and economic institutions. The United Nations (UN) estimates that between 1980 and 1988 alone, Angola lost some $30 billion due to the war—six times its 1988 gross domestic product.[5] Given the disturbing intensity of violence, one would not expect to uncover limits in the scope of external intervention in the war. In this respect, the identification of strategic restraint in the interactions of competitive interveners provides powerful evidence of the conditioning effect of fears of inadvertent escalation.

---

[2] A "least-likely" case is one in which a relationship holds despite background factors predicting otherwise (Gerring and Cojocaru 2016: 404). On the virtues of "least-likely" tests, see Gerring and Seawright (2007: 115–119).
[3] Given the difficulty of data collection on the Angolan civil war, estimates of war deaths vary significantly by source. Heldt, Wallensteen, and Nordquist (1992: 442) estimate 100,000 battle-related deaths for the period 1975–1991, with total war casualties, including indirect deaths, estimated at 300,000–500,000. Laffin (1994: 14) estimates 350,000 deaths over the same period.
[4] As quoted in Brinkman (2000: 7).
[5] UN Inter-Agency Task Force (1989: 2, 24–27).

The Angolan civil war is a highly complex case. The objective of this chapter is not to comprehensively overview the conflict, but rather to examine the strategic behaviors adopted by the competitive interveners and to assess their consequences for domestic bargaining processes. Employing process tracing, my goal is to verify the mechanisms that underlie the statistical association between competitive intervention and protracted conflict by testing the observable implications of my theory. In doing so, I aim to fulfill the second stage of my nested analysis research design by building upon my large-N cross-national findings with contextually based evidence of my theory's proposed mechanisms in action.[6] I begin at the international level of the competitive interveners to examine the degree to which the interveners constrained the scope of their assistance to domestic combatants, to determine whether this restraint was motivated by escalation fears vis-à-vis opposing interveners, and to assess whether limits on the scope of support were constructed around thresholds that signaled restraint to opposing interveners. I then turn to the domestic level of the civil war combatants to examine whether and how competitive intervention distorted bargaining processes by reducing the costs of war, balancing combatant capabilities, and amplifying information asymmetries.

The analysis that follows draws on an extensive set of primary and secondary materials. These include semi-structured interviews with former military commanders, political leaders, and diplomats who participated in the conflict; archival documents and declassified intelligence reports; and memoirs and personal accounts published by political and military veterans of the war. The chapter begins with a brief overview of the civil war and the relationships between domestic combatants and foreign interveners. Next, it examines how interveners navigated the unique strategic dilemmas inherent in competitive intervention. It then unpacks the consequences of these dilemmas for domestic bargaining processes. The chapter concludes with a summary of the evidence and an explicit consideration of how the problem of escalation and its control affected conflict dynamics in the Angolan civil war.

Overview of the War and Combatant Relationships

The origins of the Angolan civil war date back to the efforts of three national liberation movements to achieve independence from Portuguese colonial rule in the early 1960s: the Movimento Popular de Libertação de Angola (MPLA) led by Agostinho Neto, the União Nacional para a Independência Total de

---

[6] In the language of a nested analysis research design, the goal of this chapter is to proceed to "model-testing small-N analysis." See Lieberman (2005: 442–443).

Angola (UNITA) led by Jonas Savimbi, and the Frente Nacional de Libertação de Angola (FNLA) led by Holden Roberto.[7] All three movements developed guerrilla armies, but none of them established an effective fighting force.[8] The Portuguese's unrivaled weapons technology provided a decisive military advantage over the nascent rebel challengers, ensuring colonialist control throughout Angola (see Figure 5.1 for a map of the country).

On April 25, 1974, all that changed. In Portugal, a military coup organized by a group of leftist military officers overthrew the Estado Novo, ending one of the longest-surviving authoritarian regimes in Europe. The coup marked not only the beginning of the Carnation Revolution in Portugal but also the transformation of Angola's colonial struggle into a civil war. The military junta that took power in Lisbon moved quickly to grant independence to Portugal's overseas territories. Within months, all three Angolan liberation movements had signed agreements both with the transitional government and each other. Under a pact known as the Alvor Agreement, the parties committed to forming a coalition government, with plans for national elections to follow soon after. These provisions would then pave the way for Angolan independence, which was scheduled for November 11, 1975.

The agreement was hopelessly ambitious: FNLA and MPLA soldiers began fighting each other in Luanda only days after its signing, and by midyear, UNITA too had joined the fray. Clashes quickly spread throughout the country, casting the die for a military solution to political disagreements. As violence erupted, external states mobilized support for their favored sides. Foreign meddling in Angolan affairs was nothing new—transfers of weapons and financial aid to the guerrilla armies had been a feature of the anticolonial struggle since the 1960s.[9] But in the power vacuum left by the collapse of the Portuguese administration, the scope of external intervention increased dramatically.

On one side of the battlefield stood the FNLA and UNITA, backed by the US, South Africa, and Zaire; on the other stood the MPLA, backed by Cuba and the Soviet Union. American aid had begun flowing into Angola as early as January 1975, and by July a covert operation, IA Feature, was established to provide some $31.7 million in military assistance.[10] Motivating Washington's

---

[7] Each group organized associated military forces: the MPLA's Forças Armadas Populares de Libertação de Angola (FAPLA), UNITA's Forças Armadas de Libertação de Angola (FALA), and the FNLA's Exército de Libertação Nacional de Angola (ELNA). In what follows, I simply refer to the groups' main political organizations (MPLA, UNITA, and FNLA) to cut down on the great array of acronyms found in the literature on the war.

[8] This was the perception of the US intelligence community at the time. See NSC Interdepartmental Group for Africa (1975: 1–2, 21).

[9] As a few examples: in the 1960s, the Congo, Soviet Union, and Yugoslavia were supporting the MPLA's liberation efforts; China had trained and armed Savimbi and other UNITA guerrillas; and Zaire and the United States were actively backing the FNLA.

[10] For details on IA Feature, see Stockwell (1978: 206).

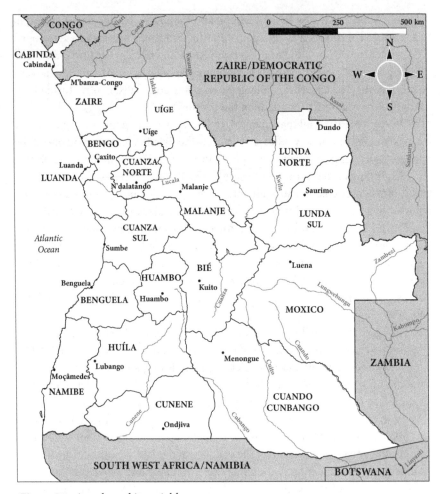

Figure 5.1 Angola and its neighbors.

entry into the war were fears over Soviet expansionism in southern Africa. American policymakers worried that a victory for the communist-aligned MPLA increased the chances of "heavy Soviet influence in independent Angola, continued instability in Angola beyond independence, an unstable Zaire, and a general destabilization of the area." They warned of "another country added to the list of those that deny us access to ports and airfields for our Navy and Air Force. In addition to enjoying such access, the Soviets might be given military facilities."[11]

---

[11] "Talking Points for Secretary Kissinger, NSC Meeting on Angola" (June 27, 1975).

Their assessment was correct. As former Deputy Head of the Soviet Ministry of Foreign Affairs Anatoly Adamishin explains, "[a]part from ideological motives, geopolitical interests were gaining more and more weight: the aim was to capture strategic ground in the South of the African continent to oppose the United States."[12] Air and naval access in Angola allowed the Soviets to monitor shipping lanes around the Cape of Good Hope and into the South Atlantic.[13] This was a critical seaway that transferred much of the West's oil supply from the Persian Gulf.

American officials began privately coaxing South Africa to join the anti-MPLA alliance.[14] Pretoria needed little encouraging. The collapse of Portuguese colonial administration threatened to empower black liberation movements fighting against the apartheid regime's control of South West Africa (today known as Namibia). A former German colony, South West Africa fell under a South African mandate following Germany's defeat in the First World War. Pretoria ruled it as a fifth province and sought to stamp out the activity of a nascent liberation movement known as the South West Africa People's Organization. For South African policymakers, the danger posed by this *swart gevaar* (black threat) was magnified by a second: the *rooi gevaar* (red threat). As Portuguese authority receded from southern Africa, Pretoria worried it would be replaced by Soviet influence. The persistent fear of the apartheid regime concerned the consequences of communist-sponsored black troops, which would enjoy vastly superior numbers and, with the largess of the Soviet Union, access to modern weapons.[15]

In October 1975, Pretoria made its move: some 3,000 South African Defense Force (SADF) troops joined up with UNITA in a mechanized column to begin advancing on Luanda from the south; Operation Savannah—the code name given to the military invasion—had begun. Meanwhile, Zairian President Mobutu Sese Seko threw his support behind his brother-in-law, Holden

---

[12] Adamishin (2014: 6).
[13] Shubin (2008: 72). Tu-95RTs reconnaissance aircraft periodically deployed to Angola to monitor the South Atlantic, while the Soviet West Africa naval patrol used Luanda for crew rest, logistics, and ship repairs. See CIA (n.d.: 1).
[14] South African recriminations strongly suggest American enticement. As the then defense minister PW Botha decried to South African Parliament in 1978, "I know of only one occasion in recent years when we crossed a border, and that was in the case of Angola when we did so with the approval and knowledge of the Americans. But they left us in the lurch. We are going to retell the story: the story must be told of how we, with their knowledge, went in there and operated in Angola with their knowledge, how they encouraged us to act and, when we had nearly reached the climax, we were ruthlessly left in the lurch." See Republic of South Africa, Debates of the House of Assembly (April 17, 1978: col. 4852). Statements by American politicians likewise suggest US encouragement of the South African offensive. For example, US Senator Barry Goldwater is reported as saying that "[t]here is no question but that the CIA told the South Africans to move into Angola and that we would help with military equipment" (as quoted in Wolfers and Bergerol 1983: 8).
[15] For a discussion of how South Africa's threat perception dictated its security strategy, see Anderson and Bell (2023).

Roberto, bolstering an FNLA force advancing from the north. For American, South African, and Zairian officials alike, it was hoped that the anti-MPLA coalition would reach Luanda by November 11 to seize control of the country in time for Angolan independence.

However, with the defensive capability provided by Soviet arms, as well as the deployment of an elite Angolan unit—the Ninth Brigade, which had received extensive training in the Soviet Union—the MPLA succeeded in beating back the FNLA offensive in the north.[16] A decisive battle took place on the eve of independence between the MPLA and the FNLA at Quifangondo, roughly thirty kilometers from Luanda. MPLA forces inflicted a devastating beating on an advancing FNLA column. Discipline among FNLA troops rapidly collapsed, and "what started as a military withdrawal degenerated into a scramble for the border."[17] On January 4, 1976, the FNLA's main basing area at Carmona was overrun, signaling the group's total collapse as a fighting force and its exit as a meaningful participant in the war.

Yet while the MPLA enjoyed battlefield victories in the north, the combined South African/UNITA army proved too powerful to halt in the south. By November 6, 1975, the latter had advanced some 800 kilometers, capturing the port cities of Benguela and Lobito in what the former chief of the Central Intelligence Agency's (CIA) Angola Task Force has described as "the most effective military strike force ever seen in black Africa."[18] The MPLA was quickly faced with what amounted to a severe military crisis as UNITA forces positioned themselves to begin threatening the capital.

Under siege in Luanda, the MPLA appealed for urgent assistance from its patrons. Increasing shipments of Soviet arms were already being transferred to MPLA units as early as December 1974, and by late summer 1975, a handful of Cuban advisors had arrived in Angola to begin training MPLA recruits.[19] In the wake of Operation Savannah, however, this trickle of military aid turned into a flood: between November 1975 and March 1976, the Soviet Union established an air-and-sea bridge that coordinated the deployment of some 36,000 Cuban soldiers and the transfer of hundreds of millions of dollars' worth of military equipment to reinforce MPLA positions.

As Cuban forces armed with Soviet military hardware poured into Angola, the specter of a full-blown conventional war between South African and Cuban

---

[16] Members of the Ninth Brigade had been sent to the Soviet Union in March 1975, where they were put through higher officer courses. The brigade returned to Angola in late August aboard a Soviet ship, along with its kit of armored cars (BRDM-2s), artillery (82-mm mortars and 76-mm guns), and antiaircraft weapons. See Shubin (2008: 40) and Gleijeses (2002: 268).

[17] George (2005: 90–91).

[18] Stockwell (1978: 191). Spies (1989: 149) estimates that SADF-backed forces were in control of 80% of Angolan territory by this time.

[19] Westad (1996: 24); Gleijeses (2002: 261); Zubok (2007: 252).

forces loomed large. International opinion also turned against what was seen as an aggressive invasion by a racist South African apartheid state. On December 19, the US Senate adopted the Clark Amendment, which blocked additional covert funding for the Angolan conflict. Washington was forced to abandon the South African force it had encouraged to invade Angola and to terminate its own clandestine operations in that country. This was followed on January 22, 1976 by a vote at the Organization of African Unity (OAU) that formally recognized the MPLA regime, rendering the South African adventure an illegal occupation. The writing was on the wall: the SADF withdrawal began; by February 11, the UNITA capital at Huambo fell, and Savimbi returned his rebels to the Angolan bush.

But the conflict was far from over. The next fifteen years would see continued fighting between the MPLA and UNITA in a civil war sustained by external patrons who not only continued to transfer weapons, money, and equipment but also sent their own forces into combat. Initially concentrated in the southeast of the country, fighting soon spread throughout Angola's countryside and into its urban centers, imposing an ever-growing toll. And yet, despite billions in aid from Soviet coffers and the deployment of tens of thousands of Cuban troops, the MPLA proved unable to crush the UNITA insurgency. And despite regular SADF incursions into Angola and the provision of American military hardware, UNITA failed to overthrow the MPLA regime.[20] Instead, the conflict settled into a bloody war of attrition, in which neither side proved capable of military victory nor willing to sue for peace.

Figure 5.2 provides a visual summary of the primary domestic combatants and competitive interveners of interest to the analysis that follows. While the FNLA was a participant in the early stages of the war, the group was inconsequential following its defeat at Quifangondo.[21] Small bands of FNLA fighters did continue to operate from bases along the Zairian border, but they never again posed a threat to the MPLA regime. Indeed, as early as February 1976, the MPLA's defense minister, Iko Carreira, had declared northern Angola "completely liberated."[22] For these reasons, I limit my analysis to the conflict's primary domestic combatants, the MPLA and UNITA.

---

[20] The Clark Amendment, which barred aid to rebel groups engaged in Angola, remained in effect only until its repeal in July 1985. Further, the force of the Amendment was blunted by the fact that Washington continued to transfer "gray market" and "dual use" equipment, channeled aid through third-party countries (including Morocco, Israel, and Zaire), and actively vetoed international efforts to sanction South African interventions. From 1986 onward, the US provided UNITA with military hardware valued at tens of millions of dollars per year.

[21] As George (2005: 90) puts it, "[t]he repercussions of this battle would far exceed the losses in men and material [...] for within days it became clear that the psychological blow inflicted on Roberto's soldiers had broken their will to fight on. In fact it is no exaggeration to say that the battle of Quifangondo destroyed the FNLA."

[22] As quoted in Gleijeses (2002: 338–339).

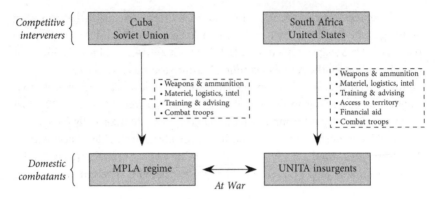

Figure 5.2 Relationships between primary domestic combatants and competitive interveners during the Angolan civil war, 1975–1991.

Similarly, while Zaire participated in the opening salvos of the war by supporting the FNLA, it would eventually expel Roberto and his rebel forces in accordance with an MPLA-Zairean peace accord that committed both states to end support for insurgencies in each other's countries. Accordingly, I focus my analysis on the conflict's primary competitive interveners: on one side, the US and South Africa, and on the other, the Soviet Union and Cuba.

Strategic Restraint During Competitive Intervention in the Angolan Civil War

From 1975 to 1991, external interveners spent billions of dollars and lost thousands of lives fighting in the Angolan civil war. Clearly, for all parties to the conflict, the battle for Luanda was worth significant sacrifices. Yet, the protracted character of the fighting presents a puzzle. If external interveners stood to gain from the victory of their domestic clients, why would they choose to invest in the conflict at a level that resulted in a costly stalemate?

This section explains how the escalation dilemma at the heart of competitive intervention complicated and prolonged foreign participation in the war. While all of the interveners had important strategic interests at stake in the Angolan conflict, none were willing to entertain the idea of a war against each other. Their challenge, therefore, was to pursue their individual interests while avoiding direct confrontation. In line with theoretical expectations, the interveners found ways to regulate their competition by tacitly and explicitly communicating, by adopting patterned behaviors, and by constraining the scope of their interventions. Yet while limits served to manage escalation risks, they simultaneously prevented the conferral of decisive military advantages. The net result was a protracted civil war. In what follows, I elaborate on the form and function of the interveners' strategic restraint in the Angolan case.

"Advisory" versus "Combat" Missions

Despite committing billions of dollars' worth of aid to the war, neither the US nor the Soviet Union deployed combat troops to the Angolan theater. As US Secretary of State Henry Kissinger explained to the Subcommittee on African Affairs of the Senate Committee on Foreign Relations, the Angolan conflict was "of a type in which diplomacy without leverage is impotent, yet direct military confrontation would involve unnecessary risks."[23] As was the case with other hotspots during the Cold War, the impossible stakes of direct US–Soviet confrontation precluded sending American or Soviet troops to decisively shift the balance of power between the domestic combatants—this despite the tremendous effect even a small deployment could have on the outcome of the war.

However, simply delivering military equipment to their Angolan clients proved problematic. As the former chief of the CIA's Angola Task Force, John Stockwell, explains, domestic combatants "were not able to organize the logistical systems necessary to deploy [weapons] or to develop the communications, maintenance, combat leadership, and discipline to organize an effective military effort."[24] Many Angolan fighters lacked even basic shooting skills, possessed no formal military training, and had little combat experience. "[B]eyond a certain point," one CIA report observes, "equipment itself—without the trained men to use it—became ineffectual."[25] Consequently, Washington and Moscow faced a dilemma: How could they provision effective military aid without committing their own forces?

Their solution was to draw a distinction between "advisory missions," which involved training client forces, and "combat missions," which involved direct participation in the conflict. This distinction has commonly been observed by intervening states as a means to communicate restraint—ostensibly because of the "non-combat" role played by advisors. Accordingly, both the US and Soviet Union deployed personnel that became deeply involved in the management of

---

[23] Kissinger (1976: 181).
[24] Stockwell (1978: 176).
[25] CIA (March 1977: 17).

the conflict.[26] These advisors performed a number of functions: they instructed and organized domestic combatant forces; they undertook strategic and tactical planning; they serviced combat vehicles and equipment; and (in the case of Soviet advisors) they served as technicians for advanced weapon systems, including antiair batteries.[27]

The arrival of military advisors was critical to the combat effectiveness of both the MPLA and UNITA. It was active US–Soviet participation in the conflict that directly contributed to the domestic combatants' fighting capacities. But by drawing a distinction between "advisory" and "combat" missions, the great powers established an observable threshold that could control escalation: the deployment of "advisors" was acceptable; the deployment of "combat troops" was prohibited. This enabled both sides to support their domestic clients while ensuring that direct confrontations between their troops would be avoided.

To reinforce the distinction, foreign advisors were strictly prohibited from participating in combat. Sergej Kolomnin, a Soviet officer who served in Angola, notes that "[Soviet advisors] were told time and again that we should only instruct, train and advise [...] but not fight."[28] Lieutenant (ret.) Vyacheslav Barabulya, who served as a Soviet translator in Angola from 1986 to 1988, likewise confirms that Soviet advisors "didn't take a direct part in combat action."[29] Lieutenant Colonel (ret.) Igor Zhdarkin explains that during his deployment in 1986, Angolan battalions "were regularly sent out to clear the territory of the enemy. [...] We often also helped them prepare for actual operations but didn't participate ourselves, thank god."[30] Upon coming under fire, Soviet advisors were instructed to withdraw. Petr Khrupilin, a senior member of the Soviet military mission in Angola, explains that "[a]s a rule, [Soviet] advisors in the Angolan brigades moved to the rear when there were military operations."[31] Similarly, Barabulya notes that his unit "had BTR-60PB armored troop carriers and BMP-1 infantry combat vehicles [that] stood in fortified structures (caponiers)

---

[26] While the Clark Amendment barred US advisory missions in Angola, they were active prior to its passing in 1976 and following its repeal in 1985.

[27] While detailed information about the scale of the American advisory mission remains classified, a monograph prepared by the Russian Ministry of Defense provides figures that reveal how large these advisory missions could grow. It notes that 10,985 Soviet military advisors served in Angola from late 1975 to January 1, 1991 (Zolotarev 2000: 104). Unfortunately, yearly figures are not provided, but available oral histories suggest advisors usually served deployments of two years (e.g., see the biographies of contributors in Shubin and Tokarev 2011). Thus, it is reasonable to assume that some 500–1,500 Soviet advisors were deployed in Angola each year from 1976 to the end of 1990. A declassified CIA (October 1985: 7) report suggests as much, estimating year-end totals of 500 Soviet advisors deployed in 1976, rising to 1,750 advisors deployed by 1982. Also see CIA (February 1988: 10), which estimates 1,200 Soviet advisors were deployed each year by 1981.

[28] Kolomnin (2005: 188).
[29] Barabulya (2011: 167).
[30] Zhdarkin (2011: 117).
[31] Khrupilin (2000: 6), as quoted in Gleijeses (2013: 187).

all the time, ready for rapid evacuation."[32] As one Angolan commander recalls, "the Soviet military advisors didn't want to fight. They wanted to get out of harm's way, they wanted to leave."[33]

For their part, American advisors simply avoided the front lines altogether. Former Director of Central Intelligence William Colby writes that between 1975 and 1976, training was conducted outside of Angola "as no CIA officers were permitted to engage in combat or train there."[34] Stockwell concurs that the CIA was prohibited from deploying advisors inside Angola, though he claims "we did it anyway." However, he does not dispute the claim that advisors avoided combat: "[n]o CIA staffers were killed or suffered any discomfort worse than malaria."[35] The CIA, he explains, let "others run the serious risks."[36] Likewise, following the repeal of the Clark Amendment in July 1985, US military advisors instructed their clients far from the front, basing in southeastern Angola at the UNITA headquarters in Jamba. Daniel Fenton, a former senior analyst at the CIA, recalls that advisors "talked only to Savimbi and his chosen few. They lived in a compound, and they had no real freedom of movement."[37]

Cuban advisors who were forward deployed at MPLA base camps also avoided combat. As SADF Major General (ret.) Roland de Vries explained to me, "one thing that we found was that every time we became heavily engaged with a [MPLA] brigade the Cuban commanders and Soviet advisors were flown out by chopper."[38] Colonel (ret.) Jan Breytenbach, another veteran of the war, likewise observed the tendency of Cuban advisors to retreat: "Cuban advisors, when they saw [Angolan troops] jumping, they were off like a shot. [...] [W]hen things start getting wrong then they get out. This is part of the way they operate—to get away from it; not to give support when the fight is going on. [...] We always found remnants of them—cigarettes and booze and what have you. They were there, but they were gone."[39] Interviews with conscripted MPLA troops confirm this tendency to avoid combat. As one former government soldier put it, "[i]n battle [the Cubans] stayed behind and the Angolans were pushed to the front."[40] Another recounts that "[t]hey pushed us to the front. They'd say 'you are the master of this land.'"[41]

---

[32] Barabulya (2011: 169). Recalling his experiences during Operation Protea, de Vries (2013: 267) writes that "[t]he Russian military advisors and their families abandoned Xangongo in such haste that we found their breakfasts lying untouched on dining room tables; clothes were still flapping in the wind on washing lines."
[33] As quoted in Gleijeses (2013: 231).
[34] Colby (1978: 422).
[35] Stockwell (1978: 177).
[36] Stockwell (1978: 247).
[37] As quoted in Gleijeses (2013: 309).
[38] Interview, Major General (ret.) Roland de Vries. September 9, 2014. Telephone.
[39] Interview, Colonel (ret.) Jan Breytenbach. June 20, 2014. George, Western Cape, South Africa.
[40] Farmer, May 2008, Huambo, Angola, as quoted in Pearce (2017: 18).
[41] Participant of group interview, October 2008, Huambo, Angola, as quoted in Pearce (2017: 20).

The South Africans likewise withdrew their advisors upon coming under fire. As Breytenbach, who served as an advisor and military trainer in Angola, explained to me, "[t]he first thing you get sorted out is your escape route to get out—then you carry on. But you must be able to get away quickly. [...] [W]hen things start getting wrong, then you must get out. And you always have a plan for getting out. You always have a standby plane or vehicle or something that you can get into and be gone."[42]

The decision to withdraw advisors had immediate tactical consequences on the battlefield, as the morale of the domestic combatants suffered. Nonetheless, withdrawal when under fire was a universal response for foreign military advisors deployed on the front lines. While disadvantageous from a tactical perspective, the need to maintain a clear distinction between "advisory" and "combat" missions was of paramount importance for escalation control between the competitive interveners.

Defensive Deployment Patterns and Force Postures

While the US and Soviet Union restricted their ground presence to military advisors, both Cuba and South Africa maintained prolonged deployments of combat troops that saw action against UNITA and the MPLA, respectively. Naturally, the proximity of their military forces risked direct confrontations, whether due to accidents, misunderstandings, or miscommunication. To manage this risk, both Cuba and South Africa adopted deployment patterns and force postures designed to signal restraint and communicate limited objectives.

When Operation Savannah was launched in October 1975, Pretoria sought to propel an anti-MPLA coalition to power in Angola.[43] The SADF seized cities, established control over the Moçâmedes and Benguela railway lines, and held onto Angola's coastal ports. However, the rapid (and unexpected) deployment of Cuban forces in November 1975 transformed the tactical situation on the ground. The SADF was no longer fighting a ragtag guerrilla army—the Cubans presented a conventional threat. As the SADF–UNITA force began operating on increasingly longer supply lines, its commanders became concerned that logistics would struggle to sustain an escalation of the war.[44] The arrival of the

---

[42] Interview, Colonel (ret.) Jan Breytenbach. June 20, 2014. George, Western Cape, South Africa.

[43] An internal SADF summary provides a chronology of four phases for the 1975 Operation Savannah invasion: "Phase One: Land and cities must be brought under UNITA/FNLA control. Phase Two: Occupation and pacification [skoonmaak, lit. cleansing] of the south-western corner of Angola, including cities like Sá da Bandeira and Moçâmedes. Phase Three: Attack on harbor cities Benguela-Lobito and opening of the Benguela railway before 11 November. Phase Four: Conquest of Luanda." See "Op Savannah: Opsomming van Gebeure tot 10 Jan 76" (January 13, 1976), as quoted in Miller (2016: 183).

[44] Steenkamp (1989: 54).

Cubans meant that the northward campaign would now require committing greater resources to preserve South African control of conquered territory. This was a cost that Pretoria was unwilling to pay—the SADF would not become an occupying force. Yet, if UNITA was to seize power in Luanda, it would of course need to capture territory from the MPLA. The challenge for Pretoria, then, was to find a way to increase UNITA's territorial control while clearly communicating that it did not entertain the idea of fighting battles against the Cubans to hold on to Angolan cities.

The SADF's solution was to adopt an in-and-out deployment pattern. South African troops would attack enemy bases in southern Angola, project UNITA's power into captured areas, and then withdraw shortly thereafter. During an interview, Breytenbach noted that territory could be held "for quite a while [...] because it [would] take them quite a while to bring in enough troops to kick us out again." But South African decision-makers were cognizant of the fact that holding on to Angolan territory would be viewed as the first step in a coordinated campaign to push deeper into Angola. If Pretoria had undertaken such a strategy, Breytenbach explained, "the Russians would come back *en masse*."[45] Consequently, in the aftermath of Operation Savannah, the SADF prioritized mobility—rapid offensives and withdrawals. Brigadier General (ret.) George Kruys writes that "operations were planned in detail in terms of time in, time out and exactly what was to be achieved while in Angola as well as how the operation was to be coordinated and executed."[46] De Vries concurs, noting that while cross-border operations varied in intensity and duration based on operational circumstances, "two principles applied to all: ground must be seized but not occupied, and a force must not become bogged down in grinding battles— the rule was to go in fast and then get out fast again upon completion of the mission."[47] Territory was to be held only as long as tactical advantage flowed from it.[48]

For their part, the Cubans adopted defensive force postures that signaled their own restraint in Angola.[49] From 1976 onward, most Cuban troops were assigned to garrison duties in Angola's main cities, with the bulk of these forces located in or around Luanda. Beginning in 1979, the largest single concentration of Cuban troops outside the capital was located along a defensive line that ran roughly along the Moçâmedes Railway (discussed in more detail in the next subsection). Even as SADF units raided in and out of southern Angola throughout the

---

[45] Interview, Colonel (ret.) Jan Breytenbach. June 20, 2014. George, Western Cape, South Africa.
[46] Kruys (2001: 13).
[47] De Vries (2013: 75).
[48] For a discussion of these ideas, see Scholtz (2013: 247–251).
[49] A US intelligence assessment prepared in 1985 notes that most Cuban forces "avoid an active combat role and are employed primarily in defensive postures." See CIA (November 1985a: 2).

1980s, Cuban forces remained in their defensive positions and arrayed along the defensive line. They did not launch counterattacks, interfere with SADF logistical lines, or make any attempt to prevent South African attacks on the MPLA.[50] Cuban President Fidel Castro also took care to highlight the defensive orientation of his forces in public speeches, raising its salience for domestic and international audiences alike. For example, during one public rally held in Bayamo, Cuba in July 1982, Castro warned that, should South African troops "strike deeply into Angola *and reach our lines*, we will fight with all our might against these parasitic, racist mercenaries."[51] Similarly, in an official statement published in the Cuban press the following month, Castro warned "that Cuban troops would go into action 'with all forces available' *if* South African columns approached the Cubans' defensive positions."[52] In effect, Castro sought to make clear his desire to avoid escalating the Angolan conflict into a regional war. While they would assist the MPLA in the counterinsurgency campaign against UNITA, the Cubans had little appetite for direct confrontation with the South Africans.

These deployment patterns and defensive force postures were costly signals for both sides of the war. The defensive orientation adopted by Cuban troops enabled UNITA to establish a foothold in southern Angola from which it could operate with greater ease and mobility against the MPLA. At the same time, because the SADF was unwilling to occupy conquered areas, the MPLA could recapture lost territory upon their withdrawal. The net result was a predictable to and fro: South African forces would cross the border into Angola and, after a brief battle, enemy forces would retreat; UNITA would then claim a military victory against the MPLA and the SADF would be withdrawn; upon South African forces vacating the area, the MPLA would attack UNITA positions to recapture lost cities; the guerrillas would then melt back into the countryside, and the cycle would repeat once more.[53]

Yet, while tactically disadvantageous for the purposes of helping their domestic clients prevail in the war, these deployment patterns and force postures were necessary for the purposes of controlling escalation. As one veteran and former commanding officer of the war, Major General (ret.) Gert Opperman, explained to me, "instead of continuing and doing what you believed had to be done from a military point of view, you had to withdraw. [...] I think one of the constant

---

[50] George (2005: 120, 141); de Vries (2013: 106).
[51] As quoted in Vasquez (1982: A18). Emphasis added.
[52] Jaster (1989: 95). Emphasis in original.
[53] Interview, Colonel (ret.) Jan Breytenbach. June 20, 2014. George, Western Cape, South Africa. Commanders' accounts of military operations are replete with examples of SADF units handing over responsibility for captured territory to UNITA. See, for example, de Vries (2013: 303, 310, 316), who also notes that liaison teams were attached to all UNITA forces, which facilitated the handovers.

factors to be considered was: would it result in unnecessary escalation of the war? [...] [I]t might make sense from a military point of view, a tactical point of view, but from a strategic point of view that would be exactly the type of escalation that we would like to prevent."[54]

Geographic Areas of Contestation and Control

In addition to predictable deployment patterns and defensive force postures, the interveners also exploited geographic and topographic features of the Angolan countryside to manage escalatory risks. In particular, natural and human-made markers were used to limit the geographic scope of competition between the interveners' forces. Perhaps the most observable manifestations of this strategic use of physical terrain were Cuba's establishment of a defensive line that ran roughly along the Moçâmedes Railway, stretching from the Atlantic coast in the west to Menongue in the east, and South Africa's establishment of the so-called "area of dispute" in south-central Angola (see Figure 5.3).[55]

From January 1979 until the spring of 1988, Cuba did not allow its troops to operate south of the Moçâmedes Railway, though MPLA battalions regularly did. As Major General (ret.) Johann Dippennar explained to me, Cuban forces were positioned behind Angolan units "[a]ll the time, or sometimes in the front in the defensive positions, but in an advisory capacity, not behind the weapons."[56] In fact, Cuba's official policy dictated that its troops were not to operate in Cunene or southern Cuando Cubango provinces.[57]

For their part, the South Africans responded to Cuba's reticence by containing their own operations to south-central Angola. De Vries explained to me that "strategically, [the SADF] established an area of dispute from the [Namibian] border, along the Cunene River, and up to Techamutete, Cuvelai, those areas."[58] This territory was designated a "hunting ground" for the SADF. South African forces would regularly conduct in-and-out operations into the provinces of Huila, Cunene, and Cuando Cubango, but would always remain south of the Cuban defensive line. The reason for these geographic limits? Escalation risks.

---

[54] Interview, Major General (ret.) Gert Opperman. June 23, 2014. Pretoria, Gauteng, South Africa.

[55] The defensive line was not manned continuously across its entire 700-kilometer span. Rather, Cuban troops were stationed at key points where enemy units were expected to advance—mainly along paved roads. These points included Moçâmedes, Lubango, Matala, Kuvango, and Menongue. See Gleijeses (2013: 214).

[56] Interview, Major General (ret.) Johann Dippenaar. June 30, 2014. Pretoria, Gauteng, South Africa.

[57] George (2005: 119–120).

[58] Interview, Major General (ret.) Roland de Vries. September 9, 2014. Telephone. Also see de Vries (2013: 116–117, 125). Breytenbach (2002: 247) likewise writes that SADF control was established in "Cunene Province east of the Cunene River and as far north as Cassinga."

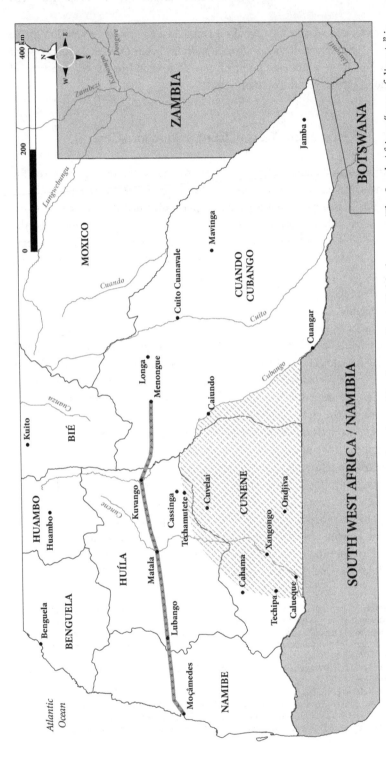

Figure 5.3 Southern Angola. The Cuban defensive line is indicated by the gray line with black crosses. The South African "area of dispute" is indicated by the gray diagonal slashes.

As de Vries put it, "[t]here were constraints placed on the tactical commanders [...] in terms of how far you could go. Can you attack Menongue? No. Can we attack Cuito Cuanavale from the west? No. Rather, stay on the eastern side of the river so that the war does not escalate."[59]

The buffer zone virtually eliminated the risk of Cuban–South African confrontation. The Cubans left the SADF free to roam south of the defensive line, while the South Africans made sure to avoid approaching it. In an interview, Breytenbach explained to me that "[i]n the beginning, we had some Cubans with Operation Savannah, when we went into Angola for the first time. But I think that we gave them such a bloody nose that they stayed away from us after that. You had Cubans in the rear areas, where they were training others as well, but when I was there, we never had Cuban formations operating against us."[60] Adamishin provides an alternative view: the Cubans never crossed the defensive line, he suggests, because they "effectively restrain[ed] the enemy with the simple fact of their presence."[61] Regardless of interpretation, the reality on the battlefield was one of strategic restraint and escalation control. Indeed, between January 1979 and January 1988, there was not a single clash between South African and Cuban ground forces despite their deep and sustained involvement in the war.

Targets

As one former MPLA soldier recounts, "[i]t was an international war. The MPLA with the Cubans, UNITA with the South Africans. But it was mostly Angolans who died."[62] Indeed, a theme that emerged repeatedly during field research was the critical role of selective targeting on the part of the interveners during the war. Naturally, targeting an opposing intervener's troops or advisors risked retaliation in kind. Thus, to avoid costly escalation with each other, the interveners distinguished between "acceptable" and "prohibited" targets. Here, the threshold that served to constrain escalation was centered on nationality: Angolan targets (MPLA and UNITA) were distinct from South African–American and Cuban–Soviet targets.

South African leaders were keenly aware that operations against Angolan forces could be perceived as actions against Cuba or even the Soviet Union. Consequently, cross-border raids "had to be played very carefully, because the conflict could have developed into a regional war," as de Vries put it. "We didn't

---

[59] Interview, Major General (ret.) Roland de Vries. September 9, 2014. Telephone.
[60] Interview, Colonel (ret.) Jan Breytenbach. June 20, 2014. George, Western Cape, South Africa.
[61] Adamishin (2014: 6).
[62] Participant of group interview, October 2008, Huambo, Angola, as quoted in Pearce (2017: 20).

really want to fight against Cubans—that was not part of the idea."[63] To those ends, South African engagements stopped short of confrontations with Cuban troops, and also avoided interactions with Cuban and Soviet advisors that were forward deployed with MPLA units. This was recognized by their opponents on the other side. "[T]he Russians were no worse at apartheid than we were," remarked former South African Ambassador Vic Zazeraj, "their officers were not living in the same camp as the rest of them. [...] [T]hey would make sure that they were a few kilometers off to the side."[64] This is confirmed in accounts by Soviet advisors. For example, Barabulya, whose tour of duty in Angola included forward deployment in Cuito Cuanavale, notes that the Soviet encampment was seven kilometers from the besieged city.[65]

That the South Africans were selective in their targeting procedures was appreciated by Soviet advisors. The account of Zhdarkin, who served in Angola from 1986 to 1988, is worth quoting at length:

> The South Africans, by the way, being remarkable gentlemen, had bombarded only the Angolan brigades. In other words, I think the bombardment of our camp wasn't part of their plans. Perhaps they didn't want to risk international complications or confrontation with the Soviet Union, or something like that. But this evidently applied only to our own camp, whereas with all the others it was war as usual. So, if the Soviet advisor goes to his brigade and walks into a bombardment there, nothing can be done—war is war!
>
> The South Africans sent us an ultimatum before 11 March 1988 stating: "Soviets, leave Cuito Cuanavale, we don't want to touch you." These leaflets were in English. The Angolans brought the leaflets to us and asked us to translate them because they couldn't decipher the message. Those leaflets were packed inside hollow artillery shells, like propaganda! Their warning was precise, concrete and clearly written. "Soviets, we don't want to touch you. Go away. Leave, please. We want right now to cut up these Angolans."[66]

For their part, the Soviets reciprocated this strategic restraint by reiterating the non-combat role of their advisors. As Adamishin relates, "[w]e limited ourselves to sharp protests and what was evidently more effective, serious warnings directly to the South Africans repeated through KGB channels. We consistently held to the 'stay out' line, politely declining calls to bomb or otherwise hit South African bases in Angola or airfields in Namibia during an aggravation of the situation."[67]

[63] Interview, Major General (ret.) Roland de Vries. September 9, 2014. Telephone.
[64] Interview, Ambassador (ret.) Victor Zazeraj. July 4, 2014. Johannesburg, Gauteng, South Africa.
[65] Barabulya (2011: 168).
[66] Zhdarkin (2011: 161).
[67] Adamishin (2014: 29–30).

The Cubans likewise avoided direct confrontations with South Africans. For example, in 1976, when South African forces were withdrawing from Angola in the aftermath of the OAU vote against their invasion, the Cubans left time and space for their escape. In Castro's words, "[w]e kept pushing, pushing and pushing until they withdrew completely from Angola, without fighting. This is the battle that we won without bloodshed. Because we gave them time, and kept applying psychological pressure [...] and they withdrew."[68] During later stages of the conflict, the reaction of Cuban forces to South African incursions into Angola was muted. Aside from verbal protests, no action was taken to directly confront South African forces.

Like their Soviet counterparts, the Cubans also maintained a general separation from the broader Angolan population in self-contained enclaves. Hatzky documents the "strict inclusion and exclusion mechanisms" that were "designed to segregate" Cubans and Angolans. For example, accommodations were purposefully built for the Cubans, who "lived in them separated from the Angolan population, only leaving to go to work." Day-to-day life largely played out in "controlled spaces reserved exclusively for the Cubans," providing protection from external threats and the wider war.[69]

It is also notable that the competitive interveners avoided targeting each other's strategic communication and logistical lines: there were no large-scale air or naval operations to interdict supply lines at the strategic level. As de Vries writes, "[t]o any impartial observer this obvious neglect by the enemy was astounding." Yet here again, the need to control escalation dominated strategic decision-making. "Perhaps," de Vries wryly suggests, "the reason for this was to make sure that the fighting did not arouse too much anger in the breasts of the major world powers."[70]

Encounters between intervening forces in the air were equally rare. As Scholtz writes, "the war in Angola was not characterized by great aerial battles. In fact, there were only four encounters in the air between South African and Cuban aircraft."[71] These four encounters were hardly dogfights: no planes were shot down and no casualties were inflicted on either side. Instead of confronting each other, the two sides tended to keep their distance. The account of Lieutenant (ret.) Anatoliy Alekseevsky, who served in Angola between 1986 and 1988, is typical: "[o]nce when the Cubans encountered the [SADF] Mirages, they almost entered aerial combat, but the South Africans simply left, ran away. They could

---

[68] "Reunión del Comandante en jefe con los políticos para analizar la situación de las troupas Cubanas en la RPA" (December 9, 1987: 5–6), as quoted in Gleijeses (2013: 34).
[69] Hatzky (2015: 217–225).
[70] De Vries (2013: 106–107).
[71] Scholtz (2013: 402–403).

see from the MiGs' flight pattern that these weren't Angolans. The Cubans didn't insist on aerial combat and returned to base."[72]

Likewise, air battles between Soviets and South Africans did not occur. While most of the military transport planes and their crews operating in Angola were Soviet, the Soviet military mission did not allow its pilots to fly in combat zones.[73] As the CIA reported in October 1985, Moscow "was not inclined [...] to take on South African aircraft, despite sufficient opportunities."[74] Nor did South African air crews entertain the idea of confronting Soviet-piloted aircraft. As Zazeraj explained to me, "[t]here was an unspoken rule that if it was a Russian pilot or even a Cuban pilot, the South African Air Force wouldn't interfere with them too much. [...] [W]e didn't want to get into a dogfight with them. [...] [I]f we were to deliberately engage and shoot down a Soviet plane that was not a threat to us—that would have worried us, because we did not want to draw them into the war any more. You don't want to scratch the bear and create a problem that you can't solve."[75]

Restraint in the Final Months of the War

Much has been made of the final months of the Angolan civil war. Owing to a large-scale MPLA offensive against UNITA in the southeast of the country—and subsequent efforts by the SADF to halt it—the period between October 1987 and March 1988 would see heavy fighting around Cuito Cuanavale, a desolate but strategically valuable town on the western banks of the Cuito River, as well as the approval of a determined Cuban advance into Cunene Province—the first time Cuban troops had moved into the southwest since January 1979. Over the last three decades, this culminating period of the conflict has been mythologized, with both sides claiming victory on the battlefield and, by extension, in the war.[76]

On its face, the increase in the intensity of fighting in the final months of the conflict would appear to challenge my argument that fears of large-scale confrontations with one another led third-party interveners to constrain the scope of their support to Angola's domestic combatants. After all, participation by Cuban and South African forces in sustained combat risked inadvertent escalation between the external interveners, and the Cuban advance into the

---

[72] Alekseevsky (2011: 178).
[73] Gleijeses (2013: 357).
[74] CIA (October 1985: 12).
[75] Interview, Ambassador (ret.) Victor Zazeraj. July 4, 2014. Johannesburg, Gauteng, South Africa.
[76] As one example, Castro—with typical flair—has suggested that "the history of Africa will have to be written before and after Cuito Cuanavale" (as quoted in Steenkamp 1989: 163). For a discussion of the contested narratives of the final months of Cuban–South African confrontation in Angola, see Baines (2014: chapter 6).

southwest violated the tacit agreement that maintained a buffer zone demarcated by the Cuban defensive line. In this sense, the actions of the interveners crossed thresholds that had constrained the scope of their support to Angola's domestic combatants, representing an escalation of the war.

Yet while it is true that the intensity of the war increased between the fall of 1987 and the spring of 1988, it is precisely for this reason that the highly constrained nature of Cuban–South African confrontation is so striking. Indeed, despite ample opportunity to enlarge the conflict, the competitive interveners proved remarkably adept at avoiding decisive confrontations with each other. In what follows, I review the final months of competitive intervention in the Angolan theater in detail to demonstrate the lengths to which Cuba and South Africa went to prevent a larger war.

During the early spring of 1987, South African military intelligence began picking up signals that foreshadowed a large MPLA offensive against UNITA: thousands of tons of military supplies were being stockpiled in and around Cuito Cuanavale, suggesting that the town was being developed as a base area for an advance into the southeast. Alarmed by the growing threat this posed to their domestic client, SADF strategists began planning an intervention to halt the advance. An internal debate developed around the question of whether South African forces should confront the MPLA offensive west of the Cuito River, which would enable the SADF to break through to the MPLA's rear areas, or east of it, which would counter the MPLA's forces head-on.

Despite agreement that the western assault option would bypass the MPLA's concentrations in the east, cut their communications, sever their logistics, and threaten their supply lines, it was not well received by the high command. A top secret planning document, written on June 5, 1987 on behalf of the chief of the army, sheds light on why this was the case. The document's general guidelines for operational planning explain that "[t]he central idea is to let the [MPLA's] offensive fail without totally committing the [Republic of South Africa]."[77] It stresses that "operations must not provoke revenge attacks" and that "the conflict must not be allowed to escalate beyond the capacity of the [...] SADF in general."[78] A western attack on Cuito Cuanavale risked clashes with Cuban forces manning the end of the Cuban defensive line at Menongue and would have required advancing into territory never before contested by SADF troops. Consequently, the decision was made to confront the offensive from the east. UNITA units were to serve as a screen to protect South African artillery teams that would pummel the advancing MPLA units from afar. This led to a series of battles along the Lomba River, a major physical obstacle to be crossed by the MPLA

---

[77] H Leër/D OPS/309/1, "Beplanning: Op Modular" (1987: para 5e).
[78] H Leër/D OPS/309/1, "Beplanning: Op Modular" (1987: para 16e).

on their southeastern march. The combined UNITA–SADF force successfully halted the offensive, and by October 5, the remaining MPLA units were ordered to withdraw northwards back toward Cuito Cuanavale.

Having successfully stopped the MPLA advance, a counteroffensive was planned to preclude a renewed offensive against UNITA later that fall. However, debate once again broke out over the question of whether the SADF should attack Cuito Cuanavale from the west, which would enable the SADF to envelope the remaining MPLA brigades, or attack from the east, which would require a head-on clash. As before, the eastern attack option was clearly tactically disadvantageous, yet it was adopted. De Vries, who was designated the commander for a possible assault from the west, explains why:

> I then conducted the joint operational planning cycle, and our proposed course of action was to attack Cuito Cuanavale from the west early in November. But during the presentation of our plans, the chief of the defense force, General Jannie Geldenhuys, said no—we had to remain on the eastern side of the river. And what I surmised from that exchange is that they were very apprehensive about escalating the war. [...] [T]hey were still pussyfooting and making sure that they didn't escalate the war into a regional war. [...] [A] small trigger could trigger that war into a massive, escalated, high intensity battle.[79]

De Vries' interpretation accords with a statement given by Geldenhuys during a press interview after the counteroffensive had begun, in which he voiced a desire to avoid "unnecessary escalation of the war after the mission had been fulfilled already."[80] Lieutenant General Kat Liebenberg, then the chief of the army, also shared these views, emphasizing his concern over "the possibility of the war in Angola escalating beyond proportion."[81]

Notably, South African efforts to control escalation were reciprocated by their Cuban opponents. Indeed, when the MPLA's offensive began in mid-August 1987, no Cuban forces participated—the offensive was entirely composed of MPLA units and Soviet advisors. As battles raged along the Lomba River in September and October, the nearest Cuban military unit was stationed some 350 kilometers from the fighting. In mid-November, as the SADF began its counteroffensive to push the MPLA back toward the Cuito River, a group of approximately thirty Cuban military advisors was sent to Cuito Cuanavale—yet still no combat troops were deployed. On December 5, 1987, a further 106 Special

---

[79] Interview, Major General (ret.) Roland de Vries. September 9, 2014. Telephone.
[80] As quoted in Scholtz (2013: 283–284).
[81] De Vries (2013: 409).

Forces and 15 officers were sent to the town, but these forces were tasked with reorganizing the MPLA's command structure, defense, and artillery positions.[82]

It was only in late January 1988, by which time the SADF and UNITA had driven the Angolans back to a small bridgehead at Tumpo, just across the river from Cuito Cuanavale, that some 1,500 Cuban combat troops joined to stiffen the MPLA's defense.[83] The majority of these units were placed in rear positions, west of the Cuito River and in the third (and last) defensive line that protected the city.[84] This was a force posture that clearly signaled Castro's limited objectives at Cuito Cuanavale and demonstrated that while he would not allow the destruction of the remaining MPLA brigades, he was unwilling to force a decisive battle for the town.

A limited clash did occur between the SADF and a small group of Cuban troops that were attached to an Angolan unit on February 14, 1988—"the first time since the Battle of Cassinga a decade previously that South Africans and Cubans would come eye to eye on the battlefield," as Scholtz describes it.[85] Cuban troops also manned artillery deployed on the western side of the Cuito River and piloted combat aircraft in defense of Cuito Cuanavale. But as Gleijeses writes, "[n]o climatic battle was fought at Cuito Cuanavale. The South Africans did not launch a major assault on the town; nor did the Cubans and the [MPLA] surge from the town to push them back to Mavinga."[86] These were far from decisive encounters between the competitive interveners—largely because that was precisely what both sides sought to avoid. Indeed, in one SADF planning document produced on December 8, 1987, there is a warning to avoid engaging in any "decisive battle."[87] Similarly, operational instructions issued at the brigade level noted that "decisive fighting must be avoided."[88] Meanwhile, the Cubans did not attempt an attack on SADF positions outside Cuito, nor did they interfere when South African forces withdrew from the front.[89]

Castro was unwilling to confront the South Africans in direct clashes at Cuito Cuanavale, so he adopted an indirect approach instead. While a limited number of Cuban troops helped stiffen the MPLA's defense in the southeast, he

---

[82] Gleijeses (2013: 398, 408, 423). Colonel (ret.) Vyacheslav Mityaev (2011: 28), who served as a Soviet military advisor and who was stationed in Cuito Cuanavale at the time, confirms that Cuban troops did not take part in the MPLA's offensive.
[83] Gleijeses (2013: 423).
[84] Scholtz (2013: 316); "Gesamentlike militere aksies deur RSA en UNITA magte teen FAPLA magte in die sesoe militere streek van angola vanaf desember 1987 tot maart 1988" (n.d.: para 13c).
[85] Scholtz (2013: 330).
[86] Gleijeses (2013: 425).
[87] SWAGM VHK/309/1 (Op Moduler) Memorandum, "Op Beplanning Volgens H Leer Riglyne" (1987: para 4iii).
[88] "Gesamentlike militere aksies deur RSA en UNITA magte teen FAPLA magte in die sesoe militere streek van angola vanaf desember 1987 tot maart 1988" (n.d.: para 46b).
[89] De Vries (2013: 134, 138).

ordered a major combat formation to advance in the southwest. Between March and May 1988, thousands of Cuban troops reinforced with hundreds of tanks, armored cars, and artillery pieces began moving into Cunene Province—a territory they had been expressly forbidden from entering for nearly a decade. These troops, including the vaunted 50th Division, were joined by thousands of MPLA soldiers who began integrating with the Cubans at the battalion level.[90]

Why did Castro advance in the southwest? Certainly the strategy was not without risks—the chance of misperception or miscalculation was high, as a number of thresholds that had been exploited to limit South African–Cuban confrontation were becoming blurred. But the crafty Cuban leader had realized that Pretoria could not respond to the Cuban advance—the bulk of South African forces were tied down in the southeastern battle for Cuito Cuanavale. His aim, therefore, was to pry the SADF out of southeastern Angola without the need to directly challenge South African military power. To those ends, Castro ensured that the movement of Cuban troops into Cunene Province was matched with a determined diplomatic offensive on the issue of a joint termination of Cuban and South African participation in the Angolan conflict.[91] In effect, his bold move in the southwest sought to shore up his bargaining position *without* a fight. In the words of Chester Crocker, the lead negotiator of the American delegation during the 1988 peace talks, "the potent Cuban force was primarily a political demonstration in keeping with Castro's 'strutting cock' school of grand strategy."[92] Castro admitted as much to Gorbachev in March 1988, when he explained that "we are not doing this in order to win a war but to guarantee a just and reasonable political negotiation that will allow Angola to preserve its sovereignty, its integrity and its peaceful development, as well as assure the independence of Namibia."[93]

To signal his limited intentions, Castro carefully calibrated the advance. Cuban units pushed forward slowly, and SADF troops noticed that advance patrols of Cuban units were "quite careful and cagey."[94] And while the power of Castro's southern advance stemmed from the threat it posed to Namibia, the archival record makes clear that Castro never envisioned an attack across the border. Indeed, as early as December 3, 1987, he had told his generals that he did "not intend to cross the border with troops."[95] Two weeks later, he explained

---

[90] Gleijeses (2013: 420, 429).
[91] Specifically, negotiations centered around the implementation of the so-called "linkage policy": the idea that South Africa's relinquished control of South West Africa/Namibia (as per UN Security Council Resolution 435) was to be linked to the withdrawal of Cuban troops from Angola.
[92] Crocker (1992: 371).
[93] "Castro to Gorbachev" (March 3, 1988: 15), as quoted in Gleijeses (2013: 418).
[94] This description was offered by SADF Commandant Jan Hougaard, as quoted in Bridgland (1990: 349).
[95] "Reunión del Comandante en Jefe" (December 3, 1987: 88), as quoted in Gleijeses (2013: 454).

that "[a]n invasion of Namibia by our army would have very serious political repercussions. [...] We cross the border, and there would be an international scandal."⁹⁶ The limited aims of the Cuban advance are also confirmed by Soviet sources. For example, Adamishin writes that the Soviets "had an understanding with the Cubans that they would act cautiously and would not cross the Angolan-Namibian border in any circumstance."⁹⁷ Notably, even South African military intelligence understood Castro's objectives to be limited, interpreting the southwestern advance to be a "predominantly defensive strategy."⁹⁸

Cuban MiG-23s did penetrate northern Namibia's airspace in May 1988, but they did so cautiously, never attacking ground targets, never venturing closer than twenty kilometers from SADF airbases, and always making their presence known well in advance. As Brigadier General (ret.) Dick Lord explains, "[a]lthough we did think they might attack [SADF] bases, the high altitudes they were flying at were not conducive to surprise. They were always within our radar cover. [...] We decided that they wanted to test our pilots' reaction times."⁹⁹ But there were to be no dogfights: "there was a ban on air-to-air combat which might escalate the war," explains Commandant Jan Hougaard.¹⁰⁰

Similarly, there were to be no decisive confrontations between ground forces: both sides "skillfully avoided contact," as Crocker puts it.¹⁰¹ The South Africans offered no resistance to the Cuban advance, with the exception of a few brief skirmishes that took place between April and June 1988, mainly around the Calueque dam installation (which supplied northern South West Africa/Namibia with water and which had been defended by South African troops for several years). Notably, these were highly constrained interactions that were often the product of mistakes by advance patrols rather than deliberate actions. For example, on April 18, the first such skirmish occurred when an SADF unit bumped into a Cuban patrol, resulting in the death of an SADF major. A second clash occurred on May 4, when a reconnoitering SADF unit, operating approximately fifty kilometers inside Angola, approached a Cuban forward observation post. The South Africans were "surprised" by the resulting firefight, explains Hougaard, "because we thought we controlled the area opposite Ovamboland."¹⁰² A third skirmish occurred on May 22, when an

---

⁹⁶ "Reunión del Comandante en Jefe" (December 15, 1987: 36), as quoted in Gleijeses (2013: 454).
⁹⁷ Adamishin (2014: 59).
⁹⁸ MI/204/3/A6/8 (1988: para 3a). De Vries (2013: 169) notes that it was apparent to SADF intelligence staff "that the Cuban division did not have either the will or the heart to launch a major offensive into SWA/Namibia; it seemed their offensive moves and statements were more sabre rattling than anything else."
⁹⁹ As quoted in Bridgland (1990: 344).
¹⁰⁰ As quoted in Bridgland (1990: 352).
¹⁰¹ Crocker (1992: 371).
¹⁰² As quoted in Bridgland (1990: 343). Ovamboland lies in the northernmost segment of Namibia, lying on the Angola–Namibia border.

134 WARS WITHOUT END

advance team of SADF troopers ran into a group of Cubans walking down a road toward them. And a fourth and final clash occurred on June 26–27, when the SADF shelled a Cuban forward-operating base at Techipa, provoking a retaliatory Cuban air strike on the Calueque dam that has been described as "a very academic attack" and "measured retaliation."[103]

That was the full extent of Cuban–South African confrontation. In Crocker's words, "[l]ike scorpions in a bottle, the rival forces avoided each other's sting."[104] Having pushed the limits of their "cooperative competition," the two sides began to concentrate on political negotiations. Only sixteen days later, on July 13, representatives from Angola, Cuba, and South Africa had initialed an agreement stipulating fourteen principles for establishing the basis for peace, including the linked withdrawals of the SADF from South West Africa/Namibia and Cuban forces from Angola.[105] A ceasefire was declared on August 8, followed by a formal signing ceremony on August 22, during which time a Joint Military Monitoring Committee—comprising members from all three countries—was established to further negotiate the peace and ceasefire terms of reference. These efforts culminated on December 22, when the foreign ministers of Angola, Cuba, and South Africa signed the Tripartite Accord, a peace agreement that formally ended the latter two countries' competitive intervention in the civil war.[106]

Other Explanations

The empirical record provides ample support for the theory's proposed mechanisms at the international level. Interveners constrained the scope of their support to domestic combatants; they did so owing to escalation concerns vis-à-vis opposing interveners; and the limits they observed were constructed around thresholds that signaled restraint. Nonetheless, there may be concerns that interveners restricted their level of support for reasons other than escalation control. Accordingly, in this section, I address alternative explanations for the competitive interveners' strategic restraint.

First, it might be posited that the provision of aid was limited owing to intervener resource or logistical constraints. This argument is hard to square with some stylized facts from the case. The US and Soviet Union were great powers with global power projection capacity.[107] South Africa was a regional hegemon

---

[103] The former quotation is from SADF Brigadier General (ret.) Dick Lord, as quoted in Bridgland (1990: 362); the latter quotation is from Crocker (1992: 372).
[104] Crocker (1992: 371).
[105] The principles were formally approved by the respective governments one week later. See "Principles for a Peaceful Settlement in Southwestern Africa" (July 20, 1988).
[106] For the full text of the agreement, see UN Security Council (1988).
[107] For perspective, total Soviet aid to the MPLA is estimated to have reached $15 billion by 1988 (George 2005: 281). Soviet military expenditure for that year *alone* is estimated to have exceeded

that at the time occupied South West Africa/Namibia, which borders Angola.[108] And Cuba enjoyed the largess of the Soviet Union, which not only armed and equipped Cuban forces but also helped ferry them across the Atlantic.[109] Consequently, decisions to continually invest in the conflict at a level that generated stalemate, rather than decisive military advantages, confound analysis until one accounts for escalation fears among the competitive interveners.

Second, it might be argued that domestic pressure to limit the scope of intervention explains the competitive interveners' behaviors. This argument is largely limited to intervening states headed by meaningfully accountable leaders facing antiwar publics. Such characteristics do not apply to Cuba or the Soviet Union. Nor do they apply to South Africa, where a repressive apartheid regime exploited its "almost unlimited powers of surveillance, arrest, and detention" to counter domestic threats to its rule.[110] But the argument does find some support in the case of US participation in the war. In the aftermath of its defeat in Vietnam, there was little domestic appetite for large-scale intervention in the developing world—an outcome that has come to be dubbed "Vietnam Syndrome."[111] And while US aid began flowing to Angolan rebels as early as January 1975, the signing of the Clark Amendment in 1976 barred further funding for the conflict, thereby terminating the CIA's IA Feature operation. Here, domestic politics directly affected US intervention behavior. However, American money and arms would begin flowing to UNITA once more following the repeal of the Clark Amendment in July 1985. And notably, the renewed aid program continued to observe the thresholds previously established in the war. Indeed, only military advisors, not combat troops, were deployed to Angola; advisors were prohibited from participating in combat; and US personnel were positioned far from the front, basing at UNITA's headquarters at Jamba.[112] All the more striking is that these thresholds were sustained even as the Reagan Doctrine, which explicitly called for the "roll back" of Soviet-sponsored communist

---

$315 billion (US Department of State 2000: 103). Similarly, American aid to UNITA is estimated to have totaled $250 million between 1986 and 1992 (Wright 2001: 575, note 2). US military expenditure in 1992 *alone* is estimated to have exceeded $300 billion (US Department of State 2000: 109).

[108] South Africa's expenditure on arms, equipment, and troops exceeded the *combined* total of its regional rivals of Angola, Botswana, Mozambique, Tanzania, Zambia, and Zimbabwe—a coalition known as the Frontline States—in every year from 1975 to 1989. Economically, South African gross domestic product also kept pace—and regularly exceeded—that of the entire anti-apartheid coalition. For additional details, see Anderson and Bell (2023: 406–407).

[109] George (2005: 260) estimates that Soviet support to Cuban forces amounted to $4–5 billion annually.

[110] US National Intelligence Estimate (1972: 3). Even at the height of popular unrest, township protests, and boycotts during the mid-1980s, the threat posed to the apartheid regime remained limited. See Herbst (1988).

[111] Herring (1981).

[112] Gleijeses (2013: 309).

regimes around the world and which has been seen as "signaling the end of the so-called 'Vietnam Syndrome,'" became a major element of US foreign policy.[113] Indeed, even as the Reagan administration openly advocated for a UNITA victory, welcomed Savimbi to the White House, and supplanted South Africa as the rebel group's primary patron, existing thresholds were maintained. This suggests that while domestic antiwar sentiment played a role in limiting US intervention in the early years of the Angolan conflict, escalation concerns took center stage following the resumption of US aid in 1985.

Finally, it might be suggested that the interveners simply lacked motivation to sufficiently invest in the civil war. This argument is unpersuasive. For the US and Soviet Union, Angola represented one of the "hot" front lines of the Cold War given its vast natural resource wealth, its strategic air and naval facilities, and its significance for the balance of power in southern Africa.[114] For South Africa, the outcome of the conflict was of existential significance due to deep-seated fears that a defeat in Angola would mark the beginning of the end of the apartheid regime, representing the first domino in a cascade that would first liberate South West Africa/Namibia before propelling black nationalism to the seat of power in Pretoria.[115] And while the strategic interests of the Cubans are the subject of dispute—some stress Castro's ideological conviction to the exportation of revolution and "internationalist solidarity," others suggest the Cubans served at the behest of the Soviet Union—no one can doubt the significance of the scale of their intervention: the tiny island nation maintained a deployment of tens of thousands of troops for over a decade, peaking at 55,000 troops in 1988.[116] By war's end, some 337,033 Cuban soldiers and approximately 50,000 Cuban civilian advisors would serve in the country, making the Angolan campaign the longest and most comprehensive foreign engagement in Cuba's history.[117]

---

[113] Copson and Cronin (1987: 43). On the Reagan Doctrine in Angola, see McFaul (1989).

[114] "Talking Points for Secretary Kissinger, NSC Meeting on Angola" (June 27, 1975); NSC Interdepartmental Group for Africa (1975: 63–65); "Memorandum for Director of Central Intelligence from Frederick L. Wettering" (April 5, 1985: 1, 3); Shubin (2008: 72); Adamishin (2014: 6).

[115] Interview, Major General (ret.) Gert Opperman. June 23, 2014. Pretoria, Gauteng, South Africa. For a similar view from former South African Foreign Minister Pik Botha, see South Africa Department of Foreign Affairs (June 23, 1981: 25–26). The documentary record is also clear: South Africa's objective was to install UNITA at the seat of power in Luanda. For a discussion, see Gleijeses (2013: 244–250). Also see Miller (2016: 183) and Minister Botha's comments in "Samesprekings: Staatspresident met die Kabinet van die Oorgangsregering van Nasionale Eenheid (Orne) van SWA" (May 21, 1986: 11).

[116] Compare, for example, Gleijeses (2006) and Mumford (2013: 62). Economic interests also likely played a role in Havana's decision to intervene. The prospect of gaining access to Angola's rich supply of natural resources, especially oil, was significant for Cuba, which possessed few raw materials of its own. Havana's need to generate new sources of hard currency to improve its trade balance with Western Bloc countries was another motivating factor. For a discussion, see Eckstein (1980) and Hatzky (2015: 82–83).

[117] The figures are from George (2005: 324, note 1), which cites a speech delivered by Raul Castro on May 27, 1991. Based on Cuban archival records, some 2,077 Cubans died in Angola between 1975 and 1991. See Gleijeses (2006: 138).

In short, the interests at stake for interveners in the Angolan civil war cannot be dismissed as inconsequential; the outcome of the war *mattered*. To understand why they limited the scope of their support to the domestic combatants requires an explicit account of the strategic dilemmas that are specific to competitive intervention.

Domestic Bargaining Distortions and Protracted War

Strategic restraint successfully regulated confrontation between interveners in Angola. Yet, the limits it entailed had tactical implications for the domestic combatants. The withdrawal of advisors undermined the morale of government and rebel forces, geographic limits restricted the area of effect of supporting troops, and the need to avoid engagements with an opposing intervener frustrated domestic clients. In meetings with their Cuban counterparts, the MPLA expressed frustration that Cuban aviation "performed combat sorties only in the operational areas of Cuban forces, but did not support Angolan troops, though both MiGs and helicopters were available."[118] Military commanders were likewise frustrated. De Vries recalls that "more and more we found that the politics and diplomacy up high started interfering with the mission and the tactics down below. It became a serious case of micro-managing the battlefield."[119] The imperative of escalation control at the strategic level dominated decision-making at the tactical level.

What effect did this strategic restraint have on domestic bargaining processes? In line with theoretical expectations, the empirical evidence suggests that competitive intervention introduced three types of bargaining distortions: it subsidized the domestic combatants' costs of war; it balanced their military capabilities; and it amplified information asymmetries. The net result was a protracted civil war.

Aid as a Subsidy for War

My theory contends that competitive intervention prolongs conflicts by subsidizing the domestic combatants' costs of war. As their costs of war decline, combatants' willingness and ability to fight increase. This reduces the set of negotiated agreements that both sides prefer to fighting, thereby encouraging continued conflict. The Angolan case provides strong empirical support for these arguments.

---

[118] Shubin (2008: 93).
[119] De Vries (2013: 367).

Throughout the conflict, aid provided by the competitive interveners subsidized the vast majority of the domestic combatants' costs of war. Consider, for example, that as early as 1979, South African military intelligence estimated that its supplies, training, and organizational aid generated 90% of UNITA's combat power.[120] As the rebel group grew in size, so too did Pretoria's level of support. In 1989, Brigadier General Tony da Costa Fernandes, a top UNITA official, told reporters that South Africa had provided the group with military aid valued at $80 million annually.[121] Beyond training, arming, and equipping the rebel force, Pretoria also regularly assumed the direct costs of UNITA's war effort, deploying SADF troops into Angola to degrade MPLA defenses, to counter government offensives, and to seize territory on behalf of the rebels.

US support played a similar role. Prior to the passing of the Clark Amendment in 1976, the CIA's covert aid program provided UNITA with over $30 million in money, arms, and equipment. Following its repeal in July 1985, US aid flows to UNITA amounted to tens of millions of dollars of support each year. This included everything from small arms and light weapons to advanced military hardware, such as antiaircraft weapons and antitank missile systems. In his assessment of the effect of this support to UNITA over the course of the war, Hoekstra finds the provision of military aid and training to have been crucial to the rebel group's capacity to "wage a large and sustained campaign against the Angolan government."[122]

The Soviet Union's support to the MPLA was similarly comprehensive. A report by the US Senate Select Committee on Intelligence concluded that the MPLA was "clearly propped up by international forces. [...] A quick glance at the magnitude of foreign assistance in terms of men, arms, and advice suggests how deeply dependent on external military strength is the MPLA."[123] Technically, the Soviet Union "sold" the weapons it transferred to Luanda. However, 85–90% were provided on credit—a debt that remained unpaid as the Soviet Union collapsed.[124] As Adamishin recalls, "[t]he main thing that [MPLA leader] dos Santos wanted to hear—and heard—was the practically complete satisfaction of Angolan requests for new deliveries of weapons and other aid which had gone into his lion's share in form [sic] of credits and, in my memory, simply not repaid."[125] Soviet decision-making on military aid deliveries amounted to a "bureaucratic rubber-stamping process."[126] Moscow

---

[120] MI/203/4/0502, "Angola: UNITA invloed op die Angolese situasie en RSA-hulp sedert Operasie Savannah" (1979: para 21).
[121] As quoted in Ottaway (1989).
[122] Hoekstra (2018: 982).
[123] Senate Select Committee on Intelligence (1986: 3).
[124] Gleijeses (2013: 515, 521).
[125] Adamishin (2014: 18).
[126] Adamishin (2014: 30).

also provided the weapons and equipment used by Cuban troops deployed to Angola—again, free of charge.[127]

Cuban support to the MPLA government subsidized its war effort both directly and indirectly. A remarkable 377,033 Cuban troops rotated in and out of Angola for one and a half decades from 1975 onward, training MPLA soldiers, participating in the fight against UNITA, and protecting Angolan oil facilities in the Cabinda enclave.[128] Importantly, Havana paid the salaries of all its troops stationed in Angola.[129] Cuban support also included the deployment of nearly 50,000 civilian advisors, technicians, doctors, and educators—the so-called "internationalists" and *cooperantes*—that provided civil aid to support nation-building in the fields of health, education, manufacturing, engineering, agriculture, administration, and construction.[130] This was an extraordinary example of South–South cooperation during the East–West conflict of the Cold War. Indeed, Cuban aid did not merely help defend Luanda from UNITA's encroachments, but also helped to build the rudiments of a public administration in the country, including a network of state-run social services designed to help win over the support of the civilian population.[131]

US intelligence officials explicitly linked external aid flows to the domestic combatants' bargaining stances and willingness to continue fighting. An "increased Soviet and Cuban commitment," one report notes, "hardened political views in Luanda. President dos Santos until recently had seemed willing to swap a Cuban troop withdrawal for independence in Namibia. He is now insisting publicly that South African support to UNITA must end as well."[132] Improved military performance, enabled by "considerable Soviet and Cuban help," rendered the MPLA's leadership "even more determined to pursue a

---

[127] Gleijeses (2013: 521).

[128] In what can only be described as a paradoxical twist of the Angolan war, Cuban troops were protecting the oil installations of US corporations. Revenues generated from these American oil facilities were in turn used by the MPLA government to fund its war against the American-backed UNITA rebels. The irony was not lost on Cuban soldiers: as one officer put it, "[w]e never thought we would be protecting American interests" (as quoted in Brooke 1986: 3).

[129] Gleijeses (2013: 521).

[130] In her study on Cuban civil aid to Angola, Hatzky (2015: 153–154) notes that estimates of the number of Cuban civil aid workers deployed to Angola vary somewhat between sources. One internal set of statistics uncovered at the Cuban Ministerio para la Inversión Extranjera y la Colaboración Económica cites a total of 44,206 aid workers; another unpublished study from the archive of the Instituto de Historia de Cuba puts the number at 48,957. Unlike Cuban soldiers, whose salaries were paid by Havana, Cuban aid workers' salaries were paid by Luanda beginning in 1977. However, the MPLA often failed to make payments, imposing financial strain on Havana. See Gleijeses (2013: 82–84, 521) and Hatzky (2015: 181–188).

[131] All civil aid workers underwent basic military training either before or during their stay in Angola, and many were obligated to remain armed at all times. For the MPLA, the Cuban civilians' military training was an added bonus, as it meant these aid workers could be deployed to regions that were under threat of UNITA attack. See Hatzky (2015: 159, 225–231).

[132] "Angola-USSR-South Africa: Growing Conflict" (December 5, 1983: 12).

military solution to the insurgency."[133] The provision of external support was also assessed to positively impact Luanda's morale and willingness to continue to fight under conditions of battlefield stalemate.[134] Meanwhile, staffers from the Senate Select Committee on Intelligence, who visited Savimbi's headquarters at Jamba, described the continuation of external aid as a "most important principle" underlying UNITA's strategic and operational planning.[135] UNITA's capacity to maintain successful military operations, fueled by foreign military assistance, was understood to harden Savimbi's political demands.[136] In a letter to US President Reagan, written in September 1986, Savimbi himself tied external aid, battlefield victories, and political success together:

> Over the past three months, our armed forces have destroyed some twenty-five of the enemy's [S]oviet-made aircraft which is more than their total aircraft loss for the entire 1985. Thanks to your help, this represents a very important military achievement for us, a step forward in our efforts to persuade the other side to accept a negotiated political settlement to the conflict. But we still see no concrete signs of the MPLA's willingness to accept a just, peaceful settlement, unless, of course, we increase the military pressure for the months to come.[137]

Two years later, and just one month after the agreement on the linked withdrawals of South African and Cuban troops, Savimbi requested that Washington pledge to continue its aid to UNITA as long as the conflict was not settled in a manner satisfactory to his movement.[138] In a reply, Reagan assured Savimbi that the US had "no intention of making our assistance to you a bargaining chip"; that "there will be no unilateral disengagement by the United States as long as the government in Luanda continues to receive billions in military assistance from abroad"; and that the US was "not negotiating peace between South Africa and the MPLA government in order to free the latter to make war on UNITA."[139]

Little wonder, then, that Angola's domestic combatants chose to sustain their war efforts rather than sue for peace. External aid subsidized the costs of fighting and insulated both the MPLA and UNITA from the burden of sustaining their respective war efforts. It thereby encouraged the combatants to fight on in the interest of receiving greater concessions from their opponent in the future.

---

[133] CIA (November 1985b: 1–2).
[134] CIA (February 1985: 7).
[135] Senate Select Committee on Intelligence (1986: 6).
[136] CIA (January 1984: 11).
[137] Letter from Savimbi to Reagan (September 9, 1986: 1).
[138] Letter from Savimbi to Reagan (September 19, 1988: 2).
[139] Letter from Reagan to Savimbi (October 24, 1988: 1).

Balancing Combatant Capabilities

My theory posits that competitive intervention encourages continued fighting by balancing combatant capabilities. The provision of countermeasures capable of curtailing an opponent's military advantages precludes decisive confrontations and instead generates battlefield stalemates. Under such conditions, combatants must fight additional battles to acquire more information about their opponent and to signal capability and resolve. This ensures that they avoid settling on inequitable terms, but also prolongs the war. The Angolan case provides considerable empirical evidence in support of these arguments.

Throughout the conflict, government forces enjoyed superior conventional military strength relative to their rebel challengers. With the largess of the Soviet Union, the MPLA's arsenal came to encompass a wide variety of tanks and tank destroyers (PT-76s, T-34s, T-54s, T-55s, T-62s, and SU-100s), infantry fighting vehicles and armored cars (BMD-1s, BMD-2s, BMP-2s, BRDM-2s, BTR-50s, BTR-60s, and BTR-152s), self-propelled multiple rocket launchers (BM-21 Grads), aircraft (An-12s, An-26s, Mi-17s, Mi-25s, MiG-21s, MiG-23s, Su-20s, Su-22s, Su-25s, and Yak-40s), and artillery (D-30s and M-46s). The MPLA also acquired air search and height finding radars, self-propelled anti-aircraft guns (ZSU-23-4s and ZSU-57-2s), and a variety of mobile surface-to-air missile systems (including ground-mounted SA-2s, tracked and wheeled SA-3s, SA-6s, SA-8s, SA-9s, and SA-13s, and man-portable SA-7s, SA-14s, and SA-16s).[140] This equipment was organized into twenty-three brigades trained by thousands of Cuban instructors in camps across Angola, while a contingent of Soviet advisors—"the nerve center of MPLA military operations"—developed all strategic and operational military plans and also helped to train government forces.[141] This was a formidable force—among the most sophisticated in all of sub-Saharan Africa—with staggering qualitative and quantitative advantages over UNITA.

How could Savimbi's meager rebel forces possibly survive against the MPLA onslaught? Declassified intelligence reports, archival documents, and participant memoirs are unanimous: external support was the critical lifeline that enabled UNITA to counter the MPLA's military advantages and, thereby, continue to participate in the war. In Adamishin's assessment, "the UNITA rebels could not have re-emerged out of the bush" were it not for South African support.[142] Hoekstra concurs, arguing that external support "had a major positive

---

[140] A full inventory of Soviet hardware transferred to the Angolan government during the war can be found in Stockholm International Peace Research Institute (2020).
[141] Senate Select Committee on Intelligence (1986: 3).
[142] Adamishin (2014: 6). Also see MI/203/4/0502, "Angola: UNITA invloed op die Angolese situasie en RSA-hulp sedert Operasie Savannah" (1979: para 21).

effect on UNITA's war prospects by greatly increasing the rebel group's operational capabilities."[143] To confront Angolan armored elements, UNITA relied on artillery and antiarmor weapons provided by South Africa, as well as antitank weapons provided by the US. To provide protection from air strikes, UNITA relied on American surface-to-air missile systems—a capability Savimbi himself called "decisive" in repelling MPLA offensives.[144] To open new fronts and to stretch government supply lines, UNITA relied on South African logistical support, air drops, and operational planning. And to train his troops, Savimbi relied on a sprawling network of South African and American training camps located in southern Cuando Cubango and South West Africa/Namibia.[145] Taken together, the capabilities afforded to UNITA by its external backers ensured what the CIA described as a "relatively even match despite an imbalance of forces."[146]

By the mid-1980s, UNITA fielded an army of roughly 60,000, with a mix of guerrilla, semi-regular, and regular troops. Guerrillas were generally lightly armed, equipped with assault rifles (AK-47s), 7.62-mm machine guns (PKs), 60-mm mortars, and grenade launchers (RPG-7s). Semi-regular troops were more heavily equipped, possessing 82-mm mortars, heavy machine guns (12.7-mm and 14.5-mm), and surface-to-air missile systems (SA-7s). Finally, the regular battalions were the most heavily armed, utilizing all of the above weapons in addition to 120-mm mortars and 106-mm recoilless antitank rifles. Significantly, these regulars, organized in 1,000-man battalions, proved themselves capable of conventional tactics, directly opposing the MPLA's mechanized task forces and capturing territory from government troops.[147]

But perhaps most important of all, when the tide of battle turned against them, UNITA battalions relied on South African forces to reinforce their positions and to push back MPLA advances. As Adamishin puts it, "[w]hen UNITA was in trouble the South Africans went [into] action."[148] Hoekstra concurs, noting that on "multiple occasions" South African intervention "directly prevented a looming rebel defeat."[149] Former South African Defense Minister Magnus Malan acknowledges that, had the SADF not intervened, Savimbi's rebels would have been soundly defeated.[150] A summary of the MPLA's 1987 offensive, prepared by US intelligence officials, is typical: the MPLA "was making some progress

---

[143] Hoekstra (2018: 982).
[144] As quoted in Claiborne (1987: A28).
[145] This included eleven installations run by the South Africans, such as the Guerrilla Warfare School run by Breytenbach in South West Africa/Namibia. The Americans sent instructors to train UNITA recruits following the repeal of the Clark Amendment. They were stationed a few miles outside Savimbi's main base area at Jamba. See Gleijeses (2013: 229, 309).
[146] CIA (February 1985: iv).
[147] Senate Select Committee on Intelligence (1986: 1–2); CIA (July 1983: 1).
[148] Adamishin (2014: 11).
[149] Hoekstra (2018: 982).
[150] See Claiborne (1987: A28).

toward its main objective [...] until checked last week with the help of direct South African military intervention."[151] While UNITA forces could slow government advances, it was South African support that enabled the "larger scale" operations that kept the rebels in the fight.[152]

The same balancing function was played by the MPLA's patrons. As the rebels' strength improved, the MPLA's military advantages declined. By 1983, US intelligence assessed that a Cuban withdrawal "would paralyze the Angolan Army and enable UNITA to win the war outright."[153] To counter this growing threat, Cuba enhanced its deployment. As an interagency assessment explained, the "increase in Cuban military personnel was in response to the significant expansion of the UNITA insurgency in Angola and, to a lesser extent, to numerous South African military operations in the southern part of the country."[154] Improvements in the military performance of government units was likewise attributed to "more extensive Soviet involvement in planning and directing combat operations," which enabled the MPLA to take advantage of "[b]etter trained and organized Angolan forces" as well as "more effective use of large quantities of Soviet weapons, especially aircraft."[155] Soviet- and Cuban-flown transport aircraft played an essential role in the rapid redeployment and concentration of MPLA forces to counter UNITA offensives.[156] With Soviet guidance and provision, Luanda also constructed an expansive air-defense belt to deter South African air operations. Stretching from Moçâmedes on the Atlantic coast to Cuito Cuanavale in the east, the air-defense system mirrored the Cuban defensive line on the ground.[157]

And as with their rebel opponents, when the going got tough, the MPLA relied on foreign troops for its rescue. The deployment of Cuban soldiers in the fall of 1975 was critical to the MPLA's survival in the early phases of the war. Throughout the 1980s, the Cuban defensive line played a key role in deterring deeper South African strikes in the Angolan heartland. And perhaps most dramatically of all, the arrival of Cuban reinforcements to the besieged town of Cuito Cuanavale in January 1988 was a turning point in what would become one of the most intense, but ultimately stalemated, battles of the war.

Free from the threat of battlefield defeat, the MPLA could dig in its heels and drive a harder bargain. As the CIA explained, "[t]he alternative of a negotiated power-sharing arrangement with UNITA has been publicly refused by the

---

[151] CIA (September 1987: 1).
[152] CIA (September 1987: 2).
[153] CIA (July 1983: iv).
[154] CIA (November 1985a: 3).
[155] CIA (n.d.: 3); also see CIA (April 1986: 15); CIA (June 1986: 3).
[156] CIA (April 1986: 17).
[157] Senate Select Committee on Intelligence (1986: 3).

MPLA. It is likely to be considered, in our view, only when the government is either under extreme military pressure or believes it can negotiate from a position of strong military advantage."[158] The balancing dynamics inherent in competitive intervention precluded both possibilities.

In short, external aid from the competitive interveners served to balance combatant capabilities in ways that prolonged the war. Soviet MiGs flown by MPLA pilots were repelled by American antiaircraft weapons fired by UNITA troops. Rebel assaults were repulsed by Cuban-trained MPLA counterinsurgency units, while government offensives were halted by South African-trained UNITA mortar teams. And when threatened with destruction, both domestic combatants relied on their patrons' armed forces for survival. As US intelligence analysts put it in a report written in 1986, "[f]or both UNITA and the government, the importance of the main outside backers seems likely to us to increase if only to offset the other's role. Savimbi probably will seek improved antitank and antiaircraft weapons to compensate for government superiority, and Pretoria may be required to commit forces again to defend UNITA's sanctuary and rear bases."[159] It was precisely in these ways that external aid provided by the competitive interveners precluded decisive military advantages, thereby generating battlefield stalemates that prolonged the war.

Amplifying Information Asymmetries

My theory holds that competitive intervention distorts domestic bargaining processes by amplifying information asymmetries. As information asymmetries grow, uncertainty over relative strength and resolve increases, encouraging continued fighting. The Angolan case provides empirical evidence in line with these propositions.

At least three types of information problems, introduced by competitive intervention, can be identified. First, secrecy shrouded the external aid programs that constituted the primary source of military power generated by the domestic combatants. This created considerable uncertainty about relative capabilities. In the lead up to Operation Savannah, for example, Pretoria gave no signs that it was planning to back the rebels, let alone that it would send its forces deep into Angola. As the CIA reported, "both UNITA and the South African government made a major effort to keep the South African operation secret."[160] Opperman explained to me that South African officials "had hoped that by going in covertly,

---

[158] CIA (April 1986: 15).
[159] CIA (April 1986: 18).
[160] CIA (March 1977: 24).

we would prevent the situation from escalating much more rapidly."[161] Pretoria's participation was rapidly detected by all sides in the conflict, but the degree to which South Africa was involved remained unclear.[162] In a heavily redacted report prepared in 1977, even the CIA acknowledged that "[t]he extent of South African aid to UNITA has been difficult to assess."[163] As late as 1986, American intelligence was "unable to put a dollar figure on South African assistance."[164] This led the CIA to assess that Luanda "underestimates UNITA's fundamental military and political strength and the depth of South Africa's commitment, which guarantees a continuation of the conflict."[165] For their part, UNITA and the South Africans likewise struggled to estimate the strength of their opponents. Savimbi acknowledged that it was "very difficult to get information about the Cubans. They used different radio transmissions from the MPLA and a different code which was very difficult to break."[166] An SADF military report similarly notes that although commanders "were aware of the areas where the respective [MPLA] and other hostile forces, such as the Cuban regiment, were deployed, uncertainty often existed at a very late stage regarding the identification of force positions, as well as their strength and composition, and the main equipment they possessed."[167] In short, the inability to fully observe the scope of support provided to the MPLA and UNITA impeded estimates of their relative military strength.

Second, the scope of external aid flowing to the domestic combatants varied over the course of the war. Pretoria's support to UNITA was subject to significant temporal variation: from a covert invasion of South African forces during Operation Savannah to an initial withdrawal just a few months later, followed by the establishment of a military aid program that varied in scope over the next twelve years.[168] US aid also experienced upheavals, with strong support in 1975 before the taps turned off following the passage of the Clark Amendment in 1976, only to resume once more in 1985. The variable nature of military aid flows, together with questions about the reliability of UNITA's external support, encouraged Luanda in its view that time was on its side and that "the best move

---

[161] Interview, Major General (ret.) Gert Opperman. June 23, 2014. Pretoria, Gauteng, South Africa.

[162] Four SADF soldiers were captured in Angola on December 13, 1975. Just three days later, they were paraded in front of international media in Luanda. The resulting condemnation from abroad and public humiliation at home forced the apartheid regime to publicly acknowledge participation in the Angolan war. See Baines (2012).

[163] CIA (July 1983: 7).

[164] CIA (June 1986: 9).

[165] CIA (February 1987a: 10).

[166] As quoted in Bridgland (1986: 278).

[167] "Gesamentlike militere aksies deur RSA en UNITA magte teen FAPLA magte in die sesoe militere streek van angola vanaf desember 1987 tot maart 1988" (n.d.: para 8).

[168] On the fluctuations of South African aid to UNITA over the course of the war, see Hoekstra (2018).

in the near term is to sustain the pressure on the insurgents, minimize risks, and, at all costs, avoid a major defeat."[169] At the same time, Cuban and Soviet support was likewise subject to change. The number of Cuban troops deployed to Angola fluctuated from 36,000 in April 1976 to less than 24,000 just one year later. As the threat posed by UNITA grew, so too did the Cuban deployment, reaching 30,000 by early 1983 before peaking at 55,000 by the late 1980s.[170] Similarly, Moscow delivered varying quantities and qualities of weapons and equipment to bolster the MPLA and Cuban troops throughout the war. This "volatility" in support, as the CIA described it, was explicitly cited as complicating the agency's own estimates of the likely outcomes of MPLA offensives.[171]

Finally, uncertainty over how, when, and to what extent the interveners might join their clients in combat complicated estimates of likely battlefield outcomes. Former US Secretary of State Henry Kissinger, for example, notes that "[t]he scale of the Soviet effort was unexpected, and the intervention of Cuban combat forces came as a total surprise."[172] Indeed, that the MPLA could capture and hold Luanda in 1975 is attributable to the unforeseen deployment of Cuban combat troops. Having secured the MPLA's control of the capital, however, Cuban forces decreased the level of their participation in the war. Savimbi noticed that "[u]p to 1978 most of the fighting was being done by the Cubans and not by the MPLA," but that following that date the former "began to concern themselves mostly with logistics, intelligence, protecting the MPLA military convoys, and flying helicopters and MiGs."[173] Only a few years later, this once again changed when Cuban troops rejoined MPLA counterinsurgency teams to counter a growing UNITA threat. As they began taking casualties, analysts questioned how long Cuban resolve could last.[174] It is perhaps for this reason that Castro's bold advance into southwestern Angola in early 1988 caught American policymakers, South African military commanders, and UNITA guerrillas completely unprepared.[175]

The same is true of South African deployments in support of UNITA. The MPLA, Cubans, and Soviets considered an SADF intervention to be "unlikely" in 1975, under the assumption that Pretoria would not jeopardize détente with neighboring black African states—an important policy goal pursued by South

---

[169] CIA (February 1987a: 7–8).
[170] These troop numbers are reported in Gleijeses (2013: 215, 421, 516).
[171] CIA (June 1986: 12).
[172] Kissinger (1999: 815).
[173] As quoted in Bridgland (1986: 270).
[174] Former deputy chief of staff intelligence of the SADF, General (ret.) Chris Thirion, explains the logic: "[t]he war was costly for the Cubans. Confronted with rising costs in blood and money they would leave Angola. Granted, the weapons were given by the Soviet Union. But the Soviets, too, might eventually tire and decide to cut their losses." As quoted in Gleijeses (2013: 248).
[175] Gleijeses (2006: 136–137).

African Prime Minister John Vorster.[176] Thereafter, major MPLA offensives would often stall upon the unexpected arrival of SADF reinforcements. Under the terms of the Lusaka Accords, signed by Pretoria and Luanda in 1984, South Africa agreed to withdraw its ground forces from Angola, provided that Cuban troops did not move into the areas vacated by the SADF. But it was not long before SADF Recces were caught during a botched attack on Angolan oil facilities in Cabinda, revealing that South Africa had in fact been violating the Lusaka Accords by carrying out attacks disguised as UNITA rebels.[177]

In short, external aid programs were shrouded in secrecy, there was variation in the quality and quantity of military assistance provided over time, and there was uncertainty over how, when, and to what extent the interveners might join their domestic clients in combat. Taken together, these features of competitive intervention in the Angolan civil war complicated the domestic combatants' efforts to estimate the relative capabilities and resolve of their opponent. The net result was a protracted civil war.

Other Explanations

The cross-national analyses reported in Chapter 4 identify two potentially competing domestic-level explanations for protracted war in Angola: the state's regime type and the number of warring factions participating in the conflict. Specifically, democracy is substantively and statistically associated with longer civil wars. Likewise, the number of rebel factions participating in a conflict is positively correlated with conflict duration. These results dovetail with arguments found in the wider literature.[178] However, neither explanation can account for protracted fighting in Angola.

Arguments linking democratic regime types to longer conflicts fail to explain the duration of the Angolan civil war for the simple fact that post-independence Angola has never been a democracy. To the contrary, from 1975 to 1991, Angola had an average polity score of −6.82, indicating an autocratic regime type based on the widely employed data compiled by the Polity Project.[179] Throughout the same period, Freedom House consistently classified the Angolan state as "not

---

[176] CIA (March 1977: 18). On Vorster's détente agenda, see Miller (2016).

[177] The failed covert mission, codenamed Operation Argon, is recounted in detail in Steyn and Söderlund (2015: chapter 10). It came just one month after the last South African soldier withdrew from Angola under the terms of the Lusaka Accords.

[178] For example, Merom (2003) argues that democracies are constrained in their ability to fight ruthlessly against insurgencies; Mueller (2005) argues that democracies suffer from greater casualty sensitivity relative to authoritarian regime types; Cunningham (2011) shows that bargaining in multiparty civil wars is more difficult; and Christia (2012) highlights how multiparty civil wars can experience shifting combatant alliances that prolong fighting.

[179] Marshall and Gurr (2020).

free," based on aggregate assessments of the country's protection of political rights and civil liberties.[180] It was not until September 1992 that the country's first general elections were held. However, as discussed below, those elections were mired in controversy. More generally, Angolan citizens have seen little change in their political and civil rights since 1992. The state has been ruled by the MPLA since 1975; authorities have systematically repressed political dissent; and abuse at the hands of state security forces remains common.[181] In short, Angola is not, nor has it ever been, a democracy. Consequently, arguments linking democratic regimes to longer conflicts cannot account for the protracted character of the Angolan civil war.

The connection between multiparty wars and longer periods of fighting likewise fails to account for the duration of the Angolan conflict. While the war began as a three-way contest between the MPLA, UNITA, and the FNLA, the latter group was quickly eliminated. Indeed, following its devastating defeat at the Battle of Quifangondo, which occurred on the eve of Angolan independence on November 10, 1975, the FNLA ceased to be a meaningful participant in the conflict.[182] By February 1976, the FNLA had been eliminated from the Angolan theater.[183] Thereafter, the civil war was fought exclusively between the MPLA regime and its UNITA rivals. Consequently, arguments linking multiparty contests to protracted fighting cannot explain the duration of the Angolan civil war—for virtually the entire conflict period, there was only one rebel faction.

Summary

At the domestic level of the civil war combatants, competitive intervention subsidized the costs of fighting, balanced military capabilities, and increased information asymmetries. These distortions of the bargaining process increased the combatants' willingness and ability to fight, precluded decisive military advantages, and increased uncertainty over relative strength and resolve. Indeed, it is notable that throughout the war, the MPLA conditioned talks on UNITA's severing of links with South Africa. For its part, UNITA conditioned talks on the withdrawal of Cuban troops from Angola. In the interim, both sides reiterated their refusal to bargain and committed themselves to a military solution to the conflict. Even in the mid-1980s, as violence reached new heights in what was a brutally violent war of attrition, the CIA confidently reported that the prospects for MPLA–UNITA reconciliation were "virtually nil."[184]

---

[180] Freedom House (2023).
[181] Freedom House (2022).
[182] George (2005: 90).
[183] Gleijeses (2002: 338–339).
[184] CIA (June 1986: 13).

It is therefore not surprising that the *internal* peace agreement signed between the MPLA and UNITA in 1991 was preceded by the Tripartite Accord, an *external* agreement signed between Angola, Cuba, and South Africa in December 1988. It was only after an international agreement that terminated competitive intervention was reached that a domestic settlement became possible. Tellingly, Adamishin writes that negotiations over the linked Cuban and South African withdrawals "began only after everyone agreed to exclude the internal issues of Angola from the agenda."[185] Indeed, the Tripartite Accord is silent on the question of a domestic settlement.

That external aid distorted the domestic bargaining process is manifest in the remarkable fact that Angolan President José dos Santos and UNITA leader Jonas Savimbi met *for the first time* only in June 1989—some fourteen years after the start of the war, but just six months after the signing of the Tripartite Accord. The rival leaders' meeting concluded with a temporary ceasefire under the Gbadolite Declaration, though the agreement broke down quickly.[186] Notwithstanding renewed fighting, serious bargaining continued. Nudging the talks along, in October 1990 the US stipulated that its assistance to UNITA would be subject to termination if the MPLA undertook the reforms necessary to bring peace to Angola.[187] For its part, the Soviet Union—amid its own crumbling economy—announced publicly that it was considering cutting all military aid to the MPLA. These moves on the part of the remaining competitive interveners instigated significant movement in the domestic combatants' bargaining positions. In December 1990, Savimbi announced that UNITA no longer demanded explicit recognition by the MPLA. In response, the MPLA indicated its willingness to transition to a multiparty political system with competitive elections. Crucially, this new round of negotiations explicitly linked a domestic agreement with the termination of outside aid. In that context, the pace of bargaining quickened, and by May 1991 UNITA and the MPLA had signed the Bicesse Accords, a comprehensive treaty that included stipulations for political reconciliation, elections, and military monitoring.

Tragically, the peace agreement would break down following presidential elections in the fall of 1992. Savimbi, alongside eight other opposition parties, protested that the election had been neither free nor fair—a claim that

---

[185] Adamishin (2014: 60).

[186] On the diplomatic fiasco caused by Zairian leader Mobutu Sese Seko's mishandling of the Gbadolite meeting, see McCormick (1991: 3-4).

[187] This stipulation was formalized in the Solarz amendment to the annual Intelligence Authorization bill, through which US covert aid to UNITA was channeled. The amendment passed the House of Representatives and was added to the bill, though the bill itself was vetoed by US President George Bush for unrelated reasons. Nonetheless, the US State Department claimed the administration still chose to follow the "spirit" of the amendment (McCormick 1991: 9).

was denied by a UN monitoring mission in Angola.[188] Yet while the conflict would eventually relapse, in no small part due to Zaire's re-entry into the war, South Africa and Cuba respected their obligations as stipulated by the Tripartite Accord and the US and Soviet Union stayed true to their commitments to terminate aid. With the end of competitive intervention, the first phase of the Angolan civil war was officially over.

Conclusion

This chapter presented evidence that verifies the observable implications of my theory of competitive intervention at both the international and domestic levels. First, the empirical record shows that the interveners constrained the scope of their support to the domestic combatants. Second, participants of the war confirm that this restraint was motivated by escalation fears vis-à-vis opposing interveners. Third, limits constructed around thresholds—such as distinctions between advisory and combat missions, geographic areas of control and contestation, defensive and offensive deployment patterns and force postures, and acceptable and prohibited targets—were demonstrated to have effectively regulated confrontation between the interveners. Finally, intervener restraint was found to prevent the conferral of decisive military advantages while simultaneously distorting domestic bargaining processes by subsidizing combatants' war costs, balancing their capabilities, and enhancing information asymmetries. Through these international- and domestic-level channels, competitive intervention was found to prolong the Angolan civil war.

A central claim of my theory is that the escalation dilemma inherent to competitive intervention leads interveners to refrain from providing the level of support necessary to achieve positive objectives, such as battlefield victories, and instead provide a level of support sufficient only to achieve negative objectives, such as avoiding battlefield defeats. Putting this argument to the test, I asked interviewees whether they thought South Africa did enough for UNITA during the Angolan civil war. "We did help them a lot," Opperman responded. "We provided them with a lot of material support; a lot of financial support; we gave them an international platform, which they would not have had. So yes, we

---

[188] Margaret Anstee, who headed the UN mission in Angola, issued a public statement that explained that "[t]he United Nations considers that while there were certainly some irregularities in the electoral process, these appear to have been mainly due to human error and inexperience. There was no conclusive evidence of major, systematic or widespread fraud, or that the irregularities were of a magnitude to have a significant effect on the results officially announced on 17 October [1992]. Nor, in view of their random nature, could it be determined that such irregularities had penalized or benefited only one party or set of parties." As quoted in UN Security Council (1992: para 20). For her firsthand account of the collapse of the Angolan peace process, see Anstee (1996).

really helped them a lot." But when I asked whether South Africa ever tried to ensure UNITA would prevail on the battlefield, he gave a negative response: "I don't think we ever had the real option of getting them to win the civil war—that would have been beyond our means. Getting them to control the whole country and to keep them in place, despite the troop and armaments escalation from the other side, just wouldn't have been possible. I don't think that was really an option for us."[189] When I asked Dippenaar the same question, he echoed Opperman's response. "I think there are a number of cases where UNITA could have done better if they were better equipped and better trained, where they could have taken over," he explained. But while "the possibility was always there," he acknowledged that South Africa was hamstrung by escalation concerns: "[t]he threat against the country from abroad [...] was building up all the time."[190]

Brigadier General (ret.) Deon Fourie, who served on the staff of the chief of the army during the 1980s, told me that South African military and political leaders wanted "to try and save UNITA from the consequences of Cuban and Soviet intervention. [...] [T]he feeling [was] that we didn't want to abandon UNITA to any unpredictable fate, but we didn't want to go right into central Angola and get into serious trouble." By "serious trouble," Fourie was referring to direct confrontation with Cuban and Soviet forces: "we didn't want to get involved in a full-scale campaign, a full-scale war," he explained. "We just wanted to save UNITA and then leave them."[191] Dave Steward, former director-general of the South African Communication Service, reiterated this sentiment: "[a UNITA victory] would have been nice," he explained, but in light of escalation fears, South African military assistance sought a more limited objective: to ensure UNITA could continue "holding the line."[192]

The archival record suggests that Cuba likewise pursued the more limited objective of avoiding defeat in Angola. Castro saw the Cuban deployment as a deterrent to South African invasion rather than as a fighting force to help the MPLA prevail in its civil war with UNITA. In fact, as early as January 1979, Cuba had ended its participation in the fight against UNITA, withdrawn Cuban advisors from MPLA counterinsurgency units, and limited Cuban participation to making recommendations and observing. This decision proved costly: UNITA enjoyed a period of recovery and development, as the MPLA failed to maintain the pace of operations set by the Cubans. By late 1979, Savimbi had moved UNITA's headquarters from northern South West Africa/Namibia to

---

[189] Interview, Major General (ret.) Gert Opperman. June 23, 2014. Pretoria, Gauteng, South Africa.
[190] Interview, Major General (ret.) Johann Dippenaar. June 30, 2014. Pretoria, Gauteng, South Africa.
[191] Interview, Brigadier General (ret.) Deon Fourie. June 16, 2014. Pretoria, Gauteng, South Africa.
[192] Interview, Dave Steward. June 6, 2014. Johannesburg, Gauteng, South Africa.

Jamba in southeastern Angola; in September 1980, he captured Mavinga; and by May 1981, he had repulsed the MPLA's attempts to retake captured cities. Disturbed by UNITA's resurgence, in December 1981 the Cubans agreed to reassign military advisors to the war against UNITA. However, Castro ensured that his combat troops remained north of the Cuban defensive line.[193] And even in the final months of the conflict, as Cuban troops advanced in the southwest for the first time in a decade, the actions of front line forces render plain Castro's limited objectives. A decisive confrontation to ensure the MPLA a military victory over UNITA was not worth a conventional war with South Africa; the risk of inadvertent escalation with the SADF necessitated a carefully calibrated approach.

In short, while interveners on both sides of Angola's civil war sought to advance their national interests during the conflict, the need to control escalation and avoid direct confrontations vis-à-vis interstate rivals constrained their ability to confer decisive military advantages on domestic clients. At the same time, it is precisely because they enjoyed the support of competing external backers that government and rebel forces faced neither the resource constraints inherent in war nor the threat of defeat at the hands of their opponent. The net result was a bloody and protracted war, with little hope for compromise or resolution.

---

[193] Gleijeses (2013: 110, 192, 194–195).

6
The Afghan Communist–Mujahideen Civil War, 1979–1992

When Soviet leaders ordered troops to Afghanistan in December 1979, they believed it would be a short war. But while it was expected that Soviet troops would return home within a matter of months, Moscow soon found itself mired in a protracted counterinsurgency campaign.[1] Much has been written about the Soviet experience in Afghanistan, but to date, most research has focused on the Politburo's decision to intervene in 1979 and to withdraw in the late 1980s.[2] This chapter poses a different question: Why did the war last so long?

This is an important question not only for explanations of the conflict but also for our understanding of competitive intervention. While US–Soviet rivalry in Afghanistan is often cited as the archetypal Cold War "proxy war," scholars have overlooked the ways in which the escalation dilemma at the heart of competitive intervention affected its dynamics and outcomes. Battlefield victory was a matter of life and death for the communist government and its rebel challengers in the mujahideen.[3] For the competitive interveners, on the other hand, the need to control escalation and avoid large-scale confrontations necessitated more limited aims. In line with this book's theoretical expectations, the interveners signaled strategic restraint by drawing distinctions between geographic areas of contestation and control, offensive and defensive force postures, and the qualitative characteristics of different weapon systems. This served to regulate the interveners' competition with one another and helped to avoid a regional war between them. But it simultaneously—and paradoxically—prevented the conferral of decisive military advantages on Afghanistan's domestic combatants. The net result was a stalemated conflict that neither side was capable of winning, yet that neither side was willing to lose.

---

[1] Soviet Foreign Minister Andrei Gromyko told Soviet Ambassador to the US Anatoly Dobrynin that the intervention was "only for a month, we'll do everything and leave quickly" (as quoted in Mlechin 2006: 436). Soviet General Secretary Leonid Brezhnev also believed this, arguing that troops would be out of Afghanistan within months (see Liakhovskii 1995: 356).

[2] On the Soviet decision to intervene, see Westad (1996) and Gibbs (2006); on the decision to withdraw, see Mendelson (1998), Halliday (1999), Grau (2007), and Kalinovsky (2011).

[3] There are many accepted spellings for the name of the Afghan resistance. For clarity, I have used a standardized "mujahideen" in this chapter, including in quotations where alternate spellings appear in the original.

Like the Angolan civil war discussed in the previous chapter, the Afghan conflict is an important case for this book for a number of reasons. First, it presents a "least-likely" test for my argument relating escalation fears to intervener restraint. The communist–mujahideen war was one of the bloodiest conflicts of the Cold War period, killing an estimated 800,000–1.2 million Afghans,[4] generating some 5.5 million refugees,[5] and rendering another 2 million people internally displaced.[6] In an effort to stamp out the insurgency, Afghan and Soviet forces unleashed an exceptionally violent campaign, which included the mass depopulation and physical destruction of entire villages.[7] In light of this brutality, the suggestion that the war presents evidence of "restraint" will undoubtedly strike some as improbable. Yet, it is precisely because of the level of violence seen in Afghanistan that the restraint of the competitive interveners vis-à-vis *one another* is so remarkable. Despite their widespread mistreatment of Afghans—government, guerrilla, and civilian alike—external interveners went to extraordinary lengths to avoid mutual clashes that risked further enlarging the conflict. It is in this respect that the case provides powerful evidence of the conditioning effect of escalation fears during competitive intervention in civil wars.

Second, the case provides an opportunity to test my theory while relaxing the assumption that interveners ultimately seek to see their domestic client through to victory. A common refrain in analyses of the Afghan conflict is that Washington did not seek to "beat" the Soviets in Afghanistan, but rather aimed to "bleed" them in a costly quagmire.[8] I consider whether these more limited objectives liberated US or Soviet policymakers from the escalation dilemma my theory identifies. The case evidence is clear: the contradictory pressures of competitive intervention constrained American and Soviet policymaking alike. Whether in pursuit of absolute victory or more limited objectives, the need for strategic stability dominates tactical choices under conditions of competitive intervention.

Third, the case is valuable for its historical and policy significance. Many have attributed the Soviet withdrawal from Afghanistan to the American and Pakistani covert aid program, codenamed Operation Cyclone, which supported

---

[4] Kalinovsky (2011: 1). Other estimates are roughly in this range, including Grau and Nawroz (1995: 19) who report 1.3 million dead, and Sliwinski (1989: 39) who reports 1–1.5 million dead.

[5] Grau and Nawroz (1995: 19). Again, other estimates are roughly in this range. Sliwinski (1989: 54), for example, reports that 33.2% of the Afghan population became refugees by 1987. Estimating the prewar Afghan population as between 12 and 15.5 million, this would amount to 3.98–5.15 million refugees.

[6] Boulouque (1999: 717). Sliwinski (1989: 54) reports that 10.9% of the Afghan population was internally displaced by 1987. Assuming a prewar Afghan population of between 12 and 15.5 million, this would amount to roughly 1.31–1.69 million internally displaced persons.

[7] On mass killings in the context of guerrilla insurgencies, including a discussion of the Afghan case, see Valentino (2004: chapter 6).

[8] On the "bleeders" within the Reagan administration, see Cordovez and Harrison (1995: chapter 8).

the mujahideen. Some have gone further, suggesting that the military pressure generated by the program not only defeated the Soviets in Afghanistan but also played a part in the collapse of the Soviet Union itself.[9] Due to this apparent "success," some analysts have pointed to Operation Cyclone as a model for US military assistance programs, including in contemporary civil wars.[10] But while it is true that American and Pakistani money and arms played a central role in the mujahideen's military campaign, the success of the covert aid program must not be exaggerated. The Soviets were not "defeated" in Afghanistan: rather than retreating under fire, Soviet leaders signed the Geneva Accords that brought their troops home at a time of relative strength and entrenched military positions. Nor were the costs imposed by the aid program so severe as to necessitate a Soviet withdrawal. In a declassified intelligence report written at the height of the war in 1987, the US Central Intelligence Agency (CIA) itself acknowledged that the war had "not been a substantial drain on the Soviet economy" and that economic costs were "unlikely [...] to be of sufficient magnitude to constitute a significant counterweight to the political and security implications the Soviets would attach to withdrawal under circumstances that could be seen as a defeat."[11] To suggest that Operation Cyclone not only defeated the Soviets in Afghanistan but that it also played a role in the disintegration of the Soviet Union itself is to present a serious misreading of history. What is more, it overlooks the ways in which American and Pakistani policymakers carefully restricted the scope of their support to the mujahideen to avoid provoking Soviet retaliation. These are important lessons not only for our understanding of the dynamics of the Afghan civil war but also for policymakers contemplating similar aid programs in contemporary conflicts.

Finally, an additional contribution of the chapter is its correction of an ill-founded narrative that is common in the literature, but which is unsupported by the documentary record. Many have argued that the Reagan administration's approval of National Security Decision Directive 166 (NSDD-166) in March 1985 was a critical juncture in the war, representing a significant escalation that

---

[9] Former US National Security Advisor Zbigniew Brzezinski, for example, has argued that the Afghan civil war "brought about the demoralization and finally the breakup of the Soviet empire." When asked if he regretted providing arms to fighters who would later use them in terrorist attacks, Brzezinski explicitly connected the US aid program to the dissolution of the Soviet Union: "What is more important in world history? The Taliban or the collapse of the Soviet empire? Some agitated Muslims or the liberation of Central Europe and the end of the Cold War?" As quoted in Le Nouvel Observateur (1998: 76). Also see Arnold (1993) and Reuveny and Prakash (1999).

[10] See, for example, Riedel (2013), Blume (2014), Boot (2016), Herbst (2017), and Pollack (2018).

[11] CIA (February 1987b: iii, v). Another report, prepared in the fall of 1984, similarly concluded that the positive benefits of consolidated control of Afghanistan—including enhanced leverage over Pakistan and Iran—outweighed non-economic domestic costs, including worsening morale among Soviet conscripts, growing drug abuse problems, and strained regime credibility among the Soviet public. See CIA (October 1984).

authorized "all means available" to defeat the Soviets in Afghanistan. I show that this claim is based on journalistic accounts that relied on interviews with former US policymakers who framed the directive as an aggressive departure from past policy. Using the declassification of NSDD-166 as an opportunity to reassess its significance, I demonstrate that the directive was not the escalatory policy change many have interpreted it to be.

The analysis that follows unpacks the strategic challenges that competitive interveners confronted in Afghanistan by drawing on a rich set of primary and secondary sources, including archival documents from the Soviet Union and United States, official histories of the Afghan campaign prepared by the Pakistani and Russian General Staffs, and declassified intelligence reports. Like the previous chapter, my objective is to examine the observable implications of my theory and to verify the processes that link competitive intervention to protracted conflict at both the international and domestic levels. In doing so, I aim to assess whether my argument continues to receive support in the manner specified by my theory in the context of a different conflict environment. Employing process tracing, I explore how the unique strategic dilemmas posed by competitive intervention affected the Afghan battlefield. Beginning at the international level, I examine whether the interveners constrained the scope of the aid they provided to domestic combatants; I identify the extent to which intervener restraint was motivated by escalation fears vis-à-vis opposing interveners; and I assess whether limits on the scope of support were constructed around thresholds that served as credible signals of restraint. Turning to the domestic level, I then consider whether and how intervener support distorted bargaining processes by reducing the civil war combatants' costs of war, balancing their capabilities, and amplifying information asymmetries.

The chapter begins with a brief overview of the war and the relationships between its primary combatants. Next, it examines how interveners regulated their competition by establishing limits to control escalation vis-à-vis one another. It then explores the consequences of competitive intervention for domestic bargaining processes. The chapter concludes with a summary of the evidence and an assessment of the escalation dilemma's significance for the Afghan civil war.

Overview of the War and Combatant Relationships

The origins of the Afghan conflict can be traced to the Saur Revolution. On April 17, 1978, a prominent leader of the communist People's Democratic Party of Afghanistan (PDPA), Mir Akbar Khaibar, was assassinated. The PDPA leadership and other leftists alleged the assassination had been ordered by the ruling

Afghan president, Mohammed Daoud Khan, and used Khaibar's funeral as an occasion for mass demonstrations. Interpreting the scale of the protest as an alarming indication of the PDPA's organization, Daoud had the party's leadership arrested. However, he moved too slowly: rebellion had already spread to the military, and on April 27, army and air force officers sympathetic to the PDPA led a coup against Daoud, who was deposed and killed. The PDPA's leadership was promptly released from prison, formed a new Revolutionary Council, and took the seat of power in Kabul (see Figure 6.1 for a map of the country).

The new Afghan leaders sought revolutionary goals for their country, calling for radical social, political, and economic reforms. Unfortunately for the PDPA, however, this vision for a fundamentally transformed Afghan society was out of touch with their fellow countrymen. Opposition to the new regime emerged quickly, as its attempts to wrestle social control from the tribal aristocracy was contested by the fiercely conservative prejudices of Afghanistan's landowners, traditional leaders, and mullahs. A collection of Islamic guerrilla groups, known as the mujahideen, began organizing to oust the communist government. The PDPA responded with repression, using the tools of mass arrests, torture, and executions. Far from stamping out the opposition, however, the PDPA's brutality unified popular resistance to its rule. On March 15, 1979, the first of what would become a series of mutinies in the Afghan Army took place in Herat. Fearful that the country was slipping from its control, the PDPA turned to the Soviet Union for help, requesting the deployment of Soviet troops to help quell the rebellion.[12]

Kabul and Moscow enjoyed friendly relations long before the onset of the civil war.[13] And while the Soviets did not play a direct role in the PDPA's coup, they had committed to the defense of the Afghan revolution under the provisions of a Treaty of Friendship, Good Neighborliness, and Cooperation, signed in December 1978.[14] During an emergency meeting of the Politburo held on March 17 and 18, Soviet leaders contemplated the PDPA's request for aid. Citing the negative impact the deployment of Soviet troops would have on détente with the US, ongoing negotiations over strategic nuclear weapons, and the planned Carter–Brezhnev summit that was to take place that June, a direct intervention was ruled

---

[12] For an overview of this period and the objectives of the PDPA's reforms, see Rubin (2002: chapter 5).
[13] Soviet military assistance to Afghanistan began as early as 1919, when Moscow provided financing and arms to support Afghan resistance to Britain during the Third Anglo-Afghan War. In February 1921, a Soviet–Afghan Treaty of Friendship was signed, followed by a neutrality and mutual nonaggression agreement in June 1931. Relations were deepened further in 1956, when the Soviet minister of defense took on the responsibility of training Afghan national military cadres. By the 1970s, hundreds of Soviet specialists and advisors worked in Afghanistan, training the Afghan Army, serving as technical assistants, and providing policy guidance.
[14] The Afghan coup was a surprise to Soviet officials in Kabul, as the PDPA's leaders had neither informed nor consulted the Soviet leadership of their plans. See Braithwaite (2011: 41–42).

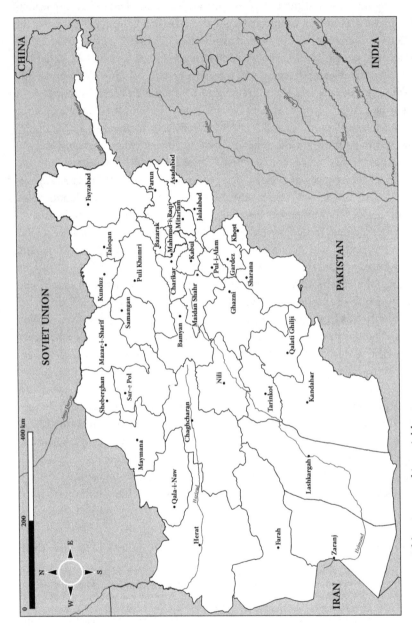

Figure 6.1 Afghanistan and its neighbors.

out.[15] However, Soviet leaders agreed to a stepped-up aid program, including the provision of additional weapons and an increased number of advisors.[16]

The Afghan Army managed to pacify Herat, but conditions continued to worsen. By the summer, mutinies had struck Jalalabad, Asmar, Ghazni, Nahrin, and even Kabul itself.[17] Further complicating matters was infighting within the PDPA. Feuding between two party leaders, Nur Muhammad Taraki and Hafizullah Amin, was intensifying as the two strongmen jockeyed for control. As tensions reached an apex, Taraki attempted to have Amin killed.[18] The plan failed, however, and with the help of a contingent of army officers, Amin had Taraki arrested. A few weeks later, on October 9, 1979, Taraki was smothered to death while tied to a bed in his jail cell.

Amin's decision to have Taraki killed shocked and angered the Soviets. Letters circulated among the Politburo leadership following the event reveal growing concern about Amin's erratic behavior, repression, and secretiveness.[19] The Komitet Gosudarstvennoy Bezopasnosti (KGB) had long-questioned whether Amin might be working for the CIA, perhaps having established ties to American intelligence services when he attended graduate school in the US.[20] Amin's refusal to accept the recommendations of Soviet political and military advisors was also deeply frustrating for Moscow, especially in light of the mujahideen's growing strength.

By early December, the head of the KGB, Yuri Andropov, began laying out the case for a direct intervention to secure the Soviet Union's interests in its southern neighbor.[21] Distrust of Amin, fears of US intentions in the Persian Gulf, and

[15] "Meeting of the Politburo of the Central Committee of the Communist Party of the Soviet Union" (March 17–19, 1979).
[16] The aid included five MI-24 attack helicopters, eight MI-8T transport helicopters, thirty-three BMP-1 infantry fighting vehicles, fifty BTR-60PB armored personnel carriers, twenty-five armored reconnaissance vehicles, fifty mobile antiair units, and one SA-9 surface-to-air missile system. The Soviets also committed to repair Afghan helicopters and aircraft, to send 100,000 tons of grain, and to raise the price they paid for Afghan natural gas from $21 to $37 per cubic meter. See "Transcript of Telephone Conversation Between Soviet Premier Alexei Kosygin and Afghan Prime Minister Nur Mohammed Taraki" (March 17 or 18, 1979); "Record of Meeting of A.N. Kosygin, A.A. Gromyko, D.F. Ustinov, and B.N. Ponomarev with N.M. Taraki" (March 20, 1979).
[17] Rubin (2002: 120).
[18] It remains unclear whether the Soviets had known about Taraki's plan. Leading up to the assassination attempt on September 14, 1979, Soviet advisors were pressuring Taraki to remove Amin from power, but officials claimed to have no knowledge of the assassination plot. See Westad (2007: 312–313).
[19] See, for example, "Gromyko-Andropov-Ustinov-Ponomarev Report to the Central Committee of the Communist Party of the Soviet Union on the Situation in Afghanistan" (October 29, 1979); "Andropov-Gromyko-Ustinov-Ponomarev Report to the Central Committee of the Communist Party of the Soviet Union on Events in Afghanistan on 27–28 December 1979" (December 31, 1979); "Personal Memorandum from Andropov to Brezhnev" (December 1979).
[20] Westad (2007: 305).
[21] "Personal Memorandum from Andropov to Brezhnev" (December 1979). The Soviet Ministry of Defense had already begun military preparations for a possible response to fighting in Afghanistan. For example, in June the Soviets sent a parachute battalion, disguised as an aviation

concern for the geopolitical consequences of "losing" Afghanistan convinced Soviet leaders that a military response had become necessary.[22] On December 12, the Politburo approved the deployment of Soviet forces in a handwritten resolution.[23] Thirteen days later, on December 25, the Soviet 40th Army—officially dubbed the "Limited Contingent of Soviet Forces in Afghanistan"—crossed the border into Afghanistan. Just before nightfall on December 27, KGB special units attacked Amin's residence at the Dar-ul-Aman Palace in Kabul, deposed him, and installed a new regime led by Babrak Karmal.[24]

The international response to the Soviet intervention was swift. Within days, US President Jimmy Carter was publicly arguing that the occupation threatened both Iran and Pakistan, the world's oil supplies, and "the stable, strategic, and peaceful balance of the entire world."[25] A few weeks later, he again hit on these themes, issuing a stern warning to the Soviets in what would come to be known as the "Carter Doctrine": the policy that any attempt to gain control of the Persian Gulf would be considered an assault on America's vital interests.[26]

Washington's anxieties were mirrored in Islamabad. From the perspective of Pakistani leaders, the Soviet intervention presented a menacing security threat. Militarily, Pakistan had always positioned its forces along its eastern border, arrayed to meet the challenge posed by its archrival, India. It had neither the infrastructure nor the military capacity to fight in the east and west simultaneously. Yet in late December 1979, the potential for a two-front war looked very real: the Soviet Union and India were linked through a Treaty of Friendship, signed on the eve of Pakistan's dismemberment in 1971, and unlike most other nonaligned countries, India was unwilling to condemn the Soviet intervention.[27]

By January 10, 1980—just two weeks after Soviet troops crossed into Afghanistan—the first US arms shipment had arrived into Pakistan for distribution to mujahideen fighters.[28] The following month, Carter's national security

---

maintenance team, to protect Soviet air squadrons based at Bagram airfield. They also sent a special detachment of KGB men, disguised as embassy service personnel, to help protect the Soviet Embassy. See "Gromyko-Andropov-Ustinov-Ponomarev Report to the Communist Party of the Soviet Union Central Committee on the Situation in Afghanistan" (June 28, 1979). For a discussion, see Carson (2018: 248–252).

[22] Westad (2007: 316), Liakhovskii (1995: 109), Kornienko (1994: 193), Halliday (1999: 678–679), and Kalinovsky (2011: 11–12, 24, 52, 214–215).

[23] See "Concerning the Situation in 'A'" (December 12, 1979).

[24] Karmal had been the former vice president and deputy prime minister of the 1978 revolutionary government, but had been exiled due to PDPA infighting.

[25] Carter (January 4, 1980). Also see "Personal Memorandum from Brzezinkski to Carter" (December 26, 1979).

[26] Carter (January 23, 1980).

[27] CIA (July 1982: 1); Yousaf and Adkin (1992: 23–24); Pakistan Air Force (2000: 26). A Special National Intelligence Estimate put the odds of Soviet intelligence and logistical support to India at 70%, should India express an interest in attacking Pakistan. See Director of Central Intelligence (1984: 13).

[28] Cogan (1993: 76).

advisor, Zbigniew Brzezinski, traveled to Pakistan where he met with Pakistani President Muhammad Zia-ul-Haq. Together, the two men worked out the details of an expanded aid program to support the Afghan insurgency. Codenamed Operation Cyclone, the program would see the US government finance the CIA to covertly purchase arms and equipment from other third-party states, including Britain, China, Egypt, and Israel, as well as from the US itself. The Saudi government would match this funding, dollar for dollar. The CIA would then coordinate the distribution of arms, equipment, and financial aid to the Pakistani Inter-Services Intelligence (ISI). For its part, the ISI would manage the distribution of military aid to the mujahideen, which it channeled through an alliance of seven political parties—four Islamic fundamentalist and three moderate traditionalist—that positioned themselves as representatives of the various mujahideen commanders in the field.[29] Pakistan would also provide sanctuary and training to mujahideen fighters, who were permitted to establish base camps and stockpile supplies on Pakistani territory.[30]

The war's center of gravity was in the east, along the Afghanistan–Pakistan border. Here lay the Afghan capital, the strategic airfield at Bagram, and the major north–south roadway that linked the Soviet Union to Kabul.[31] The majority of counterinsurgent forces were deployed in the east, whether garrisoned in cities or in the hundreds of mutually supporting guard posts that protected supply lines from Mazar-i-Sharif to Kandahar. Offensive operations were likewise concentrated in the east, reflecting the counterinsurgents' efforts to deny the mujahideen its Pakistani sanctuary by sealing the border.

Throughout the war, the mujahideen mostly operated outside major Afghan cities, avoiding set-piece battles in favor of small-unit ambushes and asymmetric attacks on major roadways, supply lines, and outposts. The conventional, theater-level offensives initially employed by the counterinsurgents failed to thwart these guerrilla tactics. Over time, however, Afghan and Soviet forces adapted to their foe. While the rebels proved remarkably resilient, they suffered repeated losses as communist forces exploited their complete domination of the air to bomb mujahideen base camps, perform reconnaissance, and provide convoy security, tactical lift, mining, and air support operations. Helicopter-borne

---

[29] Most of the military aid was transported by sea to the port of Karachi, though some of it was flown in to Islamabad. Major ISI warehouses were located near Rawalpindi and Quetta. Smaller depots, which were controlled by the mujahideen, were scattered along the Afghan–Pakistani border region.

[30] For an overview of the aid network, see Yousaf and Adkin (1992: 81–84).

[31] The aforementioned roadway was the eastern section of the Highway 1 ring road, stretching from Mazar-i-Sharif to Kandahar. This section of the highway is also the route of the above-ground oil pipeline that stretched from the Soviet Union to Bagram airfield.

Spetsnaz teams, backed by columns of motorized infantry, proved especially effective in hammer-and-anvil operations. The counterinsurgents also sought to eliminate the mujahideen's civilian support network in the Afghan countryside by destroying unfriendly population centers. Cropland and pastures were burned and mined, and entire villages were leveled to the ground. By the fall of 1984, pro-government forces had achieved considerable military success, leading one mujahideen commander, Ahmed Shah Massoud, to comment that it had "become a very hard war, far harder than before. [...] Their commandos have learned a great deal about mountain guerrilla warfare and are fighting much better than before."[32] Afghan government forces, supported by Soviet artillery and air power, began taking the lead in frequent operations against mujahideen base areas. Throughout 1985 and 1986, the counterinsurgents' successes continued, especially as the 40th Army's troop numbers reached their peak level of 108,800 personnel.[33]

Yet try as they might, Afghan and Soviet forces proved unable to eliminate the mujahideen. Frustrated by the stalemate, Moscow began searching for a way out. In May 1986, Soviet leaders engineered a change in the Afghan leadership, replacing Karmal with the head of the Afghan secret police, Mohammad Najibullah. The latter proposed a ceasefire under the Soviet-orchestrated policy of "National Reconciliation," but there were no political breakthroughs. Following several meetings of the Politburo over the course of 1987, the decision was made to bring Soviet soldiers home. During a visit to Washington in December of that year, Gorbachev announced that Moscow was prepared to withdraw its forces. By April 1988, a United Nations (UN) mediated agreement was reached. The settlement, known as the Geneva Accords, included provisions for the withdrawal of Soviet troops, slated to begin on May 15, 1988 and end on February 15, 1989.

Moscow abided by the withdrawal timetable, but the war was not yet over. While agreeing to serve as "guarantors" of the Accords, the American and Soviet sides failed to reach agreement on "negative symmetry"—the mutual cessation of arms supplies to the domestic combatants. The US and Pakistan had demanded that Moscow terminate all forms of military aid to the Kabul regime upon withdrawal; the Soviets rejected this idea. In response, the US and Pakistan claimed the right to continue to supply the insurgency as long as the Soviets supplied Kabul. Accordingly, competitive intervention continued to afflict the Afghan conflict, with the PDPA regime proving itself capable of retaining control of Kabul even in the absence of Soviet troops.

---

[32] As quoted in Girardet (1984).
[33] Russian General Staff (2002: 26).

It would take an exogenous shock—an attempted coup in the Soviet Union in August 1991—to bring the competitive intervention to an end. As the Soviet Union disintegrated from within, Moscow and Washington finally agreed to "negative symmetry," pledging to mutually terminate aid to their domestic clients by the end of 1991. Pakistan, however, was not party to the agreement. The Najibullah regime was doomed, as the military balance swung decisively in the mujahideen's favor. On April 16, 1992, Kabul fell.

Figure 6.2 provides a visual overview of the relationships between the primary domestic combatants and competitive interveners relevant to the analysis that follows. While the war saw the participation of a number of different third-party states, I limit my analysis to the major players in the Afghan conflict: in the domestic realm, the communist PDPA government and the mujahideen insurgents;[34] and in the international realm, the Soviet Union, Pakistan, and the United States.[35] While limiting the analysis to these primary actors may risk

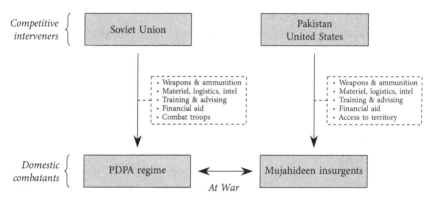

Figure 6.2 Relationships between primary domestic combatants and competitive interveners during the Afghan civil war, 1979–1992.

---

[34] Here I include the many Sunni mujahideen parties that composed the majority of the insurgency in Afghanistan, but exclude the Hazara Shiite mujahideen parties. The Hazaras did not possess the logistical capacity or the military supplies to wage sustained operations, and for their part, communist forces were by and large content to allow the Hazaras to remain isolated and autonomous during the war.

[35] Many states played a secondary role in the Afghan conflict, mainly by selling or donating weapons and equipment. Included on this list are Britain, China, Egypt, and Israel. Saudi Arabia was an important funder of the mujahideen, matching US contributions in cash, but it did not play an operational role. As Prince Turki put it, "[w]e don't do operations. We don't know how. All we know how to do is write checks" (as quoted in Coll 2005: 72). Finally, another state excluded in the analysis below is Iran. Sharing a 900-kilometer long border with Afghanistan, it was impossible for Iran to avoid the war entirely. However, the Iranian role was relatively limited for three reasons: first, the Afghan–Iranian border areas are dominated by open terrain, which made it difficult for rebels to find shelter; second, the Iran–Iraq War held most of Iran's attention during the Afghan conflict; and third, the majority of Iranian military aid went to the Hazara Shiite resistance that played a relatively minor role in the conflict. On Iran's limited role, see Defense Intelligence Agency (n.d.: 18–19).

oversimplification, it is necessary to render the case tractable. Moreover, no generality is lost: the case is examined from the perspective of those who had the most to gain—and the most to lose—during the war.

Strategic Restraint During Competitive Intervention in the Afghan Civil War

From 1979 to 1992, the Soviet Union, the US, and Pakistan spent tens of billions of dollars in an attempt to influence the outcome of the Afghan civil war. For the Soviets, the costs proved even greater, including some 13,833 dead, 49,985 wounded, and 311 missing in action.[36] Clearly, the battle for Afghanistan's future was significant for all sides. It is for this reason that the protracted nature of the conflict is perplexing. Given the stakes of the war and the high costs of fighting, why would the interveners continue to invest in the conflict at a level that resulted in a painful and persistent stalemate?

In accordance with theoretical expectations, this section demonstrates that escalatory risks conditioned the scope of intervener support for the domestic combatants in ways that prolonged the civil war. While the interveners had important national interests at stake in the conflict, they found themselves ensnared by the escalation dilemma that distinguishes competitive intervention from other configurations of external support. In what follows, I explain how they navigated this dilemma, highlighting the form and function of strategic restraint during the Afghan conflict.

Geography, Borders, and Conflict Containment

One of the most striking features of the Afghan case is that while Soviet leaders set essentially no restrictions on the application of military force within the borders of Afghanistan, they carefully calibrated their military presence along the Afghanistan–Pakistan border. Their restraint in this regard is especially notable given the critical role that Pakistani sanctuary and support played in the mujahideen's war effort. Indeed, it was Pakistan that served as the conduit for almost all of the mujahideen's military supplies; that administered the refugee camps that served as the guerrillas' primary recruitment pools; and that provided the safe haven behind which tens of thousands of resistance

---

[36] These are the official Russian figures. See Russian General Staff (2002: 309). There is some variation in estimates across sources. Braithwaite (2011: 140–143), for example, estimates 14,427 Soviet fatalities.

fighters could rest, recover, and refit for operations. In short, terminating the mujahideen's sanctuary in Pakistan was a necessary prerequisite for victory, yet Soviet forces avoided actions that meaningfully threatened Pakistani territory. Why?

As is often the case during competitive intervention, it was escalation concerns that hamstrung Moscow's military objectives. To terminate the mujahideen's safe haven would have required sending Soviet ground forces into Pakistan, risking a military response from Islamabad. Soviet military strength dwarfed that of Pakistan's, but the possibility of confrontation worried Soviet leaders on two fronts: first, it would mean a significant expansion of their war effort, as the civil war in Afghanistan became a regional war in South Asia; and second, the onset of a regional war risked a global confrontation with Washington given the existence of a US–Pakistan mutual security agreement. While vague on details, the 1959 US–Pakistan Agreement of Cooperation required Washington "to take such action, including the use of armed forces," in the event that Islamabad came under attack by communist troops.[37] The impossible stakes of direct clashes between American and Soviet forces, however remote, were simply too great for Moscow to consider attacking Pakistan. To avoid inadvertent escalation, Soviet troops would have to stay on the Afghan side of the border.

To ensure stability in the border regions, and to avoid accidental Soviet–Pakistani skirmishes, Moscow established a simple rule for its commanders: no combat operations could take place within five kilometers of the border without explicit permission from Soviet military leadership.[38] Offensive raids into Pakistan were forbidden, as were "hot pursuit" operations over the Afghanistan–Pakistan border. These geographic limits were strictly enforced, and cross-border adventures were punished by the high command.[39]

---

[37] For the full text of the agreement, see "Agreement of Cooperation Between the Government of the United States of America and the Government of Pakistan" (1959). The section quoted above continues, "as may be mutually agreed upon, and as envisaged in the Joint Resolution to Promote Peace and Stability in the Middle East." Section 2 of the Joint Resolution to which the agreement refers limits the US defense commitment to assisting "nations requesting assistance against armed aggression from any country controlled by international Communism." This was a not-too-subtle qualifier that ensured the US would not need to come to Pakistan's defense in the event of an India–Pakistan war.

[38] Grau and Jalali (2005: 661). Also see Kozlov (1997), Grau (2004: 142, 149), and Kalinovsky (2011: 44).

[39] There is evidence of at least one border violation by the 15th Spetsnaz Brigade under the command of Lieutenant Colonel Babushkin, which during an operation against a mujahideen logistics base in Krer, Afghanistan, crossed the border into Pakistan. This "forbidden cross-border vendetta," as Grau and Jalali describe it, had not been approved by the high command. When parts of the brigade became pinned down by mujahideen fire, Babushkin was forced to request gunship and medevac support, thereby disclosing his location. Upon learning of the incident, the Soviet military leadership was furious. Following an investigation by the KGB and a formal inquiry, Babushkin was found guilty, relieved of his command, and sent back to the Soviet Union. For a full account of this incident, see Grau and Jalali (2005).

To maintain pressure on Islamabad, an exception was made for Soviet and Afghan aircraft operating in the border regions—I discuss this exception in the following subsection. But for the tens of thousands of ground forces fighting in the war, combat was restricted to the Afghan side of the border.

The tactical consequences of the Soviet border rules cannot be overemphasized. As Charles Cogan, the former chief of the Near East and South Asia Division of the CIA's Directorate of Operations puts it, "[t]he Pakistani border constituted a sort of psychological Yalu River, behind which the resistance could regroup in relatively safe haven."[40] Forbidden from eliminating the mujahideen's base infrastructure at its source, Soviet troops were forced to try to seal the 2,250-kilometer border to prevent military supplies from flowing into Afghanistan. Given their woefully inadequate numbers and the border region's rough, mountainous terrain, this was an impossible task—and the Soviet military leadership knew it. During a Politburo meeting on November 13, 1986, Foreign Minister Gromyko complained that "[t]oo long ago we spoke on the fact that it is necessary to close off the border of Afghanistan with Pakistan and Iran. Experience has shown that we were unable to do this in view of the difficult terrain of the area and the existence of hundreds of passes in the mountains." Viktor Chebrikov, then the chief of the KGB, agreed that Gromyko was "partly right," but argued that "the failure in the closing is also tied to the fact that not everything was done that could have been." The chief of the general staff of the Soviet Armed Forces, Marshal Sergei Akhromeyev, concurred: "[fifty-thousand] Soviet soldiers are stationed to close off all passages where cargo is transferred across the border. [...] [W]e can maintain the situation at the current level, but we need to look for a way out and resolve the question [...] We must go to Pakistan."[41]

US policymakers understood that escalation fears constrained the Soviet Army's geographic areas of operation and tactical efficiency. In a cable to US Secretary of State George Shultz, sent in June 1981, the American Embassy in Kabul noted that "none of the previous Soviet approaches [to dealing with the mujahideen] have worked," and that the Soviets might employ stronger measures against Pakistan, such as "cross-border raids or mini-invasion." But it concluded that embassy officials "continue to doubt that the Soviets wish to risk a major confrontation with the US at this moment, no matter how tempting it might be to blast the mujahideen out of the Parachinar Salient."[42] The CIA likewise observed the Soviets' inability to close the Afghan–Pakistani border, and it too raised the possibility of increased Soviet pressure on Islamabad—including

---

[40] Cogan (1993: 79).
[41] "Meeting of the Politburo of the Central Committee of the Communist Party of the Soviet Union" (November 13, 1986).
[42] "Cable from American Embassy Kabul to Secretary of State" (June 1, 1981: para 8–9).

cross-border operations and the seizure of Pakistani territory. But the agency also concluded that "the Soviets would probably try to control the escalation by limiting their attacks to insurgent bases and supply lines, not striking deeply into Pakistan, and trying to avoid clashes with the Pakistan Army that could trigger a larger conflict and provoke sharp international censure."[43] In another report, the agency assessed that Moscow was unwilling "to face the military risks and political consequences of a significant expansion of hostilities into Pakistan or Iran. [...] We believe, therefore, that the Soviets will continue for at least the next year or so to try to make progress against the insurgents without a major expansion of their forces or of the geographic scope of the war."[44]

Notwithstanding the confidence of American officials, Islamabad remained deeply afraid of the possibility of deeper Soviet incursions. As the former head of the ISI's Afghan Bureau, Brigadier (ret.) Mohammed Yousaf explains:

> As a soldier, I find it hard to believe that the Soviet High Command was not putting powerful pressure on their political leaders to allow them to strike at Pakistan. [...] The Soviet Union, however, held back from any serious escalation. I had to ensure that we did not provoke them sufficiently to do so. A war with the Soviets would have been the end of Pakistan and could have unleashed a world war. It was a great responsibility, and one which I had to keep constantly in mind during those years.[45]

For his part, Zia insisted that Pakistan had "to be careful" and could not allow the conflict to become a "free-for-all."[46] He repeatedly stressed that "[t]he water in Afghanistan must boil at the right temperature"—a metaphor that succinctly captured his concern about conflict spillover.[47] While he was willing to support the opposition against the Soviets, it was critical that the mujahideen avoid provocative actions that could cause the pot to "boil over" into Pakistan.

One type of provocative action that went beyond the pale was an attack on Soviet soil. Indeed, the importance attached to geographically bounding the Afghan conflict stands out clearly in American and Pakistani responses to mujahideen attacks inside Soviet territory in April 1987. That month, three ISI-equipped teams of mujahideen slipped across the Amu Darya river into the Soviet Union. The first crept toward an airfield near Termez in Uzbekistan and, upon getting within range of their target, launched a barrage of rockets; the second ambushed a Soviet convoy along a border road; and the third attacked an

---

[43] CIA (July 1982: 6). Also see Director of Central Intelligence (1984: 8–9).
[44] CIA (March 1985: 3).
[45] Yousaf and Adkin (1992: 49–50).
[46] "Cable from American Embassy Islamabad to Secretary of State" (November 29, 1984: para 4).
[47] As quoted in Yousaf (1991: 17).

industrial site some ten miles into Soviet territory. It remains unclear where the idea to run these operations came from. Yousaf claims it was pushed by former CIA Director William Casey.[48] However, Milton Bearden, a CIA field officer who served in Pakistan from 1986 to 1989, makes clear that the CIA had no involvement in the planning and execution of the attacks; he also absolves Casey of authorizing the operations.[49] Moreover, at the time of the attack, Casey had already stepped down as director of the CIA, forced to resign in January 1987 due to the growth of a brain tumor. And while it is true that the US sanctioned cross-border propaganda operations beginning in late 1984, distributing Korans translated into local dialects in Soviet Central Republics, attacks on Soviet soil not only risked massive escalation, they were also prohibited by American law.[50] That the CIA gave the ISI extensive satellite reconnaissance on Soviet targets inside Afghanistan but refused to provide satellite photos of the Soviet Union itself also casts doubt on Yousaf's claims.[51]

Regardless of whether the attacks were the product of miscommunication between the CIA and ISI, or the independent initiative of Yousaf and the mujahideen, the cross-border operations generated an immediate response from Washington and Islamabad. The Americans stressed to their Soviet counterparts that they had never sanctioned military attacks on Soviet soil and demanded that their Pakistani partners end the attacks. "Please don't start a third world war by conducting these operations inside Soviet territory," Bearden told Yousaf.[52] The Pakistanis also panicked, with Zia ordering an end to all such operations at once. That same month, Yousaf was passed over for a promotion to major general; he would "retire" shortly thereafter.[53] In his own

---

[48] Yousaf and Adkin (1992: 189).
[49] Bearden and Risen (2003: 282–289).
[50] The Koran initiative was an extension of an ongoing propaganda campaign inside Afghanistan. In the mid-1980s, the United States Agency for International Development (USAID) funded a University of Nebraska at Omaha project that printed explicitly violent textbooks for elementary school students in Afghanistan. Printed in Dari and Pashtu, these textbooks sought to foment Islamic militancy and resistance to the Soviet occupation. In one third-grade mathematics textbook, for example, children were presented with the following subtraction problem: "One group of mujahideen attack 50 Russian soldiers. In that attack 20 Russians were killed. How many Russians fled?" In a fourth-grade mathematics textbook, children were asked: "The speed of a Kalashnikov bullet is 800 meters per second. If a Russian is at a distance of 3,200 meters from a mujahid, and that mujahid aims at the Russian's head, calculate how many seconds it will take for the bullet to strike the Russian in the forehead." Staff were aware of this violent content, but chose to ignore it. As one USAID official later put it, "I think we were perfectly happy to see these books trashing the Soviet Union" (as quoted in Stephens and Ottaway 2002). For a discussion and further examples of the violent content in these textbooks, see Davis (2002: 92–93).
[51] Coll (1992a: A24).
[52] As quoted in Yousaf and Adkin (1992: 206).
[53] Yousaf and Adkin (1992: 211–212). Yousaf claims he had "long before decided to retire if not promoted," suggesting that his decision to leave the ISI was voluntary. Whether the timing of his "early retirement" was coincidental or not remains unclear, however. Also see Bearden and Risen (2003: 289).

reflections, Yousaf acknowledges that the attacks "caused the water temperature to come perilously close to boiling. [...] There was, for a short while, a real fear among the politicians that the Soviet Union and Pakistan might go to war. It was a dangerous game."[54]

These responses underscore the importance attached to the geographic limits that contained fighting within Afghanistan's borders. To avoid enlarging the conflict into a regional war, the interveners imposed boundaries on operations both for their own troops and for their domestic clients—even when doing so undermined tactical efficiency.

Deployment Patterns and Force Postures: Avoiding Engagements and Communicating Restraint

In addition to observing geographic limits, the competitive interveners also communicated restraint by adopting defensive force postures. This manifested as limits imposed on the size and orientation of Soviet and Pakistani forces, as well as highly restrictive rules of engagement that were explicitly designed to avoid confrontations along the Afghanistan–Pakistan border.

Consider first the limited nature of the Soviet ground force in Afghanistan, and the signals it provided to the opposing interveners. Given the weakness of the Kabul regime, Moscow accepted that it was impossible to keep Soviet soldiers out of the fight. But as they took on combat duties, limits had to be found to communicate restraint. To those ends, operations involving the participation of Soviet troops were carefully calibrated and controlled, with strong top-down command and clear signaling of intentions. Isby notes that between 1980 and 1983, "the war ran at a very deliberate pace. All but urgent calls for air strikes had to go through Kabul, leading to at least a one-day wait. Ground units responded even more slowly, and all movements were well advertised in advance."[55] From 1984 onward, regional commands could order tactical ground force actions, but the slow tempo and telegraphing of the Soviet Army's movements persisted throughout the war.

Moscow also restricted the size of its deployment and the infrastructure that supported it. As one internal assessment prepared by the US Army observes, "the Kremlin obviously imposed limitations on the size of the Soviet force deployment. [...] The Soviet name for their forces in Afghanistan, 'Limited Contingent', was as real as it was propagandistic."[56] At its peak, the 40th Army never exceeded 108,800 personnel (or roughly 2% of the total available troops of the Soviet

---

[54] Yousaf and Adkin (1992: 189–190).
[55] Isby (1988: 80).
[56] US Army (1989: 2).

military).⁵⁷ The majority of these troops were assigned to defensive positions in cities, on airfields, and along logistical lines. Less than a third were available for offensive combat.⁵⁸ As Yousaf explains, Soviet force dispositions "indicated a mainly static, defensive posture."⁵⁹

The tactical inefficiency of the limited Soviet deployment was self-evident to Moscow. As Kalinovsky explains, "it was obvious that there were often not enough troops to carry out the 'hold' part of their clear-and-hold strategy."⁶⁰ But as is common during competitive intervention, escalation concerns dominated Soviet decision-making. As former KGB officer Vladimir Kuzichkin recalls, "[w]hen we began to get bogged down, of course, the army argued for more troops. The Soviet general staff wanted at least twice as many—to seal off the frontier with Pakistan and get better control along the border with Iran. But the Politburo ruled that out. By then, it feared provoking a serious Western reaction."⁶¹ A surge of Soviet troops risked a reciprocal escalation in American and Pakistani participation in the war. Consequently, troop levels remained capped at 108,800 personnel—strategic stability trumped tactical advantage.

The restricted size and defensive force posture of Soviet ground forces served as a credible signal of restraint for Moscow's rivals in Washington and Islamabad. Yousaf recalls seeing "no evidence that [the Soviets] wished to escalate the war in terms of numbers."⁶² The US intelligence community reflected on a similar point in a number of assessments throughout the war. For example, a Special National Intelligence Estimate prepared in 1984 put the probability of Soviet air strikes or hot-pursuit actions along the Afghan–Pakistani border at 40%. But given that a large-scale operation against Pakistan would require "new deployments and some weeks of preparation," it concluded that a major Soviet attack was "very unlikely," assigning a probability of just 5%.⁶³ In another report prepared the following year, the CIA again noted that large-scale operations against Pakistan would require "[m]ajor improvements in air and logistical facilities and the deployment of additional forces." Undertaking such preparations "would provide more warning of an impending attack."⁶⁴ The agency was confident that it could detect a Soviet decision to escalate, highlighting that it was "very likely

---

⁵⁷ This is the official figure reported in Russian General Staff (2002: 26). Other sources estimate slightly higher numbers. Westad (2007: 357), for example, estimates an upper bound of 120,000 troops.
⁵⁸ Grau (2007: 247, 250). Note that this figure relates to the composition of Soviet forces prior to the start of their withdrawal from Afghanistan in 1988. The number of battalions available for offensive combat decreased significantly as the withdrawal unfolded.
⁵⁹ Yousaf and Adkin (1992: 48).
⁶⁰ Kalinovsky (2011: 44).
⁶¹ Kuzichkin (1982: 34).
⁶² Yousaf and Adkin (1992: 48).
⁶³ Director of Central Intelligence (1984: 13).
⁶⁴ CIA (April 1985: 4, 23); also see CIA (October 1983: 18).

to see the military and logistic moves to implement such a decision well before they effectively changed the scope of the war or seriously increased the threat to Pakistan."[65]

Defensive force postures were also adopted by the Soviets in the skies above the Afghan–Pakistani border. As noted above, an important exception to the geographic limits observed by the interveners was the use of air strikes by Afghan and Soviet aircraft within the border regions of Pakistan. In their efforts to stem the tide of men and war materiel crossing the border, communist aircraft violated Pakistani airspace and conducted bombing raids on Pakistani territory. Importantly, however, these incursions were limited in terms of their targets and their geographic depth. As an official history prepared by the Pakistani Air Staff explains, "[t]he employment of air power by the Soviets was limited to hit and run raids against undefended and exposed targets in the border belt." Afghan and Soviet aircraft would fly parallel to the Afghan–Pakistani border, darting across only a few miles to bomb mujahideen convoys and base camps before returning to Afghan airspace. Because Pakistan Air Force (PAF) fighter aircraft were committed only in the event of an actual ingress, this in-and-out air strike strategy ensured an "impossibly short reaction time for any effective interception." Even when air incursions did establish contact with PAF fighters—sometimes within visual range—Soviet and Afghan pilots would not challenge Pakistani aircraft. As the Air Staff describes, "[t]he moment the enemy intruders noted that the PAF aircraft had been committed, they would turn around and exit."[66]

For their part, the Pakistanis responded to Soviet reticence by signaling their own defensive intentions. While Islamabad warned Moscow and Kabul of its intention to defend its borders, it undermined this rhetoric by demonstrating a firm determination to avoid direct clashes. As the CIA observed, "[t]he Pakistanis *could* inflict serious losses on small Soviet or Afghan forces operating in the border region in chance encounters or if there were time enough to use their better knowledge of the terrain to set up ambushes, but it is clear [redacted] Islamabad fears such clashes would provoke a large Soviet response."[67] Rather than attempt to deter Soviet border violations with a forward defense, Pakistan settled for a more careful approach. As Air Commodore (ret.) A. Hameed Qadri explains, "[t]he dictates of defense policy required adaptation of a defensive posture, and exercise of restraint."[68]

---

[65] CIA (January 1986: 11).
[66] Pakistan Air Force (2000: 37, 41, 59). The PAF did lose one F-16 during the war, but this was a friendly fire incident that occurred in April 1987.
[67] CIA (July 1982: 7). Emphasis added.
[68] Qadri (1998).

The PAF, for example, adopted an explicitly defensive force posture with highly restrictive rules of engagement. PAF pilots were not permitted to engage in "hot pursuit" of Soviet–Afghan aircraft and were forbidden from entering Afghan airspace. Qadri recalls that PAF pilots "were specifically instructed to avoid engagements."[69] Indeed, as the Air Staff explains, "[t]he PAF was under orders to use all the means it could to avert an intensified air war directly with the Soviet air power. That was a distinct possibility and if it had materialized, Pakistan's Afghan war policy would have suffered a serious setback. [...] [T]he overriding political consideration was that the PAF involvement should be kept to a minimum. Pakistan did not wish to escalate this conflict."[70]

Higher commands carefully monitored the progress of interceptions and watched nervously as PAF fighters approached enemy aircraft. As Qadri relates, "[s]uch was the caution exercised by the higher command that almost everyone who mattered monitored the progress of interceptions from Section Operations Centre and Northern Air Command Headquarters. It almost amounted to breathing down the necks of our controllers by the senior staff, which restricted the freedom of combat controllers. [...] As the [Combat Air Patrols] were maintained in depth with strict instructions to avoid engagement, the whole exercise was one of extreme frustration for the controllers and pilots."[71]

The caution of the higher command is confirmed by some basic data on the frequency and intensity of PAF combat air patrols (see Table 6.1). Over the course of the Soviet intervention in Afghanistan, the PAF recorded some 2,476 air violations involving 7,589 enemy aircraft. In response, PAF squadrons committed to the defense of Pakistan's western airspace flew 10,939 sorties and logged 13,275 flying hours. And yet, despite the high number of airspace violations and the high intensity of PAF combat air patrols, only *eight* intruding aircraft—one-tenth of 1% of all recorded violators—were ever shot down.[72] To put this figure in context, consider that in 1987 the CIA estimated Soviet *peacetime training* attrition to be seventy tactical aircraft *per year*.[73]

The restrictive rules of engagement imposed by the senior Pakistani leadership negatively affected the morale of PAF pilots. Pakistani air crews watched with frustration as Afghan and Soviet aircraft bombed border targets within Pakistani territory while their own rules of engagement prevented them from retaliating. As the Air Staff relates, "[a] fleeting encounter with the enemy would

---

[69] Qadri (1998).
[70] Pakistan Air Force (2000: 62–63).
[71] Qadri (1998).
[72] An account of each confrontation is provided in Pakistan Air Force (2000: 44–55). It remains unclear what the mix of downed Afghan versus Soviet piloted planes was during the war. At least one Soviet and three Afghan pilots were shot down. The nationalities of the other four are unknown.
[73] CIA (February 1987b: 7).

Table 6.1 Pakistan Air Force air defense effort during the Afghan civil war. Data from Pakistan Air Force (2000: 70).

Squadron	Sorties	Hours
9 SQN	2,221	3,701:40
14 SQN	1,825	2,585:20
26 SQN	2,479	2,394:25
15 SQN	2,521	2,142:10
11 SQN	346	896:15
17 SQN	628	824:05
23 SQN	737	563:50
5 SQN	108	141:30
18 SQN	20	27:25
Total	**10,939**	**13,275:40**

soon lead to utter despair when the enemy aircraft, after dropping their ordnance on mujahideen camps, would cross over leisurely to the other side. This adversely affected the squadron pilots' spirits. Day and night they were engaged in what they thought was a largely fruitless activity, severely constrained as it was by the [rules of engagement]."[74] The Pakistani media also harshly criticized the PAF's failure to challenge airspace violations, putting "tremendous pressure on PAF personnel."[75]

Nonetheless, the higher command remained committed to its strategy of exercising restraint and avoiding escalation. At the tactical level, strict rules of engagement would continue to limit the freedom of pilots and combat controllers. As the Air Staff explains, Pakistan "did not wish to escalate the Afghan conflict under any circumstances. Doing anything else would have been strategically counterproductive."[76]

Weapons, Military Aid, and Fears of Escalation

By observing geographic limits, adopting defensive force postures, and imposing restrictive rules of engagement, the interveners successfully avoided direct clashes between their military forces. But for Pakistan and the US, an additional dilemma complicated participation in the war: to keep the pot "boiling,"

[74] Pakistan Air Force (2000: 39).
[75] Qadri (1998).
[76] Pakistan Air Force (2000: 58).

the mujahideen required weapons and other war materiel; yet, to prevent the pot from "boiling over," the scope of their support needed careful calibration.[77] National Security Council (NSC) memos and intelligence assessments warned that Pakistan's role in the covert aid program risked Soviet retaliation.[78] How could Islamabad and Washington effectively assist the mujahideen while at the same time manage escalation?

Zia struck on a solution: escalation risks could be managed by exploiting the qualitative characteristics that distinguish different weapon systems. All weapons flowing to the mujahideen, he argued, should be "battlefield credible"— that is, plausibly captured on the Afghan battlefield. As former US Congressman Clarence Long explains, "[i]f it was American made, the Soviets would trace it to Pakistan and [Zia] didn't want that. He suggested we get foreign-made guns."[79] If the weapons used by the mujahideen were battlefield credible, Pakistani and American officials could plausibly deny supplying them. This served a critical function: "it gave Soviet leaders face-saving space to continue to abstain from retaliation."[80]

The battlefield credible distinction suited the Americans. CIA Deputy Director John McMahon worried about the implications of American-made weapons killing Soviet soldiers in Afghanistan. There was a risk, he argued, of provoking Soviet retaliation.[81] US officials understood that the aid program "could not be so provocative, or so blatant, as to invite a major Soviet reaction against Pakistan."[82] Indeed, Fred Iklé, who served as the undersecretary of defense for policy, recalls that "the danger of such a Soviet escalation was carefully considered by those of us in Washington who dealt with American aid for the Afghan resistance fighters."[83] Accordingly, CIA operators were instructed to abide by the battlefield credible distinction. To those ends, they began to purchase weapons from states with access to Soviet-model armaments, including Egypt (a former Soviet client), Israel (which possessed stockpiles of Soviet weapons captured from Arab armies), and China (a former Soviet ally and beneficiary of Soviet military aid). When it was discovered that there was insufficient supply available

---

[77] In a memo to US Secretary of State George Shultz, Under Secretary of State for Political Affairs Lawrence Eagleburger makes explicit reference to this idea: "the problem is to keep the pot boiling without having it boil over." See "Memorandum from Lawrence Eagleburger to George Shultz" (November 24, 1982: 2).

[78] See, for example, "Memorandum from Thomas Thornton to Zbigniew Brzezinski" (September 24, 1979: 2); CIA (January 1980: 3–4).

[79] As quoted in Woodward and Babcock (1985).

[80] Carson (2018: 268).

[81] Ottaway (1986). McMahon allegedly told US Senator Malcolm Wallop that the military aid program could not be "too successful."

[82] Cogan (1993: 80).

[83] Iklé (2005: 134, note 6).

for purchase, the CIA also began producing large quantities of Soviet-model weapons in Egyptian ordinance factories.[84]

The battlefield credible rule remained in place without contestation from 1980 to 1983, with the arms provided to the mujahideen restricted to relatively low-technology weapons such as rifles, mines, grenade launchers, and light antiaircraft weapons.[85] By the mid-1980s, however, it was becoming increasingly clear that more would have to be done to assist the insurgency. Pro-government forces had adjusted their tactics and began to more successfully exploit their dominance of the skies. Gunships with armored underbellies attacked mujahideen positions with near-impunity, while helicopter-borne Spetsnaz teams began taking the war to the remote valleys and mountain peaks where the mujahideen had established base camps. Reeling from this military pressure, mujahideen commanders began requesting increased aid—especially more effective air defense weapons—in August 1983.[86]

Fearful that the insurgency was at risk of defeat, voices inside and outside of Washington began lobbying the Reagan administration to meet the mujahideen's requests. Initially, these efforts focused on the provision of American-made Redeye or Stinger ground-to-air missiles. However, the CIA blocked both weapons on no uncertain terms—they clearly violated the battlefield credible rule and could be easily traced back to Washington.[87] A third option, the British-made Blowpipe, was suggested as a plausibly deniable alternative. However, the weapon was tactically suboptimal: it had a terrible performance record and it required operators to manually guide a missile onto a target, leaving them vulnerable to counterattack. This left a fourth option: the Swiss-made Oerlikon cannon. Like the Blowpipe, it presented a plausibly deniable alternative, but it too was tactically disadvantageous: the gun weighed hundreds of pounds, requiring multiple mules to transport it over Afghanistan's rough, mountainous terrain; it was also an expensive option, with unit costs of $1 million per gun and shells running $50 each.[88] As the then-CIA station chief in Islamabad, Howard Hart, put it, the selection of the Oerlikon was "tactically stupid."[89] Nonetheless, congressional supporters of the mujahideen persevered, and beginning in the summer of 1984, the CIA relented to a limited test of the Oerlikon in Afghanistan. As predicted, it had little effect on the battlefield, and over the course of 1984, the plight of the mujahideen worsened.

Meanwhile, the CIA continued to express concern about Soviet retaliation against Pakistan. In October 1984, the agency requested that a Senate resolution

---

[84] Cordovez and Harrison (1995: 68–69).
[85] Lundberg (2008: 28–29).
[86] Kuperman (1999: 222).
[87] Woodward and Babcock (1985).
[88] Yousaf and Adkin (1992: 87).
[89] As quoted in Whittle and Kuempel (1997).

demanding further aid to the mujahideen amend its calls for "material assistance" to the lesser pledge of "effective support."[90] That same month, Deputy Director for Intelligence Robert Gates penned a classified memo that warned that "the Soviets are likely to learn about [American aid increases] through leaks [...] What impact will this have on the Soviets as they consider their options? [...] Sharp and steady increases [in insurgent activity] over a period of two years, month to month, would suggest that more of the same is not enough and that the Soviets would have to consider more seriously more dramatic action."[91] The Pentagon also remained worried about Soviet retaliation. According to Iklé, officials worried that "one million Soviet troops" might march on Pakistan.[92]

Notwithstanding these fears, in the spring of 1985 the Reagan administration began to reassess its strategy. The Soviets had slowly increased the number of Spetznaz deployed to Afghanistan and had continued to pacify the mujahideen's rural support network. Cut off from local support and pressed in the remote valleys and mountainous terrain where their base camps were located, the insurgents' military outlook looked increasingly grim. Intelligence reports from agents recruited in the Soviet Defense Ministry warned that Soviet hard-liners were pushing to attempt to "win" the war within two years.[93] American officials increasingly feared that a sharp escalation by the Soviets would put the continued viability of the mujahideen at risk. In March 1985, the Reagan administration responded by signing NSDD-166, which augmented US aid to the mujahideen.

In the existing literature, NSDD-166 has been pointed to as a watershed document that shifted US objectives in Afghanistan, setting the foundation for significant American escalation of the war. Mendelson, for example, writes that with the signing of NSDD-166, "US policy goals shifted from harassment to defeat of the Soviets."[94] Garthoff writes that NSDD-166 "[set] the objective of driving the Soviet forces out of Afghanistan."[95] Hershberg writes that, with the approval of the directive, "Washington escalated its objectives [...] seeking to achieve a military victory that would drive [the Soviets] out."[96] And Maley, quoting a phrase that is commonly recited in the literature, writes that the directive "approved the use of 'all means available' to remove Soviet forces from

---

[90] Lundberg (2008: 37).
[91] Gates (1984: 1–2).
[92] As quoted in Kuperman (1999: 223).
[93] Schweizer (1994: 212–213); Mendelson (1998: 97). These intelligence reports were erroneous. As Kalinovsky (2011: 87) points out, no Soviet sources support their conclusions. Nonetheless, the intelligence likely weighed on US decision-makers.
[94] Mendelson (1998: 69).
[95] Garthoff (1994: 712).
[96] Hershberg (2003: 27).

Afghanistan."⁹⁷ Numerous other examples of this characterization of NSDD-166 can be found.⁹⁸

Prior to its declassification, however, the top secret directive remained shrouded in secrecy. Consequently, researchers were compelled to rely on journalistic accounts that drew on interviews with former US policymakers to glean details about its contents, most of whom framed the directive as aggressive and escalatory. For example, it was in one of the first reports on NSDD-166 that *The New York Times* reporter Leslie Gelb—citing administration officials—claimed that the directive authorized "all means available" to get the Soviets out of Afghanistan.⁹⁹ Subsequent reporting by *The Washington Post* correspondent Steve Coll crystallized perceptions of NSDD-166 as a critical juncture in US policy and objectives in Afghanistan.¹⁰⁰

The declassification of NSDD-166 provides an opportunity to reassess these claims. An examination of the original document reveals that the phrase "all means available" does *not* appear in NSDD-166. And while it is correct that the directive calls for an improvement in the military effectiveness of the Afghan resistance, there is no discussion of a need to send high-technology, US-made equipment. The directive does note that the "ultimate goal" of US policy "is the removal of Soviet forces from Afghanistan and the restoration of its independent status."¹⁰¹ However, this was not new: Soviet withdrawal was *already* the stated objective of US policy in Afghanistan.¹⁰² It is also striking that NSDD-166 does not specify mujahideen victory as a US objective.¹⁰³ Instead, the document identifies a more limited goal: to "[p]revent the defeat of an indigenous movement which is resisting Soviet aggression."¹⁰⁴ In short, NSDD-166 was not the escalatory policy change many have interpreted it to be: the priority remained focused on avoiding defeat, rather than on ensuring victory.

---

⁹⁷ Maley (2021: 66).
⁹⁸ See, for example, Pear (1988), Ottaway (1989), Cordovez and Harrison (1995: 160), Kuperman (1999: 227), Coll (2005: 127), and Lundberg (2008: 40). Some of these authors also mistitle the directive as "Expanded US Aid to Afghan Guerrillas" (its actual title is "US Policy, Programs and Strategy in Afghanistan").
⁹⁹ Gelb (1986).
¹⁰⁰ Coll (1992a, 1992b). Coll's reporting is cited in discussions of NSDD-166 by a number of scholars, including Cogan (1993), Garthoff (1994), Mendelson (1998), Kuperman (1999), Hershberg (2003), and Lundberg (2008). Other scholars cite Coll's bestselling book, *Ghost Wars*, which itself draws on his earlier reporting. See, for example, Wilson (2008) and Carson (2018).
¹⁰¹ National Security Decision Directive 166 (1985: 1).
¹⁰² See National Security Decision Directive 75 (1983: 4), which preceded NSDD-166 by over two years.
¹⁰³ National Security Decision Directive 166 (1985: 1).
¹⁰⁴ National Security Decision Directive 166 (1985: 2). Emphasis added. The concluding sentence of the paragraph from which this quotation is drawn repeats this language: "[i]t is vital that such indigenous resistance movements *not be defeated* by Soviet counterinsurgency efforts" (emphasis added).

That is not to say there was no adjustment to US policy—the dollar value of US aid rose from $122 million in 1984 to $250 million in 1985.[105] But officials in Washington and Islamabad remained unwilling to violate self-imposed limits on the types of weapons provided to the mujahideen. By exploiting the qualitative characteristics of different weapon systems—namely, their "battlefield credibility"—the US and Pakistan could continue to back the Afghan opposition while simultaneously controlling escalation vis-à-vis the Soviet Union.

The Stinger and Escalation Control in Afghanistan

It was in March 1986—a full year *after* NSDD-166—that a landmark policy decision was made that deepened US and Pakistani participation in the Afghan civil war: for the first time, the mujahideen would be provisioned with high-technology, US-made Stinger antiaircraft missiles. This was a weapon that crossed the "battlefield credible" threshold that had been exploited to communicate restraint and control escalation since the start of the war. For that reason, it is important to investigate the factors that motivated its approval. The Stinger decision was an escalation—it was an action that crossed a threshold that determined the existing limits of the war—and in that regard it cuts against my argument that competitive interveners avoid escalating the scope of their support to domestic combatants in fear of reprisals from interstate opponents. However, as I elaborate below, approval of the Stinger cannot be separated from the dire military situation that confronted the mujahideen in early 1986. In this important respect, I argue, the Stinger was an effort to maintain balance on the battlefield—in particular, by countering the counterinsurgents' supremacy in the air.

As the war continued into 1985, the struggle facing the mujahideen looked increasingly grim. As Grau explains, by this time "[t]he [m]ujahideen were badly battered and close to breaking."[106] Lundberg agrees: "[i]t seemed possible the rebels would lose."[107] The Afghan Army had regained its composure, stepping up its participation in the conflict and taking the lead in frequent operations against mujahideen base areas. Soviet troop levels also reached their peak during this period, buoyed by an influx of additional Spetsnaz units and armored MI-24 Hind attack helicopters. Between April and June 1985, the Afghan Army, supported by Soviet aviation and artillery, undertook a series of ambitious offensives against resistance bases in the Kunar, Maidan, and Panjshir valleys.

---

[105] Roy (1991: 35); Lundberg (2008: 37).
[106] Grau (2004: 141).
[107] Lundberg (2008: 23).

In July, an offensive in Paktia province relieved the garrison of Khost and pushed to clear Zhawar, an important basing complex comprising a series of interconnected caves and tunnels on the Afghan–Pakistani border.[108]

As the opposition continued to lose ground, the Pakistani brass began to fear the Soviets might win in Afghanistan. Yousaf recalls that any strong offensive toward Zhawar "always produced squeals of alarm from both politicians and the military in Islamabad." With this latest push, "[t]he Soviet/Afghan forces had shown that their tactics and techniques were improving, they had been able to penetrate into areas long held to be inaccessible, and had they been able to close right up to the border and destroy our bases there, the entire campaign might have been put in jeopardy."[109] In September 1985, Pakistan's vice chief of army staff, General Mirza Aslam Beg, told an American delegation outright that he thought "the rebels were losing the war."[110] These views were also taking hold in American policy circles. Morton Abramowitz, the former director of the Bureau of Intelligence and Research at the US State Department, became "increasingly disturbed by evidence that the resistance was losing."[111] As former Secretary of State George Shultz explains in his memoirs, "Spetsnaz troops had hurt the mujahideen freedom fighters, and there had been no major victories for the Afghan resistance for months. [...] The Soviets seemed to be winning."[112]

The key to the counterinsurgents' success, it was widely understood, was their air superiority. As one report prepared for the US Army explained, the "substantial improvement" of the counterinsurgents' performance during the mid-1980s "occurred in a regimen of virtually complete Soviet dominance in the air." Indeed, the mujahideen had no meaningful defensive capacity to counter Afghan–Soviet gunships, vertical envelopments, and aerial assaults. "This dominance is of critical importance to effective counterinsurgency operations," the report continued, "since a significant majority of such missions depend on reliable air transportation and combat support."[113] Mujahideen commanders stressed their need for improved antiair weapons to counter Afghan–Soviet air power. Abramowitz recalls "a lot of complaints about helicopters."[114]

As pressure to respond to the counterinsurgents' air power increased, American proponents of the mujahideen—led by Iklé, his Coordinator for Afghan Affairs Michael Pillsbury, and Senator Orrin Hatch—once again returned to the subject of antiair weapons.[115] But this time they would not settle for second-class,

[108] Russian General Staff (2002: 26–27, 33); Braithwaite (2011: 214).
[109] Yousaf and Adkin (1992: 162, 164).
[110] Lundberg (2008: 67–68).
[111] Cordovez and Harrison (1995: 195–196).
[112] Shultz (1993: 691–692).
[113] Alexiev (1988: 33).
[114] As quoted in Lundberg (2008: 68).
[115] Cordovez and Harrison (1995: 194); Lundberg (2008: 23).

foreign-made arms. Citing the Afghan–Soviet advance on Zhawar as evidence to bolster their argument, the American policymakers were determined to earn approval for the US-made, state-of-the-art Stinger.[116]

From a tactical perspective, the Stinger was an obvious choice. First, it was an easy to use, "fire and forget" man-portable air defense system that fired an infrared homing surface-to-air missile. Second, it had a range of up to five miles and an effective ceiling of 10,000 feet, which compared very favorably to the two-mile range and 7,500-foot ceiling of the Soviet-made SA-7. Third, it weighed just 34.5 pounds, making it easy to carry in the mountainous Afghan terrain. And fourth, it was relatively cheap to produce at just $30,000 per unit.

However, from a strategic perspective, the provision of the Stinger made many US policymakers nervous. The intelligence community remained wary, with one official warning that "[w]hen this weapon gets in and if helicopters start getting shot out of the sky with regularity, we've got a problem. [...] A weapon like this could force the Soviets to become more indiscriminate in their use of force. They could begin much more bombing. It could change the equation radically."[117] Another administration official highlighted that "[o]ne of the important things is restraint and that includes restraint on our part [...] and restraint by the Soviet Union. You've got to consider what they haven't done to Pakistan and others. [...] Afghanistan is on their border, and you have to believe the Soviets could, if they chose, march in with sufficient troops to do the job."[118] Worryingly, political-military simulations run by the NSC suggested that the Soviets might escalate if large numbers of Stingers were sent into Afghanistan.[119]

Another issue was whether the Pakistanis would ever approve the Stinger. Zia had long opposed it, arguing that it contradicted the battlefield credible threshold.[120] It was Islamabad, after all, that faced the immediate threat of Soviet retaliation. Pillsbury and Iklé had first set out to get Zia's approval of the Stingers in May 1985, highlighting for the Pakistani leader that the mujahideen could not effectively operate in Afghanistan due to a lack of adequate antiair capabilities. Zia would not commit, however. "He hemmed and hawed," recalls Iklé, because "he was cautious at that point."[121] The next month, Pillsbury again visited Pakistan, this time accompanied by Hatch, for another meeting with Zia. During this visit, the Pakistani leader did agree to request the missiles from the

---

[116] Cordovez and Harrison (1995: 200).
[117] As quoted in Woodward and Babcock (1985).
[118] As quoted in Woodward and Babcock (1985).
[119] The details of these simulations remain largely classified, but see the available materials in Situation Support Staff, White House Office of Records, Box 1, IN-HIS 1-5 Afghanistan Game (1 and 2), Ronald Reagan Presidential Library and Archive.
[120] Yousaf and Adkin (1992: 181).
[121] As quoted in Cordovez and Harrison (1995: 195).

Reagan administration; however, it was understood that they were solely for use by Pakistani forces, not the mujahideen.[122]

Over time, however, military realities began chipping away at Zia's conviction to stick with the battlefield credible distinction. Soviet and Afghan government offensives had made 1985 the bloodiest year of the war. ISI officials were increasingly vocal in their calls for more effective aid for the mujahideen, especially antiaircraft weapons. This domestic pressure was matched by renewed external pressure in January 1986, when Pillsbury and Hatch made yet another visit to Pakistan. The US delegates, emphasizing the Stinger's military utility, stressed the "moral obligation" to supply it to the mujahideen.[123] Under this sustained pressure, Zia finally relented. It had become clear to the Pakistani leader that something had to be done to bolster the resistance. As Yousaf explains, "heavy fighting along the border with Pakistan [...] frightened everybody into forgetting the risks and giving us [the ISI] what we wanted."[124]

However, the American delegation still required CIA approval. Upon returning to the US, Hatch called Director Casey personally to brief him on Zia's decision, spurring Casey to call a meeting to discuss authorizing the weapon. During the meeting, the highly charged nature of the Stinger debate revealed itself once more when Thomas Twetten, the deputy chief of the CIA's Near East and South Asia Division, vetoed approval of the weapon. Discussion broke down and the meeting ended without consensus.[125] But under sustained pressure from Iklé, Pillsbury, and Hatch, the CIA eventually dropped its opposition to the Stinger, and in March 1986 the Reagan administration approved its distribution to the mujahideen. It would still be a number of months until the weapon appeared on the Afghan battlefield—it was first used on September 25, 1986—but the bureaucratic battle over the Stinger was over.

The Stinger decision crossed the "battlefield credible" threshold that had previously limited the scope of US and Pakistani support to the mujahideen. In this respect, it constitutes an escalatory action that runs contrary to this book's theoretical expectations. However, the decision to approve the Stinger cannot be divorced from the stark military realities that faced the mujahideen beginning in 1985. US and Pakistani policymakers worried that opposition forces were losing the war. Without the ability to counter air attacks, the insurgents could not meaningfully compete against Afghan–Soviet airborne counterinsurgency operations. In this regard, the decision to approve the Stinger was informed by the need to provision a defensive capability that would balance against the

---

[122] Cordovez and Harrison (1995: 195).
[123] Lundberg (2008: 76).
[124] Yousaf and Adkin (1992: 182).
[125] Kuperman (1999: 234).

counterinsurgents' air supremacy—indeed, proponents of the Stinger pointed to Afghan–Soviet advances as "evidence that the missiles were needed."[126]

It is also notable that quantitative and qualitative controls were still placed on the delivery of the Stinger following its approval. First, only 250 launchers and 1,000 missiles were provided.[127] These limits frustrated mujahideen commanders, such as Abdul Haq, who questioned the impact the Stinger could have on the war: "How could we stop all the Soviet aircraft because we have twenty-five or thirty Stingers? No, it is impossible."[128] Second, approval only extended to the FIM-92A variant (Stinger Basic), not the FIM-92B variant (Stinger POST)—this, despite the fact that the FIM-92A was known to struggle with countermeasures regularly employed by the Soviets, such as the use of flares, infrared beacons, and baffles on aircraft exhausts.[129] In effect, even as they crossed the battlefield credible threshold, US officials still put constraints on their support for the mujahideen.

Other Explanations

The empirical record largely conforms with the theory's proposed mechanisms at the international level. Evidence reveals that the competitive interveners constrained the scope of their support to the domestic combatants; that escalation concerns vis-à-vis opposing interveners motivated these choices; and that limits were constructed around thresholds that signaled restraint. The Stinger decision counts against the theory, though in an important sense it is the exception that proves the rule: the "battlefield credible" threshold limited arms supplies from 1980 to 1986; the decision to violate that threshold was made in the context of growing concern that the mujahideen would be defeated; the decision was met with rancorous debate, centered on escalation concerns, within the US and Pakistani governments; and even after approval was granted, significant constraints were placed on the provision of the weapons. Nevertheless, there may be lingering concerns that external support was curtailed for reasons other than escalation control. Hence, in this section, I address alternative explanations for the competitive interveners' strategic restraint.

First, it might be argued that logistical or resource constraints better explain the scope of support. This argument is unpersuasive. As great powers, the US

---

[126] Cordovez and Harrison (1995: 200). Also see Lundberg (2008: 38).
[127] Cordovez and Harrison (1995: 198).
[128] As quoted in Kemp (1988: 380).
[129] While the FIM-92A uses an infrared seeker, the FIM-92B uses a dual infrared/ultraviolet seeker, resulting in significantly higher resistance to enemy countermeasures, such as flares. See Kuperman (1999: 231, 248, and note 145). Isby (1990: 58) finds that "although none of the Soviets' countermeasures were totally successful, the Stinger [...] did not succeed in forcing Soviet helicopters out of the sky." Also see Braithwaite (2011: 205).

and Soviet Union possessed unparalleled power projection capabilities. Moreover, the Soviet commitment of combat forces was facilitated by a shared border with Afghanistan. Even at its peak, the "Limited Contingent" never exceeded 2% of the total available troops of the Soviet military.[130] Nor was the war a meaningful drain on the Soviet economy, as the CIA itself acknowledged.[131] And while US support to the mujahideen has been described as "the biggest bequest to any Third World insurgency," Washington's annual spending on the war never exceeded one-quarter of 1% of its annual military expenditure.[132] For its part, Pakistan shouldered little of the war's financial burden—all arms, equipment, and funding were provided by the US and Saudi Arabia—while its shared border with Afghanistan facilitated the provision of sanctuary, training, and logistical support to the mujahideen.[133] For all these reasons, claims that logistical constraints or resource limitations provide a more compelling explanation for the competitive interveners' strategic restraint are unconvincing; concerns about escalation played the crucial role.

Second, it might be posited that the competitive interveners' behaviors can be attributed to domestic pressure to restrict the scope of intervention. There is little evidence to support such claims. Indeed, during the war, both Washington and Moscow had to contend with *hawkish* domestic pressure—in the US, criticism from conservative, anticommunist constituencies (especially under President Carter), and in the Soviet Union, post-Stalin factionalism split along hawk/dove lines.[134] For its part, Pakistan was a military dictatorship under martial law; the military governed the country, and Zia controlled the military.[135] The Pakistani president faced a "fragmented domestic political opposition" that "lack[ed] the cohesion and credibility to pose a serious challenge to his rule."[136] Meanwhile, most Pakistanis approved of his refusal to recognize the Afghan communist regime.[137] Thus, the notion that domestic pressure was a primary factor that constrained the scope of intervention in Afghanistan is uncompelling. The empirical record instead indicates that concerns about escalation took center stage.

---

[130] Russian General Staff (2002: 26).
[131] CIA (February 1987b: iii, v). Estimates suggest that Moscow spent no more than 1–3% of its annual defense expenditure on the Afghan war. See CIA (May 1985: 14) and Dameyer (1988: 35).
[132] The quotation is from Girardet (1987). US aid to the mujahideen is estimated to have reached $630 million in 1987 (Cordovez and Harrison 1995: 157). Total US military expenditure that same year is estimated to have exceeded $285 billion (US Department of State 2000: 109).
[133] Yousaf and Adkin (1992: 81–84).
[134] Carson (2018: 244).
[135] Martial law was imposed in Pakistan following Zia's overthrow of Pakistani Prime Minister Zulfikar Ali Bhutto on July 5, 1977. Civilian government would not resume until 1988 following Zia's death in an aircraft crash.
[136] CIA (March 1984: iii).
[137] CIA (March 1984: 1).

Finally, it might be argued that strategic restraint in Afghanistan simply reflected "low stakes" in the outcome of the war from the perspective of the competitive interveners. This argument is difficult to sustain in light of the numerous geopolitical and national security motivations driving participation in the war. Soviet leaders, for example, feared the consequences of "losing" Afghanistan to the United States.[138] They worried that the overthrow of the PDPA regime would negatively affect their credibility with other client states elsewhere in the world.[139] They expressed concerns that the US might attempt to establish intelligence centers or station Pershing missiles in Afghanistan, close to the Soviet Union's "most sensitive [i.e., southern] borders."[140] And they speculated about the possibility of a US invasion of the Persian Gulf in response to the Iranian Revolution, "which threatened to cardinally change the military-strategic situation in the region to the detriment of the interests of the Soviet Union."[141] Ironically, at the same time that Moscow worried about American expansionism in the Persian Gulf, Islamabad and Washington feared aggressive Soviet intent in Afghanistan. Memoirs of top Pakistani officials vividly portray the sense of existential threat that pervaded Islamabad:

> Pakistan felt insecure. India was on her eastern flank, an enormous nation of 800 million hostile Hindus, with whom Pakistan had fought three times. To the west lay Afghanistan and the Soviets, a communist superpower whose army was now deployed within easy reach of the mountain passes into Pakistan. Potentially, it was a highly dangerous strategic situation. India and the Soviet Union were allies; should they combine, Pakistan faced the prospect of being squeezed out of existence.[142]

Acquiescing to the Soviet occupation was not an option for Pakistan: doing so would mean the elimination of a buffer against further Soviet incursions in the

---

[138] These fears were accentuated by speculation that Afghan leader Hafizullah Amin was a CIA agent. As noted above, the KGB questioned whether Amin might have established ties to American intelligence services when attending graduate school in the US. At best, Amin could not be trusted to follow the instructions of his Soviet advisors; at worst, Amin might have been planning what Soviet General (ret.) Leonid Shebarshin called "doing a Sadat on us"—that is, a wholesale defection from the Soviet camp (as quoted in Westad 2007: 316). A similar description is offered by Cordovez and Harrison (1995: 4), who highlight Soviet fears of what they call "an American-supported Afghan Tito."

[139] Halliday (1999: 678); Kalinovsky (2011: 11–12, 24, 52).

[140] The quotation is Soviet General (ret.) Leonid Shebarshin, as quoted in Westad (2007: 316). Also see Liakhovskii (1995: 109), Cordovez and Harrison (1995: 47), and Kalinovsky (2011: 214–215).

[141] Kornienko (1994: 193). Liakhovskii (1995: 109) recounts discussion of a CIA effort to create a "new Great Ottoman Empire" that would have threatened the southern Soviet Republics. That the Carter administration had moved naval forces to the Persian Gulf in the fall of 1979 only reinforced Soviet concern.

[142] Yousaf and Adkin (1992: 23–24); also see Pakistan Air Force (2000: 26).

region. Special concern revolved around the possibility of communist expansion into Pakistan's Northwest Frontier Province and Baluchistan, both of which were subject to Afghan territorial claims.[143] Washington shared these anxieties, perceiving the Soviet intervention as "an extremely grave challenge" to the wider Persian Gulf region and—critical to that part of the world—Middle East oil.[144] Indeed, only days after the Soviet intervention had begun, US President Carter was publicly arguing that "[a] Soviet-occupied Afghanistan threatens both Iran and Pakistan and is a steppingstone to possible control over much of the world's oil supplies."[145] Only a few weeks later, during a State of the Union address, Carter would explicitly link the Soviet intervention in Afghanistan, Middle East oil, and US national interests:

> The Soviet effort to dominate Afghanistan has brought Soviet military forces to within 300 miles of the Indian Ocean and close to the Straits of Hormuz, a waterway through which most of the world's oil must flow. The Soviet Union is now attempting to consolidate a strategic position, therefore, that poses a grave threat to the free movement of Middle East oil. [...] Let our position be absolutely clear: an attempt by any outside force to gain control of the Persian Gulf region will be regarded as an assault on the vital interests of the United States of America, and such an assault will be repelled by any means necessary, including military force.[146]

So intense was American concern that Thomas Thornton, then the NSC director of South Asian affairs, recalls that "careful measurements were made on maps throughout Washington to determine how much closer the Soviet Union was to the Straits of Hormuz and other exotic sites in the petro-world."[147] For the Carter administration, the Persian Gulf was a "third strategic zone" on par with Europe and Asia, rendering the Soviet intervention in Afghanistan "the most serious threat to peace since the Second World War."[148] These views persisted into the Reagan administration, which viewed Afghanistan as a central theater in the global campaign to "roll back" Soviet influence.[149] In short, the argument that strategic restraint in Afghanistan simply reflected "low stakes" in the outcome of the war is unpersuasive—it finds little support in the empirical record.

---

[143] CIA (January 1980: 4, July 1982: 1); Yousaf (1991: 16); Cordovez and Harrison (1995: 61).
[144] The quotation is Carter's National Security Adviser Zbigniew Brzezinski. See "Personal Memorandum from Brzezinkski to Carter" (December 26, 1979).
[145] Carter (January 4, 1980).
[146] Carter (January 23, 1980).
[147] As quoted in Cordovez and Harrison (1995: 55).
[148] Carter (January 23, 1980). Also see Carter (1995: 481–482).
[149] As Westad (2007: 331) writes, "[t]he Reagan approach was in many ways a continuation of the policies and methods developed by Carter's National Security Adviser Zbigniew Brzezinski and his staff."

To understand the form and function of intervener participation in the conflict necessitates an appreciation for the strategic dilemmas intrinsic to competitive intervention.

Domestic Bargaining Distortions and Protracted War

By limiting the geographic boundaries of their military operations, adopting defensive deployment patterns and force postures, and restricting the scope of their support to "battlefield credible" aid, Pakistan, the US, and the Soviet Union signaled restraint in their contest with one another. This restraint preserved strategic stability between the competitive interveners, limited the risk of direct confrontation, and helped to control escalation. Yet as the analysis above makes clear, the limits observed by the interveners simultaneously constrained the tactical efficiency of the support provided to the domestic combatants. Rather than confer decisive military advantages to enable their clients to prevail on the battlefield, the interveners provided a level of support sufficient only to prevent their defeat. What were the effects of these behaviors on domestic bargaining processes?

In this section, I turn to the domestic level of the civil war combatants to consider the distortionary effects of competitive intervention on domestic bargaining. In line with theoretical expectations, I identify three types of bargaining distortions introduced by this form of external meddling in Afghanistan: it subsidized the domestic combatants' costs of war; it balanced their capabilities; and it amplified information asymmetries. Taken together, these distortions increased the domestic combatants' willingness and ability to continue fighting while decreasing the set of negotiated settlements acceptable to both the Kabul regime and its mujahideen challengers. The consequences of these effects for the duration of the Afghan conflict were significant.

Aid as a Subsidy for War

My theory contends that external aid provided by competitive interveners subsidizes the costly learning process of war by reducing domestic combatants' costs of fighting. As war costs decline, the relative value of war increases. This prolongs conflict by shrinking the set of mutually acceptable bargains preferred to war while bolstering combatants' willingness and ability to fight. The Afghan case provides strong empirical support for these propositions.

Throughout the conflict, the communist regime in Kabul was heavily subsidized by Moscow, both directly and indirectly. While the prewar government already depended on Soviet aid, the civil war amplified this dependency. To be clear, the PDPA government retained its autonomy vis-à-vis the Soviets—indeed, Elias' research on defiant local partners in counterinsurgency wars has found that "there was no marked increase in the rate of substantive compliance from Afghans when compared to other local counterinsurgents responding to requests from intervening allies."[150] But the survival of the Afghan communist regime hinged on continuous inflows of Soviet aid. By 1989, for example, "nearly all of Kabul's food and fuel was donated by the USSR."[151] Moscow provided virtually all economic, technical, and development assistance received by Kabul.[152] It also advised on all aspects of Afghan government policy, with thousands of specialists and technicians overseeing national defense, foreign affairs, internal affairs, and the intelligence service.[153] Soviet advisors distributed aid, worked in mines and natural gas installations, prepared bureaucratic memorandums, and even wrote speeches for Afghan politicians. As Kalinovsky observes, the Soviet role was so extensive that "[c]ontemporary western commentators interpreted the 'Sovietization' of Afghanistan after the invasion as part of a broader plan to make Afghanistan a virtual republic of the USSR."[154]

Soviet support in the military sphere was similarly comprehensive. The Afghan army had all but collapsed as an effective fighting force in the early years of the war, with defections reducing its strength to less than half of its pre-war numbers.[155] Those that remained were ill-equipped and poorly trained for counterinsurgency operations. This necessitated that Soviet troops, rather than Afghan government soldiers, carry the bulk of the combat burden.[156] Soviet advisors, serving at the battalion level, took direct control of Afghan military forces' administrative and operational activities, and made "all decisions concerning operations, organization, promotions, and transfers of officers."[157] With Soviet training and support, Afghan troop numbers would recover; by the mid-1980s, government forces proved capable of taking the lead in frequent offensive operations. But they remained dependent on Moscow for equipment, arms, training, command and control, and logistical support. Indeed, an estimated 95% of Afghan military equipment was supplied by the Soviet Union.[158] Technically,

---

[150] Elias (2020: 216). Unfortunately, her data only extends from 1978 to 1980. However, the finding is notable in that this early period was arguably the time of greatest weakness for the PDPA amid factional fighting and army desertions.
[151] Rubin (2000: 1792).
[152] CIA (December 1984: 4).
[153] CIA (December 1984: 4).
[154] Kalinovsky (2011: 31).
[155] Jalali and Grau (1999: xvi).
[156] Tahir-Kheli (1980: 3); Kalinovsky (2011: 30).
[157] CIA (December 1984: 4).
[158] Tahir-Kheli (1980: 3).

much of this equipment was "sold" to the Afghan state, with Kabul accumulating over $10 billion in debt owed to Moscow during the war. This debt remained unpaid as the Soviet Union collapsed, however, and was eventually forgiven by the Kremlin.[159] Even after the withdrawal of Soviet combat troops, the Afghan government's war effort was characterized by a "near complete dependence on Soviet supply."[160]

For their part, the mujahideen's war effort was also massively subsidized by external aid. Islamabad trained over 80,000 mujahideen in camps run by Pakistani military instructors on Pakistani soil.[161] All arms and equipment, save for what was captured on the battlefield, were supplied and paid for by foreign patrons. US funding for the rebels saw exponential growth over the years, eventually becoming "the largest CIA military support operation since Vietnam."[162] All told, estimates suggest that the US alone funneled over $3 billion in aid to the mujahideen.[163] This was matched by Saudi Arabia, dollar for dollar. So comprehensive was the external aid reaching the mujahideen that it even included hundreds of mules shipped from Tennessee to Pakistan for use in transporting equipment, food, and medical supplies into Afghanistan.[164]

What was the effect of the competitive interveners' subsidization of the domestic combatants' war efforts? As anticipated by the theory, declassified intelligence reports, archival documents, and statements by the combatants themselves directly link external aid to the domestic combatants' willingness and ability to continue fighting. In a Special National Intelligence Estimate, for example, the CIA reasoned that Kabul "will continue to resist mujahideen pressure so long as the Soviet Union remains willing and able to continue its massive military supply program and the regime's internal problems remain manageable."[165] Soviet specialists likewise observed that "[Afghan troops] seemed confident only when they were near Soviet troops."[166] And Kabul itself warned that it would be unable to continue the war without Soviet support, emphasizing the need for military assistance "both practically and psychologically"—that is, both to strengthen capabilities and resolve. This was understood to be crucial for improving the regime's bargaining position: if it could hold off mujahideen assaults, the latter would "have to enter into negotiations [...] to work out the

---

[159] BBC News (2007).
[160] CIA (November 1989: 1).
[161] Yousaf and Adkin (1992: 29).
[162] Lundberg (2008: 37).
[163] Riedel (2014: xi).
[164] Pear (1988); Cordovez and Harrison (1995: 337); Grau (2004: 140).
[165] CIA (November 1989: iii).
[166] See "Nasha bol'—Afganistan [Our Pain—Afghanistan]," interview with Yurii Gankovskii (1989: 4), as quoted in Kalinovsky (2011: 28).

future government arrangement in Afghanistan, which they steadfastly refuse to do at this time."[167]

The same was true for the insurgents. As one analyst put it, "[t]he arms question is basic to mujahideen morale. Without arms they are discouraged; with them, they seem prepared to endure inordinate hardship indefinitely."[168] The CIA concurred, explicitly linking the provision of weapons and training to the mujahideen's aggressiveness on the battlefield.[169] In one National Intelligence Estimate on the prospects of the resistance, the agency concluded that "[t]he insurgency could not continue at the present level without outside support."[170] Because most mujahideen groups had only small reserves of ammunition and weapons, a decline in external support would mean that the "insurgents would have to reduce significantly their attacks on road convoys, and some bands would stop fighting altogether. Over time, the lack of such weapons could seriously affect both the willingness and the ability of large numbers to continue fighting."[171] In a secret memo on the critical importance of Pakistani aid, Secretary of State George Schultz put it more bluntly: "without Zia's support, the Afghan resistance, key to making the Soviets pay a heavy price for their Afghan adventure, is effectively dead."[172]

In short, external aid subsidized the costly learning process of war for both the Afghan communist regime and its insurgent opponents. As their costs of war fell, the domestic combatants' willingness and ability to keep fighting increased. The net result was a protracted conflict with little hope for negotiated agreement.

Balancing Combatant Capabilities

My theory holds that competitive intervention prolongs civil wars by shifting domestic combatants' military capabilities toward parity. This balancing dynamic generates battlefield stalemates by precluding decisive confrontations while enabling the opposing sides to avoid military defeat and, thereby, stay in the fight. Under such conditions, combatants forgo negotiated agreement to avoid settling on inequitable terms. The Afghan case provides considerable evidence in support of these arguments.

Despite the overwhelming firepower advantage enjoyed by Afghan government and Soviet troops, the mujahideen controlled much of the rural

---

[167] "Meeting of the Politburo of the Central Committee of the Communist Party of the Soviet Union" (January 23, 1989). Also see Rashid (1989a: 20).
[168] US Bureau of Intelligence and Research (1982: 9).
[169] CIA (May 1985: iv, 18).
[170] CIA (October 1983: 7).
[171] CIA (October 1983: 17).
[172] "Memorandum from George Shultz to Ronald Reagan" (November 29, 1982: 2).

countryside throughout the war. The rebels established shadow administrations, collected taxes, set prices, and dictated curfews.[173] These accomplishments were remarkable considering the low military capacity of the resistance at the start of the conflict. Indeed, when the civil war began, mujahideen fighters were poorly armed, relying primarily on Lee-Enfield bolt-action rifles from the First World War and Martini-Henry single-shot breech-loading rifles from the 1880s.[174] Recruits were unpaid volunteers with little (if any) formal military training. How was it possible that this ragtag militia could survive and control territory amid a war with a communist government backed by a great power?

Mujahideen accounts of combat during the war highlight the fundamental role of external aid in balancing the counterinsurgents' military advantages.[175] Foreign backers significantly improved the resistance's armaments, equipment, and skills. By the early 1980s, most battles featured the use of AK-47 assault rifles; 82-mm and 107-mm mortars (82-BM-37s and M1938s); 122-mm howitzers (D-30s); 75-mm and 82-mm recoilless rifles (B-10s and B-11s); antitank grenade and rocket launchers (RPG-7s and RPG-18s); an assortment of light, medium, and heavy machine guns (including RPKs, PKs, and DshKs); single- and multiple-barrel 107-mm rocket launchers (BM-1s and BM-12s/Type 63s); and the extensive use of antivehicle mines. Recoilless rifles and grenade launchers were used with devastating effect against armored personnel carriers and infantry fighting vehicles; heavy machine guns shot up enemy supply convoys; mortars, howitzers, and rocket launchers enabled offensive attacks against fortified security posts, garrisons, and airfields; and tactical radios, flares, and smoke grenades helped coordinate units located in different areas of operation. The RPG—described by Jalali and Grau as "a great equalizer"—proved especially effective against enemy armor and trucks, and was also used to counter low-flying helicopters.[176] The mujahideen were likewise proficient in the use of landmines—Soviet soldiers customarily rode on top of their armored carriers, rather than inside of them, as it proved safer to do so.[177] And critical to countering the counterinsurgents' air supremacy, the mujahideen also received 14.5-mm antiaircraft guns (ZPU-1s) and surface-to-air missiles, including SA-7s and—beginning in the fall of 1986—FIM-92A Stingers.

Balancing dynamics were explicitly linked to the domestic combatants' willingness and ability to keep fighting by American and Pakistani officials. As one CIA report explained, "[t]he insurgency could not continue at the present level

---

[173] US Bureau of Intelligence and Research (1982: 6).
[174] Grau (2004: 134–135).
[175] See the accounts of mujahideen fighters compiled in Jalali and Grau (1999).
[176] Jalali and Grau (1999: 66).
[177] As Jalali and Grau (1999: 53) explain, "[a] powerful antitank mine blast might merely hurl the soldiers off the APC whereas it would almost certainly kill everyone inside."

without outside support. [...] [W]ithout antitank rockets, heavy machine guns, and modern landmines—most of which come from foreign sources through Pakistan—insurgent capabilities would begin to decline within months."[178] The mujahideen's ability to control the Afghan countryside was understood to depend on "access to strong external support and open borders."[179] A reduction in the relative military capabilities of the insurgency was expected to negatively affect mujahideen morale.[180] Yousaf notes that "without the intelligence provided by the CIA, many battles would have been lost, and without the CIA training of our Pakistani instructors, the mujahideen would have been fearfully ill-equipped to face—and ultimately defeat—a superpower."[181] It was also understood that the mujahideen's relative military capabilities dictated their bargaining position. As one Special National Intelligence Estimate put it, a "unilateral US cutoff of support to the resistance would alter the military balance in favor of the regime and give it the upper hand in dictating the terms of political arrangements."[182] But so long as American and Pakistani aid continued to flow to the resistance, "most major commanders [would] refuse to negotiate with the PDPA."[183]

At the same time, the weapons provided to the mujahideen were insufficient to directly contest the conventional superiority of Soviet and Afghan government forces. The rebels could overrun government administrative centers, but they could not resist counterattacks. Where they were compelled to hold ground, the insurgents were overwhelmed by superior artillery, air power, and large numbers of mechanized troops backed by ample armor. The mujahideen found it impossible to hold onto large bases and staging areas and were frequently forced to pull back over the Pakistani border.

For its part, the PDPA regime was reliant on Moscow for continued survival. As one National Intelligence Estimate explained, in the event of a unilateral cut in Soviet aid, the regime would not "last long in power."[184] Yet the level of aid flowing to communist forces was insufficient to stamp out the insurgency. The limited size of the 40th Army undermined efforts to expand Kabul's area of physical control. Yousaf relates that, at the time, he "thought it a little strange that in terms of numbers the Soviet pressure had not increased much since 1979. [...] It seemed they were not prepared to commit substantial additional formations to the war. If this deduction was true, it could be a critical factor for the success of

---

[178] CIA (October 1983: 7).
[179] CIA (May 1985: iv).
[180] CIA (November 1989: 6).
[181] As quoted in Coll (1992b).
[182] CIA (November 1989: iii).
[183] CIA (November 1989: 4).
[184] CIA (November 1989: 6).

future mujahideen operations."[185] Indeed, while Soviet and Afghan government troops could clear insurgent strongholds, they could not hold onto liberated territory. When major operations were conducted in one part of the country, forces had to be drawn from other areas, leaving them vulnerable to insurgent counterattack. The mujahideen learned to wait for enemy troops to depart an area before returning to re-establish control.[186] As the Russian General Staff admits, "[t]his happened repeatedly."[187] The counterinsurgent force was also far too small to close the Afghan–Pakistani border, which served as the lifeline of the mujahideen. Hundreds of passageways remained open, providing a steady transfer of men, money, and weapons between the battlefields of Afghanistan and the sanctuaries of Pakistan. Meanwhile, the slow tempo and telegraphed movement of the Soviet Army undermined its military effectiveness. As Yousaf explains, "[t]here was no discernible attempt at surprise; the entire effort was slow-moving and ponderous, enabling the mujahideen to fight or disappear at their will."[188]

In sum, external aid from the competitive interveners served to balance combatant capabilities rather than confer decisive military advantages. As capabilities shifted toward parity, battlefield stalemates set in. Since neither the PDPA regime nor the mujahideen were meaningfully threatened with defeat, neither side was compelled to negotiate an end to the conflict. Protracted warfare was the net result.

Amplifying Information Asymmetries

My theory posits that competitive intervention delays the information-transmission function of warfighting by amplifying information asymmetries. Uncertainty about the quality and quantity of aid received by the domestic combatants, their ability to bring aid to bear on the battlefield, and their capacity to detect covert transfers to their rival complicate estimates of relative capability and resolve. This generates divergent expectations about likely battlefield outcomes, resulting in continued fighting. The Afghan case provides strong support for these propositions.

---

[185] Yousaf and Adkin (1992: 46).

[186] In a passage marked by frustration, Russian Captain (ret.) Khabarov recalls that "[t]hroughout the whole of that war practically every operation ended in the same way. Military operations began, soldiers and officers died, Afghan soldiers died, the mujahideen and the peaceful population died, and when the operation was over our forces would leave, and everything would return to what it had been before." See Liakhovskii and Nekrasov (2007: 33), as quoted in Braithwaite (2011: 223).

[187] Russian General Staff (2002: 26).

[188] Yousaf and Adkin (1992: 53).

Two key sources of uncertainty can be identified. First, levels of aid provided to the domestic combatants were subject to both obscurity and variation. The US covert aid program, for example, was shrouded in various degrees of secrecy over the course of the war. Carson identifies three periods.[189] During the first, "effective secrecy" (1980–1984), it was never clear how much support was arriving for the mujahideen, nor from where it originated. This was by design: the "battlefield credible" distinction, which required arms to be of Soviet origin, sought to purposefully obfuscate the level of foreign participation in the war.[190] During the second, "open secrecy" (1984–1986), it became more difficult for the US to deny involvement. The aid program had become the subject of discussion in popular media, not least due to the expansion of US support under NSDD-166. Nonetheless, the program remained covert, enabling the US to continue to obscure the level of aid it provided to the mujahideen. With the provision of the US-made Stinger missile in the fall of 1986, the US aid program entered an "overt" period (1986–1991). But here again, the quantity of aid provided to the resistance was concealed.

Even if it were possible for pro-government forces to fully observe the inflow of supplies destined for mujahideen storehouses in Pakistan, there were reasons to question how much aid would actually make it onto Afghan battlefields. The influx of money and arms into the hands of often destitute mujahideen fighters brought with it opportunities for graft and profiteering. The ISI sought to limit corruption in the aid pipeline by punishing transgressions when they were uncovered—Yousaf, for example, writes that "[i]f a Party could not control its commanders in this respect then their share [of military aid] would be cut." Nonetheless, he admits that "there is probably no commander in Afghanistan who has not, at some time, sold or bartered weapons."[191] The role of corruption as a source of uncertainty cannot be pushed too far: while there was illicit smuggling in the aid pipeline, the fungibility of weapons in Pakistani bazaars arguably made it easier for commanders to get the supplies they needed in the face of inconsistencies in arms availability from the ISI.[192] Still, even US officials

---

[189] Carson (2018: chapter 7).
[190] As Coll (1992b) explains, "[s]ecrecy shrouded the logistics pipeline."
[191] Yousaf and Adkin (1992: 104–105). Yousaf qualifies this statement by noting that "[s]ometimes, in an emergency, it was the only way to obtain food, evacuate a casualty, or secure urgently needed ammunition."
[192] Grau (2004: 139) explains: "Often the aid that was available was inappropriate for the individual mujahideen commander. For example, a commander might arrive in Pakistan seeking antitank mines, only to discover that no antitank mines were available, but heavy machine gun ammunition was being distributed. The commander might have no heavy machine guns, but he would take the ammunition anyway and take it down to the bazaar and sell it. There would be a resultant hue and cry that the mujahideen were selling aid for personal gain. Actually, what usually happened was that the commander would then take the money to buy the antitank mines at the bazaar, where everything always seemed to be available."

struggled to monitor what happened to their money, arms, and supplies once they landed in Pakistan.[193] This underscores the challenges communist forces faced in estimating external aid flows to the mujahideen.

Soviet support to Kabul was overt from the start, but it too varied in quantity and quality over time.[194] The 52,000 personnel that composed the initial intervention force was not intended to fight a counterinsurgency campaign—instead, it was ordered to play a passive role, garrisoning major cities and protecting military bases to enable the Afghan Army to pursue the mujahideen. But as Moscow quickly discovered, the Afghan Army had disintegrated due to defections and purges of its officer corps. As a result, Soviet forces were soon bearing the brunt of combat duties. Between 1980 and 1985, Soviet forces were engaged in sustained combat, often in cooperation with Afghan units, but sometimes without them. The overall size of the Soviet force grew to some 81,800 troops, reinforced with thousands of armored cars and tanks, as well as hundreds of aircraft and helicopters. In early 1986, the force grew again, reaching a peak strength of 108,800 personnel backed by some 29,000 major pieces of equipment, four aviation regiments, and three helicopter regiments. Yet at this time, the Soviets began to play a largely supportive role, backing Afghan government-led offensives when necessary and undertaking large-scale operations less frequently. In a report prepared that summer by the Directorate of Intelligence, it was acknowledged that "substantial uncertainties" surrounded the CIA's own assessments of Soviet strategy in Afghanistan, the possibility of an increased military effort against the mujahideen, and the likelihood of a withdrawal of Soviet forces.[195] And indeed, some 15,000 troops were withdrawn in the latter half of 1986, preceding the eventual withdrawal of all Soviet forces between May 1988 and February 1989—a withdrawal that few had anticipated.

Uncertainty and miscalculations about future battlefield outcomes directly contributed to prolonged fighting. For example, with the departure of Soviet troops, most observers, the mujahideen, and even the CIA itself believed Kabul would quickly collapse.[196] In light of the regime's seemingly dismal military prospects, major mujahideen commanders were assessed to be highly unlikely to enter into a bargained agreement with the PDPA, pushing instead to ensure its total demise.[197] However, government troops would prove remarkably successful at defending against mujahideen attacks, including at a major battle at

---

[193] Cordovez and Harrison (1995: 206).
[194] The troop estimates that follow are drawn from Russian General Staff (2002: chapter 1).
[195] CIA (July 1986: 9–13).
[196] In an estimate prepared in March 1988, the CIA wrote that it "judge[d] that the Najibullah regime will not long survive the completion of Soviet withdrawal even with continued Soviet assistance. The regime may fall before withdrawal is complete." See CIA (March 1988: 1). This estimate needed to be revised the following year. See CIA (November 1989: 1–2 and note 3).
[197] CIA (March 1988: 6).

Jalalabad. "I was dead wrong about Najibullah," US President George H. W. Bush told UN Secretary General Javier Pérez de Cuéllar, "I thought he would fall when the Soviet troops withdrew."[198] Underlying Najibullah's success was the unexpected scope of support the Soviet Union continued to provide to Kabul. As one analyst, writing in the fall of 1989, put it, "Moscow's commitment in economic and military aid to the Kabul regime has been vastly underestimated by the West and Pakistan."[199] Like the US covert aid program, the inability to fully observe the quantity and quality of aid provided to Kabul amplified information asymmetries concerning the domestic combatants' relative capabilities. This generated divergent expectations about the likely outcome of the war, thereby encouraging continued fighting.[200]

A second source of uncertainty concerned the willingness of Pakistan to continue to support the mujahideen with sanctuary. Pakistan's role was understood to be "crucial" to the war effort, given that "[t]he loss of Pakistani support would severely affect the ability of the resistance to continue."[201] Yet, even its allies in the CIA could not express confidence in Islamabad's participation in the conflict over the long term.[202] Pakistan was vulnerable to Soviet meddling in its internal politics, to cross-border strikes, and to the threat of a larger Soviet invasion; to the ever-present threat of conflict with India; and to a breakdown in relations with the US over its illicit nuclear weapons program. Under the weight of this pressure, it was reasonable for communist forces to question whether Islamabad might seek to placate its opponents by exiling the mujahideen party organizations present on its soil. This would force the parties to move their headquarters to other countries, such as Saudi Arabia, where their ability to support the mujahideen would be severely constrained. Pakistan might also close down rebel camps or otherwise make it more difficult for them to operate from bases located on Pakistani territory—an action that would have crippled the mujahideen's war effort. In this respect, questions over the reliability of Islamabad's support generated considerable uncertainty about the viability of the mujahideen's prospects over the long term, encouraging the PDPA regime and its Soviet allies that they were positioned to win the war of attrition—that "time was on their side."[203]

In sum, competitive intervention amplified information asymmetries during the Afghan civil war. The secret and variable nature of aid flows, together

---

[198] "Note of the Secretary-General's luncheon with George Bush" (June 4, 1990), as quoted in Kalinovsky (2011: 193).
[199] Rashid (1989b: 22).
[200] As one Afghan official put it at the time, "[t]he Soviet Union is giving us oxygen—bread and weapons—to defend ourselves." As quoted in Rashid (1989b: 23).
[201] CIA (October 1983: 18–19). Also see CIA (July 1982: 1).
[202] CIA (October 1983: 7, 18).
[203] Steele (1986: 10–11).

with questions about the reliability of external support, complicated estimates of the domestic combatants' military capabilities and ability to keep fighting. This increased uncertainty about relative strength and resolve, thereby increasing the relative value of continued warfare.

Other Explanations

How do other domestic-level accounts of protracted fighting fare in explaining the Afghan conflict's duration? Recall that the cross-national results reported in Chapter 4 identify two potentially competing explanations. First, democratic regime types were found to impart a statistically and substantively significant positive effect on conflict duration. Second, multiparty conflicts were found to be longer than wars fought between just two belligerents. I consider both alternatives in turn.

Arguments linking democratic regime types to protracted conflict cannot explain the persistence of the Afghan civil war given that Afghanistan has never been a democracy. Indeed, at no point prior to, during, or after the conflict was the Afghan state coded as possessing a democratic regime type in the widely employed regimes data compiled by the Polity Project.[204] Nor was the Afghan state ever coded as "free," based on aggregate assessments of the country's political rights and civil liberties compiled by Freedom House.[205] During the war, government torture of citizens, impressment of youth into the Afghan Army, and disregard for the life and liberty of civilians were widespread; criticism of the regime risked detention; media was government owned and operated; travel was restricted; and religious organizations were surveilled.[206] In short, the PDPA operated a highly repressive, authoritarian regime. For this reason, arguments linking democratic states to longer internal conflicts fail to explain the duration of the war.

By contrast, the theorized relationship between multiparty conflicts and longer durations does find empirical support in the Afghan case.[207] Recall that the mujahideen alliance was composed of seven political parties—four Islamic fundamentalist and three moderate traditionalist—which maintained headquarters-in-exile in Peshawar, Pakistan. Each party was affiliated with, though separate from, mujahideen commanders in the field. However, as a rule, every mujahideen commander was required to belong to one of the seven

---

[204] Marshall and Gurr (2020).
[205] Freedom House (2023).
[206] Gastil (1982: 261, 1986: 256); McColm et al. (1990: 27–28).
[207] On multiparty conflicts and protracted civil war, see Cunningham (2011).

parties to receive arms, ammunition, and training.[208] Local antagonisms—ethnolinguistic, sectarian, and local—influenced patterns of party loyalty among the mujahideen fighters.[209]

Initially, the anticommunist war had a unifying effect on the resistance. The various parties and their local commanders "understood their common cause to be more important than their cultural differences, and they often provided support for each other."[210] However, as the power of the mujahideen groups increased relative to their communist rivals, new logics of rebel alliance politics began to set in. As Christia explains, constituent mujahideen groups "began to worry more about their *own* power and survival instead of their alliance."[211] As these intra-alliance power concerns increasingly took hold, defections began to occur. The resulting fragmentation of the alliance increased the number of independent warring parties. This weakened the overall resistance effort, thereby contributing to the prolongation of the war.[212]

Notably, however, evidence suggests that external aid played a key role in fomenting in-fighting and shifting alliance dynamics within the Afghan resistance. Recall that Pakistan's ISI controlled the flow of money and arms to the mujahideen; by Zia's insistence, all US aid was channeled through this shadowy agency.[213] This suited the Americans. As Vincent Cannistraro, a former CIA operations officer and intelligence official on the NSC staff put it, "[t]he CIA believed they had to handle this as if they were wearing a condom."[214] However, this meant that the US exercised little control over the aid once it landed in Pakistan. Yousaf insists that the ISI's allocation decisions were "all related to battlefield competence."[215] But it is known that the political allegiances of the various mujahideen parties also mattered. In particular, Islamabad favored the fundamentalist parties in general, and Hekmatyar's Hezb-i-Islami in particular, over the moderate parties.[216]

---

[208] Yousaf and Adkin (1992: 40).
[209] Tarzi (1991: 484).
[210] Canfield (1989: 640–641). Also see Tarzi (1991: 485) and Yousaf and Adkin (1992: 33).
[211] Christia (2012: 111). Emphasis added. Specifically, minimum winning coalition dynamics took hold, in which constituent groups sought to form alliances that were large enough to win the war, but also small enough to maximize their own share of postwar power.
[212] For an extensive overview of these shifting intra-mujahideen alliance dynamics, see Christia (2012: chapter 4).
[213] Yousaf and Adkin (1992: 81, 96–97, 102).
[214] As quoted in Coll (1992b).
[215] Yousaf and Adkin (1992: 104).
[216] The fundamentalist parties had a preexisting working relationship with the ISI, having served as useful tools against the Pashtun-dominated Afghan monarchy and the Daoud regime prior to the communist takeover. The ISI's anti-Pashtun bias was rooted in the territorial conflict between Islamabad and Kabul over Pashtun areas straddling the Afghan–Pakistani border. By favoring the fundamentalists, the ISI could minimize the quantity and quality of aid that would end up in the hands of local Pashtun tribal leaders, who were largely allied with the moderate traditionalist groups. There was also an ideological affinity between the fundamentalists and the ISI in their mutual drive

The uneven allocation of weapons and ammunition fueled schisms within the alliance. In a Special National Intelligence Estimate, the CIA highlighted the role of external aid in fomenting infighting. Some mujahideen commanders, it explained, "believe they are not receiving their fair share of military supplies and expect they will be denied any significant political role once the fighting is over. Consequently, the focus of some commanders on strengthening their local positions has reduced the vigor with which they have attacked the regime."[217] Tarzi contends that Pakistan's control over the flow of money and arms "played the most important role in affecting the relative power position of the various resistance groups."[218] In effect, the unequal distribution of external aid from the ISI to the mujahideen alliance's various factions was itself a key factor driving intra-alliance power asymmetries.[219]

This suggests an important relationship between external aid and the multiparty character of the Afghan civil war: foreign military assistance fomented rebel in-fighting and the splintering of the mujahideen alliance, which in turn rendered the conflict a multiparty contest. This made bargaining more difficult, as more actors needed to be incorporated into the bargaining process, which meant more information needed to be collected from the battlefield before a mutually agreeable settlement could be reached.[220] This is an additional distortionary effect of external aid on domestic bargaining processes that is unanticipated by the theory, but which complements the theory's proposed mechanisms that link competitive intervention to protracted civil wars via domestic bargaining distortions.

Summary

Competitive intervention in the Afghan conflict decreased the domestic combatants' costs of war, shifted their relative military capabilities toward parity, and enhanced information asymmetries. In these ways, it distorted domestic bargaining processes in ways that increased combatants' willingness and ability to fight, precluded decisive military advantages, and increased uncertainty over relative strength and resolve. With a constant stream of aid, supplies, and weapons, the civil war combatants could continue fighting beyond their

---

for a pan-Islamic regional bloc that could challenge Indian dominance. See Cordovez and Harrison (1995: 162) and Tarzi (1991: 493).

[217] CIA (November 1989: 2).
[218] Tarzi (1991: 492–493).
[219] This is somewhat overlooked in Christia's analysis of the Afghan case because she treats the involvement of external actors as an extension of the power of local mujahideen groups (see Christia 2012: 103).
[220] Cunningham (2011).

domestic material constraints. At the same time, the protection conferred by Soviet troops and the sanctuary provided by Pakistani territory ensured that neither the Afghan communist government nor its mujahideen challengers faced the threat of defeat at the hands of their opponent.

That competitive intervention distorted the domestic bargaining process is made clear by the fact that negotiations between the mujahideen and the Afghan communist government did not occur at any point during the war. Under Karmal, the Afghan regime ruled out any possibility of negotiating with the rebels, while olive branches extended under Najibullah—such as a ceasefire proposal in January 1987—were quickly rebuffed by the rebels. "We will continue to fight," mujahideen leader Mohammed Nabi Mohammedi declared, "until Najibullah is thrown out and a complete Islamic government is established in Moslem Afghanistan."[221] The mujahideen *never* accepted the idea of sharing power with the Afghan communists, nor of joining a broad-based transitional government under UN auspices. Even following the signing of the Geneva Accords, the mujahideen were "virtually unanimous in their refusal to have anything to do with communists."[222] For its part, Kabul was in no hurry to share power. As Kalinovsky explains, "[t]he presence and protection of Soviet troops allowed [Afghan government] leaders to move slowly with regard to National Reconciliation."[223]

Consequently, negotiations to end the conflict took place exclusively at the international level, convened between the governments of Afghanistan, Pakistan, the Soviet Union, and the United States. This was a decidedly odd arrangement, in which one side of the civil war—the mujahideen—was excluded from deliberations over the future of the country for which it was fighting. Issues critical to resolving the domestic conflict, such as the demobilization and reintegration of fighters, trust-building measures, and reconstruction, were absent from the Geneva Accords. Upon its signing, the then chairman of the mujahideen alliance, Gulbuddin Hekmatyar, reiterated his determination to overthrow the Kabul regime, criticizing the Accords as "ineffective" and "flawed." The agreement, he argued, "can neither result in the just and lasting solution of the crisis, nor can it terminate the war, nor can it result in a voluntary return of refugees."[224]

Adding to the peculiarity of the talks, Pakistan did not recognize the Kabul regime as a legitimate negotiating partner and refused to meet with the Afghan delegation in person. This meant that talks took place indirectly in the form

---

[221] As quoted in Lee (1987: A1). Mohammedi was the founder and leader of Harakat-i-Inqilab-i-Islami.
[222] Girardet (1988).
[223] Kalinovsky (2011: 107).
[224] As quoted in Girardet (1988).

of "proximity talks," with the lead UN mediator, Diego Cordovez, shuffling between rooms to deliver messages between delegations. When it came time to sign the Geneva Accords, Pakistani and Afghan representatives entered the Council Chamber of the UN's Geneva headquarters through opposite doors. Islamabad even refused to sign on the same page as Kabul.[225]

A final tragic twist to the negotiation saga was the role played by the great powers. Despite signing the Geneva Accords, which committed them "to invariably refrain from any form of interference and intervention in the internal affairs" of Afghanistan, both sides immediately made it clear that they were fully prepared to violate them. In a press briefing that followed the signing ceremony, US Secretary of State George Schultz stated that while the US was "prepared to meet restraint with restraint," Washington had "made clear to Soviet leaders that, consistent with our obligations as guarantor, it is our right to provide military aid to the resistance."[226] Just two weeks later, in an official statement addressed to the UN Secretary General, the Soviet government issued its own warning: "Before the ink on the signatures to the Geneva documents was even dry, statements began to be heard which contradicted the spirit and the letter of the Geneva agreements. [...] Any deviation from the agreed provisions as written could harm the cause of the Afghan settlement, and tarnishes the moral authority of a State violating an obligation which it entered into in full view of the whole world."[227] Whether aid flows were halted for any period of time is unclear, but within months, both sides had succumbed to the collaboration problem inherent in competitive intervention. Defending their actions as retaliatory given violations by the other side, both interveners resumed the flow of weapons, equipment, and financial aid to the domestic combatants.[228]

It is little surprise, then, that the Geneva Accords failed to end the Afghan civil war. Without an *external* agreement between the competitive interveners, a lasting *internal* agreement between the domestic combatants was impossible. So long as the Afghan government and the mujahideen faced neither the resource constraints inherent in war nor the threat of defeat at the hands of their opponent, the domestic bargaining process had little hope of getting off the ground. It would take the dissolution of the Soviet Union—and thereby the termination of competitive intervention—to end the communist–mujahideen civil war. As

---

[225] For a detailed overview of the Geneva Accords negotiations, see Cordovez and Harrison (1995).
[226] For the full set of remarks delivered by Secretary Schultz, see "Agreements on Afghanistan" (1988: 55).
[227] UN General Assembly (1988: 3).
[228] For a sense of the scale of this continuing aid, consider that a 600-truck convoy ran weekly resupply missions between the Soviet Union and Afghanistan. The Soviets also maintained an air bridge to Kabul, flying in everything from food and assault rifles, to medicine and SCUD missiles. See Grau (2007: 258).

Soviet arms and funding dried up, Afghan government forces quickly collapsed. On April 16, 1992, the mujahideen captured Kabul.

Conclusion

This chapter presented empirical evidence that verifies each of the international- and domestic-level observable implications of my theory of competitive intervention. First, interveners in the Afghan civil war constrained the scope of their support to the domestic combatants. Second, this restraint was motivated by escalation fears vis-à-vis opposing interveners. Third, strategic limits in the scope of external aid were constructed around thresholds—geographic areas of contestation and control, deployment patterns and force postures, and the qualitative characteristics of different weapon systems—to signal mutual restraint. Finally, intervener restraint prevented the conferral of decisive military advantages while simultaneously distorting domestic bargaining processes by subsidizing the costs of war, balancing combatant capabilities, and enhancing information asymmetries. In these ways, competitive intervention prolonged the civil war.

The historical record also provides confirmatory evidence for one of the key assertions of this book: that the escalation dilemma at the heart of competitive intervention warps an intervener's positive objectives, such as the pursuit of battlefield victories, into negative objectives, such as the avoidance of battlefield defeats. Consider, for example, how one former KGB general describes the Soviet experience: "we are bogged down in a war we cannot win and cannot abandon. It's ridiculous. A mess."[229] Lieutenant General (ret.) Boris Gromov puts it this way: "[t]here is no basis for saying that the 40th Army suffered a defeat, just as there is no basis for saying we scored a military victory in Afghanistan."[230] Moscow admitted that the war entailed an unwelcome cost, but determined that the price of alternative policies would be even higher.[231] Their opponents understood well the dilemma that confronted them. As Yousaf puts it, "[t]o win in the field would have meant a vast escalation of men, money, and equipment. There was no way that Gorbachev was even going to contemplate such a price."[232] Knowing they could not prevail over the mujahideen without significantly enlarging the war, the Soviets resigned themselves to simply avoiding defeat.

[229] As quoted in Kuzichkin (1982: 33).
[230] Gromov (1994: 330–332), as quoted in Kalinovsky (2011: 37).
[231] CIA (March 1985: 1).
[232] Yousaf and Adkin (1992: 216).

The Pakistanis also appreciated the contradictory nature of their participation in the war. As the Pakistani Air Staff puts it, their objective was "confrontation and provocation avoidance—it was like walking on a tight rope."[233] In their account of the war, it is made clear that "Pakistan was not trying to win the war for the Afghani people." Instead, the aim was "to provide several kinds of moral, material and diplomatic support to the Afghan resistance" while being sure "to avoid a direct or escalated involvement in the war."[234] Notably, this restraint was apparent to Moscow at the highest levels: in a meeting with Najibullah in 1987, Gorbachev noted that "in Pakistan they understand they ought not to play dangerous games with the Soviet Union. They see the limits."[235]

For the American side, the story is less straightforward. US participation in the early periods of the war certainly *was* constrained by escalation fears. There was a need to avoid provoking Soviet retaliation against Pakistan—the critical source of sanctuary and resupply for the Afghan resistance—and as one official put it, "[i]f we escalate, then the Soviets go after the Pakistanis."[236] That the goal of avoiding defeat trumped the objective of ensuring victory was clear to some 60 Senators and 124 Congressmen in the fall of 1983, when they sponsored a joint House–Senate resolution that accused the Reagan administration of providing the mujahideen "with only enough aid to fight and die but not enough to advance their cause of freedom."[237] In 1985, Reagan authorized the notorious NSDD-166, which reiterated the US goal of Soviet withdrawal from Afghanistan. Yet, far from authorizing "all available means," as many have suggested, American objectives remained limited to "prevent[ing] the defeat" of the mujahideen.[238]

It was only in 1986 that the American intelligence and military services finally relented to congressional pressure to provision high-technology, American-made weaponry, symbolized by the Stinger antiaircraft missile. To be sure, this *was* an escalation of US involvement in the conflict. But as documented above, the decision to send the Stinger cannot be divorced from the increasingly dire military predicament of the mujahideen. In this regard, the increasing scope of American military aid was an effort to maintain balance on the battlefield—specifically, to provide a defensive capability that could counter the counterinsurgents' air supremacy. Even then, the decision to send Stingers was far from unanimous, with many officials continuing to worry about the possibility of Soviet reprisals. Fortunately for American and Pakistani officials, Moscow

---

[233] Pakistan Air Force (2000: 40).
[234] Pakistan Air Force (2000: 62).
[235] "Record of Conversation, Mikhail Gorbachev with Mohammad Najibullah" (July 20, 1987).
[236] As quoted in The Wall Street Journal (1984).
[237] S. Con. Res. 74 (October 6, 1983); H. Con. Res. 237 (November 18, 1983). The resolution was not put to a vote in 1983; an amended version of the resolution was passed in 1984.
[238] National Security Decision Directive 166 (1985: 2).

had already given up hopes of victory months before the first Stinger shot down a Soviet helicopter in the fall of 1986.[239]

Why did the Soviets withdraw from Afghanistan? It was not because they suffered a defeat at the hands of the mujahideen, nor because they could not afford to continue their counterinsurgency campaign.[240] Instead—and in sharp contrast to the political rhetoric surrounding the effects of the American covert aid program in general or the Stinger missile in particular—the Soviets pulled out of Afghanistan because it offered a pragmatic way to advance a larger foreign policy objective of the Gorbachev regime: improved relations with the West through perestroika. Importantly, perestroika was not a consequence of the Soviet experience in Afghanistan, but rather the culmination of a process of political change that had been building for decades in response to political, economic, and social problems that ultimately stemmed from the failure of the Soviet command economy. In short, it was not that the US and Pakistan "won" in Afghanistan—it was that the Soviets stopped competing.

---

[239] Kuperman (1999).
[240] CIA (February 1987b: iii, v).

7
Conclusion

Extensions, Implications, and Future Trajectories

Civil wars kill, maim, and displace. They destroy property, infrastructure, and institutions. They spread infectious illness and disease. They divert productive activities and services to fighting, deplete human and physical capital, and induce financial flight. They sow seeds of distrust within communities, weaken social bonds, and generate both intragroup and intergroup grievances. They weaken constraints on opportunism and encourage criminality. Even after the fighting stops, civil wars increase rates of morbidity, infant and adult mortality, and long-term disability. In an increasingly globalized and interconnected world, these consequences permeate the domestic boundaries of the states they afflict, resonating throughout international politics and around the globe.

And yet, many civil wars persist. Even when they become bogged down in protracted wars of attrition, government and rebel combatants regularly choose to continue to keep fighting. And even as the costs of participation in foreign wars grow larger, third-party interveners often continue to invest in stalemated conflicts. Precisely because the consequences associated with civil wars scale as a function of their duration, understanding why some wars go on, seemingly without end, is of pressing concern for both scholarship and policy.

This book has endeavored to explain intractable conflict and prolonged interventions by situating civil wars within the broader geopolitical environment in which they take place. It has explored the connections between subnational conflict processes, interstate competition, and the characteristics of the international system in search of new inferential leverage to better understand the behaviors of armed groups, states, and third-party interveners, as well as the consequences of their behaviors for temporal variation in the average duration and global prevalence of civil wars.

A central finding that emerges from the analysis is the critical role of competitive intervention—two-sided, simultaneous military assistance from different third-party states to both government and rebel combatants—in the dynamics and intractability of civil wars across time and around the globe. While battlefield victory may be the primary objective for a conflict's domestic combatants, the escalation dilemma inherent in competitive intervention—the desire to help one's client prevail, while at the same time control the risk of enlarged conflict vis-à-vis an opposing third-party state—leads competitive interveners to pursue more limited objectives. To manage escalation risks, interveners signal restraint in the force postures they adopt, the targets they attack, and the types of weapons they provide to a civil war's domestic combatants. This is a negotiated form of "cooperative competition" that involves processes of threshold construction and observance, costly signaling, and tacit and explicit communication about limits to the scope and scale of their participation in the conflict—as well as the behaviors that will trigger an escalation of the war. Limits serve to manage intervener relations, but they simultaneously hinder the conferral of decisive military advantages on domestic clients. Rather than ensure battlefield victories, this paradoxical dynamic of competitive intervention distorts domestic bargaining processes: it subsidizes domestic combatants' costs of war; it balances their capabilities; and it amplifies information asymmetries. Taken together, these pernicious effects increase domestic combatants' willingness and ability to fight, negate decisive military advantages, and increase uncertainty over relative strength and resolve. The net result is protracted civil war.

Indeed, competitive intervention decreases the hazard of conflict termination by more than 50% across every point in time over a civil war's duration. This is a generalizable finding: one that is applicable to the wide range of political, economic, and social contexts in which intrastate conflicts are waged. It is also a robust result: one that holds across numerous model specifications that employ alternative measures of civil war, account for potential unobserved decade-specific confounders, and control for potential unobserved conflict-specific heterogeneity.

But the significance of competitive intervention extends beyond the duration of any individual conflict—indeed, this pernicious form of external meddling helps to explain changing trends in the global prevalence of intrastate war. While many have celebrated the so-called "decline of civil war" that accompanied the post–Cold War period, it is commonly overlooked that the waning prevalence of internal conflict was to a large extent a function of their decreasing average duration, rather than a decline in their rate of outbreaks. Stated otherwise, the determinants of protracted conflict are important drivers of variation in the prevalence of civil war. Competitive intervention—a factor central to understanding the intractability of intrastate conflict—was twice as common during the bipolar Cold War period as it has been in the unipolar post–Cold War era. Bipolarity gave rise to great power rivalry between the US and Soviet Union and increased foreign adventurism among their client states. This increased the prevalence of competitive intervention. Unipolarity, by contrast, both eliminated great power competitive intervention and restrained the interventionist tendencies of weaker states. This decreased the prevalence of competitive intervention. Crucially, as competitive intervention has waxed and waned, so too have the domestic- and international-level mechanisms that link it to protracted conflict. This explains changing trends in the average duration—and thus the global prevalence—of civil war.

In this concluding chapter, I explore the relevance of these findings for one of the most violent and deadly conflicts of the twenty-first century: the Syrian civil war (2011–present). This ancillary case provides additional within-case analysis and valuable out-of-sample testing by examining the dynamics of competitive intervention in an ongoing civil war that falls outside the universe of cases included in the Extended External Support Dataset analyzed in Chapter 4. I briefly overview how the escalation dilemma at the core of competitive intervention has affected external participation in the war. Next, I explore whether and how competitive intervention in the conflict has distorted domestic bargaining processes. I then turn to consider the implications of my findings for the policy and practice of conflict management, both in Syria and in other future civil wars. I conclude by suggesting fruitful avenues for future research on civil war, interstate competition, and the nexus between them.

Extensions to a Contemporary Battlefield: The Syrian Civil War (2011–Present)

From Protests to Violent Conflict

In March 2011, a group of teenaged boys was caught writing graffiti in the Syrian city of Daraa. Their painted message, which read "the people want to bring down the regime," was inspired by the political upheavals taking place elsewhere in the Middle East as part of the Arab Spring.[1] Major unrest had not yet occurred in Syria, but it was generally understood that popular discontent with the Bashar al-Assad regime was widespread. The response from state security forces, therefore, was as swift as it was cruel: the graffiti writers were incarcerated, beaten, and tortured.

News of the young boys' plight quickly became public knowledge, sparking local demonstrations that demanded their release. The Assad regime responded with repression, using tear gas, water cannons, and even live fire to quell the discontent. Far from stamping out the nascent political movement, however, the regime's violence fanned the flames of civil disobedience. Demonstrations quickly spread to other cities, and demands for greater political reform continued to mount. As the unrest became increasingly threatening to the regime, the

---

[1] The message, "As-Shaab/Yoreed/Eskaat el nizam!" (Arabic: الشعب يريد إسقاط النظام), was a rallying cry across the Middle East during the Arab Spring.

Syrian Army was called in to suppress it. Armed protesters soon clashed with government troops, foreshadowing a coming civil war within Syrian society. In July 2011, disillusioned members of the Syrian Army began to defect from the regime, announcing the formation of the Free Syrian Army—a rebel group that, for the first time, explicitly called for the overthrow of Bashar al-Assad. Undeterred, the regime doubled down; by the fall of 2011, a full-blown insurrection was underway.[2]

In the years that followed the onset of the civil war, a dizzying array of rebel groups, insurgent militias, and external interveners emerged to make Syria one of the most complicated and destructive battlegrounds in contemporary history. In broad terms, three campaigns have driven the conflict for over a decade: violence between the Syrian government and various domestic opposition forces that call for the removal of the Assad regime; an international coalition's efforts to defeat and prevent the return of the Islamic State in Iraq and Syria (or Daesh; hereafter, ISIS); and Turkish military operations that target the Kurdish-dominated Syrian Democratic Forces (SDF) rebel organization. Amid these overlapping and interacting campaigns, a complex network of regional and global third-party interveners have entered the war in pursuit of varied objectives. Driven by their rivalrous relations with the Assad regime, and seeking increased regional influence in the Middle East, Saudi Arabia, Turkey, and Qatar have backed various rebel outfits, "moderate" and "jihadist" alike. Horrified by the brutality inflicted against civilians by both the Syrian regime and ISIS, while also wary of supporting jihadist elements in the broader Syrian opposition, Western states, such as France and the United Kingdom, have favored the Kurds. And motivated by the need to prop up a long-time ally, and thereby gain greater influence in the region, Iran has thrown its support behind the Assad regime.[3]

But the most significant case of competitive intervention in the Syrian civil war has been the contest between the United States and Russia. The Central Intelligence Agency (CIA) began supplying money, weapons, and training to anti-Assad forces under the covert Timber Sycamore program as early as 2012. By 2015, US special operations units were deployed to the country, working closely alongside partner forces inside Syria. As of the summer of 2024, US forces continued to operate in the country's northeast in support of the SDF; US troops also bolstered Syrian Free Army (formerly known as the Maghaweir al-Thowra; hereafter SFA) forces based at the al-Tanf garrison in the southeast.[4] For its

---

[2] On the internal origins of the Syrian uprising, see the contributions in Hinnebusch and Imady (2018).

[3] For a comprehensive overview of the regional and international power struggles underlying intervention in the Syrian conflict, see the contributions in Hinnebusch and Saouli (2020).

[4] The scope of US support remains comprehensive, including everything from weapons and ammunition, to military equipment and vehicles, to medical supplies and logistical support, to

part, Moscow has delivered regular shipments of weaponry to the Assad regime throughout the war. Since September 2015, it has also maintained a deployment of Russian forces in the Syrian theater. While exact numbers remain classified, the Russian defense ministry has acknowledged that over 63,000 Russian military personnel have participated in the war, including 434 generals and 25,738 officers.[5] By all accounts, this support has been critical to the survival of the Assad regime.[6]

Notwithstanding the scale and scope of their assistance to Syria's domestic combatants, however, military operations undertaken by both the US and Russia have been complicated by complementary and competing interests in the outcome of the war. While both interveners oppose ISIS and agree that Syria's civil war undermines efforts to destroy that group, they have had vastly different prescriptions for resolving it. Russia supports the Assad regime incumbent in Damascus; the US supports rebels fighting against its consolidation of control. Stated otherwise, while both interveners have a mutual enemy in ISIS, they have mutually exclusive (and competing) domestic clients.[7] The Syrian case therefore provides a fascinating window through which to observe the dynamics of competitive intervention in a contemporary conflict. In what follows, I first examine whether and how the strategic dilemmas inherent in competitive intervention have affected American and Russian behavior in the Syrian civil war. I then turn to explore the consequences of their competitive intervention for domestic bargaining processes.

Strategic Restraint During Competitive Intervention in the Syrian Civil War

As is common during competitive intervention, the desire to help their domestic clients, while at the same time avoid inadvertent escalation vis-à-vis one another, has led the US and Russia to establish limits on the scope of their support to rebel and government forces, respectively. In keeping with the predictions of this book's theoretical arguments, strategic restraint has manifested in a range of tacit and explicit agreements that seek to avoid direct confrontations through diplomatic, military, and intelligence channels.

In the air, for example, the interveners established a memorandum of understanding that mandates "maintaining professional airmanship at all times, the

---

stipends and clothing. For an unclassified breakdown of the 2025 fiscal year train-and-equip funding request, see Office of the Secretary of Defense (2024: 17–23).

[5] O'Connor (2018).

[6] See, for example, Eilam (2022: 125), Russell (2018: 1, 9), and Graham (2019: 138).

[7] On the US counter-ISIS campaign, see Wasser et al. (2021). On the Russian counter-ISIS campaign, see Lavrov (2018).

use of specific communication frequencies and the establishment of a communication line on the ground." American and Russian pilots are to operate at "safe distances" from one another, and "it is standard practice for [US pilots] to stand off until the airspace is clear."[8] These deconfliction mechanisms have had significant tactical consequences for US airpower in Syria. As one F-15E pilot, Lieutenant Colonel Brian Novchich, explained to me, "[t]here were times where we had known enemy targets—we knew exactly where they were, exactly how to go and get them and how to destroy that target—and we were unable to because of deconfliction measures with third-party actors, specifically Russia. So there were times where it even prevented us from executing a mission that would achieve an objective, because deconfliction was more important."[9]

For its part, Russia has carefully managed its interactions with US airpower. For example, while Moscow has deployed its advanced S-300 surface-to-air missile system to the Syrian theater, Russian personnel have retained full control of the weapons at all times. Moscow has not permitted Syrian crews to operate them, and it is also notable that, to date, the weapons have not been used to defend against US air and missile strikes, despite their frequent occurrence.[10] For example, the Russian air defense system did not react to US cruise missile strikes on Syria's al-Shayrat air base on April 7, 2017.[11]

Of course, deconfliction in the air still leaves the problem of where each side's bombs land. Washington and Moscow have therefore coordinated their efforts to avoid inadvertent targeting of each other's ground forces. For example, the US Pentagon has acknowledged that it has informed Russia about the locations of US Special Forces operating in Syria. While officials stress that the locations they have identified are "not specific areas, but firmly broad areas," a Pentagon press secretary has confirmed that this information sharing has taken place outside of the memorandum of understanding that deconflicts American and Russian aircraft.[12] When queried about the logic of these disclosures, the then head of the US Air Force Central Command, Lieutenant General Charles Brown, highlighted the importance of controlling escalation: "[w]e told them [the Russians] these are [...] general areas where we have coalition forces that we don't want them to strike [...] because all it's going to do is escalate things."[13]

Escalation concerns have also constrained the impact of American ground forces deployed to the Syrian theater. To control the political and physical risks

---

[8] The quotations are from Lieutenant Colonel Kristi Beckman, a spokeswoman at the US Central Command, as quoted in Ignatius (2016). Unfortunately, the text of the memorandum of understanding has not been publicly released.
[9] Interview, Lieutenant Colonel Brian Novchich. January 27, 2021. Zoom.
[10] Egozi (2020); Melman (2020).
[11] Lavrov (2018: 25).
[12] The quotation is from Lieutenant General Charles Brown, as quoted in Gibbons-Neff (2016).
[13] As quoted in Torbati (2016).

of placing American troops alongside their local partners, US advisors' positions have been restricted to "the last cover-and-concealed position from the front line of advance of the partner force."[14] Advisors are generally prohibited from direct ground combat and restricted in their movement on the battlefield.[15] As one volunteer who fought alongside Syrian opposition forces put it, "[US advisors] stayed with the command element, they weren't actually fighting." While advisors provided medical assistance and helped to coordinate air strikes and mortar fire, "they weren't putting rounds down range."[16]

Escalation concerns have likewise constrained the types of weapons that the US has provided to anti-Assad opposition groups. Even as rebel-held sections of Aleppo suffered under intense Russian bombing during the fall of 2016, US officials remained unwilling to provide heavier weapons—such as truck-mounted antiaircraft guns—that would enable defense against Russian aircraft. Former Secretary of State John Kerry justified the decision by highlighting fears that the weapons could end up killing Russian troops and thereby trigger confrontation with Moscow.[17] Former US President Barack Obama, too, cited concerns about getting pulled into a deeper conflict with Russia.[18]

Over time, the conflict witnessed a gradual progression toward nominal zones of influence and control, with reasonably well-delineated east–west geographic limits. In particular, the US and its domestic clients tacitly conceded Assad's control of central and southern Syria to the west of the Euphrates River, while Russian and Syrian forces avoided operations to the east of it, permitting the US to move its forces and allies downriver to control villages toward the Iraqi border. Since August 2016, Turkey's military occupation of Syria's northwest has represented a third competing area of influence and control.[19] Lieutenant Colonel Novchich explained to me that when he was in the Syrian theater, he "had maps that were very easy to position keep: 'you stay on this side and we stay on that side'. All of the corridors, the air routes—the entire airspace—was built to follow the deconfliction lines so you never had to really make a decision on whether you were going to cross the line or not. There was no airspace—there were no options—to do anything other than stay on your side."[20]

---

[14] The quotation is from Colonel Ryan Dillon, a spokesperson for the US-led coalition in Syria, as quoted in Snow (2017).
[15] "Direct ground combat" refers to "engaging an enemy on the ground with individual or crew served weapons, while being exposed to hostile fire and to a high probability of direct physical contact with the hostile force's personnel. Direct ground combat takes place well forward on the battlefield while locating and closing with the enemy to defeat them by fire, maneuver, or shock effect." See US Department of Defense (1994: 1–2).
[16] As quoted in Snow (2017).
[17] Miller and Entous (2016).
[18] Jaffe and Entous (2017).
[19] I discuss the Turkish occupation, and the escalatory risks it entails, in more detail in the next section.
[20] Interview, Lieutenant Colonel Brian Novchich. January 27, 2021. Zoom.

Rather than acknowledge this deconfliction as "cooperation," however, US officials have stressed their independence and autonomy. In a November 2015 interview with National Public Radio, for example, the then Supreme Allied Commander Europe, US General (ret.) Philip Breedlove, stressed that cooperation was "not the word" he would use:

> I would not use that word. We are not cooperating. We have developed a safety regime with them to ensure the deconfliction of our aircraft, et cetera, in the sky. But cooperation is not the word. [...] What I would say is that we have developed the regimens and the procedures to allow us not to come into contact and when we do, how we handle that, how we communicate, how we operate, the things that we do and don't do to be—so as to not look bellicose.[21]

Similarly, former US Secretary of Defense Ash Carter has emphasized that negotiations with Russia are "not based on trust." Instead, he explained, "[t]hey're based on a transaction and on mutual interest to the extent—and when and as we're able to identify that with the Russians."[22] Proposals for further coordination in the form of a "Joint Implementation Group" were also resisted by officials in the Pentagon and the US intelligence community.[23]

Yet efforts to control escalation have undoubtedly limited US strategic priorities in Syria. Consider, for example, efforts to punish the Assad regime's use of chemical weapons. In April 2017, former US President Donald Trump authorized missile strikes against the al-Shayrat air base in response to a chemical weapons attack in Khan Sheikhoun. In an important sense, the strikes represented a departure for American policy in Syria: it was the first time that US forces directly attacked regime targets. In other respects, however, US behavior in the lead up to the strikes was consistent with policy priorities centered on escalation control. First, the Pentagon warned Russia of the impending attack, providing time for Russian and Syrian officials to evacuate personnel and equipment.[24] Second, US military planners explicitly sought "to minimize risk to Russian or Syrian personnel located at the airfield."[25] Third, the target was unambiguous, the attack was discrete, and the strike's purpose was explicitly linked

---

[21] A full transcript of General (ret.) Breedlove's interview can be found in Inskeep (2015).
[22] A full transcript of Secretary Carter's comments can be found in US Department of Defense (2016).
[23] One leaked proposal, obtained by *The Washington Post* in July 2016, called for a joint command center in Amman, Jordan to coordinate an intensified bombing campaign against ISIS and the Nusra Front. See Terms of Reference for the Joint Implementation Group (n.d.). While meetings on the proposal between former US Secretary of State John Kerry and Russian Foreign Minister Sergey Lavrov did end with a "tentative deal," the terms of the deal were not made publicly available.
[24] Lister et al. (2017); Newmani and Hosenball (2017).
[25] The quotation is from Pentagon spokesman Captain Jeff Davis. A full transcript of his statement can be found in US Department of Defense (2017).

to the chemical weapons attack in Khan Sheikhoun.[26] Finally, in the immediate aftermath of the strikes, senior US officials publicly emphasized that the "target in this attack was not Russian. It was not the Russians. It was not their forces nor any Russian individuals."[27] Former Secretary of State Rex Tillerson also warned against extrapolating from the strikes, emphasizing that there had been "no change" in US policy or posture with respect to the broader Syrian civil war.[28] In short, even when tensions have peaked in Syria, the competitive interveners have prioritized escalation control—an outcome predicted by the theory developed in this book.

Domestic Bargaining Distortions and Protracted War

Efforts to manage escalatory risks have served to regulate confrontation between competitive interveners in the Syrian theater. However, this "cooperative competition" has also had deleterious consequences for the war's domestic combatants. The reallocation of resources across various train-and-equip programs has undermined rebel capability and morale, geographic limits have restricted the area of effect of American and Russian air support, and the interveners' need to avoid engagements with one another has undermined the effectiveness of ground operations by rebel and government forces alike. In line with theoretical expectations, these dynamics of competitive intervention have prolonged the Syrian civil war in three ways.

First, competitive intervention has subsidized domestic war costs. The Timber Sycamore program was one of the most expensive covert operations ever run by the CIA. While details remain classified, one source estimates that over $1 billion in military aid was distributed to anti-Assad opposition forces over the life of the program; another estimates the program's budget approached $1 billion *per year*.[29] Note that Timber Sycamore was separate from Washington's counter-ISIS campaign, and also separate from the Pentagon's own train-and-equip program that armed the largely Kurdish rebel forces fighting in northeast Syria, the latter of which was estimated to have cost over $2.2 billion by the fall of 2017.[30] And while the scale of Russian support to the Assad regime remains unknown, estimates suggest that Moscow has spent between $1.2 and $2 billion

---

[26] The al-Shayrat airfield was the alleged origin of the aircraft that conducted the Khan Sheikhoun chemical weapons attack.
[27] The quotation is from former Secretary of State Rex Tillerson. A full transcript of his statement can be found in US Department of State (2017).
[28] As quoted in US Department of State (2017).
[29] See, respectively, Mazzetti, Goldman, and Schmidt (2017) and Miller and DeYoung (2015).
[30] Dubin (2017).

per year on the war.³¹ For a sense of scale, consider that the Syrian government's entire state budget in 2021 amounted to just $3.86 billion.³² In light of these figures, it is hardly surprising that Syria's domestic combatants have chosen to sustain their war efforts rather than sue for peace: external aid significantly subsidizes continued fighting. As Phillips puts it, the war has been "outsourced"—domestic actors are not dependent on only local resources.³³ This insulates against the true costs of war and incentivizes the delay of negotiations in the interest of greater concessions in the future.

Second, competitive intervention has shifted the domestic combatants' military capabilities toward parity. The CIA trained and equipped tens of thousands of anti-Assad fighters, enabling opposition forces to make substantial battlefield gains against militarily superior government troops. By one estimate, CIA-backed fighters killed or wounded some 100,000 Syrian soldiers and their allies.³⁴ The US provision of tank-destroying missiles in particular proved crucial in the routing of government forces.³⁵ By the summer of 2015, the rebels were at the gates of Latakia on the northern coast, threatening Assad's ancestral homeland, while also pushing toward Damascus. US intelligence officials even began suggesting that it was "time to start thinking about a post-Assad Syria."³⁶ But this was not to be: Russian President Vladimir Putin was warily observing battlefield trends, and in September 2015 he responded to the shifting tide by deploying Russian combat forces. From that point forward, the military effectiveness of the US-trained rebels began to decline. As one analyst explains, "[US support] was potent enough to threaten Assad and draw Russian intervention, but not strong enough to prevail."³⁷ Another laments that Washington "never gave [the rebels] the necessary resources or space to determine the dynamics of the battlefield. They were drip-feeding opposition groups just enough to survive but never enough to become dominant actors."³⁸ In this context, relentless bombing by Russian aircraft slowly hollowed out rebel forces. Unwilling to risk an escalation spiral, and citing concerns about getting pulled into a larger conflict with Russia, American policymakers declined to provide the antiair weapons opposition forces requested.³⁹ Instead, US officials shifted their focus to the counter-ISIS fight, abandoning the Timber Sycamore program in the summer of 2017 and reallocating its resources to the Pentagon-run train-and-equip programs in northeast Syria and at the

---

[31] Estimates of the cost of Russian support vary. For a discussion, see Schaffner (2021).
[32] Center for Operational Analysis and Research (2020: 2).
[33] Phillips (2020: 46).
[34] As cited in Ignatius (2017).
[35] Mazzetti, Goldman, and Schmidt (2017).
[36] As quoted in Ignatius (2015).
[37] Ignatius (2017).
[38] The quotation is from Charles Lister, as quoted in Mazzetti, Goldman, and Schmidt (2017).
[39] Jaffe and Entous (2017).

al-Tanf garrison in Homs Governorate. It was in these regions that the geographic saliencies that deconflicted American and Russian aircraft were already established—a protective curtain that has continued to protect Syrian opposition forces, including the SDF and SFA. Here again, the Syrian theater has witnessed a general balancing dynamic that serves to counter decisive military advantages at critical junctures of the war. And as Hinnebusch observes, it is precisely because "external players continued to provide their clients with enough support to keep fighting and avoid defeat but not enough to defeat their opponent" that "each side still continued to hope to win" based on the belief "that the power balance was shifting in its favor."[40] Stated otherwise, the balancing dynamic that is characteristic of competitive intervention has served to increase uncertainty over future battlefield outcomes in Syria. It has thereby encouraged continued fighting, with the domestic combatants staking intransigent bargaining positions during mediation attempts under the auspices of the Geneva peace talks from 2012 to 2017 and the Astana talks from 2017 to the present.[41]

Finally, competitive intervention has enhanced information asymmetries. External military aid has been the central source of military power for the domestic combatants throughout the war. The inability to fully observe the quantity and quality of this aid has impeded estimates of the domestic combatants' relative military capabilities. Likewise, uncertainty over how and when the interveners might join their clients in combat has complicated estimates of the probability of victory. That the rebels could capture territory in areas long considered to be government strongholds is attributable to the CIA's covert aid program; that Assad could survive this onslaught is attributable to Russia's unexpected deployment of combat forces. Washington's sudden termination of the Timber Sycamore program in 2017 was an unexpected boon for government forces, yet its decision to remain alongside opposition forces based at the al-Tanf garrison and in the northeast has impeded the Assad regime's ability to consolidate its control. In short, the inability to predict the scope and duration of support that would be provided by the competitive interveners has increased uncertainty over relative strength and resolve, thereby increasing the relative value of continued fighting.

In all these ways, competitive intervention has subsidized the costs of war, balanced domestic combatants' military capabilities, and increased information asymmetries. These distortions have encouraged continued fighting in the interest of greater concessions in the future, generating a humanitarian crisis of

---

[40] Hinnebusch (2020: 10–11).
[41] Assad, for example, has insisted on demonizing the opposition as terrorists, while the opposition has refused to relinquish their calls for his removal from power.

staggering proportion: an estimated 618,000 people have been killed; some 6.7 million have been internally displaced; another 6.6 million have been rendered refugees in foreign countries; and a further 14.6 million have been left in desperate need of emergency aid.[42] It is precisely because they enjoy the support of competing external backers that the domestic combatants have faced neither the resource constraints inherent in war nor the threat of defeat at the hands of their opponent. An intractable, brutalizing, and cruel civil war has been the result.

Competitive Intervention and Future Flash Points in the Syrian Civil War

At the time of writing in the spring of 2024, global interest in the Syrian conflict had waned. After some thirteen years of continuous fighting, and in light of new geopolitical crises—the COVID-19 pandemic, the outbreak of the Russo-Ukrainian War, and rising anxiety over the future status of Taiwan—the war had "fallen off the front page" of the international agenda.[43] With the *de facto* partition of the country into distinct political domains marked by relatively static front lines, violence levels declined. Some observers began to suggest that the war had "largely abated."[44]

Yet, the seeming equilibrium that pushed Syria off the top of policy agendas did not arise due to meaningful progress in the war's domestic peace process: fighting along lines of contact between rebel groups under Turkish and American protection, on one side, and an Assad regime backed by Russian and Iranian support, on the other, continues. And while it is true that a decline in large-scale military offensives has reduced the war's intensity, violence remains endemic: an estimated 4,361 people were killed across Syria in 2023 alone.[45]

Instead, the "stable instability" that has characterized the war in recent years has resulted from external powers deepening their long-term exposure to developments in Syria in ways that are more likely to protract the conflict, rather than end it.[46] In particular, cognizant of the ongoing risks of escalation—and distracted by other geopolitical crises—external interveners have adopted a "spheres of influence" approach to the war, in which arms and influence have been roughly divided into three regions overseen by opposing foreign powers:

---

[42] Calculating accurate death tolls poses an almost insurmountable challenge in a complex war zone like Syria. These estimates are reported by the Syrian Observatory for Human Rights (2024). Estimates of the number of people displaced, rendered refugees, and in need of humanitarian aid are reported in UNHCR (2022).
[43] The quotation is from UN Secretary General António Guterres, as quoted in UN News (2021).
[44] See, for example, Polgreen (2023).
[45] Syrian Observatory for Human Rights (2023).
[46] The "stable instability" concept is adapted from Yacoubian (2021: 7).

Russia in the south and west, Turkey in the north, and the United States in the east.[47] In turn, three potential flash points risk the resumption of high-intensity fighting between Syria's domestic combatants, clashes among the war's competitive interveners, and the return of large-scale violence.

First, the potential for US–Russian confrontation remains a serious concern, especially in the eastern region of Homs Governorate. It is here that US forces, together with their SFA clients, patrol the so-called "55 kilometer area" surrounding the al-Tanf garrison.[48] To date, neither Russia nor the US has appeared willing to surrender influence in the region, nor has either side indicated a readiness to reengage the other to shape the conflict's end game. While both powers have continued to restrict the scale and scope of their operations to avoid a direct clash, the risk of inadvertent escalation remains high. Indeed, there have been a number of minor incidents between American and Russian forces on patrol in eastern Syria, including collisions between convoy vehicles.[49] US fighter jets have been scrambled to escort Russian aircraft overflying eastern Syria, while Russian pilots have "buzzed" US ground forces operating in the region.[50] More worryingly, Russia has continued to harass US-backed SFA rebels operating from the al-Tanf garrison, a base that Moscow has long called for US troops to abandon. Russian commanders have been careful to warn their American counterparts in advance of any strikes, so as to avoid US casualties.[51] But this behavior, together with a rise in Russian overflights of the al-Tanf garrison, has raised concerns that mistakes or misunderstandings might escalate into an unintended conflict between the US and Russian forces.[52] As Lieutenant General Alexus Grynkewich, combined forces air component commander for US Central Command, explains, "it's an uncomfortable situation [...] it just increases the risk of miscalculation."[53] Referring to the US–Russian deconfliction lines, Grynkewich confirms that "the phones are still ringing, the phones are still being picked up." However, he highlights that "the risk of miscalculation or someone just making a mistake is way higher than it needs to be."[54] Especially in the context of Syria's

---

[47] Hinnebusch (2020: 13); Yacoubian (2021: 12–19). Iran is another significant external intervener in the Syrian civil war, but it does not exert control over a specific territorial sphere of influence. Instead, Tehran has adopted a "forward-defense" strategy, using its proxies to project influence in strategic areas under the Assad regime's control. For a discussion of Iranian strategy in Syria, see Akbarzadeh, Gourlay, and Ehteshami (2023).

[48] The "55 kilometer area" is roughly composed of a half-circle with a radius of 55 kilometers, with the al-Tanf base at its center.

[49] See, for example, Foy, Manson, and Cornish (2020).

[50] Schmitt (2020); Starr (2022a).

[51] See, for example, Starr (2022b). According to US Air Force Major General Kenneth Ekman, US and Russian military officials speak several times a day because "neither nation wants any sort of a miscalculation." As quoted in Schogol (2020).

[52] Lubold and Gordon (2022).

[53] As quoted in Kube (2023). Also see Nissenbaum (2023).

[54] As quoted in Weisgerber (2023).

crowded battlespace environment, close proximity patrols, provocative probes, and aircraft "buzzing" present a serious risk of accidents, misinterpretations, and inadvertent escalation.[55]

A second potential flash point lies in the SDF-controlled northeast. Here, frequent skirmishes along tense, complicated lines of control hold the potential for a major escalation between the Turkish military and its Syrian National Army (SNA) client, on one side, and the US-backed SDF, on the other. Fearing the establishment of an autonomous Kurdish statelet on its southern border, Ankara has launched several major cross-border military operations against the SDF, which it views as an offshoot of its longtime domestic rival, the Partiya Karkerên Kurdistanê (PKK).[56] Nonetheless, and notwithstanding Turkish protestation—nor the strategic contradiction inherent in US support for a rebel group that is anathema to its North Atlantic Treaty Organization (NATO) ally—Washington has continued to facilitate the SDF's territorial control of northeast Syria through the provision of extensive military aid and the co-location of American troops alongside SDF patrols. Top US officials have repeatedly cautioned Turkey against escalatory dynamics, whether instigated by Ankara or the SNA, that would "[threaten] the safety of US personnel who are working with local partners in Syria."[57] However, these warnings have not eliminated the risk of US–Turkish clashes. In October 2023, for example, US F-16 fighter jets shot down an armed Turkish drone that came within 500 meters of American troops. The incident—"a rare use of force by one NATO member against another"—occurred after more than a dozen calls from US officials to their Turkish counterparts to inform the latter that American forces were in the area.[58] Should a new Turkish cross-border operation be launched against the SDF, Ankara is likely to come under heavy pressure to limit its ground operations to the border areas west of the Euphrates, so as to avoid US forces operating to its east. However, limiting the operation's geographic scope in this way would not neutralize all escalatory risks, for two reasons. First, Russian forces patrol the boundaries of the SDF's territorial control, risking Russo-Turkish confrontation.

---

[55] As Schelling (1966: 91, emphasis in original) warned long ago, "buzzing an airplane [...] does no harm unless the planes collide; they probably will not collide but they *may* and if they do the result is sudden, dramatic, irreversible, and grave enough to make even a small probability a serious one."

[56] More specifically, Turkey argues that the People's Defense Units, which makes up the bulk of the SDF force, is closely associated with the PKK. Major Turkish operations targeting the SDF have included Operation Euphrates Shield (2016), Operation Olive Branch (2018), and Operation Peace Spring (2019). More recently, it carried out a series of air strikes under Operation Claw Sword (2022) on SDF bases in northern Syria in retaliation for a bomb attack in Istanbul that killed six people on November 13, 2022.

[57] As quoted in Reuters (2022). Also see Ravid (2022) and US Department of Defense (2022a, 2022b).

[58] Copp, Lee, and Baldor (2023).

And second, renewed cross-border operations could push the SDF to reconcile with Damascus—if only temporarily—in the interest of a military partnership to counter the Turkish offensive.[59] In either scenario, a combustible mix of overlapping and competing interests complicate conflict resolution in Syria's northeast. For all parties to the conflict, the shadow of inadvertent escalation continues to loom large.

Finally, a third potential flash point is to be found in the northwest Idlib Governorate—the last major stronghold of non-Kurdish opposition forces in Syria. It is here that Turkish forces protect a number of anti-Assad opposition factions, chief among them Hay'at Tahrir al-Sham (HTS).[60] The Assad regime has repeatedly called for the end of Turkey's occupation and, with the support of Russian combat forces, has kept up its bombardment of the region in an attempt to recapture territory. But the deployment of Turkish forces to the area has effectively neutralized the potency of the government advance, emboldening HTS leader Abu Mohammed al-Jolani to vow his group "will never reconcile" with Assad.[61] More worryingly, the Turkish deployment has also led to run-ins between Turkish and Russian forces. For example, dozens of Turkish soldiers were killed when an air strike hit a military convoy entering contested terrain between the towns of al-Bara and Baluon, south of the city of Idlib, in February 2020.[62] Despite evidence of Russian culpability, Turkey proved reluctant to point a finger at Moscow, choosing instead to blame the Assad regime.[63] Accordingly, its retaliatory military incursion in Idlib Governorate carefully targeted regime, but not Russian, military positions. Yet, the stability of the Idlib front line remains contingent on the maintenance of a working relationship between Moscow and Ankara.[64] The former has repeatedly cautioned the latter to exercise "restraint" and to "avoid the escalation of tensions," warning that destabilization will "boomerang back and further complicate the security situation."[65] For now, such warnings have moderated Turkish ambitions.[66] But

---

[59] SDF leaders have confirmed "the readiness of (SDF) forces to coordinate with forces of the Damascus government to confront any possible Turkish incursion and to protect Syrian territories against occupation" (as quoted in Mroue 2022). Whether such coordination could eventually serve as a basis for longer term compromise is speculative at best.

[60] HTS emerged from Jabhat al-Nusra in 2017. It is opposed to Turkey's other key Syrian client, the SNA, with which it has had numerous running battles.

[61] As quoted in Lister (2023: 2).

[62] Gall (2020).

[63] For details on the incident, see Kemal (2021). For Turkey's statement on the incident, see Presidency Of The Republic Of Turkey (2020).

[64] This working relationship has been conducted bilaterally and as part of the Astana Forum. On the complex relationship between Turkey and Russia in the context of the Syrian civil war, see İpek and Güler (2021).

[65] The quotation is from Kremlin spokesman Dmitry Peskov, as quoted in Agence France-Presse (2022).

[66] On Russian warnings moderating Turkish ambitions in Syria, see Heller (2022).

should fighting between regime and opposition forces flare once more, the danger of Turkish–Russian clashes will return.

In short, while the scale of violence in Syria has declined over recent years, the country remains a tinderbox. Gun battles, shelling, and air strikes continue to kill and injure scores of civilians. The dangers of renewed fighting among a litany of rivalrous domestic combatants are ever-present. And risks of inadvertent clashes among competitive interveners remain potent at three potential flash points—in the northwest, the northeast, and in the eastern regions of Homs Governorate. While careful efforts to manage escalation and deconflict their forces has to date helped competitive interveners avoid major confrontations, the persistent and constrained character of their support to Syria's domestic warring parties continues to impede the path to peace. Meanwhile, the Syrian people suffer in the context of omnipresent violence and an unconscionable humanitarian catastrophe.

How can this book's theory and empirics help inform international engagement in the Syrian conflict and other future civil wars? While there are no easy solutions, in the next section I consider the policy implications of my findings for conflict management, before closing with suggestions for future research.

Policy Implications

Interventions to End Civil Wars: Assumptions and Realities

A common view held among pundits, policymakers, and political scientists alike is that military interventions can help end civil wars by facilitating negotiated agreements between domestic combatants.[67] By manipulating the costs of war and the benefits of peace, third parties can help generate "mutually hurting stalemates": conditions under which neither of the domestic combatants can win and continued deadlock is painful.[68] Such conditions encourage domestic bargaining, it is argued, by convincing one or both sides that there is no military solution to their conflict. This stands to propel a diplomatic process that ends fighting in favor of a negotiated settlement.[69]

Given the prominence of this argument, it is of little surprise that its logic was regularly deployed by those advocating for a greater US role in Syria. For example, in a leaked internal memo, some fifty-one US State Department

---

[67] See, for example, Licklider (1995), Walter (1997, 2002), Carment and Rowlands (1998), Regan (2002), Siqueira (2003), and Amegashie and Kutsoati (2007).
[68] Zartman (1985, 2000).
[69] For other examples of this argument, see Rothchild (1997) and Sisk (2009). For a critical view, see Duursma (2020).

officers called for increased US involvement in the conflict and military strikes against the Assad regime. In making their case for "a more militarily assertive US role in Syria," the memo writers contended that "the judicious use of stand-off and air weapons [...] would undergird and drive a more focused and hardnosed US-led diplomatic process." By raising the costs of the war and shifting the tide of the conflict against the Assad regime, the US could send a clear signal that "there will not be a military solution to the conflict." This, the memo authors argued, would "propel a new and reinvigorated diplomatic initiative" that would "put an end to this conflict once and for all."[70]

After years of death and destruction, the hope that a more robust intervention might deliver sustainable peace is understandable. But as this book's theory and empirics have made clear, the logic underpinning the arguments of intervention advocates is flawed. While military strikes might have increased the costs of war to Assad's regime in Syria, the active involvement of Russian forces would have more than made up for those losses. Indeed, Russia would have almost certainly been encouraged to increase its own military activity in Syria in response to American escalation. There is historical precedent for such an outcome: it was precisely when the Assad regime seemed most threatened by US-backed rebels, in September 2015, that Russia stepped up its participation in the war, actively intervening with its own combat forces. This decision proved to be critical for the regime's survival, as Assad himself has acknowledged: "Russian support of the Syrian Army [...] tipped the scales against the terrorists. [...] It was the crucial factor."[71]

These dynamics challenge both the wisdom and feasibility of arguments advocating for the creation of "mutually hurting stalemates" by third-party interveners, whether in Syria or other conflict zones afflicted by competitive intervention. Rather than render a conflict "ripe for resolution," interveners risk triggering countervailing responses from interstate rivals. Under the shadow of inadvertent escalation, the contradiction inherent in the desire to intervene and the need to control the risk of enlarged conflict prevents the conferral of decisive military advantages while distorting domestic bargaining processes. It is for these reasons that more robust interventions will often risk increasing the scope of violence inflicted by civil wars *without* solving the problems that underlie them.

---

[70] The memo was obtained by *The New York Times* in June 2016 and published in its entirety. See US Department of State Draft Dissent Memo (n.d.).
[71] See Bill Neely's interview with Assad, which was held on July 13, 2016. A full transcript of the interview is available from the state-run Syrian Arab News Agency (2016).

Sequencing of External and Internal Peace Agreements

This book's theoretical framework highlights how external military aid distorts the bargaining process of domestic combatants by subsidizing the costs of continued fighting, balancing combatant capabilities, and amplifying information asymmetries. Together, these distortions increase combatants' value for fighting, preclude decisive military advantages, and worsen information asymmetries—outcomes that prolong civil wars.

A natural corollary of this argument is that the termination of external support can serve to eliminate distortions of the bargaining process, thereby facilitating negotiated settlements between domestic combatants. This observation has important implications for the policy and practice of conflict management: it suggests that ending civil wars that are afflicted by competitive intervention will require *internal* peace agreements between domestic combatants to be preceded by *external* agreements between interveners.

Consider evidence from the case studies presented in this book. Throughout the Afghan conflict, there was little attempt to reconcile the interests of the competing belligerents. While it is true that talks were held between the Afghan government and Pakistan, the fact that Islamabad stubbornly refused to so much as acknowledge the legitimacy of the Kabul regime—to say nothing of its unwillingness to terminate aid to the mujahideen—doomed those negotiations from the start. For their part, the US and the Soviet Union were of little help: neither side participated in the talks, nor did they interrupt the flow of military aid to their respective domestic clients. With their war subsidized by external backers, neither the Afghan communist government nor its mujahideen challengers felt compelled to so much as begin negotiations with the other side. Predictably, no domestic agreement to end the war was ever reached.

In the case of the Angolan civil war, by contrast, a domestic peace process did eventually emerge. Notably, however, an internal agreement between UNITA and the MPLA only became possible after an external agreement—the Tripartite Accords—was signed between Angola, Cuba, and South Africa. Prior to that external agreement, the Angolan civil war remained hostage to the larger geopolitical struggle taking place between Cuba and South Africa over the former's withdrawal from Angola and the latter's withdrawal from South West Africa/Namibia. The Tripartite Accords addressed both issues—and did so without a single reference to the Angolan civil war. Once these international policy issues were addressed at the interstate level, meaningful progress could be made on the underlying domestic policy issues that fueled the civil war. In fact, negotiations between the MPLA and UNITA began just six months after the signing of the Tripartite Accords, resulting in a ceasefire under the Gbadolite Declaration and a peace agreement under the Bicesse Accords.

The proposition that external agreements will often need to precede internal agreements also finds support in other regions of the world. Consider, for example, the Esquipulas II Accord. This was an international agreement between Costa Rica, El Salvador, Guatemala, Honduras, and Nicaragua that provided the principles under which those states would work to cooperatively resolve the numerous conflicts that plagued Central America during the 1980s. The Accord defined a number of measures to promote national reconciliation at the domestic level—such as democratization and free elections—and, crucially, also established measures to regulate conflict at the interstate level, including the termination of all military, financial, and logistical aid to irregular forces, the non-use of territory to attack other states, negotiations on arms controls, and international verification procedures.[72] As Oliver explains, these measures "signified that the Central American presidents had agreed to play by the same set of rules [...] ensuring that everyone was taking similar measures at the same time in an effort to reduce mistrust and the perceived risk involved in pursuing peace unilaterally."[73] In this respect, the *external* considerations of the Esquipulas II Accord were the foundation for the *internal* peace agreements that were later established in El Salvador, Nicaragua, and Guatemala.[74]

The implications of these historical examples for Syria are clear: efforts to end the civil war must begin with external agreements between the competitive interveners. To be sure, the sheer number of armed groups and external actors participating in the war greatly complicates the bargaining process, rendering a lasting negotiated agreement that incorporates all parties to the conflict unlikely. Notwithstanding these challenges, however, an international agreement on Syria's future holds the potential for reducing violence against civilians while continuing to prevent the resurgence of ISIS. Recent trilateral talks between Syria, Turkey, and Russia offer some hope on this score, but any future agreement will require the inclusion of US interests to be meaningful.[75] Such an agreement will also require some difficult compromises: on the part of the US, a willingness to come to terms with the Bashar al-Assad regime and Turkish security concerns in Syria's northern border region; on the part of Russia, a readiness to discuss some form of post-conflict power-sharing between Assad and his opponents; and for all sides, a commitment to rein in regional powers to begin disentangling the myriad competing interests that continue to fuel

---

[72] For the full text of this agreement, see UN Security Council (1987).
[73] Oliver (1999: 155).
[74] It merits mention that delays in the establishment of domestic peace agreements in the aftermath of the Esquipulas II Accord were in large part driven by US opposition to the Accord—that is, continued external meddling from a global actor that was not party to the regional agreement signed by Costa Rica, El Salvador, Guatemala, Honduras, and Nicaragua.
[75] The trilateral talks, held on December 28, 2022, were the first meeting of the Turkish and Syrian defense ministers in more than a decade. See Michaelson (2022).

the war. These concessions will be hard won, and they will not bring peace to Syria overnight. But they will be a first step in the right direction. It is only when external powers end their meddling that a lasting internal settlement will be possible.

Establishing Effective Thresholds: The Risks of Ambiguity in Escalation Control

A third policy implication derived from the theory and empirics presented in this book concerns the characteristics of effective thresholds in the context of escalation control. As discussed in Chapter 2, escalation is a relational and context-dependent concept—it is conditioned by time, by place, and by the identities of belligerents. What marks any given threshold as more or less "effective" for coordinating behavior (and thereby, controlling escalation) is its conspicuousness (in the sense that it is prominent and both sides are aware of it) and its uniqueness (in the sense that it is novel, discrete, or discontinuous).[76]

Consider examples from the case studies presented in this book. During the Afghan civil war, the "battlefield credible" distinction, which required that all weapons provided to the mujahideen be plausibly captured on the Afghan battlefield, constrained US arms supplies for many years. In practice, whether an assault rifle is of Soviet or American origin would seem of little importance to its battlefield effects. But by establishing a battlefield credible distinction, US and Pakistani policymakers were sending a credible signal that they wanted to limit the scope of the war. The clarity of this signal stemmed from its conspicuous and unique characteristics: the absence of US-made military hardware on the Afghan battlefield was recognizable, it was qualitatively distinctive, and it was discrete rather than a "matter of degree."[77]

Likewise, the location of Cuba's defensive line during the Angolan civil war was no coincidence. By arraying his forces along the Moçâmedes Railway and forbidding Cuban troops from operating south of it, Fidel Castro constructed a salient political boundary—marked by a unique physical feature of the Angolan landscape—that signaled a limitation to his force's participation in the war. In turn, South Africa's tacit acknowledgment of this threshold was marked by their own avoidance of operations north of the rail line, even when doing so entailed tactically suboptimal outcomes.

By contrast, thresholds that are ambiguous, or that are open to interpretation, are less effective for the purposes of escalation control. In Syria, this point was illustrated in dramatic fashion in February 2018, when a nearly four-hour battle

---

[76] Schelling (1960: 57–58 and appendix A, 1966: 137–138). Also see Altman (2015: chapter 2).
[77] Cf. Schelling (1966: 138).

broke out between an attacking pro-Syrian government force and a defending SDF unit just outside the city of Deir ez-Zor, along the Euphrates River. Unbeknownst to both sides when the battle began, Russian mercenaries employed by the Wagner Group—a private military contractor—were operating alongside the pro-government force, while US troops were co-located with their SDF partners. The ensuing firefight resulted in the deaths of some 200–300 troops—including at least nine Russians.[78] This unprecedented event threatened to inflame already-simmering tensions, or worse still, spark a wider confrontation between Washington and Moscow.

While neither side has released a full account of the incident, evidence suggests that Russia was unaware that Wagner Group units were participating in the battle. Indeed, when US officials contacted their Russian counterparts via their deconfliction line, they were told that there were no Russian troops present in the attacking force.[79] It would take weeks for Moscow to eventually admit that there were Russian *citizens* (not Russian *troops*) killed in the battle. Reports suggest that the Russian Ministry of Defense was caught off guard by the incident, "simply dumbfounded" that it occurred at all.[80]

But another, overlooked dimension of the incident is the ambiguous geographical boundaries that demarcate areas of contestation and control in the immediate vicinity of Deir ez-Zor. As noted above, the Euphrates River has been the predominant geographic feature separating the US and its domestic clients from Russia and its Syrian government ally. By physically separating the two sides, the river has served to minimize the risk of direct confrontation. However, for reasons that remain unclear, at Deir ez-Zor—which lies on the western banks of the Euphrates River—pro-government forces were provided an exception to this general rule: they were permitted to control a small salient on the eastern banks of the river, directly across from the city.[81] Significantly, it was from this salient that the attacking force appears to have originated, and it was in this salient that the Russian mercenaries were killed. While details remain sparse, evidence suggests that ambiguity over "how far" the salient extended may have played a contributing role in the Russian deaths. Indeed, witnesses and participants to the events fail to confirm Russian mercenary participation in the attack on the SDF or that they joined in the battle at all. As one journalist from the area puts it, "[t]he Russians [...] just had the bad luck of being in the wrong place at the wrong time."[82]

---

[78] Gibbons-Neff (2018); Reuter (2018). No Americans were killed in the fighting.

[79] Former US Defense Secretary Jim Mattis testified that "the Russian high command in Syria assured us it was not their people" (as quoted in Gibbons-Neff 2018).

[80] Malkova and Baev (2019).

[81] Reuter (2018).

[82] The quotation is from Ahmad Ramadan, the founder of the *Euphrates Post*, as quoted in Reuter (2018).

For policymakers, the lessons of the February 2018 incident are clear: ambiguities in the limitations of war increase the likelihood of misinterpretation, miscommunication, and costly battlefield mistakes. To more effectively manage escalatory risks, thresholds must be constructed around focal points: conspicuous and discrete features that improve coordination among actors by minimizing ambiguity, increasing verifiability, and improving predictability, even in the absence of explicit communication.

Policymaker Perceptions and Escalation Control

A fourth policy lesson that emerges from this book's theory and empirics concerns the importance of policymakers' capacities to envision their opponent's expectations when attempting to control escalation during competitive interventions in foreign civil wars.[83] Attentiveness to a conflict's context and frames of reference plays a critical role in tacit communication and signaling, while a failure to consider an opponent's position and perspective can be dangerous and damaging. In the Angolan case, for example, Soviet advisors took care to position their encampments a few kilometers away from Angolan base areas, enabling South African forces to more easily avoid targeting Russian personnel. Similarly, in the Afghan case, the defensive force postures that were adopted by Soviet and Pakistani air crews demonstrated their limited intentions and desire to avoid costly dogfights. In both cases, a failure to interpret these signals of restraint risked disastrous consequences: escalation, direct confrontation, and mutually destructive outcomes.

In the face of uncertainty about an opponent's intentions, states must send costly signals to convey peaceful aims or to demonstrate a willingness to stand firm.[84] Yet, the clarity of these signals cannot be assumed: there is always the risk of misperception or misunderstanding, as the same signals can be interpreted differently by different observers.[85] Indeed, recent work has uncovered considerable heterogeneity in the degree to which costly signals can reassure.[86] Survey research has also revealed cross-national differences in how context affects perceptions of escalation.[87] Consequently, policymakers must take care to incorporate their opponent's position and perspective when devising signals and strategies to control escalation. This requires a consideration of how a rival

---

[83] On an opponent's perceptions and presuppositions for escalation control, see Smoke (1977: chapter 9).
[84] Signals must be costly in order to be credible in light of strategic incentives to dissemble. See Schelling (1966), Fearon (1994, 1997), and Kydd (2005: chapter 7).
[85] Jervis (2002).
[86] Kertzer, Rathbun, and Rathbun (2020).
[87] Lin-Greenberg (2023).

state understands the objective situation on the battlefield, interprets information signals, draws inferences, and reaches conclusions. It also requires that policymakers engage in an honest self-assessment of how their rival perceives them, their identities, and their interests.

The importance of self and situational awareness is made clear by cases in which interveners failed to appreciate their opponent's perspective. Consider, for example, China's entrance into the Korean War. It is now widely acknowledged that the American decision to send US forces north of the 38th parallel and to advance toward the Yalu River was critical to Mao Zedong's decision to commit Chinese forces to the conflict.[88] Mao felt immediately threatened by the US advance and feared the long-term political implications of an American presence in North Korea. Unfortunately, American policymakers failed to appreciate the veracity of Chinese signals of resolve, disregarded Beijing's security concerns, and dismissed the strategic importance of the 38th parallel as a geographic threshold that regulated the intensity of the Korean War. As a result, they were unable to anticipate how Mao would respond to the American offensive. The consequences of these failures to envision the Chinese position and perspective proved tragic: US troops were met by a massive counteroffensive and a greatly escalated war.

Thus, even when intentions appear "obvious" to policymakers on one side of a competitive intervention, it is critical that they ask whether it is also obvious for their opponent. Individuals and states tend to see their own actions as reasonable, legitimate, or benign while interpreting others' behavior as aggressive, greedy, or hostile. Controlling escalation is an *interactive* process that requires policymakers to not only adequately signal their own limited intentions but also look carefully for signs of an opponent's restraint. Both in Syria and in future civil wars, careful attention to cues and context is critical for escalation control.

Future Trajectories

This book has introduced a new concept to the study of civil war—competitive intervention—that challenges the traditional distinction drawn between *intra*state and *inter*state conflicts. By unpacking the unique strategic dilemmas that underlie this particular configuration of external meddling, it has shed new light on the international dimensions of civil war while improving our ability to understand the behaviors of armed groups, states, and third-party interveners under the shadow of inadvertent escalation. In doing so, it has helped to fill a gap in the existing literature, but much work remains to be done.

[88] For a detailed discussion of this case, see Christensen (1992).

CONCLUSION 227

In this final section, I consider avenues for future research on civil war, competitive intervention, and the changing security landscape of the international system.

Over the last two decades, there has been an explosion in research on the causes, dynamics, and consequences of civil war. Initially enamored with large-N, cross-national econometric studies, recent years have seen a decided shift from aggregated, macro-level analyses to much more fine-grained, micro-level studies employing data collected at the subnational level.[89] Some of today's most cutting-edge research forgoes cross-national data entirely, preferring instead detailed subnational analyses that disaggregate large, complex social processes into relationships pertaining to individual actions. This turn toward the microdynamics of civil war has paid considerable dividends, uncovering new insights on topics from civilian victimization and child soldiering, to rebel recruitment and rebel governance, to the organization of mass killing and genocide.[90] Together, these advances have led some analysts to suggest that subnational dataset construction should be prioritized by civil war researchers.[91]

Yet while this micro-level turn has been attended by important advances in our understanding of conflict dynamics, it risks leaving the intrastate/interstate conflict nexus largely unexplored. This book demonstrates that distinctions between civil war and interstate conflict are often misleading, and that there are inferential benefits that accrue from multi-level theoretical integration in the study of both types of conflict.[92] Future research stands to likewise benefit from integrating conflict processes across different levels of analysis, whether by contextualizing the characteristics of civil wars, examining the ways in which macro-historical processes affect conflict dynamics, or by studying the reciprocal influences of micro-, macro-, and systemic-level processes. Ultimately, this work will be empirically and conceptually taxing, and its validity will hinge on whether researchers can adequately capture the operative processes linking different levels of analysis. But further exploration of these linkages promises fruitful future research that will help to develop stronger theoretical foundations for the broader field of conflict research. Indeed, a synthesis of international relations theory with insights gleaned from the civil war literature promises new inferential leverage in the study of political violence of all kinds, while further exploration of the intrastate/interstate conflict nexus can contribute to the

---

[89] For prominent examples of earlier cross-national work, see Fearon and Laitin (2003a) and Collier and Hoeffler (2004). On the micro-level turn, see Kalyvas (2008).
[90] See, respectively, Humphreys and Weinstein (2006), Beber and Blattman (2013), Humphreys and Weinstein (2008), Arjona, Kasfir, and Mampilly (2015), and Verwimp (2005).
[91] Restrepo, Spagat, and Vargas (2006).
[92] On the latter point, see Balcells and Justino (2014).

theoretical and empirical development of both the interstate and civil conflict research fields.

These contributions will be critical to answering new questions that arise as the international system undergoes renewed change. While some believe the current unipole, the United States, will face no viable challengers in the near- to medium-term, others are not so sure.[93] The debate over the global diffusion of power and its implications for international stability has unfolded against the backdrop of Russian military interventions and Chinese military modernization. Russian President Vladimir Putin has confidently declared that "[t]he era of the unipolar world order is nearing its end."[94] Chinese President Xi Jinping has called for "justice, not hegemony."[95] Analysts increasingly warn of looming US–Russia *and* US–China "Cold Wars."[96] A central question for policymakers is whether Russia's recent aggression and China's global rise will be accompanied by new challenges to existing global governance structures, breakdowns in international diplomacy, and the proliferation of ungovernable spaces in weak states. It has been argued that Russia's invasion of Ukraine in February 2022 signaled the death of the post–Cold War liberal world order and the birth of a new realist order centered around security interests.[97] Meanwhile, a recent US intelligence threat assessment puts China's efforts to expand its global influence first on the list of global security threats.[98] What are the long-term implications of these developments for international security and civil war?

A focus on the likelihood of a direct US–Russian or US–Chinese confrontation ignores key lessons highlighted in the preceding pages. Given Russian and Chinese conventional and nuclear capabilities, strategic rivalry with the US is unlikely to manifest in high-intensity warfare.[99] While always a possibility, it is a remote one: such confrontation would be just as costly as a US–Soviet war would have been during the Cold War.[100] This suggests that great power competition

---

[93] Compare Wohlforth (1999), Brooks and Wohlforth (2008), and Beckley (2018) with Waltz (1993), Layne (1993, 2020), Mearsheimer (2010), and Posen (2011).
[94] As quoted in Isachenkov (2022).
[95] As quoted in Yao (2021).
[96] See, for example, Legvold (2014), Kroenig (2015), Black and Johns (2016), Bekkevold (2022), Osnos (2023), and Walsh (2023).
[97] Rodrik (2022).
[98] Office of the Director of National Intelligence (2021).
[99] On this point, it is interesting to note that recent work has found that Chinese strategists are relatively confident about US–China crisis stability, both now and in the future. The mutual possession of nuclear weapons is viewed by Chinese military experts as sufficient to keep future crises or conflicts limited. See Cunningham and Fravel (2015). On the origins and consequences of this confidence, see Cunningham and Fravel (2019).
[100] As Rovner (2017: 696) puts it, a future US–China war flirts with "two kinds of catastrophe": nuclear escalation or a protracted war in Asia. On the risk of Chinese nuclear escalation in the event of a conventional war with the US, see Talmadge (2017). On the merits of a US naval blockade as an option for controlling escalation in the event of a war with China, see Cunningham (2020).

in the future is likely to be broad, but shallow, with tensions manifesting in the form of indirect confrontation—that is, conflicts short of interstate war.

This book has considered one form of indirect confrontation—competitive intervention—but the transformed security landscape of the twenty-first century presents a range of additional avenues for states to compete below the threshold of war. China's growing antiaccess/area denial capabilities provide a defensive umbrella under which it can strengthen its military position in the South China Sea; Russia's exploitation of "frozen conflicts" can be leveraged to bolster its bargaining power; and Saudi Arabia's manipulation of oil prices can be used to drive out competitors and secure economic interests. At present, the dynamics of state competition in these "gray zones"—and their implications for international security broadly conceived—remain largely unexplored. In this respect, state confrontation below the threshold of war represents an exciting opportunity for future research on interstate competition amid diffusing power in the international system. A related set of research questions ask how military operations other than war—such as freedom of navigation missions, emergency response and rescue, antipiracy patrols, and humanitarian assistance and disaster relief operations—affect security competition among states.[101]

New questions also abound about the social processes underlying threshold construction, adaptation, and erosion in the context of limited wars. As discussed in Chapter 2, thresholds are social constructs, rather than objective facts. Whether a particular action is viewed as escalatory hinges on whether *social* ideas about thresholds are shared. Moreover, the existence of thresholds—and their war-limiting effects—depends on their (re)production through actors' actions and interactions. These insights suggest parallels between the study of thresholds in international security and the study of other social structures, such as norms, in international relations more broadly. They also raise a number of new and important questions for limited war scholars. How do states forge new thresholds in unique conflict environments? Which thresholds are most salient in cross-domain conflicts? And how far can combatants push shared understandings of the limits of war before thresholds begin to break down? On all these questions, limited war scholars stand to benefit from the constructivist research program, which studies the emergence, spread, and evolution of new standards of appropriate behavior, as well as the effects of norms on actors' interests, identities, and actions.[102] Given the correspondence between the study of thresholds and the study of norms, constructivist frameworks offer a formidable

---

[101] See, for example, Lin-Greenberg (2018).
[102] E.g., Florini (1996); Finnemore and Sikkink (1998); Risse and Sikkink (1999); Acharya (2004); Cortell and Davis (2005); Hoffmann (2005); Hofferberth and Weber (2015).

foundation upon which to develop a theory of the social construction of escalation and its control. Such a theory would not only deepen our understanding of escalation dynamics but would also offer a new theoretical approach to the older literature on limited war.

These contributions will pay dividends as scholars turn to questions about the relationship between emerging technologies and escalatory risks. Recent commentary has sounded the alarm about the threats posed by cyber, robotics, autonomous weapons, and remote sensing, as well as their implications for strategic stability.[103] As states come to possess the ability to precisely strike targets over vast distances and across multiple domains, their adversaries may face growing pressures to attack the radars, command and control networks, and long-range platforms that make these strikes possible.[104] Do emerging technologies create new pathways to escalation? Recent research has taken a skeptical view, finding that while technological change has enabled escalatory behavior in the past, the underlying drivers of escalation have lay elsewhere—in the realm of politics, doctrine, and strategy.[105] Moreover, some types of emerging technologies, such as drones, have been found to decrease escalatory risks by enabling "remote-controlled restraint": the ability to limit escalation in ways not possible when inhabited platforms are employed.[106] The cyber domain has also been identified as a "firebreak" that restrains escalatory pressures.[107] Yet, more work remains to be done to fully unpack how new technologies affect strategic stability. For example, how might states use emerging technologies to better signal strategic restraint? To what extent can existing thresholds be adapted to incorporate new weapon systems? Do emerging technologies risk the blurring of thresholds in cross-domain conflicts? These are exciting questions with important implications for the study of crisis signaling, deterrence, and coercion.

This book also makes a case for the renewed study of information problems as a cause of protracted conflict. Many scholars have cast doubt on the role of information problems in long wars, arguing that relative military strength and resolve should be revealed quickly on the battlefield.[108] Credible commitment problems—the inability of combatants to guarantee the terms of their

---

[103] See, for example, Brimley, FitzGerald, and Sayler (2013), Miller and Fontaine (2017), Acton (2018, 2020), and Buchanan and Cunningham (2020).
[104] The military utility of such "blinding strikes" informs the US's Joint Concept for Access and Maneuver in the Global Commons (more commonly known as the "AirSea Battle" concept). On the escalatory risks underlying this operational approach, see Rovner (2012, 2017: 703–706).
[105] Talmadge (2019).
[106] Lin-Greenberg (2022).
[107] Kreps and Schneider (2019).
[108] See, for example, Reiter (2003: 32), Fearon (2004: 290), Powell (2006: 172–176), Walter (2009: 246, 254), Blattman and Miguel (2010: 12), and Schulhofer-Wohl (2020: 34, 36).

own mutually arranged settlements—have therefore been privileged in the bargaining literature. Yet, existing work conceives of the costly learning process of war monotonically: from initial conditions, the combatants cumulatively learn about their opponent until expectations converge. This overlooks the dynamism of warfare, the changing circumstances that can radically upset calculations about relative strength and resolve, and the processes that distort the information-transmission function of fighting. The credible commitment perspective also ignores the fact that many protracted wars see little or no negotiation among combatants for many years, or even decades. Consider the case evidence presented in this book. In Angola, President José dos Santos and rebel leader Jonas Savimbi met for the first time some *fifteen years* after the onset of fighting. And in Afghanistan, neither the communist regime nor its mujahideen challengers showed any willingness to negotiate—even after more than a decade of fighting. The lack of political bargaining in these examples presents a challenge for the credible commitment perspective: it was not an inability to implement a mutually arranged settlement that protracted these wars; rather, it was an unwillingness on the part of the belligerents to negotiate at all. This suggests alternative bargaining problems were at work in these wars, and as the case evidence makes clear, information problems played a crucial role.

By departing from the established view that information problems provide a poor account of lengthy conflict, this book has demonstrated that competitive interveners' support to domestic combatants can serve as an exogenous—and variable—source of private information. Future work can explore other sources of dynamic uncertainty, such as the development of new military technologies, the entrepreneurship of battlefield commanders, and the transnational diffusion of military strategies and tactics.[109] There are also processes that punctuate or slow the information-transmission function of fighting that merit further scholarly attention. For example, many regions of the world experience rainy seasons that severely hinder transportation, decreasing the intensity of fighting or even bringing it to a halt for several months. This provides opportunities for combatants to consolidate their positions, regroup their forces, and adapt their tactics, altering the balance of power and complicating future estimates of relative strength and resolve.[110] By looking beyond the credible commitment perspective in these ways, future work stands to contribute to a small, but growing, literature on the role that information problems play in prolonging violent conflict.[111]

---

[109] On entrepreneurship in war, see Reiter (2003: 34–35). On the diffusion of military innovations, see Horowitz (2010).
[110] Empirically, conflicts in countries with rainy seasons have been found to be longer on average. See Buhaug and Lujala (2005).
[111] For examples, see Findley (2013), Spaniel and Bils (2018), and Krainin et al. (2020).

Future work can also broaden this book's empirical and theoretical findings by considering other conditions under which positive objectives, such as achieving battlefield victories, are supplanted by negative objectives, such as avoiding battlefield defeats. Many functions of violence extend beyond winning a war, and conflict actors often pursue priorities beyond victory. This is true of belligerents that directly benefit from the instability inherent in war, such as illicit networks that operate illegal economies, but it can also be true of mediators and peacekeepers that seek to help war-torn societies. Consider, for example, the motivations underlying state contributions to interventions undertaken by international organizations like the United Nations and African Union. These operations are often under-manned and under-resourced, lacking the logistical and military capacity to successfully accomplish their objectives.[112] Why do state contributors to these missions invest their resources in a suboptimal fashion? What other priorities—diplomatic leverage, economic advantage, or political influence—might they be pursuing beyond victory?[113] These are important questions not only for scholars but also for the policymakers who fund these missions.

A related set of questions concerns the relationship between competitive intervention and peacekeeping effectiveness. Both theoretically and empirically, competitive intervention and peacekeeping work at cross purposes via distinct channels: while the former introduces bargaining distortions that protract civil wars, the latter helps to overcome credible commitment problems to help prolong peace. Does competitive intervention condition the effectiveness of peacekeeping? This remains an open empirical question with significance for conflict management in countries currently afflicted by civil war.

The existing literature also demonstrates that peacekeepers tend to be deployed to some of the most difficult conflicts.[114] Yet, peacekeeping missions were deployed to just 10.5% of all conflict-years experiencing competitive intervention in the Extended External Support Dataset.[115] Peacekeepers are also notably absent from many contemporary conflicts afflicted by competitive intervention, such as Libya, Syria, and Yemen. This raises an additional set of questions about whether and how the presence of competitive intervention affects

---

[112] In addition to resource deficiencies, the culture of international peacebuilding has also been tied to inefficiencies in these operations. See Autesserre (2014).

[113] Fisher (2012), for example, attributes Ugandan President Yoweri Museveni's decision to contribute troops to the African Union Mission in Somalia (AMISOM) to a wider foreign policy "image management" strategy that is used to avoid diplomatic censure on other issues, such as domestic governance. In addition to this diplomatic leverage, Uganda also benefits by earning valuable combat experience for its troops, reputation and prestige, and reimbursement for equipment and troop allowances. On the deficiencies of the AMISOM mission, see Anderson (2014).

[114] Gilligan and Stedman (2003); Fortna (2004, 2008).

[115] Here I include both UN peacekeeping missions and regional peacekeeping missions.

the likelihood of peacekeeping deployments and other conflict management strategies.

Finally, questions abound on the issue of building a more sustainable future and a more peaceful international system. The post–Cold War decline of civil wars across the globe was a good news story for the international community, but regrettably, violence remains an ever-present feature of our contemporary international landscape. And while competitive intervention has become less common in the unipolar period, it has not yet disappeared. Consequently, researchers and policymakers must keep abreast of changing patterns of interstate competition and transfers of external military assistance to civil war combatants. As this book has stressed, these factors are central to understanding changing trends in the average duration and global prevalence of internal conflicts. While by definition domestic confrontations, civil wars are intimately tied to the dynamics of international politics.

Appendices

Appendix A: Variable Summary Statistics

Table A.1 reports summary statistics for all variables analyzed in Chapter 4.

Table A.1 Variable summary statistics.

Variable	Obs	Mean	SD	Min	Max
COMPETITIVE INTERVENTION	1,256	0.370	0.483	0	1
DEMOCRACY	1,256	0.275	0.447	0	1
POPULATION (LOGGED)	1,256	10.117	1.439	6.457	13.990
GDP PER CAPITA (LOGGED)	1,256	7.572	0.991	5.381	10.266
RUGGED TERRAIN	1,256	5.010	0.512	3.157	6.013
OIL PRODUCTION	1,256	0.583	0.493	0	1
CONTIGUOUS BORDERS	1,256	4.318	2.432	0	14
ETHNIC CONFLICT	1,256	0.670	0.470	0	1
SECESSIONIST–IRREDENTIST CONFLICT	1,256	0.470	0.499	0	1
UN PEACEKEEPING	1,256	0.060	0.237	0	1
REGIONAL PEACEKEEPING	1,256	0.058	0.234	0	1
REBEL TERRITORIAL CONTROL	1,256	0.542	0.498	0	1
NUMBER OF REBEL FACTIONS	1,256	1.354	0.797	1	8
LEGAL REBEL POLITICAL WING	1,256	0.169	0.375	0	1
NEITHER SIDE SUPPORTED	1,256	0.252	0.434	0	1
ONLY REBELS SUPPORTED	1,256	0.138	0.345	0	1
ONLY GOVERNMENT SUPPORTED	1,256	0.240	0.428	0	1
US–SOVIET COMPETITIVE INTERVENTION	1,256	0.076	0.265	0	1
LESSER POWER COMPETITIVE INTERVENTION	1,256	0.295	0.456	0	1
COMPETITIVE INTERVENTION (INCL. ALLEGED)	1,256	0.390	0.488	0	1

Appendix B: Nonproportional Hazards Diagnostics

The Cox models employed in Chapter 4 assume that the magnitude of the effect of any covariate on duration is proportional for any two conflict episodes and constant over time. Over the last twenty years, researchers have highlighted the ways in which violations of this proportional hazards assumption (PHA) threaten statistical inference of time-to-event data.[1] It is therefore important to test for nonproportionality when conducting duration analysis. Where violations of the PHA are detected, an easy corrective

---

[1] See, for example, Box-Steffensmeier, Reiter, and Zorn (2003) and Box-Steffensmeier and Jones (2004).

can be employed to relax the assumption: one simply interacts the offending variable with a function of time and includes that interaction term alongside the other covariates in the model (use of the natural log of time is convention).[2] Doing so relaxes the PHA to capture any nonlinear effects of the offending variable with respect to time.

To assess the validity of the PHA for the Cox models reported in Chapter 4, I follow best practice and run Schoenfeld residuals tests for each model.[3] Schoenfeld residuals are defined as the observed covariate values of each unit that failed, less the expected covariate values at each failure time. When these residuals are uncorrelated with survival time, the PHA is satisfied; when they are positively or negatively correlated with survival time, the PHA is violated. In this appendix, I present the results of covariate-specific tests of the null hypothesis that the impact of covariate x on the hazard of conflict termination violates the PHA, as well as the results of a global test of the null hypothesis that the combined effects of all covariates in a model violate the PHA. I bold any potential violations of the PHA and provide a brief discussion of any statistically significant nonproportional effects.

Table B.1 presents the results of Schoenfeld residuals tests for Models 1–5, as reported in Table 4.1 in Chapter 4. Potential violations of the PHA are detected in Models 2, 4, and 5 for two variables: OIL PRODUCTION and LEGAL REBEL POLITICAL WING. I therefore create interactions between each of these offending variables and (logged) time and include them in all three models in the analyses. Notably, however, the regression results reveal that only LEGAL REBEL POLITICAL WING and its interaction with time are statistically significant at conventional levels.

To assess how the effect of LEGAL REBEL POLITICAL WING varies over time, I follow best practice for evaluating covariate effects in the context of nonproportional hazards by calculating a combined coefficient for the variable and its time interaction using the Model 5 specification reported in Table 4.1 in Chapter 4.[4] I then use the combined coefficient to simulate the estimated percent change in the hazard of conflict termination given a one-unit increase in LEGAL REBEL POLITICAL WING, simulating 1,000 estimates for each day of conflict between six months and twenty years.[5] Figure B.1 plots the results, indicating the central interval of the simulation's distribution with a black line, the central 95% interval with a light gray ribbon, and the central 90% interval with a dark gray ribbon. The figure reveals that in the early stages of a conflict, the presence of a legal rebel political wing has a powerful impact on civil war duration, increasing the hazard of conflict termination by roughly 100–150% in the first year of conflict. This effect is moderated over time, however, and greater uncertainty surrounds these estimates as a war progresses. After roughly 2.5 years, the central 95% interval crosses zero; after roughly 7.5 years, the central 90% interval crosses zero as well. This suggests that the ability of rebel groups to substitute strategies of violence with nonviolent political action does indeed increase the likelihood of conflict termination, as predicted by existing work.[6] However, these positive effects on the hazard of conflict termination decline as a war persists. At the sample mean

---

[2] Note that unlike standard interaction tests, in the context of Cox duration models one includes x and the interaction $x^*\ln(t)$, but *not* $\ln(t)$ itself.
[3] Grambsch and Therneau (1994); Box-Steffensmeier and Jones (2004: 120–121, 131–137).
[4] For a discussion of this approach to assessing nonproportional hazards, see Licht (2011).
[5] To perform these simulations, I use the techniques developed by Gandrud (2015).
[6] See Cunningham, K. Gleditsch, and Salehyan (2009).

Table B.1 Nonproportional hazards diagnostics for Models 1–5.

	Model 1 (bivariate)			Model 2 (state factors)			Model 3 (conflict factors)			Model 4 (group factors)			Model 5 (fully specified)		
	χ^2	DF	p	χ^2	DF	p	χ^2	DF	p	χ^2	DF	p	χ^2	DF	p
COMPETITIVE INTERVENTION	0.00	1	0.99	0.03	1	0.86	0.07	1	0.80	0.00	1	0.98	0.04	1	0.84
DEMOCRACY				0.41	1	0.52							0.27	1	0.60
POPULATION (LOGGED)				0.05	1	0.82							0.27	1	0.60
GDP PER CAPITA (LOGGED)				0.86	1	0.36							1.31	1	0.25
RUGGED TERRAIN				2.20	1	0.14							0.71	1	0.40
OIL PRODUCTION				5.83	1	**0.02**							6.50	1	**0.01**
CONTIGUOUS BORDERS				0.50	1	0.48							0.21	1	0.65
ETHNIC CONFLICT							1.65	1	0.20				0.42	1	0.52
SECESSIONIST–IRREDENTIST CONFLICT							0.02	1	0.90				0.02	1	0.89
UN PEACEKEEPING							0.13	1	0.72				0.97	1	0.33
REGIONAL PEACEKEEPING							0.93	1	0.33				0.32	1	0.57
REBEL TERRITORIAL CONTROL										0.47	1	0.49	1.33	1	0.25
NUMBER OF REBEL FACTIONS										1.63	1	0.20	0.78	1	0.38
LEGAL REBEL POLITICAL WING										4.03	1	**0.05**	3.24	1	**0.07**
GLOBAL TEST	0.00	1	0.99	11.19	7	0.13	3.60	5	0.61	4.93	4	0.29	16.73	14	0.27

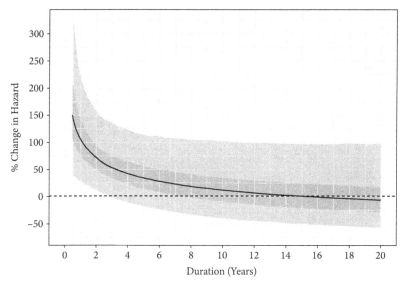

Figure B.1 Simulated percent change in the hazard of civil war termination given a one-unit change in LEGAL REBEL POLITICAL WING; simulated using Model 5. The central interval of the simulation's distribution is indicated by a black line; the central 95% interval is indicated by a light gray ribbon; the central 90% interval is indicated by a dark gray ribbon.

duration (8.59 years), the effect of LEGAL REBEL POLITICAL WING is no longer statistically significant at conventional levels.

In Table B.2, I present the results of Schoenfeld residuals tests for Models 6–10, as reported in Table 4.2 in Chapter 4. Here again, potential violations of the PHA are detected for OIL PRODUCTION and LEGAL REBEL POLITICAL WING in Models 6–7 and 9–10. I therefore include interactions between these variables and (logged) time in each regression model. As these results mirror those above, I do not discuss them further here. A potential violation of the PHA is identified for REBEL TERRITORIAL CONTROL in Model 8, which restricts the data sample to the bipolar era. I therefore include an interaction between this variable and (logged) time in the model. However, neither REBEL TERRITORIAL CONTROL nor its time interaction is found to be statistically significant in the regression model. Finally, CONTIGUOUS BORDERS, ETHNIC CONFLICT, SECESSIONIST–IRREDENTIST CONFLICT, UN PEACEKEEPING, REBEL TERRITORIAL CONTROL, and NUMBER OF REBEL FACTIONS are found to potentially violate the PHA in Model 9, which restricts the data sample to the unipolar era. Each of these variables is therefore interacted with (logged) time in the regression model. Of these, only the pairing of UN PEACEKEEPING and its interaction with time is statistically significant at conventional levels. I therefore calculate a combined coefficient for this pair and then simulate the estimated percent change in the hazard of conflict termination given a one-unit increase in UN PEACEKEEPING, simulating 1,000 estimates for each day of conflict between six months and twenty years. Figure B.2 plots the results. The figure shows that UN peacekeeping deployments have a substantively large, positive impact on the hazard of conflict termination. In numbers, UN peacekeeping deployments are found to increase the hazard of

Table B.2 Nonproportional hazards diagnostics for Models 6–10.

	Model 6 (CI vs. only gov't) χ^2	DF	p	Model 7 (CI vs. only rebels) χ^2	DF	p	Model 8 (bipolar era) χ^2	DF	p	Model 9 (unipolar era) χ^2	DF	p	Model 10 (disaggregated) χ^2	DF	p
COMPETITIVE INTERVENTION	0.06	1	0.81	0.06	1	0.81	0.21	1	0.64	1.87	1	0.17			
NEITHER SIDE SUPPORTED	0.27	1	0.61	0.27	1	0.61									
ONLY GOVERNMENT SUPPORTED				0.50	1	0.48									
ONLY REBELS SUPPORTED	0.16	1	0.69												
US–SOVIET COMPETITIVE INTERVENTION													0.00	1	0.99
LESSER POWERS													0.05	1	0.82
COMPETITIVE INTERVENTION															
DEMOCRACY	0.27	1	0.61	0.27	1	0.61	0.04	1	0.84	1.64	1	0.20	0.26	1	0.61
POPULATION (LOGGED)	0.27	1	0.61	0.27	1	0.61	0.60	1	0.44	0.44	1	0.51	0.29	1	0.59
GDP PER CAPITA (LOGGED)	1.01	1	0.31	1.01	1	0.31	0.72	1	0.40	1.47	1	0.23	1.34	1	0.25
RUGGED TERRAIN	0.61	1	0.44	0.61	1	0.44	0.01	1	0.92	1.76	1	0.18	0.71	1	0.40
OIL PRODUCTION	6.47	1	**0.01**	6.47	1	**0.01**	0.02	1	0.90	3.83	1	**0.05**	6.53	1	**0.01**
CONTIGUOUS BORDERS	0.20	1	0.65	0.20	1	0.65	0.84	1	0.36	7.85	1	**0.01**	0.20	1	0.65
ETHNIC CONFLICT	0.37	1	0.54	0.37	1	0.54	0.31	1	0.58	7.45	1	**0.01**	0.42	1	0.52
SECESSIONIST–IRREDENTIST CONFLICT	0.04	1	0.84	0.04	1	0.84	0.10	1	0.75	2.85	1	**0.09**	0.02	1	0.89
UN PEACEKEEPING	1.04	1	0.31	1.04	1	0.31	0.26	1	0.61	5.90	1	**0.02**	0.97	1	0.32
REGIONAL PEACEKEEPING	0.31	1	0.58	0.31	1	0.58	0.27	1	0.61	1.66	1	0.20	0.32	1	0.57
REBEL TERRITORIAL CONTROL	1.57	1	0.21	1.57	1	0.21	3.08	1	**0.08**	2.89	1	**0.09**	1.32	1	0.25
NUMBER OF REBEL FACTIONS	0.82	1	0.37	0.82	1	0.37	0.40	1	0.53	4.88	1	**0.03**	0.79	1	0.37
LEGAL REBEL POLITICAL WING	2.99	1	**0.08**	2.99	1	**0.08**	0.04	1	0.85	3.00	1	**0.08**	3.23	1	**0.07**
GLOBAL TEST	16.62	16	0.41	16.62	16	0.41	11.63	14	0.64	29.66	14	**0.01**	16.79	15	0.33

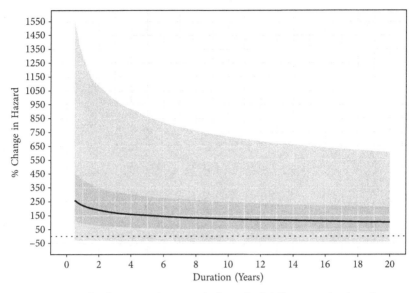

Figure B.2 Simulated percent change in the hazard of civil war termination given a one-unit change in UN PEACEKEEPING; simulated using Model 9 (unipolar era). The central interval of the simulation's distribution is indicated by a black line; the central 95% interval is indicated by a light gray ribbon; the central 90% interval is indicated by a dark gray ribbon.

conflict termination by roughly 250% in the early months of a war. However, the magnitude of this effect declines over time. An additional caveat is that considerable uncertainty surrounds this finding: the central interval of the simulation's distribution fails to reach statistical significance at the $p < 0.05$ level at all simulated points in time (though it does remain statistically significant at the $p < 0.1$ level across all simulated points in time). Taken together, these results provide tentative evidence of the ameliorative effects of peacekeeping on civil war duration in a sample constrained to the unipolar era.[7]

Table B.3 presents the results of Schoenfeld residuals tests for Models 11–15, as reported in Table 4.3 in Chapter 4. As before, potential violations of the PHA were detected in Models 11–14 for OIL PRODUCTION and LEGAL REBEL POLITICAL WING. Accordingly, I include interactions between these variables and (logged) time in each model. As these results once again mirror those above, I do not discuss them further here. Potential violations were also detected for the dummy indicators for the 1950s and 1990s in Model 12, which includes decade fixed effects, and I therefore include an interaction between these variables and (logged) time in the regression model. Lastly, potential violations of the PHA were identified for UN PEACEKEEPING and REBEL TERRITORIAL CONTROL in Model 15, which employs a case inclusion strategy that drops the 1,000 cumulative battle-related deaths criterion. Both of these variables and their interactions with time were found to be statistically significant. I therefore calculate combined coefficients for each variable and its respective time interaction, and then

---

[7] On the relationship between UN peacekeeping deployments and conflict duration, see Ruggeri, Dorussen, and Gizelis (2017) and Kathman and Benson (2019).

Table B.3 Nonproportional hazards diagnostics for Models 11–15.

	Model 11 (incl. alleged)			Model 12 (decade FEs)			Model 13 (frailty)			Model 14 (2 year rule)			Model 15 (25 threshold)		
	χ^2	DF	p	χ^2	DF	p	χ^2	DF	p	χ^2	DF	p	χ^2	DF	p
COMPETITIVE INTERVENTION				0.01	1	0.94	0.04	1	0.84	0.20	1	0.65	1.78	1	0.18
COMPETITIVE INTERVENTION (INCL. ALLEGED)	0.03	1	0.87												
DEMOCRACY	0.34	1	0.56	0.21	1	0.65	0.27	1	0.60	1.71	1	0.19	0.33	1	0.57
POPULATION (LOGGED)	0.28	1	0.60	1.33	1	0.25	0.27	1	0.60	0.11	1	0.74	2.39	1	0.12
GDP PER CAPITA (LOGGED)	1.14	1	0.29	2.11	1	0.15	1.31	1	0.25	0.38	1	0.54	2.29	1	0.13
RUGGED TERRAIN	0.75	1	0.39	0.17	1	0.68	0.71	1	0.40	2.26	1	0.13	1.01	1	0.32
OIL PRODUCTION	6.56	1	**0.01**	4.25	1	**0.04**	6.50	1	**0.01**	4.20	1	**0.04**	0.01	1	0.94
CONTIGUOUS BORDERS	0.24	1	0.62	0.12	1	0.73	0.21	1	0.65	0.43	1	0.51	1.27	1	0.26
ETHNIC CONFLICT	0.33	1	0.56	0.04	1	0.85	0.42	1	0.52	0.92	1	0.34	2.49	1	0.12
SECESSIONIST–IRREDENTIST CONFLICT	0.04	1	0.84	0.02	1	0.88	0.02	1	0.89	0.22	1	0.64	0.63	1	0.43
UN PEACEKEEPING	0.89	1	0.35	2.21	1	0.14	0.97	1	0.33	0.82	1	0.37	5.39	1	**0.02**
REGIONAL PEACEKEEPING	0.15	1	0.70	0.54	1	0.46	0.32	1	0.57	0.00	1	0.97	0.95	1	0.33
REBEL TERRITORIAL CONTROL	1.27	1	0.26	1.32	1	0.25	1.33	1	0.25	1.74	1	0.19	5.58	1	**0.02**
NUMBER OF REBEL FACTIONS	0.72	1	0.40	0.46	1	0.50	0.78	1	0.38	1.10	1	0.30	0.40	1	0.53
LEGAL REBEL POLITICAL WING	3.02	1	0.08	4.42	1	**0.04**	3.24	1	0.07	3.91	1	**0.05**	1.32	1	0.25
1940S DUMMY				0.14	1	0.71									
1950S DUMMY				4.52	1	**0.03**									
1960S DUMMY				1.75	1	0.19									
1970S DUMMY				0.12	1	0.73									
1980S DUMMY				1.79	1	0.18									
1990S DUMMY				6.18	1	**0.01**									
GLOBAL TEST	16.49	14	0.28	33.03	20	**0.03**	16.73	14	0.27	19.34	14	0.15	23.45	14	**0.05**

use the combined coefficients to simulate the estimated percent change in the hazard of conflict termination given a one-unit increase in each variable, using the same technique as described above. Figure B.3 plots the results. The figure reveals that UN

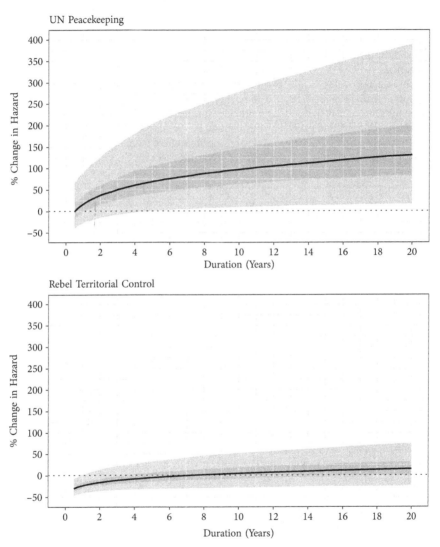

Figure B.3 Simulated percent change in the hazard of civil war termination given a one-unit change in UN PEACEKEEPING and REBEL TERRITORIAL CONTROL; simulated using Model 15 (threshold of twenty-five battle-related deaths). The central interval of each simulation's distribution is indicated by a black line; the central 95% interval is indicated by a light gray ribbon; the central 90% interval is indicated by a dark gray ribbon.

PEACEKEEPING imparts a positive effect on the hazard of conflict termination—an effect that grows larger over time. The uncertainty surrounding these estimates also declines with time, with effects becoming statistically significant around the one-year ($p < 0.1$) and five-year ($p < 0.05$) marks. These results, which align with existing studies, provide additional evidence of the peace-inducing effects of peacekeeping. REBEL TERRITORIAL CONTROL, on the other hand, is found to negatively affect the hazard of conflict termination in the early stages of a war. However, this effect moderates with time and is rendered statistically insignificant at the $p < 0.05$ level within one year of fighting; it is statistically indistinguishable from zero at the $p < 0.1$ level after roughly 3.5 years of fighting.

In sum, testing the validity of the PHA and making modeling adjustments to account for its potential violation reveals a number of interesting time-dependent effects for three variables included in the models reported in Chapter 4. First, the existence of a legal rebel political wing is found to exert a positive influence on the hazard of conflict termination in the early stages of a war. However, this positive effect fades over time and becomes statistically indistinguishable from zero after roughly 7.5 years. UN peacekeeping deployments also impart a positive effect, though the magnitude and statistical significance of their relationship with conflict duration varies over time and as a function of the data sample that is employed. Finally, rebel territorial control is found to decrease the hazard of conflict termination. However, this latter effect is only identified in a data sample that drops the 1,000 cumulative battle-related deaths criterion. What is more, it is found to moderate quickly, becoming statistically insignificant within just a few years of fighting.

Appendix C: Increasing the Conflict Episode Intermittency Window

This book's case selection strategy records a conflict's start date as the day on which the UCDP Armed Conflict Dataset inclusion criteria are met. A conflict is considered terminated once it ceases to meet these inclusion criteria for one full year. However, as noted in Chapter 4, it is reasonable to ask whether a one-year lull in fighting is sufficient to merit coding a conflict as "terminated." Moreover, a two-year intermittency rule has at times been employed in the existing literature.[8] This appendix therefore tests whether my results are sensitive to alternative measures of conflict termination. It replicates all Models 1–10 (as reported in Tables 4.1 and 4.2 in Chapter 4) using a two-year intermittency rule. As with the original analyses, I examine each model specification for violations of the PHA, interacting any potential violations with the natural log of time. I report estimated coefficients and robust standard errors for all models in Tables C.1 and C.2. I then evaluate the substantive significance of my results in Figures C.1 and C.2, which plot the

---

[8] See, for example, Fearon (2004), Sambanis (2004), Cunningham, K. Gleditsch, and Salehyan (2009), Cunningham (2011), and Wucherpfennig et al. (2012).

estimated percent change in the hazard of conflict termination given a one-unit increase in variables of interest.[9]

Results confirm that this book's empirical findings are consistent with theoretical predictions regardless of whether a one- or two-year intermittency rule is used to identify conflict terminations. Turning first to Table C.1 and Figure C.1, I find that the substantive effect of competitive intervention is increased and remains statistically significant across all models when using the two-year rule. Using the coefficients reported for a fully specified model (i.e., Model 5C), competitive intervention is found to reduce the hazard of conflict termination by an average of 64% relative to conflicts that were not afflicted by this form of external meddling. The results identified for the

Table C.1 Cox model estimates; replication of core results using a two-year intermittency rule.

	Model 1C (bivariate)	Model 2C (state factors)	Model 3C (conflict factors)	Model 4C (group factors)	Model 5C (fully specified)
COMPETITIVE INTERVENTION	−0.810*** (0.244)	−1.008*** (0.251)	−0.928*** (0.235)	−0.761*** (0.246)	−1.021*** (0.239)
DEMOCRACY		−0.678** (0.332)			−0.506 (0.323)
POPULATION (LOGGED)		−0.183** (0.091)			−0.136 (0.099)
GDP PER CAPITA (LOGGED)		−0.005 (0.126)			0.085 (0.135)
RUGGED TERRAIN			1.695** (0.742)		−0.060 (0.189)
RUGGED TERRAIN*LN(T)			−0.241** (0.103)		
OIL PRODUCTION			0.903 (1.021)		1.294 (1.055)
OIL PRODUCTION*LN(T)			−0.092 (0.136)		−0.159 (0.138)
CONTIGUOUS BORDERS			−0.012 (0.042)		−0.008 (0.043)

continued

[9] Note that log-transformed covariates are interpreted as percentage, rather than unit, increases.

Table C.1 continued

	Model 1C (bivariate)	Model 2C (state factors)	Model 3C (conflict factors)	Model 4C (group factors)	Model 5C (fully specified)
ETHNIC CONFLICT			−0.126 (0.237)		−0.138 (0.266)
SECESSIONIST–IRREDENTIST CONFLICT			−0.173 (0.227)		−0.156 (0.273)
UN PEACEKEEPING			0.801*** (0.307)		0.572* (0.342)
REGIONAL PEACEKEEPING			0.525 (0.351)		0.758** (0.363)
REBEL TERRITORIAL CONTROL				0.262 (0.198)	0.247 (0.205)
NUMBER OF REBEL FACTIONS				−0.581*** (0.207)	−0.715*** (0.202)
LEGAL REBEL POLITICAL WING				2.531*** (0.938)	2.475** (1.006)
LEGAL REBEL POLITICAL WING*LN(T)				−0.286** (0.135)	−0.300** (0.145)
NUMBER OF CONFLICTS	130	130	130	130	130
NUMBER OF TERMINATIONS	109	109	109	109	109
OBSERVATIONS	1,365	1,365	1,365	1,365	1,365

Note: Coefficient estimates with robust standard errors, clustered on conflict, in parentheses. *$p < 0.1$; **$p < 0.05$; ***$p < 0.01$.

control variables are also largely in line with those reported for a one-year intermittency rule, though the relationship between democracy and conflict duration is rendered more tenuous ($p = 0.117$), while regional peacekeeping deployments are found to increase the hazard of conflict termination by 113% relative to conflicts that did not receive a regional peacekeeping deployment.

Table C.2 and Figure C.2 likewise confirm that results are consistent when using both the one- and two-year intermittency rules. These models compare the duration effects of competitive intervention to other configurations of external support, constrain the data sample by time period, and disaggregate the competitive intervention variable. Substantively, the two-year intermittency window once again tends to increase the magnitude of the effects of the competitive intervention indicator variables, while the statistical significance of the estimated relationships is maintained. This underscores the robust relationship between competitive intervention and civil war duration while confirming that my findings are insensitive to alternative measures of conflict termination.

APPENDICES 245

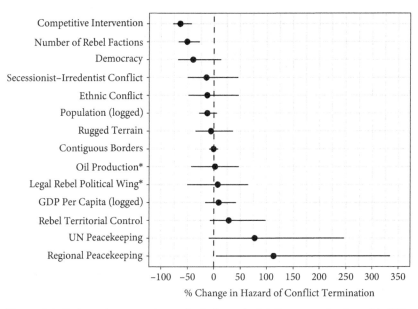

Figure C.1 Estimated percent change in the hazard of civil war termination with 95% confidence intervals; replication of core results using a two-year intermittency rule. Note that the changes in hazard for OIL PRODUCTION and LEGAL REBEL POLITICAL WING, which vary as a function of time, are estimated at the sample mean duration.

Table C.2 Cox model estimates; replication of additional results using a two-year intermittency rule.

	Model 6C (CI vs. only gov't)	Model 7C (CI vs. only rebels)	Model 8C (bipolar era)	Model 9C (unipolar era)	Model 10C (disaggregated)
COMPETITIVE INTERVENTION	−0.989*** (0.289)	−1.068*** (0.288)	−1.023*** (0.264)	−1.182** (0.517)	
NEITHER SIDE SUPPORTED	0.026 (0.261)	−0.053 (0.273)			
ONLY REBELS SUPPORTED	0.079 (0.295)				
ONLY GOVERNMENT SUPPORTED		−0.079 (0.295)			

continued

Table C.2 continued

	Model 6C (CI vs. only gov't)	Model 7C (CI vs. only rebels)	Model 8C (bipolar era)	Model 9C (unipolar era)	Model 10C (disaggregated)
US–SOVIET COMPETITIVE INTERVENTION					−0.735* (0.407)
LESSER POWERS COMPETITIVE INTERVENTION					−1.088*** (0.263)
OTHER CONTROLS INCLUDED?	YES	YES	YES	YES	YES
NUMBER OF CONFLICTS	130	130	94	66	130
NUMBER OF TERMINATIONS	109	109	64	45	109
OBSERVATIONS	1,365	1,365	856	509	1,365

Note: Coefficient estimates with robust standard errors, clustered on conflict, in parentheses. *$p <$ 0.1; **$p < 0.05$; ***$p < 0.01$.

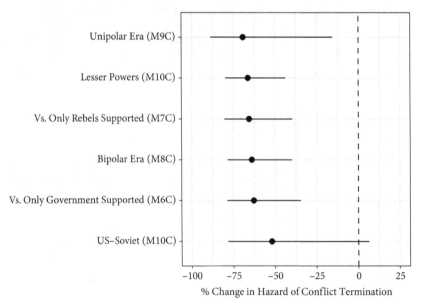

Figure C.2 Estimated percent change in the hazard of civil war termination with 95% confidence intervals; replication of additional results using a two-year intermittency rule.

Appendix D: Relaxing the 1,000 Cumulative Battle-Related Deaths Criterion

The dynamics of minor and major conflicts often differ. Consequently, studying different varieties of violence in the same empirical model risks increasing both the bias and variance of estimates. This book's definition of civil war seeks to minimize these concerns by requiring conflicts to inflict at least 25 battle-related deaths per year *and* a minimum of 1,000 cumulative battle-related deaths over the course of their full duration. The latter criterion serves to minimize concerns over unit heterogeneity and ensure that cases are sufficiently alike to merit meaningful comparisons.[10] Nonetheless, it is reasonable to ask whether and how the results may be affected by dropping the cumulative battle-related deaths criterion. Given that one would not expect competitive intervention to afflict minor conflicts—such as coups, violent riots, or isolated terrorist attacks—I anticipate that the inclusion of these additional low-fatality and short-duration conflicts will increase the magnitude of the effect of competitive intervention on civil war duration. To test that expectation empirically, this appendix replicates all Models 1–10 (as reported in Tables 4.1 and 4.2 in Chapter 4) using a threshold of twenty-five battle-related deaths per year *without* a cumulative battle-related deaths requirement. As with the original analyses, I examine each model specification for violations of the PHA, interacting any potential violations with the natural log of time. I report estimated coefficients and robust standard errors for all models in Tables D.1 and D.2. I then evaluate the substantive significance of my results in Figures D.1 and D.2, which plot the estimated percent change in the hazard of conflict termination given a one-unit increase in variables of interest.

Table D.1 Cox model estimates; replication of core results without a 1,000 cumulative battle-related deaths criterion.

	Model 1D (*bivariate*)	Model 2D (*state factors*)	Model 3D (*conflict factors*)	Model 4D (*group factors*)	Model 5D (*fully specified*)
COMPETITIVE INTERVENTION	−0.814*** (0.154)	−0.983*** (0.157)	−0.877*** (0.151)	−0.731*** (0.159)	−0.954*** (0.155)
DEMOCRACY		−0.352* (0.180)			−0.329* (0.169)
POPULATION (LOGGED)		−0.295*** (0.095)			−0.152*** (0.056)
POPULATION (LOGGED)*LN(T)		0.033** (0.015)			

continued

---

[10] On the use of battle-related death thresholds as a tractable way for scholars to address concerns about unit heterogeneity, see Anderson and Worsnop (2019).

Table D.1 *continued*

	Model 1D (bivariate)	Model 2D (state factors)	Model 3D (conflict factors)	Model 4D (group factors)	Model 5D (fully specified)
GDP PER CAPITA (LOGGED)		0.046 (0.071)			−0.004 (0.074)
RUGGED TERRAIN		−0.218** (0.086)			−0.263*** (0.092)
OIL PRODUCTION		0.113 (0.143)			0.148 (0.148)
CONTIGUOUS BORDERS		0.010 (0.023)			0.014 (0.025)
ETHNIC CONFLICT			−0.852*** (0.272)		−0.285* (0.149)
ETHNIC CONFLICT*LN(T)			0.138*** (0.046)		
SECESSIONIST-IRREDENTIST CONFLICT			−0.202 (0.137)		0.103 (0.151)
UN PEACEKEEPING			−1.604** (0.631)		−1.201* (0.634)
UN PEACEKEEPING*LN(T)			0.321*** (0.097)		0.232** (0.099)
REGIONAL PEACEKEEPING			0.167 (0.259)		0.131 (0.265)
REBEL TERRITORIAL CONTROL				−1.064*** (0.275)	−1.049*** (0.289)
REBEL TERRITORIAL CONTROL*LN(T)				0.163*** (0.047)	0.133*** (0.047)
NUMBER OF REBEL FACTIONS				−0.641*** (0.154)	−0.715*** (0.149)
LEGAL REBEL POLITICAL WING				0.346*** (0.130)	0.328** (0.141)
NUMBER OF CONFLICTS	365	365	365	365	365
NUMBER OF TERMINATIONS	337	337	337	337	337
OBSERVATIONS	1,754	1,754	1,754	1,754	1,754

Note: Coefficient estimates with robust standard errors, clustered on conflict, in parentheses. *$p < 0.1$; **$p < 0.05$; ***$p < 0.01$.

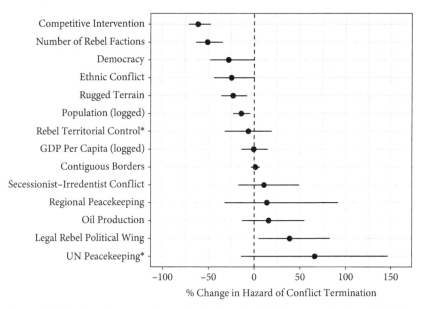

Figure D.1 Estimated percent change in the hazard of civil war termination with 95% confidence intervals; replication of core results without a 1,000 cumulative battle-related deaths criterion. Note that the changes in hazard for REBEL TERRITORIAL CONTROL and UN PEACEKEEPING, which vary as a function of time, are estimated at the sample mean duration.

Empirical results align with theoretical expectations when the 1,000 cumulative battle-related deaths criterion is dropped. Turning first to Table D.1 and Figure D.1, I find that the substantive effect of competitive intervention is indeed increased and remains statistically significant with the lower threshold. In a fully specified model that controls for a suite of state-, conflict-, and group-level factors (Model 5D), competitive intervention is found to reduce the hazard of conflict termination by an average of 61% relative to conflicts that were not afflicted by this form of external meddling. This confirms the strong relationship between competitive intervention and protracted conflict, regardless of the fatality threshold one employs.

With respect to the control variables, my findings are largely in line with previous results, with the exception that the effect of a number of factors that were previously statistically indistinguishable from zero are now statistically significant. In particular, population size, rugged terrain, and ethnic conflict are found to impart significant negative effects on the hazard of conflict termination. UN peacekeeping and rebel territorial control are also found to initially impart negative effects on the hazard, but as indicated by each variables' interaction with (logged) time, these effects moderate as a conflict endures. At the sample mean duration, neither variable imparts a statistically significant effect on the hazard. Legal rebel political wings, on the other hand, are found to increase the hazard of conflict termination by 39%.

Table D.2 and Figure D.2 likewise confirm that results are consistent when dropping the 1,000 cumulative battle-related deaths criterion. These models compare the duration effects of competitive intervention to other configurations of external support, constrain the data sample by time period, and disaggregate the competitive intervention variable. In line with theoretical expectations, the lower threshold once again often increases the magnitude of the effects of the competitive intervention variables. The statistical significance of the estimated relationships is likewise strengthened, as indicated by the tighter confidence intervals for each model estimate. This underscores the robustness of the relationship between competitive intervention and intractable conflict, even when dropping the 1,000 cumulative battle-related deaths criterion.

Table D.2 Cox model estimates; replication of additional results without a 1,000 cumulative battle-related deaths criterion.

	Model 6D (CI vs. only gov't)	Model 7D (CI vs. only rebels)	Model 8D (bipolar era)	Model 9D (unipolar era)	Model 10D (disaggregated)
COMPETITIVE INTERVENTION	−0.864*** (0.185)	−0.670*** (0.202)	−1.047*** (0.198)	−0.779*** (0.287)	
NEITHER SIDE SUPPORTED	1.274*** (0.296)	1.483*** (0.297)			
NEITHER SIDE SUPPORTED*LN(T)	−0.158*** (0.048)	−0.161*** (0.046)			
ONLY REBELS SUPPORTED	−0.240 (0.503)				
ONLY REBELS SUPPORTED*LN(T)	0.008 (0.078)				
ONLY GOVERNMENT SUPPORTED		0.195 (0.187)			
US–SOVIET COMPETITIVE INTERVENTION					−0.770** (0.309)
LESSER POWERS COMPETITIVE INTERVENTION					−0.988*** (0.168)
OTHER CONTROLS INCLUDED?	YES	YES	YES	YES	YES
NUMBER OF CONFLICTS	365	365	202	196	365
NUMBER OF TERMINATIONS	337	337	169	168	337
OBSERVATIONS	1,754	1,754	1,036	718	1,754

Note: Coefficient estimates with robust standard errors, clustered on conflict, in parentheses. *$p < 0.1$; **$p < 0.05$; ***$p < 0.01$.

APPENDICES 251

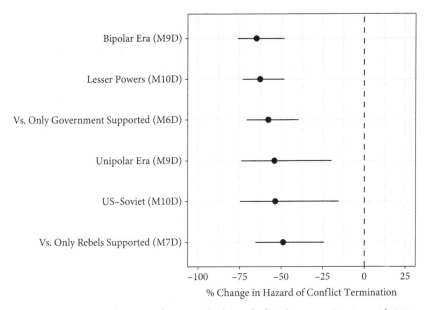

Figure D.2 Estimated percent change in the hazard of civil war termination with 95% confidence intervals; replication of additional results without a 1,000 cumulative battle-related deaths criterion.

Appendix E: Trends in the Yearly Incidence, Average Duration, and Prevalence of Intrastate Conflicts without a 1,000 Cumulative Battle-Related Deaths Criterion

In Figure 4.6 of Chapter 4, I plot the yearly incidence, average duration, and prevalence of civil wars using coding criteria that require conflicts to inflict at least 25 battle-related deaths per year *and* a minimum of 1,000 cumulative battle-related deaths over the course of their full duration. The figure reveals that the global prevalence of civil war has been predominantly driven by changes in the average duration of conflicts, rather than the incidence rate of conflicts.

However, it is reasonable to ask whether results differ when employing a lower threshold that relaxes the 1,000 cumulative battle-related deaths criterion. To answer that question, Figure E.1 reproduces Figure 4.6 using the lower threshold requirement. It confirms that the prevalence of intrastate conflict has indeed been predominantly driven by changes in the average duration of conflicts, rather than the incidence rate of conflicts, even when relaxing the 1,000 cumulative battle-related deaths criterion. While there has been some interannual variability, the incidence of conflict has generally remained low over time, with the exception of the early 1990s, when the number of new conflict outbreaks spiked following the collapse of the Soviet Union. Notably, however, at precisely the same time that the incidence of conflict increased, the prevalence of conflict decreased. These contradictory trends suggest an unavoidable conclusion: trends in the prevalence of conflict are predominately driven by average conflict duration. Indeed, trends in the former largely mirror trends in the latter, rising between 1946 and 1990, declining between 1990 and 2000, and then slowly rising once more during the 2000s. In short, the global prevalence of internal conflict has been predominantly driven by changes in how long conflicts last, rather than how many break out each year—a result that holds regardless of the threshold criteria employed.

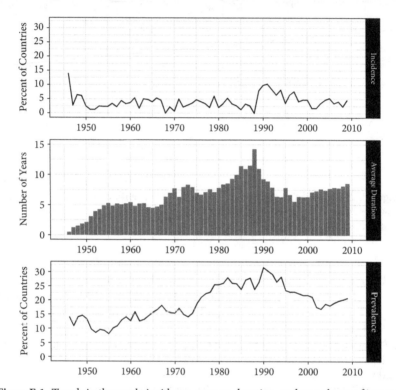

Figure E.1 Trends in the yearly incidence, average duration, and prevalence of internal conflicts without a 1,000 cumulative battle-related deaths criterion, 1946–2009.

References

Abbink, John. "Ethiopia-Eritrea: Proxy Wars and Prospects of Peace in the Horn of Africa." *Journal of Contemporary African Studies* 21, no. 3 (2003): 407–426.

Acharya, Amitav. "How Ideas Spread: Whose Norms Matter? Norm Localization and Institutional Change in Asian Regionalism." *International Organization* 58, no. 2 (2004): 239–275.

Acton, James M. "Cyber Warfare & Inadvertent Escalation." *Daedalus* 149, no. 2 (2020): 133–149.

Acton, James M. "Escalation through Entanglement: How the Vulnerability of Command-and-Control Systems Raises the Risks of an Inadvertent Nuclear War." *International Security* 43, no. 1 (2018): 56–99.

Adamishin, Anatoly. *The White Sun of Angola*. Translated by Gary Goldberg and Sue Onslow. 2nd Edition. Moscow, Russia: Vagrius, 2014.

Agence France-Presse. "Russia Warns Turkey Against 'Destabilizing' Syria." November 22, 2022.

"Agreement of Cooperation Between the Government of the United States of America and the Government of Pakistan." 10 U.S.T. 317, March 5, 1959.

"Agreements on Afghanistan." *Department of State Bulletin* 88, no. 2135 (June 1988): 54–60.

Ahram, Ariel I. *Proxy Warriors: The Rise and Fall of State-Sponsored Militias*. Stanford, CA: Stanford University Press, 2011.

Akbarzadeh, Shahram, William Gourlay, and Anoushiravan Ehteshami. "Iranian Proxies in the Syrian Conflict: Tehran's 'Forward-Defence' in Action." *Journal of Strategic Studies* 46, no. 3 (2023): 683–706.

Akcinaroglu, Seden, and Elizabeth Radziszewski. "Expectations, Rivalries, and Civil War Duration." *International Interactions* 31, no. 4 (2005): 349–374.

Alekseevsky, Anatoliy Eduardovich. "Memories of War in Angola." In *Bush War: The Road to Cuito Cuanavale*, edited by Gennady Shubin and Andrei Tokarev, 171–181. Johannesburg: Jacana, 2011.

Alexiev, Alexander. *Inside the Soviet Army in Afghanistan*. Santa Monica, CA: RAND Corporation, 1988.

Allison, Paul D. " Bias in Fixed-Effects Cox Regression with Dummy Variables." Department of Sociology, University of Pennsylvania, 2002.

Altman, Dan. *Red Lines and Faits Accomplis in Interstate Coercion and Crisis*. PhD Dissertation, Massachusetts Institute of Technology, 2015.

Amegashie, J. Atsu, and Edward Kutsoati. "(Non)Intervention in Intra-State Conflicts." *European Journal of Political Economy* 23, no. 3 (2007): 754–767.

Anderson, Noel. "Competitive Intervention, Protracted Conflict, and the Global Prevalence of Civil War." *International Studies Quarterly* 63, no. 3 (2019): 692–706.

Anderson, Noel. "Peacekeepers Fighting a Counterinsurgency Campaign: A Net Assessment of the African Union Mission in Somalia." *Studies in Conflict & Terrorism* 37, no. 11 (2014): 936–958.

Anderson, Noel, Benjamin E. Bagozzi, and Ore Koren. "Addressing Monotone Likelihood in Duration Modelling of Political Events." *British Journal of Political Science* 51, no. 4 (2021): 1654–1671.

Anderson, Noel, and Mark S. Bell. "The Limits of Regional Power: South Africa's Security Strategy, 1975–1989." *Journal of Strategic Studies* 46, no. 2 (2023): 404–426.

Anderson, Noel, and Alec Worsnop. "Fatality Thresholds, Causal Heterogeneity, and Civil War Research: Reconsidering the Link Between Narcotics and Conflict." *Political Science Research and Methods* 7, no. 1 (2019): 85–105.

"Andropov-Gromyko-Ustinov-Ponomarev Report to the Central Committee of the Communist Party of the Soviet Union on Events in Afghanistan on 27-28 December 1979," December 31, 1979. National Security Archive, George Washington University.

"Angola-USSR-South Africa: Growing Conflict," December 5, 1983. Fortier, Donald R.: Files, RAC Box 14, Soviet Project [2 of 2]. Ronald Reagan Presidential Archives.

Anstee, Margaret Joan. *Orphan of the Cold War: The Inside Story of the Collapse of the Angolan Peace Process, 1992-93*. New York, NY: St. Martin's Press, 1996.

Arjona, Ana, Nelson Kasfir, and Zachariah Mampilly. *Rebel Governance in Civil War*. New York, NY: Cambridge University Press, 2015.

Arnold, Anthony. *The Fateful Pebble: Afghanistan's Role in the Fall of the Soviet Empire*. Novato, CA: Presidio, 1993.

Art, Robert J. *A Grand Strategy for America*. Ithaca, NY: Cornell University Press, 2003.

Autesserre, Séverine. *Peaceland: Conflict Resolution and the Everyday Politics of International Intervention*. New York, NY: Cambridge University Press, 2014.

Aves, Jonathan. "The Caucasus States: The Regional Security Complex." In *Security Dilemmas in Russia and Eurasia*, edited by Roy Allison and Christoph Bluth, 175–187. London: Royal Institute of International Affairs, 1998.

Axelrod, Robert. *The Evolution of Cooperation*. New York, NY: Basic Books, 1984.

Baines, Gary. *South Africa's "Border War": Contested Narratives and Conflicting Memories*. London, UK: Bloomsbury, 2014.

Baines, Gary. "The Saga of South African POWs in Angola, 1975-82." *Scientia Militaria* 40, no. 2 (2012): 102–141.

Balcells, Laia, and Patricia Justino. "Bridging Micro and Macro Approaches on Civil Wars and Political Violence." *Journal of Conflict Resolution* 58, no. 8 (2014): 1343–1359.

Balcells, Laia, and Stathis N. Kalyvas. "Does Warfare Matter? Severity, Duration, and Outcomes of Civil Wars." *Journal of Conflict Resolution* 58, no. 8 (2014): 1390–1418.

Balch-Lindsay, Dylan, and Andrew J. Enterline. "Killing Time: The World Politics of Civil War Duration, 1820-1992." *International Studies Quarterly* 44, no. 4 (2000): 615–642.

Balch-Lindsay, Dylan, Andrew J. Enterline, and Kyle A. Joyce. "Third-Party Intervention and the Civil War Process." *Journal of Peace Research* 45, no. 3 (2008): 345–363.

Baldor, Lolita C. "US Navy Seizes Suspected Iranian Missile Parts Set For Yemen." *Associated Press*, December 4, 2019.

Bapat, Navin A. "Understanding State Sponsorship of Militant Groups." *British Journal of Political Science* 42, no. 1 (2012): 1–29.

Barabulya, Vyacheslav. "Recollections of Guns, Tanks, and Bombs." In *Bush War: The Road to Cuito Cuanavale*, edited by Gennady Shubin and Andrei Tokarev, 166–170. Johannesburg, South Africa: Jacana, 2011.

Bar-Siman-Tov, Yaacov. "The Strategy of War by Proxy." *Cooperation and Conflict* 19, no. 4 (1984): 263–273.

BBC News. "Russia Cancels Most Afghan Debt." August 6, 2007.

Bearden, Milton, and James Risen. *The Main Enemy: The Inside Story of the CIA's Final Showdown with the KGB*. New York, NY: Random House Publishing Group, 2003.

Beardsley, Kyle. "Peacekeeping and the Contagion of Armed Conflict." *The Journal of Politics* 73, no. 4 (2011): 1051–1064.

Beardsley, Kyle, and Kristian Skrede Gleditsch. "Peacekeeping as Conflict Containment." *International Studies Review* 17, no. 1 (2015): 67–89.

Beber, Bernd, and Christopher Blattman. "The Logic of Child Soldiering and Coercion." *International Organization* 67, no. 1 (2013): 65–104.

Beckley, Michael. *Unrivaled: Why America Will Remain the World's Sole Superpower*. Ithaca, NY: Cornell University Press, 2018.

REFERENCES 255

Bekkevold, Jo Inge. "5 Ways the US-China Cold War Will Be Different From the Last One." *Foreign Policy*, December 29, 2022.
Bennett, Andrew. "Causal Mechanisms and Typological Theories in the Study of Civil War." In *Transnational Dynamics of Civil War*, edited by Jeffrey T. Checkel, 205–230. New York, NY: Cambridge University Press, 2013.
Bennett, Andrew, and Jeffrey T. Checkel. "Process Tracing: From Philosophical Roots to Best Practices." In *Process Tracing: From Metaphor to Analytic Tool*, edited by Andrew Bennett and Jeffrey T. Checkel, 3–37. Cambridge, UK: Cambridge University Press, 2015.
Bennett, D. Scott, and Allan C. Stam. "The Duration of Interstate Wars, 1816-1985." *The American Political Science Review* 90, no. 2 (1996): 239-257.
Berkowitz, Jeremy M. "Delegating Terror: Principal–Agent Based Decision Making in State Sponsorship of Terrorism." *International Interactions* 44, no. 4 (2018): 709–748.
Berman, Eli, and David A. Lake, eds. *Proxy Wars: Suppressing Violence through Local Agents*. Ithaca, NY: Cornell University Press, 2019.
Betts, Richard K. "The Delusion of Impartial Intervention." *Foreign Affairs* 73, no. 6 (1994): 20–33.
Biddle, Stephen, Julia Macdonald, and Ryan Baker. "Small Footprint, Small Payoff: The Military Effectiveness of Security Force Assistance." *Journal of Strategic Studies* 41, no. 1–2 (2018): 89–142.
Bissell, Richard E. "Soviet Use of Proxies in the Third World: The Case of Yemen." *Soviet Studies* 30, no. 1 (1978): 87–106.
Black, Joseph L., and Michael Johns, eds. *The Return of the Cold War: Ukraine, the West, and Russia*. New York, NY: Routledge, 2016.
Blattman, Christopher, and Edward Miguel. "Civil War." *Journal of Economic Literature* 48, no. 1 (2010): 3–57.
Bleaney, Michael, and Arcangelo Dimico. "How Different Are the Correlates of Onset and Continuation of Civil Wars?" *Journal of Peace Research* 48, no. 2 (2011): 145–155.
Blume, Susanna. "How to Support the Opposition in Syria: New Models for Understanding Syria." *PRISM* 4 (2014): 84–93.
Boot, Max. "Cleaning Up Obama's Syria Mess." *Commentary*, November 2016.
Boulouque, Sylvain. "Communism in Afghanistan." In *The Black Book of Communism: Crimes, Terror, Repression*, edited by Stéphane Courtois, Nicolas Werth, Jean-Louis Panné, Andrzej Paczkowski, Karel Bartošek, and Jean-Louis Margolin, translated by Jonathan Murphy and Mark Kramer, 705–725. Cambridge, MA: Harvard University Press, 1999.
Bove, Vincenzo, Kristian Skrede Gleditsch, and Petros G. Sekeris. "'Oil above Water': Economic Interdependence and Third-Party Intervention." *Journal of Conflict Resolution* 60, no. 7 (2016): 1251–1277.
Box-Steffensmeier, Janet M., and Bradford Jones. *Event History Modeling: A Guide for Social Scientists*. New York, NY: Cambridge University Press, 2004.
Box-Steffensmeier, Janet M., Dan Reiter, and Christopher Zorn. "Nonproportional Hazards and Event History Analysis in International Relations." *Journal of Conflict Resolution* 47, no. 1 (2003): 33–53.
Boyle, Michael J. "The War on Terror in American Grand Strategy." *International Affairs* 84, no. 2 (2008): 191–209.
Braithwaite, Rodric. *Afghantsy: The Russians in Afghanistan 1979-89*. New York, NY: Oxford University Press, 2011.
Brass, Paul. *Theft of an Idol: Text and Context in the Representation of Collective Violence*. Princeton, NJ: Princeton University Press, 1997.
Braumoeller, Bear F. *Only the Dead: The Persistence of War in the Modern Age*. New York, NY: Oxford University Press, 2019.
Breytenbach, Jan. *The Buffalo Soldiers: The Story of South Africa's 32-Battalion, 1975-1993*. Alberton, South Africa: Galago, 2002.

Bridgland, Fred. *Jonas Savimbi: A Key to Africa*. Edinburgh, Scotland: Mainstream Publishing, 1986.
Bridgland, Fred. *The War for Africa: Twelve Months That Transformed a Continent*. Gibraltar, UK: Ashanti Publishing, 1990.
Brimley, Shawn, Ben FitzGerald, and Kelley Sayler. " Game Changers: Disruptive Technology and US Defense Strategy." Washington, DC: Center for a New American Security, 2013.
Brinkman, Inge. "Ways of Death: Accounts of Terror from Angolan Refugees in Namibia." *Africa* 70, no. 1 (2000): 1–24.
Brodie, Bernard. *Strategy in the Missile Age*. Santa Monica, CA: RAND Corporation, 1959.
Brodie, Bernard. "Unlimited Weapons and Limited War." *The Reporter* 11, no. 9 (November 18, 1954): 16–21.
Brooke, James. "Cubans Guard U.S. Oilmen in Angola." *The New York Times*, November 24, 1986, sec. A.
Brooks, Stephen G., and William C. Wohlforth. *World Out of Balance: International Relations Theory and the Challenge of American Primacy*. Princeton, NJ: Princeton University Press, 2008.
Buchanan, Ben, and Fiona S. Cunningham. "Preparing the Cyber Battlefield: Assessing a Novel Escalation Risk in a Sino-American Crisis." *Texas National Security Review* 3, no. 4 (2020): 54–81.
Buhaug, Halvard, Scott Gates, and Päivi Lujala. "Geography, Rebel Capability, and the Duration of Civil Conflict." *Journal of Conflict Resolution* 53, no. 4 (2009): 544–569.
Buhaug, Halvard, and Päivi Lujala. "Accounting for Scale: Measuring Geography in Quantitative Studies of Civil War." *Political Geography* 24, no. 4 (2005): 399–418.
Bush, George W. "Address to a Joint Session of Congress and the American People," September 20, 2001. Office of the Press Secretary. https://georgewbush-whitehouse.archives.gov/news/releases/2001/09/20010920-8.html.
Byman, Daniel. "Outside Support for Insurgent Movements." *Studies in Conflict & Terrorism* 36, no. 12 (2013): 981–1004.
Byman, Daniel, Peter Chalk, Bruce Hoffman, William Rosenau, and David Brannan. *Trends in Outside Support for Insurgent Movements*. Santa Monica, CA: RAND Corporation, 2001.
Byman, Daniel, and Sarah E. Kreps. "Agents of Destruction? Applying Principal Agent Analysis to State-Sponsored Terrorism." *International Studies Perspectives* 11, no. 1 (2010): 1–18.
"Cable from American Embassy Islamabad to Secretary of State, 'Visit of Codel Nunn: Conversation with President Zia,'" November 29, 1984. CREST: CIA-RDP90B01370R0008011 10109-1.
"Cable from American Embassy Kabul to Secretary of State, 'Soviet Pressure on Pakistan,'" June 1, 1981. Executive Secretariat, NSC: Country File, Near East and South Asia, Box 34, Afghanistan (3-6-81 to 5-19-81), Ronald Reagan Presidential Library.
Canadian Department of National Defense. " *Strong, Secure, Engaged: Canada's Defence Policy*." Ottawa, ON, 2017.
Canfield, Robert L. "Afghanistan: The Trajectory of Internal Alignments." *Middle East Journal* 43, no. 4 (1989): 635–648.
Carment, David, and Dane Rowlands. "Three's Company: Evaluating Third-Party Intervention in Intrastate Conflict." *Journal of Conflict Resolution* 42, no. 5 (1998): 572–599.
Carr, Chris. "Reverse Influence, Interdependence and the Relationship Between Supplier and Recipient in Arms Transfers." In *The Control of Arms Transfers*, edited by John Simpson, 15–30. London, UK: Arms Control & Disarmament Research Unit, Foreign and Commonwealth Office, 1977.
Carson, Austin. "Facing Off and Saving Face: Covert Intervention and Escalation Management in the Korean War." *International Organization* 70, no. 2 (2016): 103–131.
Carson, Austin. *Secret Wars: Covert Conflict in International Politics*. Princeton, NJ: Princeton University Press, 2018.

Carson, Austin, and Keren Yarhi-Milo. "Covert Communication: The Intelligibility and Credibility of Signaling in Secret." *Security Studies* 26, no. 1 (2017): 124–156.
Carter, David B. "A Blessing or a Curse? State Support for Terrorist Groups." *International Organization* 66, no. 1 (2012): 129–151.
Carter, David B., and Curtis S. Signorino. "Back to the Future: Modeling Time Dependence in Binary Data." *Political Analysis* 18, no. 3 (2010): 271–292.
Carter, Jimmy. "Address to the Nation on the Soviet Invasion of Afghanistan," January 4, 1980.
Carter, Jimmy. "The State of the Union Address Delivered Before a Joint Session of Congress," January 23, 1980.
Carter, Jimmy. *Keeping the Faith: Memoirs of a President.* Fayetteville, AR: University of Arkansas Press, 1995.
Casey, Adam E. "The Durability of Client Regimes: Foreign Sponsorship and Military Loyalty, 1946–2010." *World Politics* 72, no. 3 (2020): 411–447.
"Castro to Gorbachev," March 3, 1988. Centro de Información de las Fuerzas Armadas Revolucionarias [Archive of the Cuban Armed Forces], Havana.
Cederman, Lars-Erik, Brian Min, and Andreas Wimmer. " *Ethnic War Dataset*," n.d., 1–3.
Center for Operational Analysis and Research. "Draft Budget: The Syrian State Continues to Shrink." *Syria Update* 3, no. 37 (2020): 1–3.
Chadefaux, Thomas. "What the Enemy Knows: Common Knowledge and the Rationality of War." *British Journal of Political Science* 50, no. 4 (2020): 1593–1607.
Chapman, Thomas, and Philip Roeder. "Partition as a Solution to Wars of Nationalism: The Importance of Institutions." *American Political Science Review* 101, no. 4 (2007): 677–691.
Checkel, Jeffrey T. "Transnational Dynamics of Civil War." In *Transnational Dynamics of Civil War*, edited by Jeffrey T. Checkel, 3–27. New York, NY: Cambridge University Press, 2013.
Chenoweth, Erica, and Maria J. Stephan. *Why Civil Resistance Works: The Strategic Logic of Nonviolent Conflict.* New York, NY: Columbia University Press, 2011.
Chernick, Marc. "Peacemaking and Violence in Latin America." In *The International Dimensions of Internal Conflict*, edited by Michael Brown, 267–307. Cambridge, MA: MIT Press, 1996.
Christensen, Thomas J. "Threats, Assurances, and the Last Chance for Peace: The Lessons of Mao's Korean War Telegrams." *International Security* 17, no. 1 (1992): 122–154.
Christensen, Thomas J., and Jack Snyder. "Chain Gangs and Passed Bucks: Predicting Alliance Patterns in Multipolarity." *International Organization* 44, no. 2 (1990): 137–168.
Christia, Fotini. *Alliance Formation in Civil Wars.* New York, NY: Cambridge University Press, 2012.
CIA. "Soviet and Cuban Intervention in the Angolan Civil War." Intelligence Memorandum, March 1977. CREST: 0000518406.
CIA. "The Invasion of Afghanistan: Implications for Soviet Foreign Policy," January 1980. CREST: 0000969767.
CIA. "Pakistan: Tough Choices on Afghanistan." Directorate of Intelligence, July 1982. CREST: CIA-RDP06T00412R000200890001-1.
CIA. "Angola: The Growing UNITA Insurgency," July 1983. CREST: CIA-RDP84S00552R000300040003-1.
CIA. "Afghanistan: Prospects for the Resistance," October 1983. CREST: 0005564710.
CIA. "Angola: Near-Term Prospects." Special National Intelligence Estimate, January 1984. CREST: CIA-RDP97S00289R000200230004-9.
CIA. "Pakistan: Zia's Divided Opposition," March 1984. CREST: CIA-RDP84S00927R000300100002-9.
CIA. "Domestic Costs to the Soviet Regime of Involvement in Afghanistan," October 1984. CREST: CIA-RDP85T00287R001401010002-5.
CIA. "Afghanistan: Resisting Sovietization." Research Paper, December 1984. CREST: CIA-RDP85T00314R000400020005-2.

CIA. "Angola's Civil War: Outlook for 1985," February 1985. CREST: CIA-RDP86T00589R000100090003-5.
CIA. "Soviet Problems, Prospects, and Options in Afghanistan in the Next Year," March 1985. CREST: CIA-RDP87T00573R000200250004-1.
CIA. "The Soviet Presence in Afghanistan: Implications for the Regional Powers and the United States," April 1985. CREST: 0005445963.
CIA. "The Soviet Invasion of Afghanistan: Five Years After," May 1985. CREST: CIA-RDP86T00587R000200200003-3.
CIA. "Soviet Military Support to Angola: Intentions and Prospects." Director of Central Intelligence, October 1985. CREST: CIA-RDP87T00573R000801010001-3.
CIA. "The Cuban Presence in Angola." Interagency Intelligence Assessment, November 1985a. CREST: CIA-RDP88T00565R000600890002-7.
CIA. "Angola: Dos Santos Up Beat Before Party Congress," November 1985b. CREST: CIA-RDP85T01058R000100590001-1.
CIA. "Soviet Tactics on a 'Political Solution' in Afghanistan." Special National Intelligence Estimate, January 1986. CREST: 0005564722.
CIA. "Insurgency: 1985 in Review," April 1986. CREST: CIA-RDP97R00694R000600020001-2.
CIA. "Angola: Short-Term Prospects for UNITA." Special National Intelligence Estimate, June 1986. CREST: CIA-RDP97S00289R000200250004-7.
CIA. "Afghanistan: Are Soviet Intentions Shifting?," July 1986. CREST: CIA-RDP86T01017R000505120001-7.
CIA. "Prospects for the Angolan Civil War in 1987." Special National Intelligence Estimate, February 1987a. CREST: CIA-RDP89B00224R000501760015-2.
CIA. "The Costs of Soviet Involvement in Afghanistan," February 1987b. CREST: CIA-RDP08S01350R000300950001-0.
CIA. "Talking Points for the DDCI: Angola," September 1987. CREST: CIA-RDP89B00224R000501760003-5.
CIA. "Supporting Allies Under Insurgent Challenge: The Soviet Experience In Africa," February 1988. CREST: CIA-RDP07C00121R001000530001-0.
CIA. "USSR: Withdrawal From Afghanistan." Special National Intelligence Estimate, March 1988. CREST: CIA-RDP09T00367R000200120001-3.
CIA. "Afghanistan: The War in Perspective." Special National Intelligence Estimate, November 1989. CREST: 0005564725.
CIA. "Soviet Strategic Interests in Angola," n/d. CREST: CIA-RDP91B00874R000100030013-5.
Claiborne, William. "S. African Military Says Intervention in Angola Staved Off Rebel Defeat." *The Washington Post*, November 13, 1987.
Clausewitz, Carl von. *On War*. Translated by Michael Howard and Peter Paret. Princeton, NJ: Princeton University Press, 1989.
Cogan, Charles G. "Partners in Time: The CIA and Afghanistan since 1979." *World Policy Journal* 10, no. 2 (1993): 73–82.
Colby, William. *Honorable Men: My Life in the CIA*. New York, NY: Simon and Schuster, 1978.
Coll, Steve. "Anatomy of a Victory: CIA's Covert Afghan War." *The Washington Post*, July 19, 1992a.
Coll, Steve. "In CIA's Covert Afghan War, Where to Draw the Line Was Key." *The Washington Post*, July 20, 1992b.
Coll, Steve. *Ghost Wars: The Secret History of the CIA, Afghanistan, and Bin Laden, from the Soviet Invasion to September 10, 2001*. New York, NY: Penguin Books, 2005.
Collier, David. "Understanding Process Tracing." *PS: Political Science & Politics* 44, no. 4 (2011): 823–830.
Collier, David, and James E. Mahon. "Conceptual 'Stretching' Revisited: Adapting Categories in Comparative Analysis." *American Political Science Review* 87, no. 4 (1993): 845–855.

Collier, Paul, Lani Elliott, Håvard Hegre, Anke Hoeffler, Marta Reynal-Querol, and Nicholas Sambanis. *Breaking the Conflict Trap: Civil War and Development Policy*. Washington, DC: World Bank and Oxford University Press, 2003.
Collier, Paul, and Anke Hoeffler. "Greed and Grievance in Civil War." *Oxford Economic Papers* 56, no. 4 (2004): 563–595.
Collier, Paul, Anke Hoeffler, and Måns Söderbom. "On the Duration of Civil War." *Journal of Peace Research* 41, no. 3 (2004): 253–273.
"Concerning the Situation in 'A,'" December 12, 1979. Handwritten Note of the Central Committee of the Communist Party of the Soviet Union Politburo's Decision to Introduce Troops into Afghanistan. National Security Archive, George Washington University.
Copp, Tara, Matthew Lee, and Lolita C. Baldor. "US Shoots Down Armed Turkish Drone After It Came Too Close to US Troops in Syria." *Associated Press*, October 5, 2023.
Copson, Raymond W., and Richard P. Cronin. "The 'Reagan Doctrine' and Its Prospects." *Survival* 29, no. 1 (1987): 40–55.
Cordovez, Diego, and Selig S. Harrison. *Out of Afghanistan: The Inside Story of the Soviet Withdrawal*. New York, NY: Oxford University Press, 1995.
Cormac, Rory, and Richard J. Aldrich. "Grey Is the New Black: Covert Action and Implausible Deniability." *International Affairs* 94, no. 3 (2018): 477–494.
Cortell, Andrew P., and James W. Davis. "When Norms Clash: International Norms, Domestic Practices, and Japan's Internalisation of the GATT/WTO." *Review of International Studies* 31, no. 1 (2005): 3–25.
Cox, David R. "Regression Models and Life-Tables." *Journal of the Royal Statistical Society* 34, no. 2 (1972): 187–220.
Crocker, Chester. *High Noon in Southern Africa: Making Peace in a Rough Neighborhood*. Johannesburg, South Africa: Jonathan Ball Publishers, 1992.
Croicu, Mihai Cătălin, Stina Högbladh, Therése Pettersson, and Lotta Themnér. *UCDP External Support Project Primary Warring Party Dataset Codebook, Version 1-2011*. Uppsala, Sweden: Uppsala Conflict Data Program, 2011.
Cunningham, David E. *Barriers to Peace in Civil War*. Cambridge, UK: Cambridge University Press, 2011.
Cunningham, David E. "Blocking Resolution: How External States Can Prolong Civil Wars." *Journal of Peace Research* 47, no. 2 (2010): 115–127.
Cunningham, David E., Kristian Skrede Gleditsch, and Idean Salehyan. "It Takes Two: A Dyadic Analysis of Civil War Duration and Outcome." *Journal of Conflict Resolution* 53, no. 4 (2009): 570–597.
Cunningham, Fiona S. "The Maritime Rung on the Escalation Ladder: Naval Blockades in a US-China Conflict." *Security Studies* 29, no. 4 (2020): 730–768.
Cunningham, Fiona S., and M. Taylor Fravel. "Assuring Assured Retaliation: China's Nuclear Posture and US-China Strategic Stability." *International Security* 40, no. 2 (2015): 7–50.
Cunningham, Fiona S, and M. Taylor Fravel. "Dangerous Confidence? Chinese Views on Nuclear Escalation." *International Security* 44, no. 2 (2019): 61–109.
Dameyer, Christina. "The Myth of a Soviet Withdrawal from Afghanistan." *Middle East Insight*, February 1988, 34–41.
Davis, Craig. "'A' Is for Allah, 'J' Is for Jihad." *World Policy Journal* 19, no. 1 (2002): 90–94.
Defense Intelligence Agency. "Iranian Support to the Afghan Resistance," n.d. Excerpt from unidentified study. National Security Archive, George Washington University.
Deutsch, Karl W., and J. David Singer. "Multipolar Power Systems and International Stability." *World Politics* 16, no. 3 (1964): 390–406.
Director of Central Intelligence. "Soviet Policy Toward the United States in 1984." Special National Intelligence Estimate, 1984. CREST: CIA-RDP09T00367R000300290001-4.
Doyle, Michael W., and Nicholas Sambanis. *Making War and Building Peace: United Nations Peace Operations*. Princeton, NJ: Princeton University Press, 2006.

Dube, Oeindrila, and Juan Vargas. "Commodity Price Shocks and Civil Conflict: Evidence from Colombia." *The Review of Economic Studies* 80, no. 4 (2013): 1384–1421.

Dubin, Rhys. "The Pentagon Is Spending $2 Billion Running Soviet-Era Guns to Syrian Rebels." *Foreign Policy*, September 12, 2017.

Duursma, Allard. "African Solutions to African Challenges: The Role of Legitimacy in Mediating Civil Wars in Africa." *International Organization* 74, no. 2 (2020): 295–330.

Duursma, Allard, and Henning Tamm. "Mutual Interventions in Africa." *International Studies Quarterly* 65, no. 4 (2021): 1077–1086.

Eck, Kristine. "Repression by Proxy: How Military Purges and Insurgency Impact the Delegation of Coercion." *Journal of Conflict Resolution* 59, no. 5 (2015): 924–946.

Eckstein, Harry, ed. *Internal War: Problems and Approaches*. New York, NY: Free Press of Glencoe, 1964.

Eckstein, Susan. "Comment: The Global Political Economy and Cuba's African Involvement." *Cuban Studies* 10, no. 2 (1980): 85–90.

Egozi, Arie. "Israel Strikes Syria, Warns Russia Over Iranian Missiles." *Breaking Defense*, July 21, 2020.

Eilam, Ehud. *Israeli Strategies in the Middle East: The Case of Iran*. Cham, Switzerland: Palgrave Macmillan, 2022.

Elias, Barbara. *Why Allies Rebel: Defiant Local Partners in Counterinsurgency Wars*. New York, NY: Cambridge University Press, 2020.

Entous, Adam. "Pentagon, CIA Chiefs Don't Think Russia Will Abide by Syria Cease-Fire." *Wall Street Journal*, February 24, 2016.

Fazal, Tanisha M. "Dead Wrong? Battle Deaths, Military Medicine, and Exaggerated Reports of War's Demise." *International Security* 39, no. 1 (2014): 95–125.

Fazal, Tanisha M., and Paul Poast. "War Is Not Over: What the Optimists Get Wrong About Conflict." *Foreign Affairs* 98, no. 6 (2019): 74–83.

Fearon, James D. "Domestic Political Audiences and the Escalation of International Disputes." *The American Political Science Review* 88, no. 3 (1994): 577–592.

Fearon, James D. "Rationalist Explanations for War." *International Organization* 49, no. 3 (1995): 379–414.

Fearon, James D. "Signaling Foreign Policy Interests: Tying Hands versus Sinking Costs." *The Journal of Conflict Resolution* 41, no. 1 (1997): 68–90.

Fearon, James D. "Signaling versus the Balance of Power and Interests: An Empirical Test of a Crisis Bargaining Model." *The Journal of Conflict Resolution* 38, no. 2 (1994): 236–269.

Fearon, James D. "Why Do Some Civil Wars Last So Much Longer than Others?" *Journal of Peace Research* 41, no. 3 (2004): 275–301.

Fearon, James D., and David D. Laitin. "Ethnicity, Insurgency, and Civil War." *American Political Science Review* 97, no. 1 (2003a): 75–90.

Fearon, James D., and David D. Laitin. "Additional Tables for 'Ethnicity, Insurgency, and Civil War,'" 2003b.

Fearon, James D., and David D. Laitin. "Sons of the Soil, Migrants, and Civil War." *World Development* 39, no. 2 (2011): 199–211.

Fearon, James D., and David D. Laitin. "Violence and the Social Construction of Ethnic Identity." *International Organization* 54, no. 4 (2000): 845–877.

Feste, Karen. *Expanding Frontiers: Superpower Intervention in the Cold War*. New York, NY: Praeger, 1992.

Fettweis, Christopher J. "A Revolution in International Relation Theory: Or, What If Mueller Is Right?" *International Studies Review* 8, no. 4 (2006): 677–697.

Filson, Darren, and Suzanne Werner. "A Bargaining Model of War and Peace: Anticipating the Onset, Duration, and Outcome of War." *American Journal of Political Science* 46, no. 4 (2002): 819–837.

Findley, Michael G. "Bargaining and the Interdependent Stages of Civil War Resolution." *Journal of Conflict Resolution* 57, no. 5 (2013): 905–932.

Finnemore, Martha, and Kathryn Sikkink. "International Norm Dynamics and Political Change." *International Organization* 52, no. 4 (1998): 887–917.

Fisher, Jonathan. "Managing Donor Perceptions: Contextualizing Uganda's 2007 Intervention in Somalia." *African Affairs* 111, no. 444 (2012): 404–423.

Fitch, Asa. "U.S. Navy Ship Interdicts a Weapons Shipment in the Arabian Sea." *Wall Street Journal*, April 4, 2016.

Florini, Ann. "The Evolution of International Norms." *International Studies Quarterly* 40, no. 3 (1996): 363–389.

Fortna, Virginia Page. "Do Terrorists Win? Rebels' Use of Terrorism and Civil War Outcomes." *International Organization* 69, no. 3 (2015): 519–556.

Fortna, Virginia Page. "Does Peacekeeping Keep Peace? International Intervention and the Duration of Peace After Civil War." *International Studies Quarterly* 48, no. 2 (2004): 269–292.

Fortna, Virginia Page. *Does Peacekeeping Work? Shaping Belligerents' Choices after Civil War*. Princeton, NJ: Princeton University Press, 2008.

Fotre, Neil. "Destroyer Intercepts Arms Shipment Near Yemen." *Navy Times*, August 30, 2018.

Foy, Henry, Katrina Manson, and Chloe Cornish. "Russia Blames US for Military Convoy Crash in Syria." *The Financial Times*, August 27, 2020.

Fraiman, Keren, Austin Long, and Caitlin Talmadge. "Why the Iraqi Army Collapsed (And What Can Be Done About It)." *Washington Post*, June 13, 2014.

Freedman, Lawrence. "Ukraine and the Art of Limited War." *Survival* 56, no. 6 (2014): 7–38.

Freedom House. "Freedom in the World 2022: Angola Country Report." Washington, DC, 2022.

Freedom House. "Freedom in the World 2023: Marking 50 Years in the Struggle for Democracy." Washington, DC, 2023.

Freier, Nathan, Charles R. Burnett, William J. Cain, Christopher D. Compton, Sean M. Hankard, Robert S. Hume, Gary R. Kramlich, et al. " Outplayed: Regaining Strategic Initiative in the Gray Zone." Carlisle, PA: Strategic Studies Institute, US Army War College, 2016.

Gaddis, John Lewis. *Strategies of Containment: A Critical Appraisal of Postwar American National Security Policy*. New York, NY: Oxford University Press, 1982.

Gall, Carlotta. "Airstrike Hits Turkish Forces in Syria, Raising Fears of Escalation." *The New York Times*, February 27, 2020.

Galtung, Johan. "Violence, Peace, and Peace Research." *Journal of Peace Research* 6, no. 3 (1969): 167–191.

Gambrell, Jon. "US Navy Seizes Weapons in Arabian Sea Likely Bound for Yemen." *Associated Press*, May 9, 2021.

Gandrud, Christopher. "SimPH: An R Package for Illustrating Estimates from Cox Proportional Hazard Models Including for Interactive and Nonlinear Effects." *Journal of Statistical Software* 65, no. 1 (2015): 1–20.

Garthoff, Raymond L. *The Great Transition: American-Soviet Relations and the End of the Cold War*. Washington, DC: The Brookings Institution, 1994.

Gastil, Raymond D. *Freedom in the World: Political Rights and Civil Liberties 1982*. Westport, CT: Greenwood Press, 1982.

Gastil, Raymond D. *Freedom in the World: Political Rights and Civil Liberties 1985-1986*. Westport, CT: Greenwood Press, 1986.

Gat, Azar. "Is War Declining – And Why?" *Journal of Peace Research* 50, no. 2 (2012): 149–157.

Gates, Robert M. "Memorandum on USSR-Afghanistan: Exploring Options," October 17, 1984. Reprinted in Nomination of Robert M. Gates, Hearings Before the Select Committee on Intelligence of the United States Senate (24 September, 1-2 October 1991), S. Hrg. 102-799, Volume 2, pp. 449–450.

Gelb, Leslie. "'85 Reagan Ruling on Afghans Cited." *The New York Times*, June 19, 1986.

George, Alexander, and Andrew Bennett. *Case Studies and Theory Development in the Social Sciences*. Cambridge, MA: MIT Press, 2004.

George, Edward. *The Cuban Intervention in Angola, 1965–1991: From Che Guevara to Cuito Cuanavale.* New York, NY: Frank Cass, 2005.
Gerrard, John. " What Is a Mountain? Background Paper to Definition of Mountains and Mountain Regions." Washington, DC: World Bank, 2000.
Gerring, John. "The Mechanismic Worldview: Thinking Inside the Box." *British Journal of Political Science* 38, no. 1 (2008): 161–179.
Gerring, John. "What Is a Case Study and What Is It Good For?" *American Political Science Review* 98, no. 2 (2004): 341–354.
Gerring, John, and Lee Cojocaru. "Selecting Cases for Intensive Analysis: A Diversity of Goals and Methods." *Sociological Methods & Research* 45, no. 3 (2016): 392–423.
Gerring, John, and Jason Seawright. "Techniques for Choosing Cases." In *Case Study Research: Principles and Practices*, edited by John Gerring, 86–150. New York, NY: Cambridge University Press, 2007.
"Gesamentlike Militere Aksies Deur RSA En UNITA Magte Teen FAPLA Magte in Die Sesoe Militere Streek van Angola Vanaf Desember 1987 Tot Maart 1988 [Joint Military Actions by RSA and UNITA Forces against FAPLA Forces in the Sixth Military Region of Angola from December 1987 to March 1988]," n.d. 61 Mechanised Battalion Group Veterans Association.
Ghobarah, Hazem Adam, Paul Huth, and Bruce Russett. "Civil Wars Kill and Maim People— Long After the Shooting Stops." *American Political Science Review* 97, no. 2 (2003): 189–202.
Gibbons-Neff, Thomas. "How a 4-Hour Battle Between Russian Mercenaries and U.S. Commandos Unfolded in Syria." *The New York Times*, May 24, 2018.
Gibbons-Neff, Thomas. "Pentagon: U.S. Has Told Russia Where U.S. Special Forces Are in Syria." *The Washington Post*, February 18, 2016.
Gibbs, David N. "Reassessing Soviet Motives for Invading Afghanistan: A Declassified History." *Critical Asian Studies* 38, no. 2 (2006): 239–263.
Gilligan, Michael J., and Ernest J. Sergenti. "Do UN Interventions Cause Peace? Using Matching to Improve Causal Inference." *Quarterly Journal of Political Science* 3, no. 2 (2008): 89–122.
Gilligan, Michael, and Stephen John Stedman. "Where Do the Peacekeepers Go?" *International Studies Review* 5, no. 4 (2003): 37 54.
Girardet, Eduard. "While Most Afghan Rebels Fight the Good Fight, Some Line Their Pockets." *US News & World Report*, November 30, 1987.
Girardet, Edward. "Afghan Guerrilla Leader Holds His Own Against Soviet Offensive." *The Christian Science Monitor*, October 2, 1984.
Girardet, Edward. "Afghan Resistance Chafes at UN-Sponsored Accord." *The Christian Science Monitor*, April 11, 1988.
Gleditsch, Kristian S. "Expanded Trade and GDP Data." *Journal of Conflict Resolution* 46, no. 5 (2002): 712–124.
Gleditsch, Kristian S., and Michael D. Ward. "A Revised List of Independent States Since the Congress of Vienna." *International Interactions* 25, no. 4 (1999): 393–413.
Gleditsch, Kristian, Idean Salehyan, and Kenneth Schultz. "Fighting at Home, Fighting Abroad: How Civil Wars Lead to International Disputes." *Journal of Conflict Resolution* 52, no. 4 (2008): 479–506.
Gleditsch, Kristian Skrede. "Transnational Dimensions of Civil War." *Journal of Peace Research* 44, no. 3 (2007): 293–309.
Gleditsch, Nils Petter. "The Liberal Moment Fifteen Years On." *International Studies Quarterly* 52, no. 4 (2008): 691–712.
Gleditsch, Nils Petter, Steven Pinker, Bradley A. Thayer, Jack A. Levy, and William R. Thompson. "The Forum: The Decline of War." *International Studies Review* 15, no. 3 (2013): 396–419.

Gleditsch, Nils Petter, Peter Wallensteen, Mikael Eriksson, Margareta Sollenberg, and Håvard Strand. "Armed Conflict 1946–2001: A New Dataset." *Journal of Peace Research* 39, no. 5 (2002): 615–637.
Gleijeses, Piero. *Conflicting Missions: Havana, Washington, and Africa, 1959–1976.* Chapel Hill, NC: University of North Carolina Press, 2002.
Gleijeses, Piero. "Moscow's Proxy? Cuba and Africa 1975–1988." *Journal of Cold War Studies* 8, no. 2 (2006): 3–51.
Gleijeses, Piero. *Visions of Freedom: Havana, Washington, Pretoria, and the Struggle for Southern Africa, 1976–1991.* Chapel Hill, NC: University of North Carolina Press, 2013.
Goddard, Stacie E. *Indivisible Territory and the Politics of Legitimacy: Jerusalem and Northern Ireland.* Cambridge, UK: Cambridge University Press, 2010.
Goddard, Stacie E. "Uncommon Ground: Indivisible Territory and the Politics of Legitimacy." *International Organization* 60, no. 1 (2006): 35–68.
Gohdes, Anita, and Megan Price. "First Things First: Assessing Data Quality Before Model Quality." *Journal of Conflict Resolution* 57, no. 6 (2013): 1090–1108.
Goldstein, Joshua S. *Winning the War on War: The Decline of Armed Conflict Worldwide.* New York, NY: Dutton, 2011.
Goldstein, Joshua S., and Steven Pinker. "The Decline of War and Violence." *The Boston Globe*, April 15, 2016.
Goldstein, Joshua S., and Steven Pinker. "War Really Is Going Out of Style." *The New York Times*, December 17, 2011.
Golub, Jonathan. "Survival Analysis." In *The Oxford Handbook of Political Methodology*, edited by Janet M. Box-Steffensmeier, Henry E. Brady, and David Collier, 530–546. New York, NY: Oxford University Press, 2008.
Græger, Nina, Bertel Heurlin, Ole Wæver, and Anders Wivel. *Polarity in International Relations: Past, Present, Future.* Cham, Switzerland: Palgrave Macmillan, 2022.
Graham, Thomas. "Let Russia Be Russia: The Case for a More Pragmatic Approach to Moscow." *Foreign Affairs* 98, no. 6 (2019): 134–147.
Grambsch, Patricia M., and Terry M. Therneau. "Proportional Hazards Tests and Diagnostics Based on Weighted Residuals." *Biometrika* 81, no. 3 (1994): 515–526.
Grau, Lester, and Ali Ahmad Jalali. "Forbidden Cross-Border Vendetta: Spetsnaz Strike into Pakistan during the Soviet-Afghan War." *Journal of Slavic Military Studies* 18, no. 4 (2005): 661–672.
Grau, Lester, and Mohammed Yahya Nawroz. "The Soviet Experience in Afghanistan." *Military Review* 75, no. 5 (1995): 17–27.
Grau, Lester W. "Breaking Contact Without Leaving Chaos: The Soviet Withdrawal from Afghanistan." *The Journal of Slavic Military Studies* 20, no. 2 (2007): 235–261.
Grau, Lester W. "The Soviet–Afghan War: A Superpower Mired in the Mountains." *The Journal of Slavic Military Studies* 17, no. 1 (2004): 129–151.
Grauer, Ryan, and Dominic Tierney. "The Arsenal of Insurrection: Explaining Rising Support for Rebels." *Security Studies* 27, no. 2 (2018): 263–295.
Groh, Tyrone. *Proxy War: The Least Bad Option.* Stanford, CA: Stanford University Press, 2019.
Gromov, Boris V. *Ogranichennyi Kontingent [The Limited Contingent].* Moscow, Russia: Progress, 1994.
"Gromyko-Andropov-Ustinov-Ponomarev Report to the Central Committee of the Communist Party of the Soviet Union on the Situation in Afghanistan," October 29, 1979. National Security Archive, George Washington University.
"Gromyko-Andropov-Ustinov-Ponomarev Report to the Communist Party of the Soviet Union Central Committee on the Situation in Afghanistan," June 28, 1979. National Security Archive, George Washington University.
Guevara, Ernesto. *Guerrilla Warfare.* New York, NY: Random House, 1961.

Gurr, Ted Robert, Monty G. Marshall, and Deepa Khosla. "Peace and Conflict 2001: A Global Survey of Armed Conflicts, Self-Determination Movements, and Democracy." *Center for International Development and Conflict Management*, 2000.

H. Con. Res. 237. "A Concurrent Resolution Declaring the Support of the United States for the People of Afghanistan in Their Struggle to Be Free of Foreign Domination," November 18, 1983.

"H Leër/D OPS/309/1, 'Beplanning: Op Modular,'" June 5, 1987. 61 Mechanised Battalion Group Veterans Association Archive.

Halliday, Fred. "Soviet Foreign Policymaking and the Afghanistan War: From 'Second Mongolia' to 'Bleeding Wound.'" *Review of International Studies* 25, no. 4 (1999): 675–691.

Halperin, Morton. *Limited War in the Nuclear Age*. New York, NY: John Wiley & Sons, 1963a.

Halperin, Morton. "The Limiting Process in the Korean War." *Political Science Quarterly* 78, no. 1 (1963b): 13–39.

Hansen, Birthe. *Unipolarity and World Politics: A Theory and Its Implications*. New York, NY: Routledge, 2011.

Hatzky, Christine. *Cubans in Angola: South-South Cooperation and Transfer of Knowledge, 1976-1991*. Madison, WI: The University of Wisconsin Press, 2015.

Hauter, Jakob. "Delegated Interstate War: Introducing an Addition to Armed Conflict Typologies." *Journal of Strategic Security* 12, no. 4 (2019): 90–103.

Hegre, Håvard, Lisa Hultman, and Håvard Mokleiv Nygård. "Evaluating the Conflict-Reducing Effect of UN Peacekeeping Operations." *The Journal of Politics* 81, no. 1 (2019): 215–232.

Hegre, Håvard, Joakim Karlsen, Håvard Mokleiv Nygård, Håvard Strand, and Henrik Urdal. "Predicting Armed Conflict, 2010-2050." *International Studies Quarterly* 57, no. 2 (2013): 250–270.

Heldt, Birger, Peter Wallensteen, and Kjell-Åke Nordquist. "Major Armed Conflicts in the World, 1991." In *SIPRI Yearbook 1992: World Armaments and Disarmament*, 424–456. New York, NY: Oxford University Press, 1992.

Heller, Sam. "Turkey's Russian Red Light in Syria." War on the Rocks, December 30, 2022.

Henderson, Errol A. *African Realism? International Relations Theory and Africa's Wars in the Postcolonial Era*. Lanham, MD: Rowman & Littlefield, 2015.

Herbst, Jeffrey. "Prospects for Revolution in South Africa." *Political Science Quarterly* 103, no. 4 (1988): 665–685.

Herbst, Johnny. "Should the US Arm Ukraine? For the Answer, Look to the Soviet-Afghan War." *The Atlantic Council*, September 5, 2017.

Herring, George C. "The 'Vietnam Syndrome' and American Foreign Policy." *The Virginia Quarterly Review* 57, no. 4 (1981): 594–612.

Hershberg, James G. "The War in Afghanistan and the Iran-Contra Affair: Missing Links?" *Cold War History* 3, no. 3 (2003): 23–48.

Hicks, Kathleen H., and Alice Hunt Friend, eds. *By Other Means Part I: Campaigning In the Gray Zone*. Washington, DC: Center for Strategic and International Studies, 2019.

Hinnebusch, Raymond. "Thinking About the International Factor in the Syrian Crisis." In *The War for Syria: Regional and International Dimensions of the Syrian Uprising*, edited by Raymond Hinnebusch and Adham Saouli, 1–16. New York, NY: Routledge, 2020.

Hinnebusch, Raymond, and Omar Imady. *The Syrian Uprising: Domestic Origins and Early Trajectory*. New York, NY: Routledge, 2018.

Hinnebusch, Raymond, and Adham Saouli, eds. *The War for Syria: Regional and International Dimensions of the Syrian Uprising*. New York, NY: Routledge, 2020.

Hironaka, Ann. *Neverending Wars: The International Community, Weak States, and the Perpetuation of Civil War*. Cambridge, MA: Harvard University Press, 2005.

Hoekstra, Quint. "The Effect of Foreign State Support to UNITA during the Angolan War (1975–1991)." *Small Wars & Insurgencies* 29, no. 5–6 (2018): 981–1005.

Hofferberth, Matthias, and Christian Weber. "Lost in Translation: A Critique of Constructivist Norm Research." *Journal of International Relations and Development* 18, no. 1 (2015): 75–103.

Hoffman, Frank G. *Conflict in the 21st Century: The Rise of Hybrid Wars.* Arlington, VA: Potomac Institute for Policy Studies, 2007.

Hoffmann, Matthew J. *Ozone Depletion and Climate Change: Constructing a Global Response.* Albany, NY: State University of New York Press, 2005.

Högbladh, Stina, Therése Pettersson, and Lotta Themnér. "External Support in Armed Conflict 1975-2009: Presenting New Data." Paper Presented at the 52nd Annual International Studies Association Convention, Montreal, Canada, 16-19 March, 2011.

Horowitz, Michael C. *The Diffusion of Military Power: Causes and Consequences for International Politics.* Princeton, NJ: Princeton University Press, 2010.

Howard, Lise Morjé, and Alexandra Stark. "How Civil Wars End: The International System, Norms, and the Role of External Actors." *International Security* 42, no. 3 (2018): 127–171.

Hubbard, Ben, and Ronen Bergman. "Warning Shots: Israel Spares Hezbollah Fighters to Avert a War." *The New York Times*, April 22, 2020.

Hughes, Geraint. *My Enemy's Enemy: Proxy Warfare in International Politics.* Portland, OR: Sussex Academic Press, 2012.

Hughes, Geraint Alun. "Syria and the Perils of Proxy Warfare." *Small Wars & Insurgencies* 25, no. 3 (2014): 522–538.

Hultman, Lisa, Jacob Kathman, and Megan Shannon. "Beyond Keeping Peace: United Nations Effectiveness in the Midst of Fighting." *American Political Science Review* 108, no. 4 (2014): 737–753.

Hultman, Lisa, Jacob Kathman, and Megan Shannon. "United Nations Peacekeeping and Civilian Protection in Civil War." *American Journal of Political Science* 57, no. 4 (2013): 875–891.

Hultman, Lisa, Jacob Kathman, and Megan Shannon. "United Nations Peacekeeping Dynamics and the Duration of Post-Civil Conflict Peace." *Conflict Management and Peace Science* 33, no. 3 (2016): 231–249.

Human Security Centre. *Human Security Report 2005: War and Peace in the 21st Century.* New York, NY: Oxford University Press, 2005.

Human Security Report Project. " The Decline in Global Violence: Evidence, Explanation, and Contestation." Vancouver, BC: Simon Fraser University, 2014.

Humphreys, Macartan, and Jeremy M. Weinstein. "Handling and Manhandling Civilians in Civil War." *American Political Science Review* 100, no. 3 (2006): 429–447.

Humphreys, Macartan, and Jeremy M. Weinstein. "Who Fights? The Determinants of Participation in Civil War." *American Journal of Political Science* 52, no. 2 (2008): 436–455.

Ignatius, David. "America May Be Doomed to Cooperate with Putin." *The Washington Post*, January 12, 2016.

Ignatius, David. "Assad Nears the Tipping Point." *Washington Post*, June 4, 2015.

Ignatius, David. "What the Demise of the CIA's Anti-Assad Program Means." *Washington Post*, July 20, 2017.

Ikenberry, G. John, Michael Mastanduno, and William C. Wohlforth, eds. *International Relations Theory and the Consequences of Unipolarity.* New York, NY: Cambridge University Press, 2011.

Iklé, Fred Charles. *Every War Must End.* 2nd Revised Edition. New York, NY: Columbia University Press, 2005.

Innes, Michael A., ed. *Making Sense of Proxy Wars: States, Surrogates, and the Use of Force.* Washington, DC: Potomac Books, 2012.

Inskeep, Steve. "Gen. Philip Breedlove On How NATO Should Deal With Russia." NPR, November 2, 2015.

Interview, Ambassador (ret.) Victor Zazeraj. Johannesburg, Gauteng, South Africa, July 4, 2014.

Interview, Brigadier General (ret.) Deon Fourie. Pretoria, Gauteng, South Africa, June 16, 2014.
Interview, Colonel (ret.) Jan Breytenbach. George, Western Cape, South Africa, June 20, 2014.
Interview, Dave Steward. Johannesburg, Gauteng, South Africa, June 6, 2014.
Interview, Lieutenant Colonel Brian Novchich. Zoom, January 27, 2021.
Interview, Major General (ret.) Gert Opperman. Pretoria, Gauteng, South Africa, June 23, 2014.
Interview, Major General (ret.) Johann Dippenaar. Pretoria, Gauteng, South Africa, June 30, 2014.
Interview, Major General (ret.) Roland de Vries. Telephone, September 9, 2014.
İpek, Cemil Doğaç, and Mehmet Çağatay Güler. "Turkey and Russia in Syrian War: Hostile Friendship." *Security & Defence Quarterly* 35, no. 3 (2021): 77–92.
Isachenkov, Vladimir. "Putin Blasts US 'Hegemony', Predicts End to 'Unipolar' World." *Associated Press*, August 16, 2022.
Isby, David C. "Stinger in Afghanistan: The Soviets Try to Adapt." *Rotor & Wing International*, February 1990.
Isby, David C. *Weapons and Tactics of the Soviet Army*. New Edition. London, UK: Jane's Publishing Company, 1988.
Jackson, Richard. "The Social Construction of Internal War." In *(Re)Constructing Cultures of Violence and Peace*, edited by Richard Jackson, 61–77. New York, NY: Rodopi, 2004.
Jaffe, Greg, and Adam Entous. "Trump Ends Covert CIA Program to Arm Anti-Assad Rebels in Syria, A Move Sought by Moscow." *Washington Post*, July 19, 2017.
Jalali, Ali Ahmad, and Lester W. Grau. *The Other Side of the Mountain: Mujahideen Tactics in the Soviet-Afghan War*. Quantico, VA: The United States Marine Corps Studies and Analysis Division, 1999.
Jaster, Robert Scott. *The Defence of White Power: South African Foreign Policy under Pressure*. New York, NY: St. Martin's Press, 1989.
Jervis, Robert. "Signaling and Perception: Drawing Inferences and Projecting Images." In *Political Psychology*, edited by Kristen Renwick Monroe, 293–312. Mahwah, NJ: Lawrence Erlbaum Associates, 2002.
Jervis, Robert. "Unipolarity." *World Politics* 61, no. 1 (2009): 188–213.
Johnson, Robert. "Hybrid War and Its Countermeasures: A Critique of the Literature." *Small Wars & Insurgencies* 29, no. 1 (2018): 141–163.
Jones, Seth G. *Waging Insurgent Warfare: Lessons from the Vietcong to the Islamic State*. New York, NY: Oxford University Press, 2017.
Kahn, Herman. *On Escalation: Metaphors and Scenarios*. New York, NY: Praeger, 1965.
Kaldor, Mary. *New and Old Wars: Organized Violence in a Global Era*. 3rd Edition. Cambridge, UK: Polity Press, 2012.
Kalinovsky, Artemy M. *A Long Goodbye: The Soviet Withdrawal from Afghanistan*. Cambridge, MA: Harvard University Press, 2011.
Kalyvas, Stathis N. "'New' and 'Old' Civil Wars: A Valid Distinction?" *World Politics* 54, no. 1 (2001): 99–118.
Kalyvas, Stathis N. "Promises and Pitfalls of an Emerging Research Program: The Microdynamics of Civil War." In *Order, Conflict, and Violence*, edited by Stathis N. Kalyvas, Ian Shapiro, and Tarek Masoud, 397–421. New York, NY: Cambridge University Press, 2008.
Kalyvas, Stathis N. *The Logic of Violence in Civil War*. Cambridge, UK: Cambridge University Press, 2006.
Kalyvas, Stathis N., and Laia Balcells. "International System and Technologies of Rebellion: How the End of the Cold War Shaped Internal Conflict." *American Political Science Review* 104, no. 3 (2010): 415–429.
Kalyvas, Stathis N., and Matthew Adam Kocher. "How 'Free' Is Free Riding in Civil Wars? Violence, Insurgency, and the Collective Action Problem." *World Politics* 59, no. 2 (2007): 177–216.

Kanet, Roger E. "The Superpower Quest for Empire: The Cold War and Soviet Support for 'Wars of National Liberation.'" *Cold War History* 6, no. 3 (2006): 331–352.
Kaplan, Morton A. *System and Process in International Politics*. New York, NY: John Wiley, 1957.
Karlén, Niklas. "The Legacy of Foreign Patrons: External State Support and Conflict Recurrence." *Journal of Peace Research* 54, no. 4 (2017): 499–512.
Karlén, Niklas. "Turning off the Taps: The Termination of State Sponsorship." *Terrorism and Political Violence* 31, no. 4 (2019): 733–758.
Kathman, Jacob, and Michelle Benson. "Cut Short? United Nations Peacekeeping and Civil War Duration to Negotiated Settlements." *Journal of Conflict Resolution* 63, no. 7 (2019): 1601–1629.
Kathman, Jacob D. "Civil War Contagion and Neighboring Interventions." *International Studies Quarterly* 54, no. 4 (2010): 989–1012.
Kaufman, Stuart J. *Modern Hatreds: The Symbolic Politics of Ethnic War*. Ithaca, NY: Cornell University Press, 2001.
Kaufman, Stuart J. "Symbolic Politics or Rational Choice? Testing Theories of Extreme Ethnic Violence." *International Security* 30, no. 4 (2006): 45–86.
Kaufmann, Chaim. "Possible and Impossible Solutions to Ethnic Civil Wars." *International Security* 20, no. 4 (1996): 136–175.
Kaufmann, William W. "Limited Warfare." In *Military Policy and National Security*, edited by William W. Kaufmann, 102–136. Princeton, NJ: Princeton University Press, 1956.
Kaufmann, William W. *The Requirements of Deterrence*. Princeton, NJ: Center of International Studies, Princeton University, 1954.
Kavanagh, Jennifer, Bryan Frederick, Matthew Povlock, Stacie L. Pettyjohn, Angela O'Mahony, Stephen Watts, Nathan Chandler, John Speed Meyers, and Eugeniu Han. " The Past, Present, and Future of U.S. Ground Interventions: Identifying Trends, Characteristics, and Signposts." Santa Monica, CA: RAND Corporation, 2017.
Keels, Eric, and Krista Wiegand. "Mutually Assured Distrust: Ideology and Commitment Problems in Civil Wars." *Journal of Conflict Resolution* 64, no. 10 (2020): 2022–2048.
Kemal, Levent. "Turkey Blamed Syria For a Deadly Air Strike. Its Troops Blame Russia." *Middle East Eye*, November 5, 2021.
Kemp, Ian. "Abdul Haq: Soviet Mistakes in Afghanistan." *Jane's Defense Weekly*, March 5, 1988.
Kertzer, Joshua D., Brian C. Rathbun, and Nina Srinivasan Rathbun. "The Price of Peace: Motivated Reasoning and Costly Signaling in International Relations." *International Organization* 74, no. 1 (2020): 95–118.
Kharief, Akram. "Libya's Proxy War." Translated by George Miller. Le Monde Diplomatique, September 2020.
Khrupilin, Petr. "Mena Zvali Kamarada Pedro: Zapiski Sovetnika [My Name Was Camarada Pedro: Advisor Notes]." *Krasnaya Zvezda*, September 9, 2000.
Kissinger, Henry. "Implications of Angola for Future US Foreign Policy." Statement Made Before the Subcommittee on African Affairs of the Senate Committee on Foreign Relations, January 29, 1976. Reproduced in the Department of State Bulletin 74, no. 1 (1976): 174–182.
Kissinger, Henry. "Military Policy and Defense of the 'Grey Areas.'" *Foreign Affairs* 33, no. 3 (1955): 416–428.
Kissinger, Henry. *Nuclear Weapons and Foreign Policy*. New York, NY: Harper & Brothers, 1957.
Kissinger, Henry. *Years of Renewal*. New York, NY: Simon & Schuster, 1999.
Kohen, Sami. "Turkey Avoids Force In Armenia Strife." *The Christian Science Monitor*, June 8, 1992.
Kolomnin, Sergej. *Russkii Spetznaz v Afrike [Russian Special Forces in Africa]*. Moscow: Eksmo, 2005.

Kornienko, Georgy M. *The Cold War: Testimony of a Participant*. Translated by Svetlana Savranskaya. Moscow: Mezhdunarodnye Otnosheniya, 1994.

Kozlov, Sergei. "Karera: Novyy Vzglyad." *Soldat Udachi*, no. 7 (1997).

Krainin, Colin, Caroline Thomas, and Thomas Wiseman. "Rational Quagmires: Attrition, Learning, and War." *Quarterly Journal of Political Science* 15, no. 3 (2020): 369–400.

Krause, Keith. "Military Statecraft: Power and Influence in Soviet and American Arms Transfer Relationships." *International Studies Quarterly* 35, no. 3 (1991): 313–336.

Kreps, Sarah, and Jacquelyn Schneider. "Escalation Firebreaks in the Cyber, Conventional, and Nuclear Domains: Moving Beyond Effects-Based Logics." *Journal of Cybersecurity* 5, no. 1 (2019): tyz007.

Kreutz, Joakim. "How and When Armed Conflicts End: Introducing the UCDP Conflict Termination Dataset." *Journal of Peace Research* 47, no. 2 (2010): 243–250.

Kroenig, Matthew. "Facing Reality: Getting NATO Ready for a New Cold War." *Survival* 57, no. 1 (2015): 49–70.

Kruys, George. "Doctrine Development in the South African Armed Forces Up to the 1980s." In *Selected Military Issues with Specific Reference to the Republic of South Africa*, edited by Michael Hough and Louis Du Plessis. Pretoria, South Africa: Institute for Strategic Studies, University of Pretoria, 2001.

Kube, Courtney. "Armed Russian Jets Have Flown Over a US Base in Syria Nearly Every Day in March, US Commander Says." *NBC News*, March 22, 2023.

Kuperman, Alan. "The Stinger Missile and U.S. Intervention in Afghanistan." *Political Science Quarterly* 114, no. 2 (1999): 219–263.

Kuperman, Alan J. "The Moral Hazard of Humanitarian Intervention: Lessons from the Balkans." *International Studies Quarterly* 52, no. 1 (2008): 49–80.

Kushi, Sidita, and Monica Duffy Toft. "Introducing the Military Intervention Project: A New Dataset on US Military Interventions, 1776–2019." *Journal of Conflict Resolution* 67, no. 4 (2023): 752–779.

Kuzichkin, Vladimir. "Coups and Killings in Kabul." *Time*, November 22, 1982.

Kydd, Andrew H. *Trust and Mistrust in International Relations*. Princeton, NJ: Princeton University Press, 2005.

Lacina, Bethany. "Explaining the Severity of Civil Wars." *Journal of Conflict Resolution* 50, no. 2 (2006): 276–289.

Lacina, Bethany, and Nils Petter Gleditsch. "The Waning of War Is Real: A Response to Gohdes and Price." *Journal of Conflict Resolution* 57, no. 6 (2013): 1109–1127.

Lacina, Bethany, Nils Petter Gleditsch, and Bruce Russett. "The Declining Risk of Death in Battle." *International Studies Quarterly* 50, no. 3 (2006): 673–680.

Laffin, John. *The World in Conflict: War Annual 6*. London, UK: Brassey's Defence Publishers, 1994.

Landay, Jonathan, and Humeyra Pamuk. "Pompeo Says U.S. Seized Iranian Weapons On Way To Houthi Rebels in Yemen." *Reuters*, July 8, 2020.

Landry, Carole. "Iran Arming Yemen's Houthi Rebels Since 2009: UN Report." *Agence France-Presse*, May 1, 2015.

Lanoszka, Alexander. "Russian Hybrid Warfare and Extended Deterrence in Eastern Europe." *International Affairs* 92, no. 1 (2016): 175–195.

Lavrov, Anton. "The Russian Air Campaign in Syria: A Preliminary Analysis." CNA Occasional Paper Series. Arlington, VA: Center for Naval Analyses, 2018.

Layne, Christopher. "Coming Storms: The Return of Great-Power War." *Foreign Affairs* 99, no. 6 (2020): 42–48.

Layne, Christopher. "The Unipolar Illusion: Why New Great Powers Will Rise." *International Security* 17, no. 4 (1993): 5–51.

Le Nouvel Observateur. "Les Révélations d'un Ancien Conseiller de Carter: 'Oui, La CIA Est Entrée En Afghanistan Avant Les Russes.'" January 15, 1998.

Lee, Gary. "Afghan Chief Announces Cease-Fire: Moslem Resistance Declares It 'Trap.'" *The Washington Post*, January 2, 1987.

Lee, Melissa M. *Crippling Leviathan: How Foreign Subversion Weakens the State*. Ithaca, NY: Cornell University Press, 2020.

Legvold, Robert. "Managing the New Cold War: What Moscow and Washington Can Learn From the Last One." *Foreign Affairs* 93, no. 4 (2014): 74–84.

"Letter from Reagan to Savimbi," October 24, 1988. WHORM: Subject File, CO006 (Angola), 600000-601999, Ronald Reagan Presidential Library.

"Letter from Savimbi to Reagan," September 9, 1986. WHORM: Subject File, CO006 (Angola), 430000-449999, Ronald Reagan Presidential Library.

"Letter from Savimbi to Reagan," September 19, 1988. WHORM: Subject File, CO006 (Angola), 600000-601999, Ronald Reagan Presidential Library.

Lewis, William H. "Political Influence: The Diminished Capacity." In *Arms Transfers in the Modern World*, edited by Stephanie G. Neuman and Robert E. Harkavy, 184–199. New York, NY: Praeger Publishers, 1979.

Liakhovskii, Alexandr. *Tragediia i Doblest' Afgana [The Tragedy and Valor of Afghanistan]*. Translated by Svetlana Savranskaya. Moscow, Russia: GPI Iskona, 1995.

Liakhovskii, Alexandr, and Vyacheslav Nekrasov. *Grazhdanin, Politik, Voin: Pamyati Akhmad Shakha Masuda [Citizen, Politician, Warrior: In Memory of Ahmad Shah Masoud]*. Moscow, Russia, 2007.

Licht, Amanda A. "Change Comes with Time: Substantive Interpretation of Nonproportional Hazards in Event History Analysis." *Political Analysis* 19, no. 2 (2011): 227–243.

Licklider, Roy. "The Consequences of Negotiated Settlements in Civil Wars, 1945-1993." *The American Political Science Review* 89, no. 3 (1995): 681–690.

Lieberman, Evan. "Nested Analysis as a Mixed-Method Strategy for Comparative Research." *American Political Science Review* 99, no. 3 (2005): 435–452.

Lin-Greenberg, Erik. "Evaluating Escalation: Conceptualizing Escalation in an Era of Emerging Military Technologies." *The Journal of Politics* 85, no. 3 (2023): 1151–1155.

Lin-Greenberg, Erik. "Non-Traditional Security Dilemmas: Can Military Operations Other than War Intensify Security Competition in Asia?" *Asian Security* 14, no. 3 (2018): 282–302.

Lin-Greenberg, Erik. "Wargame of Drones: Remotely Piloted Aircraft and Crisis Escalation." *Journal of Conflict Resolution* 66, no. 10 (2022): 1737–1765.

Lister, Charles. "Turkish-Syrian Re-Engagement: Drivers, Limitations, and US Policy Implications." Middle East Institute, 2023.

Lister, Tim, Matthew Chance, Ryan Browne, and James Masters. "Shayrat: What We Know About The Syrian Airfield Hit By US Strikes." *CNN*, April 7, 2017.

Litwak, Robert S., and Samuel F. Wells, Jr., eds. *Superpower Competition and Security in the Third World*. Cambridge, MA: Ballinger Publishing Company, 1988.

Luard, Evan, ed. *The International Regulation of Civil Wars*. New York, NY: New York University Press, 1972.

Lubold, Gordon, and Michael R. Gordon. "Russian Escalations in Syria Risk Direct Conflict With U.S., Military Officials Warn." *The Wall Street Journal*, June 17, 2022.

Lujala, Päivi. "Deadly Combat over Natural Resources: Gems, Petroleum, Drugs, and the Severity of Armed Civil Conflict." *Journal of Conflict Resolution* 53, no. 1 (2009): 50–71.

Lujala, Päivi. "The Spoils of Nature: Armed Civil Conflict and Rebel Access to Natural Resources." *Journal of Peace Research* 47, no. 1 (2010): 15–28.

Lundberg, Kirsten. "The Politics of a Covert Action: The US, the Mujahideen, and the Stinger Missile." In *Living the Policy Process*, edited by Philip B. Heymann, 21–51 & 64–82. New York, NY: Oxford University Press, 2008.

Luttwak, Edward N. "Give War a Chance." *Foreign Affairs* 78, no. 4 (1999): 36–44.

Lyall, Jason. "Do Democracies Make Inferior Counterinsurgents? Reassessing Democracy's Impact on War Outcomes and Duration." *International Organization* 64, no. 1 (2010): 167–192.

Lyall, Jason, and Isaiah Wilson III. "Rage Against the Machines: Explaining Outcomes in Counterinsurgency Wars." *International Organization* 63, no. 1 (2009): 67–106.

MacFarlane, S. Neil. "Intervention in Contemporary World Politics." *Adelphi Papers* 42, no. 350 (2002).

Mahoney, James, and Gary Goertz. "A Tale of Two Cultures: Contrasting Quantitative and Qualitative Research." *Political Analysis* 14, no. 3 (2006): 227–249.

Maley, William. *The Afghanistan Wars*. 3rd Edition. London, UK: Red Globe Press, 2021.

Malkova, Irina, and Anton Baev. "A Private Army for the President: The Tale of Evgeny Prigozhin's Most Delicate Mission." *The Bell*, January 31, 2019.

Marsh, Nicholas. "Conflict Specific Capital: The Role of Weapons Acquisition in Civil War." *International Studies Perspectives* 8, no. 1 (2007): 54–72.

Marshall, Michael C. "Foreign Rebel Sponsorship: A Patron–Client Analysis of Party Viability in Elections Following Negotiated Settlements." *Journal of Conflict Resolution* 63, no. 2 (2019): 555–584.

Marshall, Monty G., and Ted Robert Gurr. *Polity5: Political Regime Characteristics and Transitions, 1800-2018*. Vienna, VA: Center for Systemic Peace, 2020.

Mazzetti, Mark, Adam Goldman, and Michael S. Schmidt. "Behind the Sudden Death of a $1 Billion Secret C.I.A. War in Syria." *The New York Times*, August 2, 2017.

McCarthy, Michael C., Matthew A. Moyer, and Brett H. Venable. *Deterring Russia in the Gray Zone*. Carlisle, PA: Strategic Studies Institute, US Army War College, 2019.

McColm, R. Bruce, James Finn, Douglas W. Payne, Joseph E. Ryan, Leonard R. Sussman, and George Zarycky. *Freedom in the World: Political Rights & Civil Liberties 1989-1990*. New York, NY: Freedom House, 1990.

McCormick, Shawn. "Angola: The Road to Peace." CSIS Africa Notes. Washington, DC: Center for Strategic and International Studies, 1991.

McFaul, Michael. "Rethinking the 'Reagan Doctrine' in Angola." *International Security* 14, no. 3 (1989): 99–135.

McKeown, Timothy J. "Case Studies and the Statistical Worldview: Review of King, Keohane, and Verba's Designing Social Inquiry: Scientific Inference in Qualitative Research." *International Organization* 53, no. 1 (1999): 161–190.

McLauchlin, Theodore. 2018. "The Loyalty Trap: Regime Ethnic Exclusion, Commitment Problems, and Civil War Duration in Syria and Beyond." *Security Studies* 27(2): 296–317.

McLauchlin, Theodore, Lee JM Seymour, and Simon Pierre Boulanger Martel. 2022. "Tracking the Rise of United States Foreign Military Training: IMTAD-USA, A New Dataset and Research Agenda." *Journal of Peace Research* 59(2): 286–296.

Mearsheimer, John J. "The Gathering Storm: China's Challenge to US Power in Asia." *The Chinese Journal of International Politics* 3, no. 4 (2010): 381–396.

Mearsheimer, John J. *The Tragedy of Great Power Politics*. New York, NY: W.W. Norton, 2001.

"Meeting of the Politburo of the Central Committee of the Communist Party of the Soviet Union," March 17, 1979. National Security Archive, George Washington University.

"Meeting of the Politburo of the Central Committee of the Communist Party of the Soviet Union," November 13, 1986. National Security Archive, George Washington University.

"Meeting of the Politburo of the Central Committee of the Communist Party of the Soviet Union," January 23, 1989. National Security Archive, George Washington University.

Meirowitz, Adam, and Anne E. Sartori. "Strategic Uncertainty as a Cause of War." *Quarterly Journal of Political Science* 3, no. 4 (2008): 327–352.

Melman, Yossi. "Why Syria Isn't Firing Its S-300 Missiles at Israeli Jets." *Haaretz*, May 15, 2020.

"Memorandum for Director of Central Intelligence from Frederick L. Wettering." National Intelligence Council, April 5, 1985. NIC #01833-85.

"Memorandum from George Shultz to Ronald Reagan, 'Visit of Zia-Ul-Haq, President of Pakistan, December 6-9,'" November 29, 1982. Near East and South Asia Affairs, Directorate, NSC: Records, RAC Box 28, Zia Visit (Pakistan), December 7, 1982 [1], Ronald Reagan Presidential Library.

"Memorandum from Lawrence Eagleburger to George Shultz, 'Pakistan and the Afghan Refugees and Freedom Fighters,'" November 24, 1982. Executive Secretariat, NSC: Country File, Near East and South Asia, Box 34, Afghanistan (7-29-82 to 5-2-83), Ronald Reagan Presidential Library.

"Memorandum from Thomas Thornton to Zbigniew Brzezinski, 'Regional Cooperation Re Afghanistan,'" September 24, 1979. Cold War International History Project Document Reader, "Towards an International History of the War in Afghanistan, 1979-1989."

Mendelson, Sarah E. *Changing Course: Ideas, Politics, and the Soviet Withdrawal from Afghanistan*. Princeton, NJ: Princeton University Press, 1998.

Merom, Gil. *How Democracies Lose Small Wars: State, Society, and the Failures of France in Algeria, Israel in Lebanon, and the United States in Vietnam*. New York, NY: Cambridge University Press, 2003.

Mesquita, Bruce Bueno de, James D. Morrow, Randolph M. Siverson, and Alastair Smith. "An Institutional Explanation of the Democratic Peace." *The American Political Science Review* 93, no. 4 (1999): 791–807.

Metternich, Nils W. "Expecting Elections: Interventions, Ethnic Support, and the Duration of Civil Wars." *Journal of Conflict Resolution* 55, no. 6 (2011): 909–937.

Metzger, Shawna K., and Benjamin T. Jones. "Getting Time Right: Using Cox Models and Probabilities to Interpret Binary Panel Data." *Political Analysis* 30, no. 2 (2022): 151–166.

"MI/203/4/0502, 'Angola: UNITA Invloed Op Die Angolese Situasie En RSA-Hulp Sedert Operasie Savannah' [Angola: UNITA Influence on the Angolan Situation and RSA Assistance since Operation Savannah]," February 15, 1979. 61 Mechanised Battalion Group Veterans Association.

"MI/204/3/A6/8 (Signal Message Form)," June 24, 1988. 61 Mechanised Battalion Group Veterans Association Archive.

Michaelson, Ruth. "Turkish and Syrian Defence and Security Officials Meet for First Time in a Decade." *The Guardian*, December 29, 2022.

Miller, Greg, and Karen DeYoung. "Secret CIA Effort in Syria Faces Large Funding Cut." *Washington Post*, June 12, 2015.

Miller, Greg, and Adam Entous. "Plans to Send Heavier Weapons to CIA-Backed Rebels in Syria Stall Amid White House Skepticism." *The Washington Post*, October 23, 2016.

Miller, James N., and Richard Fontaine. " A New Era in US-Russian Strategic Stability: How Changing Geopolitics and Emerging Technologies Are Reshaping Pathways to Crisis and Conflict." Washington, DC: Center for a New American Security, 2017.

Miller, Jamie. *An African Volk: The Apartheid Regime and Its Search for Survival*. New York, NY: Oxford University Press, 2016.

Mityaev, Vyacheslav Aleksandrovich. "The Tide Turns." In *Bush War: The Road to Cuito Cuanavale*, edited by Gennady Shubin and Andrei Tokarev, 21–33. Johannesburg, South Africa: Jacana, 2011.

Mlechin, Leonid. *Brezhnev*. Moscow, Russia: Izd-vo Prospekt, 2006.

Mohammad, Talal. "How Sudan Became a Saudi-UAE Proxy War." *Foreign Policy*, July 12, 2023.

Monaghan, Andrew. "The 'War' in Russia's 'Hybrid Warfare.'" *Parameters* 45, no. 4 (2015): 65–74.

Monteiro, Nuno P. *Theory of Unipolar Politics*. New York, NY: Cambridge University Press, 2014.

Morgan, Forrest E., Karl P. Mueller, Evan S. Medeiros, Kevin L. Pollpeter, and Roger Cliff. *Dangerous Thresholds: Managing Escalation in the 21st Century*. Santa Monica, CA: RAND Corporation, 2008.

Morgenthau, Hans J. "To Intervene or Not to Intervene." *Foreign Affairs* 45, no. 3 (1967): 425–436.

Morgenthau, Hans J. "Will It Deter Aggression?" *New Republic* 130, no. 13 (1954): 11–14.

Mott, William H. *Military Assistance: An Operational Perspective.* Westport, CT: Greenwood Press, 1999.
Mousseau, Michael. "The End of War: How a Robust Marketplace and Liberal Hegemony Are Leading to Perpetual World Peace." *International Security* 44, no. 1 (2019): 160–196.
Mowle, Thomas S., and David H. Sacko. *The Unipolar World: An Unbalanced Future.* New York, NY: Palgrave Macmillan, 2007.
Mroue, Bassem. "US-Backed Syrian Kurds to Turn to Damascus If Turkey Attacks." *Associated Press*, June 7, 2022.
Mueller, John. *Retreat From Doomsday: The Obsolescence of Major War.* New York, NY: Basic Books, 1989.
Mueller, John. "The Iraq Syndrome." *Foreign Affairs* 84, no. 6 (2005): 44–54.
Mueller, John. *The Remnants of War.* Ithaca, NY: Cornell University Press, 2004.
Mueller, John. "War Has Almost Ceased to Exist: An Assessment." *Political Science Quarterly* 124, no. 2 (2009): 297–321.
Mullenbach, Mark J. *Dynamic Analysis of Dispute Management (DADM) Project.* Conway, AR: Department of Political Science, University of Central Arkansas, 2020.
Mullenbach, Mark J. "Third-Party Peacekeeping in Intrastate Disputes, 1946-2012: A New Data Set." *Midsouth Political Science Review* 14 (2013): 103–133.
Mumford, Andrew. *Proxy Warfare.* Cambridge, UK: Polity Press, 2013.
Murray, Williamson, and Peter R. Mansoor, eds. *Hybrid Warfare: Fighting Complex Opponents from the Ancient World to the Present.* Cambridge, UK: Cambridge University Press, 2012.
"Nasha Bol'—Afganistan [Our Pain—Afghanistan], Interview with Yurii Gankovskii." *Aziia i Afrika Segodnia*, no. 6 (1989).
National Security Decision Directive 75. "US Relations with the USSR," January 17, 1983.
National Security Decision Directive 166. "US Policy, Programs and Strategy in Afghanistan," March 27, 1985.
Newman, Edward. "Conflict Research and the 'Decline' of Civil War." *Civil Wars* 11, no. 3 (2009): 255–278.
Newmani, Haider, and Alex Hosenball. "Eyewitness Says Syrian Military Anticipated US Raid." *ABC News*, April 7, 2017.
Nissenbaum, Dion. "US Says Russia's Military Actions in Syria Raise Risk of Escalation." *The Wall Street Journal*, April 25, 2023.
Nolutshungu, Sam C. *Limits of Anarchy: Intervention and State Formation in Chad.* Charlottesville, VA: University Press of Virginia, 1996.
North Atlantic Treaty Organization. "Next Steps in NATO's Transformation: To the Warsaw Summit and Beyond." White Paper. Washington, DC, 2015.
"Note of the Secretary-General's Luncheon with George Bush," June 4, 1990. Sterling Memorial Library, Pérez de Cuéllar Papers, Box 10, Folder 106.
NSC Interdepartmental Group for Africa. *Response to NSSM 224: United States Policy Toward Angola*, 1975.
O'Connor, Tom. "How Many Russian Troops in Syria? Military Reveals Full Count as U.S. Told to Leave." *Newsweek*, August 23, 2018.
Office of the Director of National Intelligence. "Annual Threat Assessment of the US Intelligence Community," April 9, 2021.
Office of the Secretary of Defense. "Justification for FY 2025: Counter-Islamic State of Iraq and Syria (ISIS) Train and Equip Fund (CTEF)." Department of Defense Budget, Fiscal Year (FY) 2025, 2024.
Oliver, Johanna. "The Esquipulas Process: A Central American Paradigm for Resolving Regional Conflict." *Ethnic Studies Report* 17, no. 2 (1999): 149–179.
"Op Savannah: Opsomming van Gebeure Tot 10 Jan 76," January 13, 1976. Terroriste Bedrywighede en Onluste: Angola, Volume 1. South African National Defense Force Archives, Group 1-HSAW Chief of Defense Force, Box 172, HSAW/82/1/1.
Osgood, Robert E. *Limited War Revisited.* Boulder, CO: Westview Press, 1979.

Osgood, Robert E. *Limited War: The Challenge to American Strategy.* Chicago, IL: University of Chicago Press, 1957.

Osnos, Evan. "Sliding Toward a New Cold War." *The New Yorker*, February 26, 2023.

Ottaway, David B. "Angolan Rebels Ask U.S. to Make Up Lost Arms Aid." *The Washington Post*, February 10, 1989.

Ottaway, David B. "Rebels' Backers on Hill Press Aid Issue." *The Washington Post*, January 16, 1986.

Ottaway, David B. "What Is 'Afghan Lesson' for Superpowers? US Policy Shifted With Decision to Supply Advanced Weapons." *The Washington Post*, February 12, 1989.

Oye, Kenneth A. "Explaining Cooperation under Anarchy: Hypotheses and Strategies." *World Politics* 38, no. 1 (1985): 1–24.

Pakistan Air Force. *The Story of the Pakistan Air Force, 1988-1998: A Battle Against Odds.* Islamabad, Pakistan: Shaheen Foundation, 2000.

Paris, Roland. "The 'Responsibility to Protect' and the Structural Problems of Preventive Humanitarian Intervention." *International Peacekeeping* 21, no. 5 (2014): 569–603.

Paul, Christopher, Colin P. Clarke, Beth Grill, and Molly Dunigan. *Paths to Victory: Detailed Insurgency Case Studies.* Santa Monica, CA: RAND Corporation, 2013.

Paul, T. V. "Influence through Arms Transfers: Lessons from the U.S.-Pakistani Relationship." *Asian Survey* 32, no. 12 (1992): 1078–1092.

Payne, James L. *A History of Force: Exploring the Worldwide Movement Against Habits of Coercion, Bloodshed, and Mayhem.* Sandpoint, ID: Lytton Publishing Company, 2004.

Pear, Robert. "Arming Afghan Guerrillas: A Huge Effort Led by U.S." *The New York Times*, April 18, 1988.

Pearce, Justin. "Global Ideologies, Local Politics: The Cold War as Seen from Central Angola." *Journal of Southern African Studies* 43, no. 1 (2017): 13–27.

Pearson, Frederic S., and Robert A. Baumann. "International Military Intervention, 1946-1988." Inter-University Consortium for Political and Social Research, Data Collection No 6035, University of Michigan, Ann Arbor, MI, 1993.

Peksen, Dursun. "Does Foreign Military Intervention Help Human Rights?" *Political Research Quarterly* 65, no. 3 (2012): 558–571.

"Personal Memorandum from Andropov to Brezhnev," December 1979. National Security Archive, George Washington University.

"Personal Memorandum from Brzezinkski to Carter," December 26, 1979. National Security Archive, George Washington University.

Petersen, Roger D. *Western Intervention in the Balkans: The Strategic Use of Emotion in Conflict.* New York, NY: Cambridge University Press, 2011.

Pfeffer, Anshel. "Smash the Bases, Spare the Men—Israel's Invisible War in Syria." *Sunday Times*, January 13, 2019.

Phillips, Christopher. "The International and Regional Battle for Syria." In *The War for Syria: Regional and International Dimensions of the Syrian Uprising*, edited by Raymond Hinnebusch and Adham Saouli, 37–49. New York, NY: Routledge, 2020.

Pickering, Jeffrey, and Emizet F. Kisangani. "The International Military Intervention Dataset: An Updated Resource for Conflict Scholars." *Journal of Peace Research* 46, no. 4 (2009): 589–599.

Pierre, Andrew J. *The Global Politics of Arms Sales.* Princeton, NJ: Princeton University Press, 1982.

Pillar, Paul R. *Negotiating Peace: War Termination as a Bargaining Process.* Princeton, NJ: Princeton University Press, 1983.

Pinker, Steven. *The Better Angels of Our Nature: Why Violence Has Declined.* New York, NY: Penguin Books, 2011.

Polgreen, Lydia. "I Went to Syria, the Country That Remade Our World, and This Is What I Saw." *The New York Times*, February 27, 2023.

Pollack, Kenneth. "Pushing Back on Iran, Part 3: The Syrian Civil War." *American Enterprise Institute*, February 14, 2018.

Popovic, Milos. "Fragile Proxies: Explaining Rebel Defection Against Their State Sponsors." *Terrorism and Political Violence* 29, no. 5 (2017): 922–942.

Posen, Barry R. "Civil Wars & the Structure of World Power." *Dædalus* 146, no. 4 (2017): 167–179.

Posen, Barry R. "Command of the Commons: The Military Foundation of U.S. Hegemony." *International Security* 28, no. 1 (2003): 5–46.

Posen, Barry R. "From Unipolarity to Multipolarity: Transition in Sight?" In *International Relations Theory and the Consequences of Unipolarity*, edited by G. John Ikenberry, Michael Mastanduno, and William C. Wohlforth, 317–341. New York, NY: Cambridge University Press, 2011.

Posen, Barry R. *Restraint: A New Foundation for U.S. Grand Strategy*. Ithaca, NY: Cornell University Press, 2014.

Posen, Barry R., and Andrew L. Ross. "Competing Visions for US Grand Strategy." *International Security* 21, no. 3 (1996): 5–53.

Powell, Robert. "Bargaining and Learning While Fighting." *American Journal of Political Science* 48, no. 2 (2004): 344–361.

Powell, Robert. "Stability and the Distribution of Power." *World Politics* 48, no. 2 (1996): 239–267.

Powell, Robert. "War as a Commitment Problem." *International Organization* 60, no. 1 (2006): 169–203.

Presidency Of The Republic Of Turkey. "We Endeavor to Resolve the Humanitarian Crisis in Syria and Ensure the Security of Our Lands," March 2, 2020.

"Principles for a Peaceful Settlement in Southwestern Africa," July 20, 1988. https://www.peaceau.org/uploads/namibia-principles-peaceful-settlement-1988.pdf.

Prunier, Gérard. "Rebel Movements and Proxy Warfare: Uganda, Sudan and the Congo (1986-99)." *African Affairs* 103, no. 412 (2004): 359–383.

Qadri, A. Hameed. "Pakistan's Afghan War Air Strategy and Operations." *Defence Journal*, 1998.

Raleigh, Clionadh, and Håvard Hegre. "Population Size, Concentration, and Civil War: A Geographically Disaggregated Analysis." *Political Geography* 28, no. 4 (2009): 224–238.

Rashid, Ahmed. "Holding His Ground." *Far Eastern Economic Review* 146, no. 43 (1989a): 20–22.

Rashid, Ahmed. "Highway Lifeline." *Far Eastern Economic Review* 146, no. 43 (1989b): 22–23.

Rathjens, George W. "Notes on the Military Problems of Europe." *World Politics* 10, no. 2 (1958): 182–201.

Rauta, Vladimir. "A Structural-Relational Analysis of Party Dynamics in Proxy Wars." *International Relations* 32, no. 4 (2018): 449–467.

Rauta, Vladimir. "Framers, Founders, and Reformers: Three Generations of Proxy War Research." *Contemporary Security Policy* 42, no. 1 (2021): 113–134.

Ravid, Barak. "CIA Warned Turkey That Strikes in Syria Endanger US Troops." *Axios*, December 7, 2022.

"Record of Conversation, Mikhail Gorbachev with Mohammad Najibullah," July 20, 1987. History and Public Policy Program Digital Archive, Gorbachev Foundation, Moscow. Translated by Gary Goldberg for the Cold War International History Project.

"Record of Meeting of A.N. Kosygin, A.A. Gromyko, D.F. Ustinov, and B.N. Ponomarev with N.M. Taraki," March 20, 1979. National Security Archive, George Washington University.

Reed, William. "Information, Power, and War." *American Political Science Review* 97, no. 4 (2003): 633–641.

Regan, Patrick M. *Civil Wars and Foreign Powers: Outside Intervention in Intrastate Conflict*. Ann Arbor, MI: University of Michigan Press, 2000.

Regan, Patrick M. "Third-Party Interventions and the Duration of Intrastate Conflicts." *Journal of Conflict Resolution* 46, no. 1 (2002): 55–73.
Reiter, Dan. "Exploring the Bargaining Model of War." *Perspectives on Politics* 1, no. 1 (2003): 27–43.
Reiter, Dan. *How Wars End*. Princeton, NJ: Princeton University Press, 2009.
Renz, Bettina. "Russia and 'Hybrid Warfare.'" *Contemporary Politics* 22, no. 3 (2016): 283–300.
Republic of South Africa. "Debates of the House of Assembly," April 17, 1978. First Session, Sixth Parliament.
Restrepo, Jorge A., Michael Spagat, and Juan F. Vargas. "The Severity of the Colombian Conflict: Cross-Country Datasets Versus New Micro-Data." *Journal of Peace Research* 43, no. 1 (2006): 99–115.
"Reunión Del Comandante En Jefe," December 3, 1987. Centro de Información de las Fuerzas Armadas Revolucionarias [Archive of the Cuban Armed Forces], Havana.
"Reunión Del Comandante En Jefe," December 15, 1987. Centro de Información de las Fuerzas Armadas Revolucionarias [Archive of the Cuban Armed Forces], Havana.
"Reunión Del Comandante En Jefe Con Los Políticos Para Analizar La Situación de Las Troupas Cubanas En La RPA [Meeting of the Commander in Chief with the Politicians to Analyze the Situation of the Cuban Troops in the People's Republic of Angola]," December 9, 1987. Centro de Información de las Fuerzas Armadas Revolucionarias [Archive of the Cuban Armed Forces], Havana.
Reuter, Christoph. "The Truth About the Russian Deaths in Syria." *Der Spiegel*, March 2, 2018.
Reuters. "Pentagon Chief Warns Turkey Against New Military Operation in Syria." November 30, 2022.
Reuveny, Rafael, and Aseem Prakash. "The Afghanistan War and the Breakdown of the Soviet Union." *Review of International Studies* 25, no. 4 (1999): 693–708.
Riedel, Bruce. *What We Won: America's Secret War in Afghanistan, 1979–89*. Washington, DC: Brookings Institution Press, 2014.
Riedel, Bruce. "Will Arming Syrian Rebels Lead to Disaster?" *Brookings Institution*, June 15, 2013.
Risse, Thomas, and Kathryn Sikkink. "The Socialization of International Human Rights Norms into Domestic Practices." In *The Power of Human Rights: International Norms and Domestic Change*, edited by Thomas Risse, Stephen C. Ropp, and Kathryn Sikkink, 1–38. Cambridge, UK: Cambridge University Press, 1999.
Rittinger, Eric. "Arming the Other: American Small Wars, Local Proxies, and the Social Construction of the Principal-Agent Problem." *International Studies Quarterly* 61, no. 2 (2017): 396–409.
Rodrik, Dani. "Ukraine Invasion Signals the Death of 'Liberal' World Order. What Will Replace It?" *South China Morning Post*, March 11, 2022.
Rosecrance, R.N. "Bipolarity, Multipolarity, and the Future." *Journal of Conflict Resolution* 10, no. 3 (1966): 314–327.
Rosenau, James N., ed. *International Aspects of Civil Strife*. Princeton, NJ: Princeton University Press, 1964.
Rosenbaum, Paul R. "Heterogeneity and Causality: Unit Heterogeneity and Design Sensitivity in Observational Studies." *The American Statistician* 59, no. 2 (2005): 147–152.
Ross, Michael L. "How Do Natural Resources Influence Civil War? Evidence from Thirteen Cases." *International Organization* 58, no. 1 (2004): 35–67.
Rothchild, Donald S. *Managing Ethnic Conflict in Africa: Pressures and Incentives for Cooperation*. Washington, DC: Brookings Institution Press, 1997.
Rovner, Joshua. "AirSea Battle and Escalation Risks." *Policy Brief*, no. 12 (2012): 1–5.
Rovner, Joshua. "Two Kinds of Catastrophe: Nuclear Escalation and Protracted War in Asia." *Journal of Strategic Studies* 40, no. 5 (2017): 696–730.
Roy, Olivier. "The Lessons of the Soviet-Afghan War." *The Adelphi Papers* 31, no. 259 (1991).

Rubin, Barnett R. *The Fragmentation of Afghanistan: State Formation and Collapse in the International System*. 2nd Edition. New Haven, CT: Yale University Press, 2002.

Rubin, Barnett R. "The Political Economy of War and Peace in Afghanistan." *World Development* 28, no. 10 (2000): 1789–1803.

Ruggeri, Andrea, Han Dorussen, and Theodora-Ismene Gizelis. "Winning the Peace Locally: UN Peacekeeping and Local Conflict." *International Organization* 71, no. 1 (2017): 163–185.

Russell, Martin. "Russia in the Middle East: From Sidelines to Centre Stage." European Parliamentary Research Service, 2018.

Russian General Staff. *The Soviet-Afghan War: How a Superpower Fought and Lost*. Translated by Lester W. Grau and Michael A. Cress. Lawrence, KS: University Press of Kansas, 2002.

S. Con. Res. 74. "A Concurrent Resolution to Encourage and Support the People of Afghanistan in Their Struggle to Be Free from Foreign Domination," October 6, 1983.

Saideman, Stephen M. "Discrimination in International Relations: Analyzing External Support for Ethnic Groups." *Journal of Peace Research* 39, no. 1 (2002): 27–50.

Salehyan, Idean. "The Delegation of War to Rebel Organizations." *Journal of Conflict Resolution* 54, no. 3 (2010): 493–515.

Salehyan, Idean, Kristian Skrede Gleditsch, and David Cunningham. "Explaining External Support for Insurgent Groups." *International Organization* 65, no. 4 (2011): 709–744.

Salehyan, Idean, David Siroky, and Reed M. Wood. "External Rebel Sponsorship and Civilian Abuse: A Principal-Agent Analysis of Wartime Atrocities." *International Organization* 68, no. 3 (2014): 633–661.

Sambanis, Nicholas. "Partition as a Solution to Ethnic War: An Empirical Critique of the Theoretical Literature." *World Politics* 52, no. 4 (2000): 437–483.

Sambanis, Nicholas. "What Is Civil War? Conceptual and Empirical Complexities of an Operational Definition." *Journal of Conflict Resolution* 48, no. 6 (2004): 814–858.

Sambanis, Nicholas, and Jonah Schulhofer-Wohl. "What's in a Line? Is Partition a Solution to Civil War?" *International Security* 34, no. 2 (2009): 82–118.

"Samesprekings: Staatspresident Met Die Kabinet van Die Oorgangsregering van Nasionale Eenheid (Orne) van SWA [Discussions: State President with the Cabinet of the Transitional Government of National Unity (Orne) of SWA]," May 21, 1986. Digital Innovation South Africa.

San-Akca, Belgin. *States in Disguise: Causes of State Support for Rebel Groups*. New York, NY: Oxford University Press, 2016.

Sandler, Todd. "International Peacekeeping Operations: Burden Sharing and Effectiveness." *Journal of Conflict Resolution* 61, no. 9 (2017): 1875–1897.

Sarkees, Meredith Reid, and Frank Wayman. *Resort to War: 1816-2007*. Washington, DC: CQ Press, 2010.

Sartori, Giovanni. "Concept Misformation in Comparative Politics." *American Political Science Review* 64, no. 4 (1970): 1033–1053.

Sawyer, Katherine, Kathleen Gallagher Cunningham, and William Reed. "The Role of External Support in Civil War Termination." *Journal of Conflict Resolution* 61, no. 6 (2017): 1174–1202.

Schaffner, Thomas. "Five Years After Russia Declared Victory in Syria: What Has Been Won?" *Russia Matters*, March 18, 2021.

Schelling, Thomas C. *Arms and Influence*. New Haven, CT: Yale University Press, 1966.

Schelling, Thomas C. "Bargaining, Communication, and Limited War." *Conflict Resolution* 1, no. 1 (1957): 19–36.

Schelling, Thomas C. *Micromotives and Macrobehavior*. New York, NY: W.W. Norton, 1978.

Schelling, Thomas C. *The Strategy of Conflict*. Cambridge, MA: Harvard University Press, 1960.

Schmitt, Eric. "U.S.-Russia Military Tensions Intensify in the Air and on the Ground Worldwide." *New York Times*, September 1, 2020.

Schogol, Jeff. "General Downplays Russian 'Harassment' of US Troops in Syria After Troubling Incidents." *Task & Purpose*, July 22, 2020.

Scholtz, Leopold. *The SADF in the Border War, 1966-1989*. Cape Town, South Africa: Tafelberg, 2013.

Schulhofer-Wohl, Jonah. *Quagmire in Civil War*. New York, NY: Cambridge University Press, 2020.

Schweizer, Peter. *Victory: The Reagan Administration's Secret Strategy That Hastened the Collapse of the Soviet Union*. New York, NY: Atlantic Monthly Press, 1994.

Senate Select Committee on Intelligence. "UNITA: A Brief Military Analysis." Draft Report, 1986. Cannistraro, Vincent: Files, Box 1, Angola (06-12-1986 to 07-23-1986), Ronald Reagan Presidential Library.

Shaver, Andrew, David B. Carter, and Tsering Wangyal Shawa. "Terrain Ruggedness and Land Cover: Improved Data for Most Research Designs." *Conflict Management and Peace Science* 36, no. 2 (2019): 191–218.

Shubin, Gennady, and Andrei Tokarev, eds. *Bush War: The Road to Cuito Cuanavale*. Johannesburg, South Africa: Jacana, 2011.

Shubin, Vladimir. *The Hot "Cold War": The USSR in Southern Africa*. London, UK: Pluto Press, 2008.

Shultz, George P. *Turmoil and Triumph: My Years as Secretary of State*. New York, NY: Charles Scribner's Sons, 1993.

Singer, J. David, Stuart Bremer, and John Stuckey. "Capability Distribution, Uncertainty, and Major Power War, 1820–1965." In *Peace, War, and Numbers*, edited by Bruce Russett, 19–48. Beverly Hills, CA: Sage, 1972.

Siqueira, Kevin. "Conflict and Third-Party Intervention." *Defence and Peace Economics* 14, no. 6 (2003): 389–400.

Sisk, Timothy D. *International Mediation in Civil Wars: Bargaining with Bullets*. New York, NY: Routledge, 2009.

Slantchev, Branislav L. "How Initiators End Their Wars: The Duration of Warfare and the Terms of Peace." *American Journal of Political Science* 48, no. 4 (2004): 813–829.

Slantchev, Branislav L. "The Principle of Convergence in Wartime Negotiations." *American Political Science Review* 97, no. 4 (2003): 621–632.

Sliwinski, Marek. "Afghanistan: The Decimation of a People." *Orbis* 33, no. 1 (1989): 39–56.

Smoke, Richard. *War: Controlling Escalation*. Cambridge, MA: Harvard University Press, 1977.

Snow, Shawn. "Boots on the Ground: Elite U.S. Troops Are in Raqqa Near the Islamic State's Front Line." *Military Times*, June 9, 2017.

Snow, Shawn. "Ship Seizures Included 'Relatively New' Iranian Surface to Air Missile Bound for Houthi Rebels in Yemen." *Military Times*, February 20, 2020.

Soifer, Hillel. "Shadow Cases in Comparative Research." *Qualitative & Multi-Method Research* 18, no. 2 (2020): 9–18.

Sousa, Ricardo Real P. "External Interventions in Post-Cold War Africa, 1989–2010." *International Interactions* 41, no. 4 (2015): 621–647.

South Africa Department of Foreign Affairs. "Besoek van Mnr Clark Aan Suid-Afrika En Suidwes-Afrika: 10-13 Junie 1981," June 23, 1981. Digital Innovation South Africa.

Spaniel, William, and Peter Bils. "Slow to Learn: Bargaining, Uncertainty, and the Calculus of Conquest." *Journal of Conflict Resolution* 62, no. 4 (2018): 774–796.

Spies, FJ du Toit. *Angola: Operasie Savannah 1975–1976*. Pretoria, South Africa: SA Weermag, 1989.

Starr, Barbara. "US Fighter Jets Escort Russian Aircraft in Eastern Syria." *CNN*, February 15, 2022a.

Starr, Barbara. "Russia Warned US It Was Going to Conduct Airstrikes on Fighters in Syria." *CNN*, June 16, 2022b.

Steele, Jonathan. "Moscow's Kabul Campaign." *Middle East Report*, no. 141 (August 1986): 4–11.
Steenkamp, Willem. *South Africa's Border War, 1966-1989*. Gibraltar, UK: Ashanti Publishing, 1989.
Stein, Arthur A. "Coordination and Collaboration: Regimes in an Anarchic World." *International Organization* 36, no. 2 (1982): 299–324.
Stein, Janice Gross. "Proxy Wars—How Superpowers End Them: The Diplomacy of War Termination in the Middle East." *International Journal* 35, no. 3 (1980): 478–519.
Stephens, Joe, and David B. Ottaway. "From U.S., the ABC's of Jihad." *The Washington Post*, March 23, 2002.
Steyn, Douw, and Arnè Söderlund. *Iron Fist From the Sea: South Africa's Seaborne Raiders 1978-1988*. Solihull, UK: Helion, 2015.
Stinnett, Douglas M., Jaroslav Tir, Paul F. Diehl, Philip Schafer, and Charles Gochman. "The Correlates of War (COW) Project Direct Contiguity Data, Version 3.0." *Conflict Management and Peace Science* 19, no. 2 (2002): 59–67.
Stockholm International Peace Research Institute. *Military Expenditure Database*, 2020.
Stockwell, John. *In Search of Enemies: A CIA Story*. New York, NY: W.W. Norton, 1978.
Sullivan, Patricia L., and Johannes Karreth. "The Conditional Impact of Military Intervention on Internal Armed Conflict Outcomes." *Conflict Management and Peace Science* 32, no. 3 (2015): 269–288.
Sullivan, Patricia L., and Michael T. Koch. "Military Intervention by Powerful States, 1945-2003." *Journal of Peace Research* 46, no. 5 (2009): 707–718.
"SWAGM VHK/309/1 (Op Moduler) Memorandum, 'Op Beplanning Volgens H Leer Riglyne'," December 8, 1987. 61 Mechanised Battalion Group Veterans Association.
Syrian Arab News Agency. "President Al-Assad's Interview with NBC News," July 14, 2016.
Syrian Observatory for Human Rights. 2023. *Highest Annual Death Toll in Three Years: 4,361 People Killed Across Syria in 2023*. Coventry, UK.
Syrian Observatory for Human Rights. 2024. *Syrian Revolution 13 Years On: Nearly 618,000 Persons Killed Since the Onset of the Revolution in March 2011*. Coventry, UK.
Tahir-Kheli, Shirin. *The Soviet Union in Afghanistan: Benefits and Costs*. Carlisle Barracks, PA: Strategic Studies Institute, US Army War College, 1980.
Talentino, Andrea Kathryn. *Military Intervention after the Cold War: The Evolution of Theory and Practice*. Athens, OH: Ohio University Press, 2005.
"Talking Points for Secretary Kissinger, NSC Meeting on Angola," June 27, 1975. Box 2, "NSC Meeting, 6/27/1975", National Security Adviser's NSC Meeting File, Gerald R. Ford Presidential Library.
Talmadge, Caitlin. "Emerging Technology and Intra-War Escalation Risks: Evidence from the Cold War, Implications for Today." *Journal of Strategic Studies* 42, no. 6 (2019): 864–887.
Talmadge, Caitlin. "Would China Go Nuclear? Assessing the Risk of Chinese Nuclear Escalation in a Conventional War with the United States." *International Security* 41, no. 4 (2017): 50–92.
Tannenwald, Nina. *The Nuclear Taboo: The United States and the Non-Use of Nuclear Weapons Since 1945*. Cambridge, UK: Cambridge University Press, 2007.
Tarzi, Shah M. "Politics of the Afghan Resistance Movement: Cleavages, Disunity, and Fragmentation." *Asian Survey* 31, no. 6 (1991): 479–495.
"Terms of Reference for the Joint Implementation Group," n.d. Draft version of proposal. Obtained by the Washington Post in July 2016. https://www.washingtonpost.com/r/2010-2019/WashingtonPost/2016/07/13/Editorial-Opinion/Graphics/terms_of_reference_for_the_Joint_Implementation_Group.pdf.
Tertrais, Bruno. "The Demise of Ares: The End of War as We Know It?" *The Washington Quarterly* 35, no. 3 (2012): 7–22.
Thaler, Kai M. "Mixed Methods Research in the Study of Political and Social Violence and Conflict." *Journal of Mixed Methods Research* 11, no. 1 (2017): 59–76.

The Wall Street Journal. "US Is Cautious in Aiding Afghan Rebels." April 9, 1984.
The White House. *The National Security Strategy of the United States.* Washington, DC, 2002.
Themnér, Lotta, and Peter Wallensteen. "Armed Conflicts, 1946-2013." *Journal of Peace Research* 51, no. 4 (2014): 541–554.
Thornton, Rod. "The Changing Nature of Modern Warfare." *The RUSI Journal* 160, no. 4 (2015): 40–48.
Tillema, Herbert K. "Foreign Overt Military Intervention in the Nuclear Age." *Journal of Peace Research* 26, no. 2 (1989): 179–196.
Tisdall, Simon. "Iran-Saudi Proxy War in Yemen Explodes into Region-Wide Crisis." *The Guardian,* March 26, 2015.
Toft, Monica Duffy. "Indivisible Territory, Geographic Concentration, and Ethnic War." *Security Studies* 12, no. 2 (2002): 82–119.
Toft, Monica Duffy. "Issue Indivisibility and Time Horizons as Rationalist Explanations for War." *Security Studies* 15, no. 1 (2006): 34–69.
Toft, Monica Duffy. *Securing the Peace: The Durable Settlement of Civil Wars.* Princeton, NJ: Princeton University Press, 2009.
Toft, Monica Duffy. "Territory and War." *Journal of Peace Research* 51, no. 2 (2014): 185–198.
Tollefsen, Andreas Forø, and Halvard Buhaug. "Insurgency and Inaccessibility." *International Studies Review* 17, no. 1 (2015): 6–25.
Torbati, Yeganeh. "U.S. Has Asked Russia Not to Attack Special Forces in Syria: Military." *Reuters,* February 18, 2016.
Trachtenberg, Marc. "Strategic Thought in America, 1952-1966." *Political Science Quarterly* 104, no. 2 (1989): 301–334.
"Transcript of Telephone Conversation Between Soviet Premier Alexei Kosygin and Afghan Prime Minister Nur Mohammed Taraki," March 17, 1979. National Security Archive, George Washington University.
Tse-Tung, Mao. "Problems of Strategy in China's Revolutionary War." In *Selected Works of Mao Tse-Tung,* edited by Committee for the Publication of the Selected Works, Vol. 1, 179–254. New York, NY: Pergamon Press, 1965.
Tubiana, Jérôme. "The Chad-Sudan Proxy War and the 'Darfurization' of Chad: Myths and Reality." HSBA Working Paper. Geneva, Switzerland: Small Arms Survey, 2008.
UN General Assembly. "The Situation in Afghanistan and Its Implications for International Peace and Security," April 29, 1988. Letter dated April 27, 1988 from the Permanent Representative of the Union of Soviet Socialist Republics to the United Nations addressed to the Secretary-General, A/43/344.
UN Inter-Agency Task Force. *South African Destablization: The Economic Cost of Frontline Resistance to Apartheid.* New York, NY: United Nations, 1989.
UN News. "Ten Years On, Syrian Crisis 'Remains a Living Nightmare': UN Secretary-General," March 10, 2021.
UN Office for the Coordination of Humanitarian Affairs. "Yemen Humanitarian Needs Overview 2019," 2018.
UN Security Council. "Agreement Among the People's Republic of Angola, the Republic of Cuba, and the Republic of South Africa (The Tripartite Accord)," December 22, 1988. S/20346.
UN Security Council. "Further Report of the Secretary-General on the United Nations Angola Verification Mission (UNAVEM II)," 1992. S/24858.
UN Security Council. "Procedure for the Establishment of a Firm and Lasting Peace in Central America (Esquipulas II Accord)," August 31, 1987. S/19085.
UNHCR. "Figures at a Glance," June 18, 2020. https://web.archive.org/web/20210424033440/https://www.unhcr.org/figures-at-a-glance.html. Accessed April 24, 2021.
UNHCR. "Syria Emergency," November 2022. https://web.archive.org/web/20230119230732/https://www.unhcr.org/syria-emergency.html.

US Army. "Lessons from the War in Afghanistan," 1989. Army Department Declassification Release. National Security Archive, George Washington University.

US Bureau of Intelligence and Research. "The Afghan Resistance Movement in 1981: Progress, But A Long Way To Go," 1982. Digital National Security Archive.

US Department of Defense. "Memorandum on Direct Ground Combat Definition and Assignment Rule," January 13, 1994.

US Department of Defense. "Press Briefing by Secretary Carter and Gen. Dunford in the Pentagon Briefing Room," July 25, 2016.

US Department of Defense. "Statement from Pentagon Spokesman Capt. Jeff Davis on US Strike in Syria," April 6, 2017.

US Department of Defense. "DOD Statement on Escalating Actions in Iraq, Syria, and Turkey," November 23, 2022a.

US Department of Defense. "Readout of Secretary of Defense Lloyd J. Austin III's Phone Call With Turkish Minister of National Defense Hulusi Akar," November 30, 2022b.

US Department of State. "Secretary of State Rex W. Tillerson's Remarks With National Security Advisor H.R. McMaster," April 6, 2017.

US Department of State. "Trafficking in Persons Report." Office to Monitor and Combat Trafficking in Persons, 2021.

US Department of State. "World Military Expenditures and Arms Transfers 1998." Bureau of Verification and Compliance, 2000.

"US Department of State Draft Dissent Memo," n.d. Draft version of dissent channel message from State Department officers to the Director of Policy Planning. Obtained by the New York Times in June 2016. https://www.nytimes.com/interactive/2016/06/17/world/middleeast/document-state-dept-syria.html.

US National Intelligence Estimate. "South Africa in a New Decade," April 1972. NIE 73-72.

US Special Operations Command. "The Gray Zone." White Paper, September 9, 2015.

Valentino, Benjamin A. *Final Solutions: Mass Killing and Genocide in the 20th Century*. Ithaca, NY: Cornell University Press, 2004.

Vanneman, Peter, and Martin James. "Soviet Intervention in the Horn of Africa: Intentions and Implications." *Policy Review*, no. 5 (1978): 15–36.

Vasquez, Juan M. "Castro Refuses to Pull Troops From Angola Until His Terms Met." *The Washington Post*, July 28, 1982.

Väyrynen, Raimo, ed. *The Waning of Major War: Theories and Debates*. New York, NY: Routledge, 2006.

Verwimp, Philip. "An Economic Profile of Peasant Perpetrators of Genocide: Micro-Level Evidence from Rwanda." *Journal of Development Economics* 77, no. 2 (2005): 297–323.

Vries, Roland de. *Eye of the Firestorm: The Namibian-Angolan-South African Border War - Memoirs of a Military Commander*. Johannesburg, South Africa: Naledi, 2013.

Wagner, R. Harrison. "Bargaining and War." *American Journal of Political Science* 44, no. 3 (2000): 469–484.

Walsh, Declan. "A 'New Cold War' Looms in Africa as US Pushes Against Russian Gains." *The New York Times*, March 19, 2023.

Walt, Stephen M. "Alliances in a Unipolar World." *World Politics* 61, no. 1 (2009): 86–120.

Walt, Stephen M. *The Origins of Alliances*. Ithaca, NY: Cornell University Press, 1987.

Walter, Barbara F. "Bargaining Failures and Civil War." *Annual Review of Political Science* 12, no. 1 (2009): 243–261.

Walter, Barbara F. *Committing to Peace: The Successful Settlement of Civil Wars*. Princeton, NJ: Princeton University Press, 2002.

Walter, Barbara F. "The Critical Barrier to Civil War Settlement." *International Organization* 51, no. 3 (1997): 335–364.

Walter, Barbara F., Lise Morje Howard, and V. Page Fortna. "The Extraordinary Relationship between Peacekeeping and Peace." *British Journal of Political Science* 51, no. 4 (2021): 1705–1722.

Waltz, Kenneth N. "Structural Realism after the Cold War." *International Security* 25, no. 1 (2000): 5–41.
Waltz, Kenneth N. "The Emerging Structure of International Politics." *International Security* 18, no. 2 (1993): 44–79.
Waltz, Kenneth N. *Theory of International Politics*. Reading, MA: Addison-Wesley, 1979.
Wasser, Becca, Stacie L. Pettyjohn, Jeffrey Martini, Alexandra T. Evans, Karl P. Mueller, Nathaniel Edenfield, Gabrielle Tarini, Ryan Haberman, and Jalen Zeman. *The Air War Against the Islamic State: The Role of Airpower in Operation Inherent Resolve*. Santa Monica, CA: RAND Corporation, 2021.
Wehrey, Frederic, and Megan Doherty. "Saving Lives in Libya's Nightmarish War." *Carnegie Endowment for International Peace*, July 16, 2019.
Weiner, Myron. *Sons of the Soil: Migration and Ethnic Conflict in India*. Princeton, NJ: Princeton University Press, 1978.
Weisgerber, Marcus. "Russian Warplanes Are 'Trying to Dogfight' US Jets Over Syria, General Says." *Defense One*, April 27, 2023.
Weisiger, Alex. "Learning from the Battlefield: Information, Domestic Politics, and Interstate War Duration." *International Organization* 70, no. 2 (2016): 347–375.
Werner, Suzanne, and Amy Yuen. "Making and Keeping Peace." *International Organization* 59, no. 2 (2005): 261–292.
Westad, Odd Arne. "Concerning the Situation in 'A': New Russian Evidence on the Soviet Intervention in Afghanistan." *Cold War International History Project Bulletin*, no. 8/9 (1996): 128–132.
Westad, Odd Arne. "Moscow and the Angolan Crisis, 1974-1976: A New Pattern of Intervention." *Cold War International History Project Bulletin*, no. 8/9 (1996): 21–37.
Westad, Odd Arne. "Rethinking Revolutions: The Cold War in the Third World." *Journal of Peace Research* 29, no. 4 (1992): 455–464.
Westad, Odd Arne. *The Global Cold War: Third World Interventions and the Making of Our Times*. Cambridge, UK: Cambridge University Press, 2007.
Whittle, Richard, and George Kuempel. "Afghan Arms Inquiry Targets Friend of Ex-Rep. Wilson." *The Dallas Morning News*, October 21, 1997.
Wilson, James Graham. "Did Reagan Make Gorbachev Possible?" *Presidential Studies Quarterly* 38, no. 3 (2008): 456–475.
Wimmer, Andreas, Lars-Erik Cederman, and Brian Min. "Ethnic Politics and Armed Conflict: A Configurational Analysis of a New Global Dataset." *American Sociological Review* 74, no. 2 (2009): 316–337.
Wimmer, Andreas, and Brian Min. "From Empire to Nation-State: Explaining Wars in the Modern World, 1816–2001." *American Sociological Review* 71, no. 6 (2006): 867–897.
Wohlforth, William C. "The Stability of a Unipolar World." *International Security* 24, no. 1 (1999): 5–41.
Wolfers, Michael, and Jane Bergerol. *Angola in the Frontline*. London, UK: Zed Books, 1983.
Woodward, Bob, and Charles R. Babcock. "US Covert Aid to Afghans on the Rise." *The Washington Post*, January 13, 1985.
Wright, George. "The Clinton Administration's Policy Toward Angola: An Assessment." *Review of African Political Economy* 28, no. 90 (2001): 563–576.
Wucherpfennig, Julian, Nils W. Metternich, Lars-Erik Cederman, and Kristian Skrede Gleditsch. "Ethnicity, the State, and the Duration of Civil War." *World Politics* 64, no. 1 (2012): 79–115.
Yacoubian, Mona. "Understanding Russia's Endgame in Syria: A View from the United States." Research Project Report. Syria Transition Challenges Project. The Geneva Centre for Security Policy, 2021.
Yao, Kevin. "China's Xi Calls for Fairer World Order as Rivalry With US Deepens." *Reuters*, April 20, 2021.
Yousaf, Mohammad. *Silent Soldier: The Man Behind the Afghan Jehad General Akhtar Abdur Rahman Shaheed*. Lahore, Pakistan: Jang Publishers, 1991.

Yousaf, Mohammad, and Mark Adkin. *The Bear Trap: Afghanistan's Untold Story*. London, UK: Leo Cooper, 1992.

Zartman, I. William. *Ripe for Resolution: Conflict and Intervention in Africa*. New York, NY: Oxford University Press, 1985.

Zartman, I. William. "Ripeness: The Hurting Stalemate and Beyond." In *International Conflict Resolution After the Cold War*, edited by Paul C. Stern and Daniel Druckman, 225–250. Washington, DC: National Academy of Sciences, 2000.

Zhdarkin, Igor Anatoliyevich. "Igor Zhdarkin Looks Back." In *Bush War: The Road to Cuito Cuanavale*, edited by Gennady Shubin and Andrei Tokarev, 94–165. Johannesburg, South Africa: Jacana, 2011.

Zolotarev, V.A., ed. *Rossiia (SSSR) v Lokal'nykh Voinakh i Voennykh Konfliktakh Vtoroi Poloviny XX Veka [Russia (USSR) in Local Wars and Armed Conflicts in the Second Half of the Twentieth Century]*. Moscow: Institute of Military History, Russian Ministry of Defence, 2000.

Zubok, Vladislav M. *A Failed Empire: The Soviet Union in the Cold War from Stalin to Gorbachev*. Chapel Hill, NC: University of North Carolina Press, 2007.

Index

For the benefit of digital users, indexed terms that span two pages (e.g., 52–53) may, on occasion, appear on only one of those pages.

Note: Page references for figures and tables are shown in bold font.

Abramowitz, Morton (Department of State, United States), 179
Adamishin, Anatoly (Ministry of Foreign Affairs, Soviet Union), 113, 125, 126, 132–133, 138–139, 141–143
Afghan civil war, **158**
   asymmetric combat, 161–162
   casualties, 154, 154 n.4, 164, 164 n.36
   center of gravity, combat, 161, 161 n.31
   CIA involvement, 174–176, 181, 188, 190–191
   civilian displacement, 154, 154 nn.5–6
   combat operations, 175
   escalation dilemma, 153–154, 201–202
   Geneva Accords, 154–155, 162, 199–201
   information asymmetries, 34–35 n.17
   international peace negotiations, 199
   international response to Soviet intervention, 160–161
   ISI involvement, 167–168, 181, 193–194, 197–198, 197 n.216
   KGB involvement, 159–160, 159–160 n.21, 184 n.139
   Koran initiative, 167–168, 167–168 n.50
   military aid, 34–35 n.17, 72–73 n.33, 157–159, 157–159 n.16, 160–161, 160–161 n.29, 162–163, 163–164 n.35, 164
   military mutinies, 157, 187–188
   negotiations, 188–192, 199–112, 221
   NSDD-166, 155–156, 193, 202
   Operation Cyclone, 154–155, 154–155 n.9, n.11, 160–161
   PDPA in-fighting, 159, 159 n.18, 159–160 n.24
   Soviet withdrawal, 162, 178, 194, 203
   Soviet-Afghan Treaty of Friendship (1921), 157 n.13
   termination of warfare, 200–201
   third-party intervention, **163**, 153, 153 n.1, 156–159, 157 n.13, 159–160, 159–160 n.21, 163–164, 163–164 nn.34–35, 187–188
   Treaty of Friendship, Good Neighborliness, and Cooperation (1978), 157–159
   See also Afghan civil war, domestic bargaining; Afghan civil war, strategic restraint
Afghan civil war, domestic bargaining
   Afghan regime, 196
   bargaining positions, 188–192, 195, 198–199
   collaboration problem, 200
   combatants, balancing of, 189–192, 191–192 n.186
   force structure, 187–188, 190
   information asymmetries, 193–196, 194–195 n.196
   military aid, 186–188, 193, 193–194 nn.191–192, 194–195
   multi-party warfare, 196–198, 197 n.211, n.216
Afghan civil war, strategic restraint
   air war, 169–171, 171 n.66, 172–173, 179–180, **173**
   antiaircraft systems, 175, 179–180, 190
   "battlefield credible" weapons, 174–175, 178, 180–182, 186, 223
   combat operations, 165–166, 165–166 n.39, 167–170, 178–179
   deployment and force postures, 164–166, 169–170, 169–170 nn.57–58, 172, 178–179, 182–183
   domestic pressure, intervening countries, 183
   escalation dilemma, 165–167, 170, 173–174, 173–174 n.77, 175–176, 180–181
   logistic/resource constraints, 182–183, 182–183 nn.131–132

Afghan civil war, strategic restraint
(*Continued*)
  loss of Afghanistan, consequences of, 184–186, 184 n.139, n.141
  military aid, 164–165, 178, 182–183
  NSDD-166, 176–177, 176 n.93, 177 n.100, n.104
  restraint signaling, 170–171, 173
  rules of engagement, 165–166, 172–173
  Stinger antiaircraft missile, 34–35 n.17, 178, 180–182, 182 n.129, 202–203
Akhromeyev, Sergei (Chief of the General Staff, Soviet Armed Forces, Soviet Union), 166
Alekseevsky, Anatoliy (Lieut., Soviet military), 127–128
al-Qaeda, 11, 74
Angolan civil war, **112**
  Alvor Agreement, 111
  "area of dispute," **124**, 123–125
  Bicesse Accords, 149, 221
  casualties, 109, 109 n.3
  CIA involvement, 113 n.14, 117, 119, 135–136, 138
  civil war, onset of, 111
  Clark Amendment (United States), 114–115, 115 n.20, 119, 135–136, 138, 145–146
  exposure of intervention, 40–41, 144–145 n.162
  final offensives, 128–132, 131 n.82, 132–134, 132–133 n.98
  Gbadolite Declaration, 149, 221
  IA Feature, 111–112, 135–136
  liberation movements, 110–111
  Lusaka Accords, 146–147, 146–147 n.177
  Moçâmedes Railway, 121–123, 123 n.55, 223
  negotiations, 132, 132 n.91, 134, 139–140, 143–144, 149
  Operation Argon, 146–147 n.177
  Operation Protea, 118–119 n.32
  Operation Savannah, 40–41, 113–114, 113 n.14, 114, 120–121, 120–121 n.43, 144–146
  peace talks, 132, 132 n.91, 134, 134 n.105, 149, 149–150 n.188, 221
  Quifangondo, battle of, 114, 115 n.21
  South Africa, 113–114, 113 n.14, 114–115
  third-party intervention, 6–7, **116**, 108–109, 111–112, 114–116, 135–137, 136–137 n.115, n.116, 150
  Tripartite Accord, 134, 149–150, 221
  withdrawal of Portugal, 111
  See also Angolan civil war, domestic bargaining; Angolan civil war, strategic restraint
Angolan civil war, domestic bargaining
  Angolan regime, 147–148
  bargaining positions, 139–140, 143–144, 148–149
  combatants, balancing of, 142–143
  force structure, 141–142, 141–142 n.145
  information asymmetries, 144–147, 146 n.174
  military aid, 137–139, 139 n.128, 139 nn.130–131
  multi-party warfare, 148
Angolan civil war, strategic restraint
  air war, 133–134, 141–142
  areas of control, **124**, 123–125, 223
  deployment and force postures, 120–123, 121 n.49, 122 n.53, 130–131
  escalation dilemma, 116–117, 122–123, 125–126, 150–152
  implications of, 137
  military advisors, 117–120, 117–118 n.27
  military aid, 117, 134–135, 134–135 n.107, n.108, 136–137
  targeting of forces, 125–128
  terminal conflict period, 128–134
Anstee, Margaret (UN Mission to Angola), 149–150 n.188
al-Assad, Bashar (President, Syria), 220
asymmetry, 2–3, 33 n.13, 161–162, 198. *See also* information asymmetries
Azerbaijan, 43

Barabulya, Vyacheslav (Lieut., Soviet military), 118–119, 118–119 n.32, 125–126
bargaining approach to war, 29–32, 30–31 n.5, n.6, 31 n.7, n.8
Bearden, Milton (CIA, United States), 167–169
Beg, Mirza Aslam (Gen., Vice Chief Army Staff, Pakistan), 179
Botha, Pik (Foreign Minister, South Africa), 113 n.14, 136–137 n.115
Breedlove, Philip (Gen., SACEUR, United States), 211
Breytenbach, Jan (Col., SADF, South Africa), 119–121, 122 n.53, 123–125 n.58, 125, 160–161
Brezhnev, Leonid (General Secretary, Soviet Union), 153 n.1

INDEX

Brown, Charles (Lt.-Gen., USAF, United States), 209
Brzezinski, Zbigniew (National Security Advisor, United States), 154–155 n.9
Bush, George H. W. (President, United States), 194–195

Cannistraro, Vincent (CIA, United States), 197
Carter, Ash (Secretary of Defense, United States), 211
Carter, Jimmy (President, United States), 160, 184–185
Castro, Fidel (President, Cuba), 121–122, 127, 128 n.76, 131–133
Chadian civil war, 43
Chebrikov, Viktor (Chairman, KGB, Soviet Union), 166
China, 226, 228
civil wars
  definition, 12, 12 n.36, 61–62
  duration and costs, 1–3, 2–3 n.8, 13–15, 81, 95, 108, 204, 219–220
  escalation, 37–38
  Esquipulas II Accord, 222, 222 n.74
  and geopolitical environment, 9, 23, 204
  peace agreements, 221–223
  prevalence and incidence, 5, 3–5, 4–5 n.19, 24–25, 49, 49 n.60, 59, **105**, 104–106, 205–206
  research on, 67, 227–228
  See also competitive intervention; EESD; historic trends in intervention
Cogan, Charles (Directorate of Operations, CIA, United States), 166
Colby, William (CIA, United States), 119
Coll, Steve (reporter, *The Washington Post*), 177
competitive intervention, **30**
  bipolar systems, 7, 28–29, 47–49, 47–48 n.52, n.55, 48 n.56, 108–109, 205–206, 228–229, 228–229 nn.99–100
  and civil war duration, **94**, **97**, 91–98, 106–107, **92**, **96**, 204–205
  definitions, 2, 8, 9–10, 12
  description of, 3, 8–9, 8–9 n.23
  domestic combatants, 6, 33–34, 33–34 n.14, 35–36, 35–36 n.20
  military aid, 22–23, 22–23 n.78, 32–33, 32 n.10, n.11, 35, 35 n.18
  and peacekeeping, 15–16, 18–19, 90, 95, 232–233
  proxy war, relationship with, 10–12

systemic pressures for, 7, 46–47, 46–47 n.48
theoretical predictions, 52–54, 52 n.72, **53**
third-party intervention, 6–7, 16–19, 24
unipolar systems, 50–52, 50 n.63, n.66, 50–51 n. 68, n. 69, 205–206
  See also Afghan civil war; Angolan civil war; asymmetry; escalation dilemma; models and methods; Syrian civil war
credible commitment problems, 15–18, 88–90, 230–232
Crocker, Chester (US lead negotiator), 132–134
Cuba, 48–49 n.58. *See also* Angolan civil war

Dippennar, Johann (Maj.-Gen., SADF, South Africa), 123, 150–151

Eagleburger, Lawrence (state department, United States), 173–174 n.77
EESD
  advantages of, 66, 66 nn.22–24
  fatality thresholds, 61–63, 62–63 n.6
  military aid, types of, 63, 63 n.10, n.14
  open source data, 65–66, 65–66 nn.16–17
  overview, 60–61
  UCDP External Support Dataset, 60–61, 61 n.2, 63 n.8, 63 nn.11–12
Ekman, Kenneth, (Maj.-Gen., USAF, United States), 216–217 n.51
escalation dilemma
  Afghan civil war, 153–154, 165–167, 170, 173–174, 173–174 n.77, 175–176, 180–181, 201–202
  Angolan civil war, 116–117, 122–123, 125–126, 150–152
  collaboration problem, 39, 45–46, 200
  covert operations as solution, 40
  definition, 37–38
  escalation in civil war, 37–38, 37–38 n.26
  escalation spiral, 38–39, 70–71, 220, 226, 230
  exposure of intervention, 40–41
  limited war, 19–21
  momentum problem, 39–40, 45–46
  restraint signaling, 6–7, 24, 41–45, 204–205, 225–226
  thresholds, 42–45, 42–43 n.37, 45–46, 223–225, 229–230
Extended External Support Dataset (EESD). *See* EESD

Fenton, Daniel (senior analyst, CIA, United States), 119
First Nagorno-Karabakh War, 43
Fourie, Deon (staff, Chief of the Army, SADF, South Africa), 151
France, 43

Gates, Robert (CIA, United States), 175–176
Gelb, Leslie (reporter, *The New York Times*), 177
Geldenhuys, Jannie (Chief of the Defense Force, SADF, South Africa), 130
Global South, 74–75
Goldwater, Barry (Senator, United States), 113 n.14
Gorbachev, Mikhail (General Secretary, Soviet Union), 202
Gromov, Boris (Lt.-Gen., Soviet Union), 201
Gromyko, Andrei (Foreign Minister, Soviet Union), 153 n.1, 166
Grynkewich, Alexus (Lt.-Gen., USCENTCOM, United States), 216–217

Haq, Abdul (mujahideen commander), 182
Hart, Howard (CIA Station Chief, Islamabad), 175
Hekmatyar, Gulbuddin (chairman, mujahideen alliance), 199
historic trends in intervention
  bipolar to unipolar transition, 72, 73, 59–60, 71–74, 72–73 n.33, 79, 205–206
  external intervention, 68, 67–68, 68 nn.28–29, 70, 79
  great power rivalry (bipolar systems), 75, 74–76, 79–80, 205–206
  lesser power intervention, 75, 76–77
  military aid, 69, 68–71
  proxy wars, 60
  unipolar systems and lesser power intervention, 78, 77–79
Hougaard, Jan (Commandant, SADF, South Africa), 133–134
hybrid war, 20–21

Iklé, Fred (Department of Defense, United States), 174–176, 180–181
India, 160, 160 n.27
indirect confrontation, 229. *See also* competitive intervention
information asymmetries
  Afghan civil war, 34–35 n.17, 193–196, 194–195 n.196

amplification of, 34–36, 54, 144–147, 192–196
Angolan civil war, 144–147, 146 n.174
conflict duration, 16–18, 230–231
private information, 30–34, 214, 231
Syrian civil war, 214
Iran, 43
Iraq, 35–36 n.19
ISIS, 35–36 n.19, 208, 211 n.23, 212–214, 222–223
Israel, 43, 43 n.45

Kerry, John (Secretary of State, United States), 210
Khrupilin, Petr (Soviet military), 118–119
Kissinger, Henry (Secretary of State, United States), 117, 146
Kolomnin, Sergej (Soviet military), 118–119
Korean War, 226
Kruys, George (Brig.-Gen., SADF, South Africa), 121
Kuzichkin, Vladimir (KGB, Soviet Union), 170

Libya, 1, 22, 43, 48–49 n.58
limited war, 19–21, 41, 229–230
Long, Clarence (Congressman, United States), 174
Lord, Dick (Brig.-Gen., SAAF), 133

Malan, Magnus (Minister of Defense, South Africa), 142–143
Mattis, Jim (Secretary of Defense, United States), 224 n.79
McMahon, John (Deputy Director, CIA, United States), 174–175
Mityaev, Vyacheslav (Col., Soviet military), 131 n.82
models and methods
  control variables, conflict-level, 88–90
  control variables, group-level, 90–91
  control variables, state-level, 86–88
  Cox model, 82–83, 83 n.5, 91–93, 92, 96, 99
  dependent variable, 85, 84, 84 n.12
  empirical results, 94, 97, 91–98, 92, 96
  explanatory variables, 84–85
  model dataset, 83–84, 84 n.10
  robustness checks, 99
  robustness checks, alleged support, 98–100
  robustness checks, conflict-specific heterogeneity, 100–101, 100–101 n.66
  robustness checks, cumulative fatality criterion, 102–103

robustness checks, decade-specific confounders, 100, 100 n.65
robustness checks, reverse causality, **104**, 103–104
robustness checks, two-year rule, 101–102

Namibia, 132–133
Novchich, Brian (Lt.-Col., USAF, United States), 208–210

Opperman, Gert (Maj.-Gen., SADF, South Africa), 122–123, 136–137 n.115, 144–145, 150–151

Pakistan. *See* Afghan civil war
peacekeeping, 15–16, 18–19, 90, 95, 232–233
Portugal, 110–111
proxy war, 10–12, 60, 153

Qadri, A. Hameed (Air-Cdre, PAF, Pakistan), 171–172

Reagan, Ronald (President, United States), 140
research design, 7–8, 55, 56 nn.74–76, 56–57 n.77, 57
Russian Federation. *See* Syrian civil war

Savimbi, Jonas (UNITA), 139–140, 144–146
Schultz, George (Secretary of State, United States), 179, 189, 200
South Africa, 113, 125–126, 135–137. *See also* Angolan civil war
Soviet Union, 75, 74–76, 113, 135–136. *See also* Afghan civil war; Angolan civil war
Steward, Dave (Director-General, South African Communication Service), 151
Stockwell, John (Angola Task Force, CIA, United States), 117, 119
Sudan, 22
Syrian civil war
 Astana peace talks, 213–214
 casualties, 214–215
 CIA involvement, 207–208, 212–214
 civil disobedience, 206–207
 flash point, SDF-Turkey, 217–218, 217–218 n.56, n.59
 flash point, Syria-Turkey, 218–219, 218–219 n.64
 flash point, US-Russia, 216–217, 216–217 n.51, n.55
 Geneva peace talks, 213–214
 insurrection, 206–207
 military campaigns, 207
 military defections, 206–207
 negotiations, 212–213, 222–223
 refugees, 1, 1 n.1, 214–215
 third-party intervention, 22, 207–208, 219–220
 See also Syrian civil war, domestic bargaining; Syrian civil war, strategic restraint
Syrian civil war, domestic bargaining
 bargaining positions, 212–214, 213–214 n.41
 combatants, balancing of, 213–214
 information asymmetries, 214
 military aid, 207–208, 207–208 n.4, 210, 212–213
 Timber Sycamore program, 207–208, 212–214
Syrian civil war, strategic restraint
 air war, 208–209, 213–214
 deconfliction, 208–211, 211 n.23
 restraint signaling, 43
 rules of engagement, 209–210, 209–210 n.15
 al-Shayrat missile strike, 211–212, 211–212 n.26
 zones of control, 210, 215–216, 215–216 n.47, 223–225

Thirion, Chris (Deputy Chief, Staff Intelligence, SADF, South Africa), 146 n.174
Thornton, Thomas (National Security Council, United States), 185–186
Tillerson, Rex (Secretary of State, United States), 211–212
Trump, Donald (President, United States), 211–212
Turkey, 43, 207

UCDP External Support Dataset, 60–61, 61 n.2, 63 n.8, 63 nn.11–12
United States
 Carter Doctrine, 160, 184–185
 Clark Amendment, 114–115, 115 n.20, 119, 135–136, 138, 145–146
 global war on terror, 74, 77–79
 IA Feature, 111–112, 135–136
 interventions, 75, 74–76, 135–136
 National Security Decision Directive 166 (NSDD-166), 155–156, 176–177, 193, 202

United States (*Continued*)
  Operation Cyclone, 154–155, 154–155 n.9, n.11, 160–161
  Reagan administration, 135–136, 155–156, 175, 176, 181, 185–186, 202
  Reagan Doctrine, 135–136
  Timber Sycamore program, 207–208, 212–214
  unipolar interventions, 78–79
  US-Pakistan Agreement of Cooperation (1959), 165, 165 n.37
  "Vietnam Syndrome," 135–136
  See also Afghan civil war; Angolan civil war; Syrian civil war
Uppsala Conflict Data Program (UCDP) External Support Dataset, 60–61, 61 n.2

Vorster, John (Prime Minister, South Africa), 146–147
de Vries, Roland (Maj.-Gen., SADF, South Africa), 119, 121, 122 n.53, 123–125, 123–125 n.58, 125–127, 130, 132–133 n.98, 137

Yemen, 1, 22, 34–35 n.16, 50–51 n. 68
Yousaf, Mohammed (Brig., ISI, Pakistan), 167, 168–169 n.53, 179, 181, 190–192, 193–194 n.191, 197, 201

Zazeraj, Vic (foreign service, South Africa), 125–126, 128
Zhdarkin, Igor (Lt.-Col., Soviet military), 118–119, 126
Zia-ul-Haq, Muhammad (President, Pakistan), 167